Social Behavior,
Natural Resources, and
the Environment

Social Behavior, Natural Resources, and the Environment

WILLIAM R. BURCH, JR.
Yale University

NEIL H. CHEEK, JR.
National Park Service and Georgia State University

LEE TAYLOR
Louisiana State University, New Orleans

HARPER & ROW, PUBLISHERS
New York, Evanston, San Francisco, London

SOCIAL BEHAVIOR, NATURAL RESOURCES, AND THE ENVIRONMENT

Copyright © 1972 by William R. Burch, Jr., Neil H. Cheek, Jr., and Lee Taylor

Standard Book Number: 06-041038-8
Library of Congress Catalog Card Number: 78-178118

CONTENTS

Biographical Notes on Editors and Contributors

William R. Burch, Jr., is Associate Professor in Sociology and Forestry at Yale University. He earned his Ph.D. at the University of Minnesota. He has published numerous articles on social change, leisure, regional planning, and natural resources. He is the author of *Daydreams and Nightmares: A Sociological Essay on the American Environment*, published by Harper & Row in 1971.

Neil H. Cheek, Jr., is Research Sociologist, National Park Service, U.S. Department of Interior and Adjunct Professor of Sociology, Georgia State University, Atlanta, Georgia. He earned his Ph.D. at Washington University. His most recent publications report on various aspects of the social organization of leisure in human societies.

Lee Taylor is Professor of Sociology and Director of the Urban Studies Institute, Louisiana State University in New Orleans. He is the author of numerous books and articles on rural life, occupational sociology, and urban planning. His most recent book is *Occupational Sociology*, published by Oxford University Press in 1968. His Ph.D. is from Louisiana State University in Baton Rouge.

Keith S. Boggs received his B.A. and M.A. at Denver University and is presently Research Sociologist with the Man-Environment Research Program at the University of Colorado. Several recent papers and articles have dealt with the diffusion of weather modification as an environmental innovation.

E. J. Bonner is Assistant Professor of Sociology at the University of Kansas. He earned his Ph.D. from the University of Colorado. His current research deals with the utilization of health resources and with role relationships in mental hospitals.

Rabel J. Burdge is presently Associate Professor of Sociology, University of Kentucky, Lexington. He received a Ph.D. from the Pennsylvania State University and has taught at Ohio State, the Air Force Academy and the University of Colorado. He is co-author of the text *Social Change in Rural Societies*. His research has been in social change, the environment, and the sociology of leisure and outdoor recreation.

James A. Christenson received his B.A. from Gonzaga University and his M.A. from Washington State University, where he is currently a Ph.D. candidate in sociology. His major areas of interests include the family and community action.

Don A. Dillman received both his M.A. and Ph.D. in sociology from Iowa State University and is now Assistant Professor of Sociology and Director of the Public Opinion Laboratory at Washington State University. His present research includes studies of the social basis of preferences for living in urban vs. rural communities and the organizational basis of public values.

William S. Folkman is Senior Sociologist and Project Leader at the Forest Service research facility in Berkeley, California, where he is responsible for a research program dealing with the man-caused forest fire problem of the arid West. His Ph.D. was earned at Cornell University.

John Forster, Ph.D., is Professor of Sociology and Chairman of the Department of Sociology, University of Alberta, Canada. Professor Forster has had a continuing interest in the Pacific, particularly in the problems of the development of small island areas, and has published widely on the subject.

Richard P. Gale is Assistant Professor of Sociology at the University of Oregon. Previous research has dealt with the role of voluntary organizations in environmental action, college student attitudes toward and involvement in environmental issues, and the effect of environmental education programs. At present, he is studying the professional socialization of architects. His Ph.D. is from Michigan State University.

J. Eugene Haas is Professor of Sociology and heads the Research Program on Technology, Man and the Environment at the Institute of Behavioral Science, University of Colorado, Boulder. The focus of his recent research is on the social consequences of large-scale weather modification programs and on the dissemination of tsunami and storm warnings.

William D. Heffernan, Ph.D., is Assistant Professor of Sociology, University of Missouri. He will complete his longitudinal study of fire prevention in 1972.

Kenneth E. Hornback received his B.S. from the University of Iowa, his M.A. from Northern Illinois University, and is currently a doctoral candidate in sociology at Michigan State University. Mr. Hornback acted as technical director for the National Environmental Organizations Directory, produced for the President's Commission on Children and Youth in cooperation with Environmental Resources, Washington, D.C. Mr. Hornback is presently developing his Ph.D. dissertation on "The Dimensions of Class Conflict in the Environmental Movement."

Samuel Z. Klausner is Professor of Sociology, University of Pennsylvania and Director for the Center for Research on the Acts of Man. He earned his Ph.D. from Columbia University. He is a consultant to the National Academy of Sciences and the National Academy of Engineering, and is the author of numerous books and articles. His most recent book is *Society and Its Physical Environment*, which was published in 1970.

Clark S. Knowlton is Professor of Sociology and Director for the Center for the Study of Social Problems, University of Utah. He earned his Ph.D. from Vanderbilt University in 1955. He has published widely on ethnic relations, delinquency, and poverty.

Robert G. Lee is completing the doctoral program in Wildland Resource Science (with a specialty in the sociology of natural resources) at the University of California, Berkeley, and is employed by the National Park Service as Research Sociologist. He received his B.S. from the University of California, Berkeley, and his M.F.S. from the Yale School of Forestry.

Richard L. Ludtke is an Assistant Professor of Sociology at the University of North Dakota, Grand Forks. He received a Ph.D. in sociology from the University of Kentucky in 1970. He has received research grants from the Corps of Engineers and the Office of Water Resources to study the social impact of various flood control plans and projects.

James McEvoy III, Ph.D., is Associate Professor of Sociology and Environmental Studies at the Davis campus of the University of California. He is Director of the Tahoe Research Group, a multidiciplinary research effort on man's impact on the natural environment. He is the author of several books and articles in the fields of political sociology and human ecology and co-editor of the forthcoming volume, *Human Ecology: An Environmental Approach.*

Richard L. Means is professor of sociology at Kalamazoo College, Michigan. His Ph.D. is in sociology from Cornell. Professor Means has published articles on a wide range of subjects, from social and theological problems to conservation. He is the author of *The Ethical Imperative: The Crisis in American Values.* His major interests continue to be in social theory and the sociology of religion.

Delbert C. Miller, Ph.D., is Joint Professor of Sociology and Business Administration at Indiana University. His special fields of interest are industrial sociology and community power structures, and he has written widely in both fields. He is the author of *International Community Power Structures,* which was published by Indiana University Press in 1970.

Denton E. Morrison received his Ph.D. at the University of Wisconsin. He is Professor of Sociology at Michigan State University. He had done research on agrarian movements, the women's liberation movement, and is presently continuing his research on the environmental movement. He is co-editor of a book of readings on research methods, *The Significance Test Controversy.*

Irving A. Spaulding has held a joint appointment at the University of Rhode Island as Professor of Sociology and Resource Economics since 1960. He earned his Ph.D. at Cornell University. He has published numerous articles on outdoor recreation, environmental issues, and methods of social research, and has a continuing interest in the study of Southeast Asia.

W. Keith Warner received his Ph.D. degree from Cornell University and is currently Professor of Sociology at Brigham Young University. His writings deal with such problems as social structure and societal development, voluntary associations as mediating mechanisms in society, organizational effectiveness, and membership participation in voluntary organizations.

G. Dale Welch is Associate Professor of Sociology at Northeastern State College, Tahlequah, Oklahoma. He earned his Ph.D. from Louisiana State University in 1970. The bulk of his research has dealt with the social aspects of environmental issues.

Preface

Earth days and hastily formed environmental impact statements suggest that the issues treated in this volume are of only recent concern to sociologists. However, the social aspects of natural resources and natural environments have long informed the sociological discourse. Early theorists such as Emile Durkheim and Herbert Spencer were concerned with the influence population-land ratios had upon social structure and social change. William Graham Sumner, Lester Ward, and Albion Small included natural resource influences in their theories. Ward was in regular dialogue with John Wesley Powell in his great and unique attempt to apply the scientific understanding of social system-ecosystem relationships in the development of the arid Western regions. In more recent times, Pitirim Sorokin (1929), Fred Cottrell (1955), and Walter Firey (1960), and a whole host of rural sociologists have been exploring the interrelations between the social order and natural resources.

Thus, the papers in this volume represent a continuation of sociological tradition, though with an awareness of contemporary problems. As such, the volume combines old and new theoretical and methodological directions. It indicates something of what we know, what we don't know, and what we need to know for understanding the unfolding relations between social behavior, natural resources, and environment. And, along the way, the volume provides a variety of direct and indirect suggestions for dealing with our problems. Hopefully, if a similar "state of art" volume appears a decade hence it will be richer for our mistakes.

This volume was stimulated by suggestions from the Development Committee of the Rural Sociological Society and has drawn upon discussions with members of the Natural Resources Committee of the Society.

We should like to acknowledge our debt to Luther Wilson for his continuing enthusiasm and to Kathleen MacDougall for her precise and "just right" editorial help.

Our special thanks is due Judith Burch, who managed to find vision and order when we were prone to despair.

W.R.B.
N.H.C.
L.T.

INTRODUCTION

The reader may be surprised and even disappointed that this volume has few references to famines in 1975, or population explosions, or territorial imperatives, or the return of ice ages and tropical ages. Indeed some may see this volume as subversive to the "subversive science."

We are not unmindful of the link between man's well-being and the well-being of the earth he inhabits. Our concern is with man as a creature of the earth whose phylogeny, as that of other species, is continuing to unfold. And as other species, *Homo sapiens* has the capacity to fail in adaptation and, therefore, destroy himself. However, it has seemed sterile if not futile to conduct investigations which seem to study everything but the specific species—man—which allegedly is the central interest. Indeed man, as other animals, is a consumer of resources and a manipulator of his ecosystem. Yet knowing this really does not tell us much about the species. Therefore, our focus is upon the behavior of man and the social and cultural systems he creates in order to survive. Such an attempt seems eminently necessary if we are to improve our long-range predictions concerning the fate of man and his nonhuman environment.

The evolutionary sweep of the species, from the early hominids to its present place in the biota of the planet, is apparently without parallel among other vertebrates. For man is one of the few species which has become almost entirely specialized with reference to the mechanisms employed in its adaptation to the challenges faced for survival. It is, of course, not unusual for a species to develop particular reproductive cycles, breeding practices, food preferences, and so on, as means of adaptation to its environment. Man has followed a similar course, but, allowing for the identifiably unique aspects of his anatomy (cranial capacity and brain mass, bipedalism, and the like), the species has evolved a means of adaptation which, though related to its biological capacities, is apparently not directly dependent upon such. Man, the self-reflexive being, seems to have found culture (the sum total of shared beliefs and values) a powerful mechanism in aiding his survival as a species.

There are few if any other species, present or past, which have been able to transcend the highly demanding and limiting ecological forces restricting the range of habitation common to such. Man is now nearly a ubiquitous species, occurring and reproducing in all of the ecologically identifiable biomes of the planet. This, of course, is not a new phenomenon. Several scholars have suggested that man was present as a predator of immense efficiency during the Pleistocene. Archaeological remains of man are being discovered in almost every climatic and topographical area. Man survived the last glaciation while many other species did not. Though it is unlikely that culture is the sole mechanism a species may utilize to transcend more narrowly limiting factors of zoogeography, it appears to be highly effective. In this book we wish to explore some of the ways in which the place of man today as one among many species is a consequence of the primacy of culture as an adaptive mechanism. We are concerned with how man approaches the nonhuman environment through culture even when the biological capacities of the species may be the more probable limiting factor in the behavior observed.

Man approaches the nonhuman environment in several characteristic ways not dissimilar from the manner in which other species approach their environments. First, the environment is the source of food supply. Secondly, it is the source of materials used for building shelters, whether they be houses or nests. Thirdly, it provides opportunities and materials for noninstrumental activities, whether play or bathing. Finally, for man and perhaps for other species, the environment is the source of energy for fuel to heat his abodes, drive off enemies of the night, and run the products of his imagination—machines. Unlike most other species, man has conceived means by which he can transcend the mere reaping of the bounty and the suffering of the cyclical variations which seem to characterize all animal and plant species. Through culture, man has been able to augment the food supply by agriculture and domestication of animals. Fiber for clothing is cultivated or created. Building materials are the object of silviculture and other accumulated sources of systematic information. The topography is varied to produce what culture identifies as aesthetically desirable. Only fossil fuels have, apparently, escaped becoming replenished through the ingenuity of the species. However, other sources of fuel energy, such as wood, water, and nuclear power, are part of the cultural capabilities of the species. In short, though the unintended consequences of some of man's actions with respect to his environment have received greatest topical attention recently, it appears that the species' primary mode of adaptation has been relatively successful as a means of coping with the ecological uncertainties of any species' survival. The irony remains that such success may prove to be the undoing of the species, but if so, then specialization would have once again shown its limitations. The sweep of the history of a species is often long. It is difficult to students of systematics in biology to determine when a subspecies may or may not have arisen. Mammals like man seem to endure as viable species for a comparatively long time. The processes of speciation continually operate. Man remains a part of this natural order. The precise relationships between the evolutionary factors of his biology and his culture remain unclear. But what is clear is that for many years the two have operated simultaneously. When one speaks of the evolutionary tracks of any species which utilizes a culture as an adaptive mechanism, then it is most difficult to disentangle one from the other. For one without the other would not work itself through in a similar fashion. For the purposes of this book, it is taken as given that a culture shared among *Homo sapiens* is similar to a culture shared among *Papio hamadryas* or *Macaca fuscata*. It is simply a mechanism by which a species adapts to its environment through time. This is not to say that all cultures for all species function in precisely the same manner. Nor do we assert that the processes internal to a culture across species function in the same manner. Our purpose is not to examine the intriguing question of cultures across species. We merely wish to note that *Homo sapiens* is not alone as a species employing culture as a means of environmental adaptation. Perhaps we can learn more about the nature of animal cultures through a comparative study with *Homo sapiens*, but our focus is somewhat narrower in this book. Whether culture will prove itself to be an effective mechanism for adaptation for the species *Homo sapiens* will not be knowable for an untold period of time. But no matter how the pages of his natural history be written, man is not man without it.

CULTURE

Culture as a concept within the realms of science is assured. Consensus regarding its particular definition is less certain. In part, definitions of concepts vary not because scientists are imprecise but because the particularities of interest and investigation vary among them. One may emphasize this or that aspect of a phenomenon and thus apparently offer a variation on a conceptualization. However, the phenomenon usually remains the same. Our concern with culture as the primary adaptive mechanism of man requires that passing attention be given to the concept.

Underlying the concept of culture as it has emerged in use among scientists is a recognition of the presence of observable patterns of behavior shared among some aggregation of animals, be it species, population, herd, or group. In a search for an explanation, when a species' language has been available as an additional modality of inquiry, investigators often seek to gain additional understandings of the shared meanings and symbol systems utilized internally among participants to account for the observed phenomena. Among *Homo sapiens* traditionally a distinction has emerged in the study of its culture between such elements (that is, such beliefs and values) and behavior—the former being relegated to culture and the latter to social organization. It has never been the investigators' intention that the phenomena under study were not equally part of the behavioral repertoire characteristic of the species. Insofar as a particular pattern of social behavior occurs only under the condition that certain beliefs and values are held by the participants, then we may speak of the classical necessary and sufficient conditions for a phenomenon to occur. But this does not mean that all animal cultures operate in the same manner. For example, we know that social mobility for individuals as well as social aggregates occurs within the societies of *Homo sapiens* and *Macaca fuscata*. That is, within a social system there occurs a change in the distribution of honor and deference among the participants which can only be accounted for by appeal to cultural variables. To avoid anthropomorphism, we do not appeal to the concept of culture as it is employed in our studies among *Homo sapiens*, but instead we appeal to a supposedly less "loaded" concept called learning. Yet phenomenologically the same behavior has occurred. Offspring of particular animals in a social aggregate share a differential place in the society as a consequence of the social behavior of the parent generation. The change in social status is perpetuated across generations in both situations. Is the one less cultural than the other? It appears a matter of definition rather than a phenomenological situation.

Irrespective of this issue, it is generally agreed that among *Homo sapiens* important components of culture are sets of shared beliefs and values as related to a wide variety of other objects in the environment, human and nonhuman.

In particular, in this book we are concerned with how man approaches the nonhuman environment through culture and social organization. To accomplish this we have provided a number of original studies conducted primarily within a single human society. Our focus is not so much upon the content of the culture as it is upon the particular processes which occur within it. Thus, the studies are important from the standpoint of what they contribute substantively to knowledge about particular examples of man, culture, and environment, and important also for the kinds of questions they raise about more abstract processes occurring within the culture of *Homo sapiens.*

The initial section indicates how man is a biocultural species, sharing certain properties with other species but diverging on other dimensions. This is followed by a section which provides detailed illustration of these differences as regards variations in the meanings imposed upon physical terrain. The third section traces how nature is incorporated into the prevailing normative system of the local community. The next section indicates how orientations toward nature vary over time and between strata and regions of a large social system. It provides evidence that, though values and beliefs may vary, they are an important determinant of the way human societies adapt to their ecosystems. The fifth section indicates how all environmental issues are ultimately reflected in the struggle over the prevailing system of authority. Two principle mechanisms of decision making in human societies—social movements and the adjustment of priorities within an established hierarchy—are discussed. Thus, in human-dominated ecosystems the biological "crises" must first be converted into social problems before they have relevance to the social system. The final section provides a theoretical overview, identifies some boundary problems, and suggests some fruitful lines for future research.

SECTION I
Man: A Biocultural Species

Man and environment are not a simple dichotomy. Both are complex. Man is at once biophysical and sociocultural and can be reduced to neither. Man's relation to the nonhuman environment at a minimum level is nurture and survival. At a maximum level, environment is a "thing" of many meanings, including leisure, recreation, and beauty. For *Homo sapiens* the nonhuman environment is instrumental and noninstrumental.

Men require certain basic functions to be operant if they are to survive. For example, respiration must occur, discharge of bodily waste products must take place, ingestion of sufficient food and water must be accomplished—all to maintain the animal in a reasonably functional state. To meet such individualistic requirements, the animal must behave in certain ways in order to obtain necessary inputs from the nonhuman environment. Though the individual requirements may vary somewhat among those in an aggregate, the manner in which such inputs are obtained, the definitions of which aspects of the nonhuman environment may be acceptable to fulfill such requirements, and the manner in which other members of the species may be employed in obtaining them are all important aspects of culture.

For example, differential food habits among various societies are well-known. The Japanese consume several species of seaweed as an important part of their diet. Though the same species are available to Americans, slight use is made of them. Throughout the world many societies exist in which the stingray is a part of the staple diet; yet North Americans rarely consume this abundant foodstuff found near their shores. Certain internal parts of food animals are infrequently consumed by various cultures. For examples, kidneys are rarely eaten by most Americans, though they are a staple of the British diet; orthodox Jews do not consume any part of cloven-hoofed animals. Examples are almost without end. Though variety of foodstuffs is available, foodstuffs are not utilized by man solely on the basis of nutritional importance, but rather on the basis of edibility as defined by the beliefs and values shared among individuals in a society. The operation of such cultural practices is not unique to our day and age, nor are they the quaint customs of some exotic group. It is an elemental property of all known human cultures, and there is some evidence that a similar phenomenon may characterize other animal cultures. Indeed, in some societies certain foods are always reserved for certain members and denied others, either through ritual or social class-based access to them. Radcliffe-Brown noted that among the Andamanese only adult males were permitted to eat turtle. The particulars of the rituals are unimportant. What is important for our purposes is that culture regulates consumption of a species in a manner analogous to mechanisms present among other species.

In addition to such matters as food consumption, there is the matter of the amount of consumption. Thus, cultures may influence not only what things in the nonhuman environment are acceptable, but also the quantities which can be safely consumed. Then, too, there are required inputs for human life which are regulated by biological necessities, though such consumption patterns may also be regulated via cultural constraints. An example is the consumption of water among households in an urban community.

Water is one of the inputs necessary for the individual animal to sustain life. The state of the technology available with respect to water utilization is a limiting factor upon the location of human communities, the patterns of growth, the density of population, and so on. Man, through culture, has been able to transport water so that he can live even at remote distances from water sources. Industrial consumption of water is the major utilization of the resources in industrial societies. The technologies employed require it for numerous operations, from cleaning of materials to heart-transferring processes. While such uses contribute to the water utilization patterns of a society, the consumption of water by individuals appears to remain based largely upon their daily requirements. Spaulding examined the water consumption patterns of households in an urban area and found that the best predictive variable was placed in the life cycle. While social class did influence somewhat the size of dwelling unit and the kinds of water-using equipment possessed, the amounts consumed were largely a reflection of the number and relative ages of the individuals in a household. Thus, the more persons in a household, the greater the consumption of water. Clearly, the number of people in a household is a function of cultural definitions about what individuals may form households. Thus, in societies which have the same technology, same settlement patterns, and so forth, and in which the household is defined as consisting of both the family of procreation and the family of orientation, the consumption of water would be greater if Spaulding's findings can be generalized. Apparently, while styles of water consumption may vary, the daily input requirements for individual members greatly influence the quantity consumed by the household as a unit of analysis. But what constitutes a household is a matter of cultural definition.

Unlike water consumption patterns, the impact of culture upon individual behavior can be clearly seen in the study conducted by Cheek. Man evolved as a species in numerous habitats. For many years, individual contact with the nonhuman environment was direct. Though it remains so today, it is now mediated by several aspects of social organization. Cheek demonstrates that, when considering a particular population of man, a substantial variation exists as to what, on a common sense level, often seems to be a matter of the nature of the beast. Moreover, the study reminds us that careful analysis is required if false conclusions based upon single variables are to be avoided. The social aggregate level of analysis is one frequently passed over in many studies. This study suggests that a reexamination of its strengths and weaknesses for sociological hypotheses may be in order. Spaulding demonstrates that biological requirements of the individual animal may determine behavior enmeshed in a cultural pattern. Cheek demonstrates that sociocultural constraints determine at an aggregate level what might be thought of as biologically regulated behavior. Spaulding is concerned with the manner in which man approaches the nonhuman environment for survival. Cheek studies the manner in which man approaches the nonhuman environment for non-instrumental aspects. Folkman examines the manner in which man approaches it as fuel and material.

The emergence of man as a dominant species during particular geological epochs is connected interestingly with the presence of controllable fire as a tool and technology. It is perhaps impossible to overestimate the importance of fire as a tool with which man approached the nonhuman environment. Its importance in the chase is well-known; its use in agricultural practices is widely known. Once various habitats began to be more or less permanently settled by man, the cultural definition of the technological uses of fire underwent a change. The more extravagant uses of fire tended to be redefined. Intentionally uncontrolled burning of woods and fields is now no longer positively sanctioned in the American society. But, as Folkman reports, man-caused fires are apparently many times greater than fires of other origin in wildland settings. What are the competing explanations for this phenomenon? Folkman suggests several possibilities. One is individual deviant behavior arising largely from idiosyncratic, pathological conditions. A second is accidental or unintended occurrences, which is the culturally preferred explanation. Finally, there is subcultural variation as an explanation. Heffernan and Welch (in Section III) present evidence on this matter. The first and last explanations are, apparently, the more powerful predictive variables.

It is apparent from these studies that the relationship between biological and cultural explanations, with respect to the nonhuman environment, requires considerably more sophistication and study. These studies collectively suggest that biological requirements of individual animals can be manifest through cultural patterns, whereas behaviors thought to stem from biological requirements are seemingly often the outcomes of cultural variables. Finally, culturally preferred explanations of apparent biopsychologically based individual behavior may be grounded instead in subcultural variations common to various geocultural regions in a society.

PAPER 1
Social Class and Household Water Consumption

IRVING A. SPAULDING

Our concern is with water consumption in urban households. There are several bases for this concern, and one is man's relationship to water. Unable to survive for long intervals without water, and subject to being overwhelmed physically by it, man could be expected to develop recurrent and rationalized practices in water use and control which would be an aspect of his way of life. This basis is critical for our research, and our other bases are related to it.

A second basis is the extent of urbanization in our society and its implications for future years. Since our society has a population predominantly urban in residence and has little foreseeable prospect for maintenance of a way of life uninfluenced by urbanization, we can predict a predominantly urban mode of living for the future. For our descendants and for ourselves, we trust that our concerns will be beneficial. Whether or not the structure of Megalopolis, described by Jean Gottman, proves to be the structure of future urbanized regions, there will presumably be water use by households of some sort or other within these regions.

A third basis for our concern is a convergence of trends of social change in such a way as to disrupt the prior integration of values in the culture of the society. Germane here are the trends of population increase and of environmental pollution. Each trend, if extended to the point that it disturbed the society's value structure,

Research on which these comments are based was financed by a grant from the Rhode Island Water Resources Research Center, pursuant to P.L. 88-379. Data pertaining to household status and quantities of water used are taken from Rhode Island Agricultural Experiment Station Bulletin 392, Household Water Use and Social Status. *Data pertaining to household status, water uses, and social values have not been published previously. The author is Professor of Resource Economics and Sociology, University of Rhode Island, Kingston, Rhode Island.*

would constitute a major "problem." Occurring "simultaneously" under circumstances in which a large contribution to the pollution problem is made by industrial and commercial activity through which employment and the goods for a high level of living are provided for the increasing population—which itself seems to press against the known limits of supply—the disturbances produced by these trends constitute one of the more perplexing problems of our society.

Our fourth basis for concern is the question about the ways in which, and extent to which, uses affecting water consumption are expressions of values within the cultural structure of our society. The pollution of water to an intolerable extent seems to strike on all fronts of man's use of water. Along with population increase, it establishes conditions in which man senses the reality, or potential, of water shortage and deprivation. This awareness stands in abrupt contrast to prior belief, whether based on reality or not, in the abundance of water. To the extent that this belief in the abundance of water was necessary for a system of water use practices and their rationalizations which were expressions of that belief, the belief was part of the value structure of the society. And to the extent that water use practices, their rationalization, and water as an artifact are incorporated into the cultural structure of a society, people have a basis for understanding both those aspects of a way of life which contribute to water resource problems and those which provide a basis for possible solutions of these problems.

The fifth basis for our concern is recognition that variety exists among human beings. Ways of living—life styles, cultures—are recognized as varying with environment to some extent, with identity and ethnicity, and with position and function within society. To the extent that recurrent and rationalized water uses are part of ways of living, they can reasonably be expected to vary as environment, identity, ethnicity, position, and function vary in the lives of people.

And, in light of all others, our sixth basis for concern with water consumption in urban households is the practical necessity for understanding the variety of facets which exist with respect to water resource problems. There is recognition, to mention a well-known distinction, that the quantity of water accounted for annually by household uses is slight when compared to the quantity accounted for by commercial and industrial uses. One might speak, figuratively, in terms of comparing a thimbleful with barrelful. But in this technological, predominantly urban, commercial society, the dependence of mankind on household uses of water, as well as upon commercial and industrial uses, prompts consideration of those household uses as but part of the total variety of facets of water resource problems and their solutions.

Research may reveal that there is among people in our society no noteworthy cultural or life style differentiation with respect to household water uses, since water for those uses seems to have been regarded, in essence, as plentiful and available and has been handled in many urbanized areas as a public utility. Yet, currently and in the future, there seem to be actual and potential shortages which may contribute to making the social scientists' perspective and knowledge about household water uses as reflections of status and life style of immediate practical importance. An indication of their ultimate importance may be suggested by Herbert J. Gans, who points out in his volume, *People and Plans* (1968), that the class position of people and their stage in the family cycle are critical characteristics to consider in urban community planning. Both of these have pertinence for households; household uses of water may vary as these factors vary.

A STUDY OF HOUSEHOLDS
IN WARWICK, RHODE ISLAND
Orientation

The research reported here is an examination of relationships between social status and factors pertinent to water use in selected households in Warwick, Rhode Island. Specific consideration is given to quantities of water used by households and to water uses and social values as they relate to the status of those households.

In Rhode Island, Warwick is a growing suburb of the capital city, Providence, and is within the Providence-Pawtucket Standard Metropolitan Statistical Area. Of two water systems serving households within the city, the one serving the larger number of households and the larger geographic area was selected to delineate census tracts within which the households studied were located. Within the 11 census tracts served exclusively by the chosen water system, the universe considered was identifiable single-dwelling housing units, each of which had an exclusive water meter. All households were charged for water according to the same pricing system. This involved a minimum annual price of $11.00 for 4,444 cubic feet (33,330 gallons) of water; the rate was $0.002475 per cubic foot. The next 10,000 cubic feet (75,000 gallons) were priced at $0.0025 per cubic foot, while the second additional unit of 10,000 cubic feet was priced at $0.0024. For additional volume, the rate was lower.

Collection of Data

Sampling and data collection were done during 1965 and 1966. From the records of the water company, 17,375 qualifying housing units were identified. With the use of housing and household data reported by tract and block (median family income and density of settlement) in the 1960 Census, a systematic stratified sample of blocks was taken within which were 3,499 dwelling units; this was approximately 20 percent of the total number of qualifying units identified. The sample slightly overrepresented blocks having a mean household size of three or more members and those having mean household values of $10,000 or more. Among the dwelling units in the blocks selected, 337 were eliminated from further consideration as being a combination of housing units, or a combination of housing unit(s) and a small business, which used a single water meter. The remaining 3,162 dwelling units were the ones for which data on total water used during 1965 were secured from the water company and to which questionnaires were sent.

Of the questionnaires sent out, 1,027 were returned, but because response was incomplete not all of them could be used for analysis.

Status of Households Studied

On the basis of information provided in the questionnaires, households were categorized by use of a status index. The index was constructed from information on current house value, household income during the prior year (1965), occupation of the household head, and education of the household head. With a range from 100 to 300, the index was used to identify three status groups: III, low status, with an index range of 100-166; II, middle status, with a range of 167-233; and I, high status, with a range of 234-300. Eight hundred and seventy-four (874) households for which indices were computed were distributed through the three categories in the above sequence as follows: 267, 440, and 167. The respective percentages are 30.55, 50.34, and 19.11 (Spaulding, 1967).

ANALYSIS OF DATA

Household Status and Quantities of Water Used

The following comments about quantities of water used and the status of households are based on an analysis of 759 households for which data were provided. Data pertaining to these households are shown in Table 1.

Data pertaining to the mean number of cubic feet of water used per household show that households of higher status use greater quantities of water than do households of lower status. For all households, the mean number of cubic feet used was 8,895. The comparable figures for status groups I and II—the high and the

TABLE 1. *Households and Mean Quantity of Water Consumed—759 Households Classified by Status Group (Selected Census Tracts, Warwick, Rhode Island, 1965)*

Households and Water Use	All Households	Status Groups		
		I	II	III
Households				
Number	759	144	390	225
Percent	100.0	18.97	51.38	29.65
Mean Cubic Feet				
Used per Household	8,895	12,358	9,059	6,429

Source: Household Water Use and Social Status, 1967; table IV, p. 10.

middle groups—were greater than this amount, while for group III—the low status group—the mean number of cubic feet used per household was less than this amount. For the status groups in sequence from I to III, the means are 12,358, 9,059, and 6,429 cubic feet. The mean for the middle status group is about 1½ times that for the low status group, while the mean for the high status group is approximately twice that of the low status group. Generalizing loosely, one can say that the middle status households use about one and one-half times as much water per household as the low status households, while the high status households use twice as much. And the high status households use about one and one-third times as much as the middle status households.

Relative to the minimum amount for which the water company charged annually—4,444 cubic feet—each status group shows a larger mean per household. The mean for the low status group, 6,429, is slightly less than 1½ times this minimum; for the middle status group the mean, 9,059, is slightly more than twice the minimum; and the mean for the high status group is almost three times the minimum. When all households are taken into consideration, the mean number of cubic feet used per household, 8,895, is in essence twice the minimum of 4,444 cubic feet.

The increase in water used is also shown by the difference between the means for the cubic feet of water used per household in each status group. The increase between the mean of status group III (low status), and that of status group II (middle status), is 2,630 feet. Between groups II (middle status) and I (high status), the increase is 3,299 cubic feet. The increase between groups II and I is 1¼ times the size of the increase between groups III and II. And with respect to the mean number of cubic feet (6,429) used in group III, the increase between groups III and II (2,630) is 40.91 percent, while the increase between groups II and I (3,200) is 51.31 percent.

Altogether the evidence indicates that households of higher status use larger quantities of water than households of lower status. This is indicated by the absolute amounts of the mean number of cubic feet used per household in each of the three status groups; it is also indicated by the relationship between these means and the minimum number of cubic feet of water for which the water company charged annually. It is further indicated by the absolute and relative size of the increase in mean cubic feet of water used between the lower status groups and the higher ones.

Variables Related to Cubic Feet of Water Used

Data pertaining to relationships between selected socioeconomic variables and cubic feet of water used per household are shown in Table 2. Four characteristics show a positive and significant correlation (*r*) with quantity of water used among the 759 households examined without regard for status. In order of decreasing

TABLE 2. *Correlation Between Socioeconomic Characteristics and Cubic Feet of Water Used per Household—759 Households Classified by Status Group (Selected Census Tracts, Warwick, Rhode Island, 1965)*

Characteristics	All Households	Status Groups		
		I	II	III
Status Index	0.327	0.142	0.105	0.226
Components of Status Index				
House value	0.273	0.244	0.154	0.175
Household income	0.330	0.168	0.178	0.288
Education of household head	0.178	0.088	-0.019	-0.019
Occupation of household head	0.218	-0.136	-0.066	-0.066
Lot Size	0.160	0.018	0.039	0.087
Household size	0.353	0.101	0.184	0.373
Feeling That Water Is a Necessity	0.089	0.001	0.023	-0.155
Correlations Significant at	0.075	0.159	0,098	0.132

Source: Household Water Use and Social Status, 1967; tables IV and VII, pp. 10 and 13.

correlation, these are household size (0.353), status index (0.327), lot size (0.160), and the feeling that water is a necessity (0.089). In addition, each component of the status index shows significant correlation with the cubic feet of water used per household. These, in order of decreasing correlation, are household income (0.330), house value (0.273), occupation of the household head (0.218), and education of the household head (0.178).

Status groups show similarities and differences with respect to relationships among these variables. For group I, with high status, only house value and household income correlated significantly with cubic feet of water used per household; the coefficients are 0.244 and 0.168 respectively. Status groups II and III, with middle and low status, are similar in the sense that significant correlations exist for the same variables; they differ in the extent of correlation. For these two groups, the significant correlations, in descreasing sequence, are for household size, household income, and house value; the respective coefficients for group II are 0.184, 0.178, and 0.154; for group III they are 0.373, 0.288, and 0.175. Consistently, the coefficients are larger for group III than for group II. The status index, itself, also correlates significantly with quantities of water used per household in these two groups; the coefficient for group III (0.226) is larger than that for group II (0.105).

With two exceptions, the highest correlations for the above variables, as they are discerned in status groups, are in the lowest status group and the lowest correlations are in the highest status group. The exceptions are for house value and for the status index. Of these two, the former correlates more highly with quantity of water used in status group I than in either status group II or group III. For the latter, the coefficient of correlation in group I is greater (but not significant) than that in group II and is smaller than that in group III.

Characteristics of the 759 households examined which did not show a positive and significant correlation with the cubic feet of water used per household were attitudes of the household head about water uses and water-using equipment as indicators of social status, the abundance of water in nature, and concern about water supply and shortage. In addition, the degree of past social mobility did not correlate positively or significantly with the quantity of water used.

Variables Related to the Social Status Index

Among the variables above which showed a positive and significant relationship to quantities of water used are those which also showed a positive and significant relationship to the status index.

TABLE 3. *Correlation Between Social Status Index and (1) Index Components and (2) Socioeconomic Characteristics—759 Households Classified by Status Group (Selected Census Tracts, Warwick, Rhode Island, 1965)*

Index Components and Characteristics	All Households	Status Groups		
		I	II	III
Components of Status Index				
House value	0.528	0.525	0.145	0.469
Household income	0.692	0.478	0.246	0.444
Education of household head	0.719	0.129	0.527	0.257
Occupation of household head	0.806	0.246	0.512	0.369
Lot Size	0.074	0.329	-0.015	0.089
Household Size	0.186	0.086	-0.019	0.145
Correlations Significant at	0.075	0.159	0.098	0.132

Source: Household Water Use and Social Status, 1967; tables V and VI, pp. 11 and 12.

Data pertaining to these are shown in Table 3. Each index component met this specification for all households and for each status group. For all households, the index components, in order of decreasing size of correlation coefficient, are occupation of household head (0.806), education of household head (0.719), household income (0.692), and house value (0.528).

RELATIONSHIPS AMONG STATUS, SOCIOECONOMIC VARIABLES, AND WATER USES

On the basis of the above correlations, it appears that, with respect to quantities of water used, house value and household income are better indicators of quantities of water used in each status group than are the education and the occupation of the household head. In addition, house value and household income are better indicators of status for the high and low status groups than are the education and occupation of the household head; for the middle status group, however, education and occupation of the household head are better indicators of status than are house value and household income. In all status groups, with one exception, each status index component is more closely related to the status index than to the quantity of water used. The exception is house value for the middle status group.

With respect to other socioeconomic variables, lot size, while significantly related to status, is not significantly related to quantity of water used in any status group. Household size, on the other hand, is consistently and more closely related to quantity of water used than to status; it is significantly related both to water used in the middle and in the low status groups and to the status index in the low status group. In no status group is the feeling that water is a necessity significantly related either to the quantity of water used or to the status index.

Hence, among the index components and other variables, house value, household income, and household size are shown to be most closely and consistently related to the quantity of water used among all households and among households in status groups. The closeness of relationship varies among variables and status groups. However, of these three, house value and household income are shown to be more closely related to the status index for households than to the quantity of water used per household. Household size is shown to be more closely related to the quantity of water used than to the status index. Despite these variations, indications are, then, that the quantity of water used by households is significantly related to their status and to their size. To the extent that status as identified here may reflect class, and to the extent that household size may reflect stage in the family cycle, the data support the point of view that class and family cycle are critical influences on quantities of water used by households. This is consistent with Gans' point of view that class and family cycle are important for urban community planning and suggests that water uses may fit into life styles in a manner which reflects social values.

HOUSEHOLD STATUS, WATER USES, AND SOCIAL VALUES

With respect to household water uses, social values, and their relationship to status, questions were raised about quantities of water for specific uses and about the importance of water-using equipment related to those uses. Household heads were asked in different places in the questionnaire to respond to each of the following questions (numbers 3 and 15 on the original questionnaire):

In your household, which of the following is the way the most water is used?

Check one: ____ a.   For cooking and beverages.
            ____ b.   For fountains and other water-using decoration.
            ____ c.   For maintenance of the house and yard.
            ____ d.   For personal cleanliness of household members.
            ____ e.   For recreation at home.
            ____ f.   For sanitation in the house and the yard.
            ____ g,   Other (specify) _____.

For your household, the most important piece of water-using equipment is the _____.

In order to relate both the responses to these questions and their implications for social values to social status, the responses were analyzed according to variations in house values, household income, and household size—the three socioeconomic variables shown above to have significant relationship to quantities of water used by households.

Three categories were established for each of these variables. For house value, the intervals were under $10,000; $10,000-19,999; and $20,000 or more. For household income, they were under $6,000; $6,000-11,999; and $12,000 or more. For household size, they were households of one or two members; of three, four, and five members; and of six or more members. The Chi-squares (X^2) were computed for distributions in the three categories for each variable and for each pair of categories within the three. Data pertaining to the use which takes the most water are reported in Tables 4, 5, and 6; those pertaining to the most important equipment are in Tables 7, 8, and 9.

On the whole, the data indicate that for both the use regarded as taking the most water and the use related to the most important equipment, greater variation exists with respect to household size than to house value or household income.

STATUS AND WATER USE

Consideration will be given first to large-quantity use. With respect to this, the relative significance of household size is shown as follows: The three distributions for categories of house value have a

TABLE 4. Responses to "In your household, which of the following is the way the most water is used?"—830 Households, Classified by 1966 House Value (Selected Census Tracts, Warwick, Rhode Island, 1965)

	House Value							
	Under $10,000		$10,000-$19,999		$20,000 or more		TOTAL	
Water Uses	N	%	N	%	N	%	N	%
Cooking and Beverages	8	6.8	16	2.7	0	0.0	24	2.9
Decoration	0	0.0	2	0.3	0	0.0	2	0.2
Maintenance	11	9.3	69	11.7	26	21.1	106	12.8
Personal Cleanliness	93	78.8	457	77.6	90	73.2	640	77.1
Recreation at Home	0	0.0	4	0.7	0	0.0	4	0.5
Sanitation	6	5.1	41	7.0	7	5.7	54	6.5
TOTAL	118	100.0	589	100.0	123	100.0	830	100.0

$x^2 = 22.70$, df = 10, $p < 0.02$. The following give x^2 for pairs of categories, where df = 5—Low-middle: 7.1164, $p > 0.05$; Middle-high: 13.0104, $p < 0.05$; Low-high: 43.4979, $p < 0.001$.

TABLE 5. Responses to "In your household, which of the following is the way the most water is used?"—786 Households, Classified by 1965 Household Income (Selected Census Tracts, Warwick, Rhode Island, 1965)

	Household Income							
	Under $6,000		$6,000-$11,999		$12,000 or more		TOTAL	
Water Uses	N	%	N	%	N	%	N	%
Cooking and Beverages	7	3.5	13	2.9	1	0.7	21	2.7
Decoration	0	0.0	2	0.4	0	0.0	2	0.3
Maintenance	36	18.1	44	9.8	21	15.5	101	12.8
Personal Cleanliness	144	72.4	360	79.8	103	75.7	607	77.2
Recreation at Home	1	0.5	2	0.4	0	0.0	3	0.4
Sanitation	11	5.5	30	6.7	11	8.1	52	6.6
TOTAL	199	100.0	451	100.0	136	100.0	786	100.0

$x^2 = 15.15$, df = 10, $p < 0.05$. The following give x^2 for pairs of categories, where df = 5—Low-middle: 12.1952, $p > 0.05$; Middle-high: 5.5807, $p < 0.05$; Low-high: 3.2318, $p < 0.05$.

TABLE 6.   Responses to "In your household, which of the following is the way the most water is used?"—827 Households, Classified by Size of Household (Selected Census Tracts, Warwick, Rhode Island, 1965)

| | Household Size | | | | | | | |
| | 1 or 2 members | | 3, 4, or 5 members | | 6 or more members | | TOTAL | |
Water Uses	N	%	N	%	N	%	N	%
Cooking and Beverages	8	3.4	11	2.3	7	5.8	26	3.2
Decoration	0	0.0	1	0.2	1	0.8	2	0.2
Maintenance	58	24.9	44	9.3	7	5.8	109	13.2
Personal Cleanliness	150	64.4	379	80.1	94	77.7	623	75.3
Recreation at Home	0	0.0	3	0.7	3	2.5	6	0.7
Sanitation	17	7.3	35	7.4	9	7.4	61	7.4
TOTAL	233	100.0	473	100.0	121	100.0	827	100.0

$x^2 = 37.61$; df = 10; $p < 0.001$. The following give x^2 for pairs of categories, where df = 5—Low-middle: 33.2231, $p < 0.001$; Middle-high: 7.3647, $p > 0.05$; Low-high: 23.8693, $p < 0.001$.

X^2 of 22.70, for which $p < 0.02$; those for household income have a X^2 of 15.15, which is not significant at the 0.05 level; and those for household size have a X^2 of 37.61, for which $p < 0.001$. (See Tables 4, 5, and 6, respectively.)

Pairs of categories will be considered in the low-middle, middle-high, and low-high sequence. Among the three pairs for house value, significant difference exists between the middle-high categories ($X^2 = 13.0104$; $p < 0.05$) and between the low-high categories ($X^2 = 43.4976$; p K 0.001). For household income, significant difference exists only between the low-middle categories ($X^2 = 12.1952$; $p < 0.05$). But for household size, significant difference exists between the low-middle categories ($X^2 = 33.2231$; $p < 0.001$) and the low-high categories ($X^2 = 23.8693$; $p < 0.001$). Households with higher house values show clear-cut differences from those with middle and low values; mixture of relationships is shown among the households of varying income levels, with no category showing conspicuously great difference from the others. Households of small size, however, are consistently different from the middle-and large-sized households. The large and consistent differences in uses are related to house value and household size rather than to household income. The

TABLE 7. Responses to "For your household, the most important piece of water-using equipment is the _____"—722 Households, Classified by 1966 House Value (Selected Census Tracts, Warwick, Rhode Island, 1965)

Equipment Classified by Water Uses	House Value							
	Under $10,000		$10,000- $19,999		$20,000 or more		TOTAL	
	N	%	N	%	N	%	N	%
Comfort	7	6.8	17	3.3	2	1.9	26	3.6
Cooking and Beverages	2	2.0	2	0.4	1	0.9	5	0.7
Decoration	0	0.0	1	0.2	0	0.0	1	0.1
Maintenance	2	2.0	10	1.9	3	2.9	15	2.1
Personal Cleanliness	60	58.8	347	67.8	69	63.8	476	65.8
Recreation at Home	2	2.0	4	0.8	0	0.0	6	0.9
Sanitation	29	28.4	131	25.6	33	30.5	193	26.8
TOTAL	102	100.0	512	100.0	108	100.0	722	100.0

X^2 = 9.22, df = 12, p $>$ 0.05. The following give X^2 for pairs of categories where df = 6—Low-middle: 6.5415, p $>$ 0.05; middle-high: 4.1414, p $>$ 0.05; low-high: 8.3939, p $>$ 0.05.

greatest differences are more prevalent between categories of household size than between categories of the other variables; this seems to indicate that stage in the family cycle may contribute more to the differences in uses than do class variables. This relationship is supported by data pertaining to beliefs about the most important piece of water-using equipment. (See Tables 7, 8, and 9.)

STATUS AND SOCIAL VALUES

In terms of their relationships to specific uses, beliefs about quantity of water used and about the most important piece of water-using equipment are regarded as reflecting association between size (quantity) and importance in the value structure of the households examined. To describe this association, X^2's were computed for the distribution of uses pertaining to the largest quantity of water used and for the distribution of uses pertaining to the most important equipment in each category for house value, household income, and household size. Since all the X^2's are greater than one would expect on the basis of chance, this evidence does not provide support for the existence of strong association between size (quantity) and importance as they relate to water uses.

TABLE 8. *Responses to "For your household, the most important piece of water-using equipment is the _____"– 683 Households, Classified by 1965 Household Income (Selected Census Tracts, Warwick, Rhode Island, 1965)*

Equipment Classified by Water Uses	Household Income							
	Under $6,000		$6,000-$11,999		$12,000 or more		TOTAL	
	N	%	N	%	N	%	N	%
Comfort	13	7.9	10	2.4	1	0.9	24	3.5
Cooking and Beverages	2	1.2	1	0.3	2	1.8	5	0.7
Decoration	0	0.0	1	0.3	0	0.0	1	0.2
Maintenance	5	3.2	6	1.4	3	2.7	14	2.1
Personal Cleanliness	99	60.7	281	68.5	72	65.5	452	66.2
Recreation at Home	1	0.6	1	0.3	1	0.9	3	0.4
Sanitation	43	26.4	110	26.8	31	28.2	184	26.9
TOTAL	163	100.0	410	100.0	110	100.0	683	100.0

$x^2 = 16.52$, df = 12, $p > 0.05$. The following give x^2 for pairs of categories, where df = 6—Low-middle: 11.8059, $p > 0.05$; middle-high: 1.4487, $p > 0.05$; low-high: 10.9413, $p > 0.05$.

However, the X^2's indicate that association between these two variables is greatest in large households and least in small households; it is also greatest for households with low income and low house value; it is intermediate for those with high income and high house value. The sequential variations in association between the two variables are regarded as nearer to being progressively consistent in the value structure with respect to family cycle stages than they are with respect to differences in class position. (See Table 10.)

Grouping the three household characteristics according to the relative size of the X^2's shows the following typologies: largest X^2's, medium house value, medium household income, and small household size; intermediate X^2's, high house value, high household income, and middle household size; smallest X^2's, low house value, low household income, and large household size. The X^2's are interpreted as indicating the greatest degree of association between size (quantity) and importance, as they relate to water uses, to be located in large households having low income and low house value. The intermediate degree of association is found in middle size households with high incomes and high house values. The smallest degree of association is

TABLE 9. Responses to "For your household, the most important piece of water-using equipment is the _____"—715 Households, Classified by Size of Household (Selected Census Tracts, Warwick, Rhode Island, 1965)

Equipment Classified by Water Uses	Household Size							
	1 or 2 members		3, 4 or 5 members		6 or more members		TOTAL	
	N	%	N	%	N	%	N	%
Comfort	15	7.3	9	2.3	1	0.9	25	3.5
Cooking and Beverages	2	0.9	1	0.2	2	1.8	5	0.7
Decoration	1	0.5	0	0.0	0	0.0	1	0.2
Maintenance	7	3.4	9	2.3	0	0.0	16	2.2
Personal Cleanliness	109	52.9	280	70.6	81	72.3	470	65.7
Recreation at Home	0	0.0	3	0.7	1	0.9	4	0.6
Sanitation	72	35.0	95	23.9	27	24.1	194	27.1
TOTAL	206	100.0	397	100.0	112	100.0	715	100.0

$x^2 = 26.91$, df = 12, $p < 0.01$. The following give x^2 for pairs of categories, where df = 6—Low-middle: 23.4248, $p < 0.001$; middle-high: 4.7612, $p > 0.05$; low-high: 17.1475, $p < 0.01$.

found in small households with middle range incomes and house values.

Despite these differentiating variations, additional evidence substantiates the lack of significant relationship between size (quantity) and importance. This is correlation (r), adjusted for small numbers, between distributions for which the X^2's were computed. Because of the small numbers involved and the nonlinear relationship among uses, the coefficients are regarded as only suggestive. Within these limitations, they tend to confirm the positive but not significant relationship between uses with which the largest quantity of water used and the importance of water-using equipment are associated. (See Table 11.)

Also, despite these differentiating variations, personal cleanliness was mentioned by the largest proportion of households as accounting for the greatest amount of water used and as having the most important equipment. Second in accounting for the greatest amount of water was maintenance, while sanitation was second in accounting for the most important equipment. Each of the other uses was never cited by as many as 10 percent of the households as paramount in

TABLE 10. X^2's and Typologies for Distributions of Water Uses Associated with Greatest Quantity of Water Used and with Most Important Water-Using Equipment—Households Classified by Socioeconomic Variables Significantly Related to Household Water Use (Selected Census Tracts, Warwick, Rhode Island, 1965)

Socioeconomic Variables	X^2's[a]	
House Value		
Under $10,000	29.7704	low
$10,000–$19,999	107.9070	high
$20,000 or more	33.2233	middle
MEAN	56.9669	
Household Income		
Under $6,000	49.2482	low
$6,000–$11,999	94.2482	high
$12,000 or more	81.1528	middle
MEAN	74.8831	
Household Size		
1 or 2 members	80.4807	high
3, 4, or 5 members	63.6103	middle
6 members or more	19.4016	low
MEAN	54.4975	
	Typologies	
Largest X's		
House Value	$10,000–$19,999	middle
Household Income	$ 6,000–$11,999	middle
Household Size	1 or 2 members	low
Middle X's		
House Value	$20,000 or more	high
Household Income	$12,000 or more	high
Household Size	3, 4, or 5 members	middle
Smallest X's		
House Value	Under $10,000	low
Household Income	Under $6,000	low
Household Size	6 members or more	high

[a]df = 5. For all values except that for households of 6 or more members, $p < 0.001$; for households of 6 or more members, $p < 0.01$.

Values for X reported here were computed without cases for the use "Comfort" associated with equipment. Values computed with these cases included were usually larger than those reported, but this variation did not alter the general pattern of relationship among the X^2's.

either respect. The implications of these relationships are yet to be explored. (See Tables 4 through 9.)

CONCLUSIONS

In conclusion, one can point out that the evidence presented here indicates three relationships. First, households of higher status

TABLE 11. Coefficients of Correlation, Adjusted for Small Numbers, Between Distributions of Water Uses Associated with Quantities of Water Used and with Importance of Water-Using Equipment—Households Classified by Socioeconomic Variables Significantly Related to Household Water Use (Selected Census Tracts, Warwick, Rhode Island, 1965)

Socioeconomic Variables	Correlation Coefficients and Level of Significance	
	r	p
House value		
Under $10,000	0.5046	$p > 0.05$
$10,000-$19,999	0.6392	$p > 0.05$
$20,000 or more	0.4706	$p > 0.05$
Household income		
Under $6,000	0.5278	$p > 0.05$
$6,000 -$11,999	0.7934	$p < 0.05$
$12,000 or more	0.5350	$p > 0.05$
Household size		
1 or 2 members	0.2610	$p > 0.05$
3, 4, or 5 members	0.7927	$p < 0.05$
6 or more members	0.6088	$p > 0.05$

For $p = 0.05$, $r = 0.7540$.

tend to use more water than households of lower status. Second, to the extent that house value and household income reflect social class and that household size reflects stage in the family cycle, quantities of water and variation in its uses seem to be more closely related to stage in the family cycle than to social class position. Third, the association between size and importance as related to water use in the value structure of the households studied is positive but not statistically significant; to these households, for these activities, the perspective of "the more the merrier" and "the bigger the better" does not apply uncritically.

Future research may well be directed toward developing understanding of household water uses relating to personal cleanliness, sanitation in house and yard, and maintenance of house and yard; these were identified most frequently in association with greatest quantities of water used and with most important water-using equipment.

REFERENCES
Ezekiel, M.
1941 Methods of Correlation Analysis, 2nd ed. New York: Wiley.

Gans, Herbert J.
    1968 People and Plans: Essays on Urban Problems and Solutions. New
        York: Basic Books.
Gottman, Jean
        Megalopolis. New York: Twentieth Century Fund.
Hagood, M., and D. Price
    1952 Statistics for Sociologists, rev. ed. New York: Holt, Rinehart &
        Winston.
Singh, R. N., and K. P. Wilkinson
    1968 Social Science Studies of Water Resource Problems: Review of Literature
        and Annotated Bibliography. Water Resources Research Institute,
        State College: Mississippi State University.
Spaulding, Irving A.
    1967 Household Water Use and Social Status. Bulletin 392, Agricultural
        Experiment Station, Kingston: University of Rhode Island.

PAPER 2

Variations in Patterns
of Leisure Behavior:
An Analysis of
Sociological Aggregates

NEIL H. CHEEK, JR.

In new areas of inquiry where theory is emergent and speculative, a search for empirical regularities often provides a heuristic beginning for more refined and sophisticated analysis. In this paper we will examine the phenomenon of going to parks. We shall identify empirical regularities associated with this phenomenon and provide some suggested hypotheses for their presence.

PARKS DEFINED

The definition of a park in sociological terms is still in the process of development. For this study, the respondent's own definition was employed. It was assumed that sufficient consensus exists within a culture so that adults could respond to the stimulus "park" and could distinguish it from "nonpark." No difficulty in this respect was experienced among respondents during either the pretest or study phases. All data reported in this paper were obtained through studies supported by the National Park Service, U.S. Department of Interior. The analysis is solely that of the author and does not reflect official interpretation in any matter.

Although dictionary definitions of a park are available, they touch only upon criteria such as land areas, ownership of lands, and so on, with no mention of behavior. Basically, the definition now commonly accepted is that a park is a geographically identifiable area of land "set aside" by members of society. In contemporary terms, such areas are for the common enjoyment of members of that society. Moreover, the designation of such land areas as parks is usually legitimated in terms of the area's symbolic significance for that society. Such symbolization usually rests upon one of three cultural values: (1) identification with, and desirability for continuity with, the past; (2) identification with contemporary expressions of the desirable; and (3) identification with a future, idealized or expected. Thus, parks are collective representations in the Durkheimian sense. Much more than land upon which members of the society gambol, they are symbolic of cultural values and beliefs shared among members of a collectivity. In this sense, parks are more sacred than secular. They symbolize the communion shared among the members of a collectivity; in this instance, a society.

A history of parks in various societies remains to be written. However, from the sketchy evidence available it appears that a park, as a sociocultural entity, has always been largely noninstrumental in character. Irrespective of ownership, parks have been used for recreation, ornamentation, or preservation. Often a particular park might serve several functions simultaneously. Throughout history parks have been places where people walked, talked, relaxed, and enjoyed themselves. This does not mean that the same kinds of people or the same social classes were found in all parks. Indeed, one important change in the history of parks was the shift from private to public ownership. Note that this is social structural shift, not necessarily accompanied by shifts in cultural values or functions of the park.

The fact that people enjoy themselves while in a park should not be dismissed lightly. What are the conditions which bring about the expectation of enjoyment? One condition is the idea of communion.[1] People in parks reaffirm their identification with others of their species, not only as conspecifics[2] but as members of a society. In parks, interaction among strangers appears to be an important social norm, and the classical anonymity of the urban area seems not to hold to the same degree. The reputed isolation and alienation of the individual from his own kind appears to be attenuated somewhat in parks. Instead, interaction is expected, enjoyed, and, at times, sought. For example, the following words were commonly used by respondents while describing their last time at the park:

warm	simple	exhilarating
casual	spontaneous	uncomplicated
free	rejuvenating	fun
crisp	relaxing	impromptu
pretty	fresh	

---

[1] For a discussion of the concept see "The Sociological Category of Communion" by Herman Schmalenbach (1961).
[2] Individual animals classified as a single species.

The content of the communications among strangers may be distinctive. During the pilot study it was observed that respondents reported passing the time of day with strangers whom they met in campgrounds, on walks, and so on, while in parks. Several interpretations of the behavior are possible. A psychologist might suggest that this kind of interaction is indicative of a minimum of personal involvement. That is, such conversation is relatively unimportant since it reveals little about the individual. Another interpretation might not disagree with the psychologist's but instead might emphasize that what is being reaffirmed in such encounters is a commonality of membership in some larger social unit. Identification among the participants is instantaneous during such encounters. What is important is not the particular detailed information about each other but the affirmation that the actors do indeed share some universe of discourse. It is this kind of communion which makes the experience of going to a park different from many other aspects of daily life, and which makes the park interesting as a social invention.

One important social structural property which may be necessary for such interaction to occur is that most people go to a park accompanied by someone else. The study found that 90 percent of the respondents had been to the park with another person, usually someone they already knew, and often a relative or close friend. Thus social interaction among strangers in a park occurs in the presence of significant others. In addition, the social interaction which occurs *within* the social groups going to a park together tends to differ from that expected outside a park.

To summarize the discussion thus far, we have suggested that people in parks share several characteristics. First, the social norm is that going to a park is done with another person. Second, it is part of the normative pattern that only certain categories of persons are eligible to accompany someone, usually relatives and friends. Finally, we noticed that social interaction occurs among strangers and is expected. Such interactions usually occur in the presence of significant others. These interactions may serve the function of reaffirming common membership in a larger social collectivity, a society.

PARK-GOING AGGREGATES

A social aggregate is comprised of people who share similar patterns of behavior, but who do not necessarily interact on a face-to-face basis. The patterns of behavior are shared because of a common culture. Like any pattern of social behavior, variability is to be expected within a population.

Lacking quantitative data from earlier historical periods, we cannot say with any certainty that the social class who went to a park is or is not similar to that found in contemporary parks. Theoretically it is reasonable to expect that a population would contain subpopulations among which park going as an important cultural activity would vary. Therefore it is necessary to identify empirically the presence of such variation within a population before proceeding with an analysis.

Table 1 shows the distribution of responses from a probability sample of adults, 18 years and older, obtained during a national study conducted in 1968. The data were obtained by interviews conducted in the respondents' homes. The sample was selected using area-probability sampling procedures and consisted of 3,587 adults. The population sampled included all adults not institutionalized or serving abroad in the armed forces of their nation. In order to learn about the relative frequency with which adults go to parks, we asked the respondents to tell us about how often they frequented parks during a calendar year. The results are seen in Table 1.

It is clear that considerable variation exists within the adult population when going to parks. Moreover, there are, as expected, some adults who reported that they never go to parks. This is, however, a relatively small percentage of the sample (about 6 percent); about 94 percent of the sample reports having gone to some park. Among those who go to parks we can identify several social aggregates—those who go once or more per month, those who go less than once a month but at least once a year, and those who go to parks but don't remember precisely how often they go, although it is not as frequently as once a year. For convenience, each of these social aggregates will be referred to throughout this article by a single term. Respectively, the social aggregates of people going to parks are *"often," "occasional," "rare,"* and *"never."*

TABLE 1.   *Frequency of Going to Parks*

	Percentage of Sample (N = 3,587)
Once or More per Month	28.1
Less than Once but Within a Year	43.9
Don't Remember but Over a Year	22.2
Never	5.6
TOTAL	99.8

In order to partly overcome the problems inherent in the use of a single variable as an index of a diffuse social process, we asked the respondents to indicate how long it had been, prior to the interview, since they were in some kind of park. When relating this distribution to the previous distribution we would expect that the answers of those persons in the *often* aggregate would be significantly different from those of the *occasional* and *rare* aggregates. The results of this cross tabulation are shown in Table 2.

TABLE 2. Recency of Last Time in Park (Percentage)

	Within a Month	Within a Year	Over a Year	Don't Remember	TOTAL	N
Park Aggregate						
Often	42.9	55.5	1.4	0.2	100.0	1011
Occasional	15.4	72.3	10.9	1.4	100.0	1576
Rare	1.0	4.3	84.6	10.1	100.0	799

It is apparent that the hypothesis is supported. Those in the *often* aggregate were significantly more recently in some park than those among the other aggregates. (The *never* aggregate is a null category empirically; therefore it is not shown in this table.) It is worthwhile noting that within the *often* aggregate at least two subgroups exist. Unlike the *occasional* and *rare* aggregates in which the distribution clusters occur at expected time intervals of respectively "within a year" and "over a year," two clusterings occur within the *often* aggregate. This suggests that some respondents in the *often* aggregate go to parks almost continuously, whereas others go to parks equally frequently during certain periods (perhaps seasons) of the year but not on a continuous basis.

SOCIAL CLASS

Parks as collective representations of a society may in their social structures reflect differences with respect to the social classes of people who go to them. However, since theoretically all members of a society would be expected at some time to participate in activities occurring in parks, all social classes should be represented. This does not deny the possibility that some kinds of parks may be the exclusive social turf, so to speak, of some social classes. Moreover, to expect the presence of all social classes in parks presupposes that the normative pattern includes a norm of unlimited accessibility for members of the society. We know that historically some parks have been for the enjoyment of a particular social grouping, such as the nobility, or the residents of a particular neighborhood, or

TABLE 3. *Income Reported (Percentage)*

	Lower (under $5,000)	Middle ($5-$9,999)	Higher ($10,000+)	No Response	TOTAL	N
Park Aggregate						
Often	18.1	45.4	34.9	1.6	100.0	1011
Occasional	25.9	43.9	28.8	1.4	100.0	1576
Rare	47.4	33.6	17.8	1.2	100.0	799
Never	67.0	23.0	8.0	2.0	100.0	201

only those who were able to pay some entry fee. Table 3 shows the distribution of gross annual family income reported by the respondents cross-tabulated with the park-going aggregate of the respondents.

Allowing for the difficulties of using access to the marketplace, measured by reported income, as the sole index of social class, it can be seen that some people from all social classes report going to some parks. Apparently, as a phenomenon per se, social class is not the factor determining the behavior. However, it is also clear from Table 3 that social class does have differential consequences regarding the frequency with which people go to parks. Thus, as the frequency of park going of an aggregate increases, the proportion of that aggregate reporting annual incomes over $10,000 increases directly. However, in no aggregate does the majority possess incomes of over $10,000. Thus, while the frequency with which an adult may go to a park is determined in part by his family's annual income, it is clear that going to parks is not solely determined by income alone.

EDUCATION

In addition to income, education may also be associated with going to parks as a social phenomenon. The effects of formal schooling upon cultural beliefs and values acquired through other mechanisms of socialization are not well understood. What does seem to occur is the establishment of peer relations among persons from differing subcultural origins. Preliminary data from another study by the author suggests that many persons have been acquainted with parks from infanthood. For such persons, going to parks is a pattern of behavior that has apparently been maintained throughout life; as adults they continue to go to parks, with infants, children, and older persons related to them. The point is that whatever differences may exist empirically among persons who go to parks as far as formal schooling is concerned, such differences may not be the most salient for predicting that behavior. On the other hand, it is known that

TABLE 4. *Education Completed (Percentage)*

	Less than High School	High School	More than High School	TOTAL	N
Park Aggregate					
Often	30.6	36.2	33.2	100.0	1011
Occasional	40.1	35.7	24.2	100.0	1576
Rare	60.4	26.2	13.4	100.0	799
Never	76.0	18.5	5.5	100.0	201

social relationships among peers strongly influence the individual's choice of behavior, particularly during the years of formal schooling and adolescence. The extent to which such influence may permanently alter previously acquired cultural patterns is not clear. However, among adults going to parks, the majority do so with relatives instead of friends. Thus, the amount of variance in going to parks which could be accounted for by the years of formal schooling acquired will require further study. However, as can be seen in Table 4, the park-going aggregates differ among themselves with respect to the distribution of education shared by respondents within an aggregate.

It is apparent from Table 4 that as the frequency with which park going increases, the proportion of the aggregate sharing formal schooling beyond high school (that is, 12 years completed) increases directly. The empirical differences among aggregates are statistically significant. However, several additional aspects of the table are noteworthy. Between the *often* and *occasional* aggregates the modal category shifts from high school completed to less than high school completed. Among the remaining aggregates, the modal category remains "less than a high school education," while the proportion of the aggregate sharing that characteristic increases until among the *rare* and *never* aggregates it becomes the most salient. This suggests that education appears to be related to park-going behavior in a manner different from income. That is, a particular level of formal schooling accounts for the major proportion of the variance within a particular aggregate. Among these aggregates, the variable also accounts for a major portion of the variance between the pairs *often-occasional* and *rare-never.* Even with these differences identified it remains clear that adults of all levels of education do in fact go to parks.

SOCIAL AGE

Among many species, recognition of a particular social status within a social grouping is necessary for certain behavior to occur among conspecifics. Thus, among many primate species, clear social distinctions exist among infants, juveniles, subadults, and adults with respect to the individual's appropriateness as a playmate, hunting partner, warrior, copulatory partner, parent, and so on. This general pattern also appears to be characteristic of *Homo sapiens*. Thus, while most individuals are capable of reproduction from puberty onward, they are not defined as potential marriage partners until some years later. In short, human aging, while continuous as with most other forms of life, is experienced by many individuals as discontinuous. Paricular segments of the continuous process tend to take on differential social meanings, symbols, and significance for both the individual and the larger group.

The population under investigation in this study is comprised of adults, 18 years and older. The age distributions of the several park-going aggregates can be seen in Table 5.

The respondents are grouped into three social age categories: 18-24; 25-49, and 50 years and older. These categories correspond roughly to, respectively, subadult, adult, and mature adult among *Homo sapiens*. Subadults are those who are capable of leaving their families of orientation and establishing families of procreation. Many individuals are completing educations, beginning work careers, and selecting marriage partners during this segment of their lives. In the segment of 25-49 years of age most individuals are recognized as adults. Most individuals (about 73 percent of both males and females) have begun a marriage by the age of 25. Many have commenced child rearing. Employment opportunities and patterns begin to stabilize for males. Throughout this period the social structural forces of work histories and family rearing are the dominant determinants for most individuals. Around the age of 50 years another segment begins. This is the social age category of mature adult. It is characterized by the termination of direct child-rearing responsibilities (for many individuals) except as grandparents, the culmination of work histories,

TABLE 5. *Social Age (Percentage)*

	Subadult (18-24)	Adult (25-49)	Mature Adult (50+)	TOTAL	N
Park Aggregate					
Often	18.1	57.6	24.3	100.0	1011
Occasional	16.6	51.2	32.1	100.0	1576
Rare	6.6	35.8	57.6	100.0	799
Never	8.0	32.8	59.2	100.0	201

TABLE 6. Comparison of Park-goers to the Population, by Social Age (Percentage)		
	Percent in U.S. Population, 1960	Percent in Parks, 1968
Social Age		
Subadult (18-24)	7.5	9.6
Adult (25-49)	32.4	32.1
Mature Adult (50+)	24.1	23.2
TOTAL	64.0	64.9

and the establishment of new behavior patterns based upon differing social structural forces. While it is not known whether these social ages per se are associated with differences in going to parks, theoretically it is to be expected that such differences will occur. Table 5 provides some interesting data with reference to this discussion.

First, it is clear by inspection that some adults of all social ages are in some parks. That is, going to parks is a social behavior participated in by some respondents in all the age categories. Second, with respect to the U.S. adult population as a whole, the number of adults going to parks is representative of the number of adults within a particular social age category in the population. This comparison is shown in Table 6. The proportion of the U.S. population which is currently under 18 years of age is approximately 35 percent.[3]

It is apparent from Table 5 that among the park-going aggregates the modal social age categories are those of adult and mature adult as compared with subadult. In other words, it appears that going to parks is behaviorally more characteristic of "older" adults than "younger" adults. Remembering the earlier discussion concerning the social norm that going to a park is participated in with significant others, this finding suggests that there may be a social structural constraint which militates against the association of subadults and adults in particular settings like parks. Although these data do not permit the observation, it would be interesting to know if the subadults went to the parks as participants in friendship groups or as members of kinship groups. The structural inhibition may lie between these two kinds of social groupings rather than between social age categories per se. During the developmental phase of another study we observed that the kinds of sentiments shared among persons while in a park tended to be the same, irrespective of age,

[3]See U.S. Bureau of the Census (1969), table 28, p. 26.

the leisure activity being pursued, and so on. What the influence, if any, of social interaction between members of structurally dissimilar social groups may be on this condition remains to be tested. The structural dissimilarity between some social groups may be either age or sex graded. That is, the normatively expected park-going group may be structurally a mixed age (adults, juveniles, and infants), mixed sex group of particular composition. Other social groups which are single age (subadults) or single sex may be comparatively unusual. If so, persons may distinguish among different kinds of parks by using such distinctions.[4]

Among the park-going aggregates the modal social age category changes between the *often-occasional* pair and the *rare-never* pair. In short, among those persons who rarely or never go to parks the modal social age category is 50 years and older. Among those who go to parks at least once within a year the modal category is 25-49 years of age. By examining the social age category of 50 years and older across the several park-going aggregates we can observe that, as the proportion of the aggregate in the category increases, the less frequently persons in the aggregate report going to parks. Moreover, when the proportions of persons in this social age category are compared statistically across aggregates, the differences between each adjacent aggregate are significant. For example, in the *often* aggregate 24 percent of the respondents were over 50 years of age. The comparable percentage in the *occasional* aggregate is 32 percent, and 58 percent in the *rare* aggregate. Clearly there is a direct relationship between location in a particular social age category and the frequency with which the adult goes to parks. The precise nature of the relationship requires further discussion.

It is clear that, as the proportion of the aggregate falling into the social age category of 50 years and older increases, the frequency with which adults go to parks in that aggregate decreases; however, it is not accurate to interpret the finding to mean that as persons become older they cease going to parks. For in both the *often* and *occasional* aggregates a substantial proportion of the adults are those over 50 years of age. These data do not permit any analysis of the park-going behavior of these mature adults when they themselves were adults in the 25-49 year category. Many now in the *rare* aggregate might have been in the *occasional* or *often* aggregate during another segment of their lives.

---

[4]This is developed more fully in my Parks, Zoos and Society (forthcoming).

SOCIAL AGE AND EDUCATION

Because social age and education both relate independently to park-going behavior, it is possible to consider the joint effects of these two variables on the frequency with which adults go to parks. We have observed that empirically the greater the proportion of an aggregate reporting more education, the more frequently the respondents in the aggregate report going to parks. With respect to social age we observed that the greater the proportion of the aggregate reporting the social age category of 50 years and older, the less frequently the aggregate reports going to parks. We now want to observe how education (or formal schooling) interacts empirically with social age and relates jointly with frequency of going to parks. The results are shown in Table 7. With social age being held constant we can examine the effects of education upon the behavior of park-going aggregates.

It is clear that within all social age categories the greater the proportion of the park-going aggregate with formal schooling beyond high school, the greater the frequency of park going reported within the aggregate. Conversely, the greater the proportion of the aggregate with formal schooling less than high school, the lower the frequency of park going within the aggregate. Apparently, when holding age constant, the effect of education on the park-going behavior of aggregates is constant. However, further examination suggests that the comparative saliency of education in determining park-going behavior among aggregates does not remain constant within all social age categories. This means that there is no direct relationship between amount of formal schooling and frequency of park going in all

TABLE 7. *Social Age, Education, and Frequency of Going to Parks (Percentage)*

	Education				
	Less than High School	High School	More than High School	TOTAL	N
Subadult					
Often	20.2	37.2	42.6	100.0	182
Occasional	31.2	42.4	26.4	100.0	268
Rare	42.3	44.3	13.4	100.0	56
Adult					
Often	25.8	41.3	32.9	100.0	586
Occasional	34.4	40.7	24.9	100.0	804
Rare	52.0	32.0	16.0	100.0	288
Mature Adult					
Often	48.8	24.5	26.7	100.0	243
Occasional	54.2	24.5	21.3	100.0	504
Rare	67.2	20.0	12.8	100.0	455

aggregates for any particular social age category. For example, the modal educational category for all aggregates within the social age category of 50 years and older is less than high school.

Any attempt at longitudinal analysis based upon cross-sectional data is always hazardous and frequently misleading. However, these data regarding the relationship between education, social age, and park-going behavior suggest that there may be no direct necessary effects between an increased general level of education in the population as a whole and an increase in the frequency of utilization of existing parks. At the very least, these data suggest the appropriateness of a careful assessment of such a proposition. Theoretically there is no necessary relationship to be expected between education and park going per se. Perhaps education combines with other variables to produce, through joint effects, differences on park-going behavior. On the other hand, as previously mentioned, an interesting observation is the apparent universality of sentiments shared among all adults with respect to park going. That is, irrespective of age, social class, or education the respondents tended to describe parks and their behavior in parks in similar terms.[5] This suggests that the social meanings attached to parks as cultural entities may be only minimally influenced by socialization processes external to the social groupings of significant others.

RESIDENCE PATTERN

The relationship between size of place and frequency of park going is shown in Table 8. It is apparent that size of place is associated with park-going behavior. Clearly, adults from all places of differing sizes go to parks. However, the comparative frequencies with which such behavior occurs tend to differ. Specifically, the modal category of places over 500,000 population is characteristic of the *often* aggregate. For all other aggregates the modal category is places under 25,000 residents. Apparently some adults in larger urban places

TABLE 8. *Size of Place (Percentage)*

	Under 25,000	25,000– 499,999	Over 500,000	TOTAL	N
Park Aggregate					
Often	30.1	23.6	46.3	100.0	1011
Occasional	46.8	18.9	34.3	100.0	1576
Rare	49.4	18.7	31.9	100.0	799
Never	56.5	12.5	31.0	100.0	201

[5]See above, pp. 30-31.

TABLE 9. Distribution of City and County Parks Among Census Regions (Percentage)

	Percent of Sample in Places over 500,000	Percent of City and County Parks[a]
Census Region		
Northeast	35.6	24.0
Northcentral	25.2	30.0
South	16.2	26.0
West	22.9	20.0
TOTAL	99.9	100.0

[a]Statistical Abstract of the United States, 1969; table 290, p. 198.

go to parks frequently and significantly more than in other aggregates. One might at first assume this finding is obvious and related to the availability of parks, believing that more parks are found in large urban areas then elsewhere. Although the data in this study do not permit a direct examination of this question, some indirect evidence can be offered. Knowing the distribution of the sample among the four census regions, we can ascertain the proportion of adults resident in places of 500,000 and over as distributed among the census regions. This distribution shows indirectly how such large urban places are distributed among the four regions. In addition, from other sources we can obtain the distribution of the approximately 30,500 city and county parks among the four census regions. These figures are given in Table 9. While these figures are not conclusive, they are instructive for the question under consideration. There is no direct relationship between the proportion of adults in large urban areas in a particular census region and the proportion of city and county parks located in that region. This suggests that frequency of going to parks in large urban areas is dependent upon factors in addition to availability alone. For example, neither these data nor those in Table 8 permit us to know whether adults in the *often* aggregate go to nearby parks more than to other parks. We do not know if adults resident in large urban areas go to outlying state parks more frequently than do those who live nearby. In short, we require additional information regarding park going, parks, and place of residence.

Even if we find empirically that nearness of parks is directly related to frequency of park going, the explanation of the relationship is not as obvious as it might at first appear. Propinquity as a motivation in human behavior does not seem to be a sufficient explanation. Moreover, since going to parks is a sociological phenomenon, the interaction constraints are likely to be important to the explanation.

It is interesting to note within the park-going aggregates that adults residing in places of differing sizes are distributed in different patterns. Within the *often* aggregate a larger proportion of adults reside in places between 25,000 and 499,999 than in any other· aggregate. This observation, in light of the discussion above, suggests that the relationship between large urban, small urban, or rural residences and going to parks is somewhat more complex than often thought.

This paper has shown the existence empirically of certain selected sociological characteristics shared by the contemporary adult members of a society concerning going to parks. It has been shown that, irrespective of a history of parks as land areas contributed by the wealthy, contemporary park going occurs among adults of all social classes, educational backgrounds, social ages, and residential patterns.

Although we do not know what, if any, relationship may exist between the frequency with which adults go to parks and, say, the strength of commitment among members of a social group or identity with a larger social collectivity, we have identified some empirical variation in the frequency of the behavior. For purposes of analysis we designated as the social aggregates, *often, occasional, rare,* and *never.* Based upon the analysis thus far, each of these social aggregates can be described further in terms of a measure of central tendency, the mode, with respect to the sociological characteristics mentioned. More extensive analysis will enable further specification of the joint effects of such variables. An example is the joint effect produced by social age and education upon frequency of park going discussed above.

TABLE 10. *Description of the Park-Going Aggregate, by Sociological Character-istic*

	Often	Occasional	Rare	Never
Sociological Characteristic				
Social class (Income)	Middle	Middle	Lower	Lower
Education	High school	Less than high school	Less than high school	Less than high school
Social age	Adult	Adult	Mature adult	Mature adult
Residence pattern	Large urban	Small urban	Small urban	Small urban

Table 10 remains a summary statement of empirical regularities. It does not constitute a set of generalizations and should not be interpreted as such. Description is merely the first step in analysis. It alone never constitutes understanding or explanation.

This paper demonstrated that the adult population of the United States is differentiated with respect to going to parks. We have observed that

1. nearly all adults go to parks at some time;
2. not all adults go to parks with the same frequency or recency; and
3. such differences in going to parks appear to be associated with similarities and differences among adults with respect to social class, education, social age, and residence.

As suggested above, these commonalities do not constitute an explanation for the behavior for its empirical variation. What is suggested is the need for further studies of the park as a form of social organization.

REFERENCES

Schmalenbach, Herman
    1961   "The Sociological Category of Communion," trans. Gregory P. Stone, in Talcott Parson et al., eds., Theories of Society vol. 1. New York: Free Press.
U.S. Bureau of the Census
    1969   Statistical Abstract of the United States. Washington, D.C.: Government Printing Office.

PAPER 3
Studying the People Who Cause Forest Fires

WILLIAM S. FOLKMAN

The inadequacies of our future timber supply, the need for more clean water, and the mushrooming armies of recreationists demanding more facilities all suggest the imperative requirements for wise management of our wildlands. Minimizing losses from fire represents a priority item in such management.

More than 90 percent of wildland fires in the United States owe their origin to man or some agency of man. Little systematic study has been made of the people responsible for such fires. However, it is apparent that the types of persons involved are diverse and their motivation even more mixed. To effect greater control over the fire problem, better understanding is needed of the complex, dynamic interrelationships between man, the fire vector, and his environment. Achieving the necessary level of understanding would require a comprehensive research program which might be summarized under the following categories:

1. the social etiology and ecology of man-caused forest fires;
2. the development and evaluation of fire prevention methods; and
3. the organization of natural resource management, especially as it relates to protection from fire.

A research program of this scope obviously involves the theory and methodology of a number of social and physical science disciplines. Here, however, I emphasize the potential sociological contributions to this area of study. In particular, I focus on research problems to be faced in investigating aspects of the first category—specifically, identifying and characterizing high-risk forest-using publics.

44

In attempting to establish causal[1] relationships between people's behavior and fire starts, a distinction is usually made between fires set deliberately and accidental fires. (Although a significant proportion of man-caused forest fires are attributed to deliberate acts of man, the vast majority, outside the Southern states, are the result of nonmalicious, unintentional acts.)

The conduct of the deliberate fire setter, quite generally, has been defined as deviant behavior. Activities of the accidental fire starter have been less frequently so defined. He may be seen as an unfortunate victim of circumstances rather than as a threat to society (Folkman 1968a:10). Studies might be concerned with how the fire control agencies—through changes of laws, Smokey Bear campaigns, and other programs—seek societal acceptance of their definition of this behavior as deviant (that is, conduct about which "something should be done"). In this they, as do those concerned with auto safety, litter control, and similar problems, seek social control through labeling as deviant previously acceptable behavior. Those familiar with recent writings in the sociology of deviance (see Becker, 1964) will recognize a number of ways in which study of the forest fire problem is dependent on deviance theory.

To label certain types of fires as accidental should not lead one to infer that they are necessarily completely unpredictable and uncontrollable phenomena. Cursory examination of fire reports indicates that, contrary to popular impressions, most accidental fires do not appear to be solely chance events. They *are not* distributed at random among different groups of the population or in different situations or at different times. These differential rates set the stage for research on why these differences exist. In the study of both accidental and deliberate fires the behavioral aspects of the fire starters—such as the climate of the family, the social forces at work in the community, the values of the society as a whole, the psychological and physical characteristics of the individual(s) involved—require attention as well as does the more frequently studied physical setting in which the event occurs.

[1]Kaufman (1967:2) suggests that, for clarity, it is necessary to note that *fire cause* is here used in a way different from its usual use in fire reporting. The traditional use of the term in fire statistics refers to the attributed origin of the fire as officially reported by the fire control agency responsible for the records. Fire cause as seen from the standpoint of this analysis has much broader implications. It is not expected that a single "cause" will be found responsible for the start of unauthorized fires, but a complex of factors which lead to fire starts. Used in this sense, the discovery of patterns of fire causation is a basic objective of behavioral studies in fire prevention.

PROBLEM DEFINITION

High hazard wildland areas are entered by a variety of people for a variety of reasons. Such people are often categorized on the basis of their use of the land or their purpose in being there—occupational, recreational, and residential being the principal categories. These may be further divided into more specific categories such as logger, construction worker, hunter, camper, summer resident, and so forth. Because of differences in the nature of their activities, the frequency and duration of their stays in the wildlands, and in the numbers of individuals involved, these various types of users are considered to represent different degrees of risk as sources of fire starts.

There is no a priori basis for assuming that this type of categorization provides the best system for grouping of high risk people. Nor is there any basis for assuming that any one system would be superior for all purposes. There is no "natural taxonomy" of forest users. Any number of characteristics might be used to identify useful homogeneous groupings. The characteristic(s) chosen would depend on the specific purposes of the research and the theoretical and methodological orientation adopted. Thus forest users, or identified fire starters, might be categorized according to demographic group memberships (sex, age, race, socioeconomic status); personality characteristics (aggressiveness, sociability, nervousness); attitudes (toward risk taking, law obedience, safety beliefs); physical attributes (health, body structure, reaction time); and/or sociological variables (group memberships, values, leader-follower patterns).

Indications from existing data, and analogy with other types of accidents (Folkman, 1966a) lead to the expectation that fire starting (accidental as well as deliberate) is not a simple random occurrence. Rather, as Suchman suggests regarding other types of accidents (Jacobs et al., 1961:47), fire starting should be seen as a complex event which involves a whole system of personal and environmental factors. The problem, therefore, is not merely to relate the incidence of fire starting to specific characteristics of people (difficult as even this is, given the limited identification of fire starters) but to determine the peculiar relationships between such characteristics and different types of environments and conditions which result in high fire occurrence.

REVIEW OF LITERATURE

Relatively few studies have been made of behavioral factors in man-caused forest fires. Most of these have focused on indigenous rural publics in the Southeastern United States where woods burning has been a strong heritage of the regional culture (Baird, 1966; Hansbrough, 1961; Jones et al., 1965; Kaufman, 1939; Shea et al., 1934, 1940; Weltner, 1942). In general, these studies have found, or accepted as established, that woods burning was a part of the culture to the extent that it was, or had been, used regularly and was supported socially, if not legally (See Table 1). Incendiarism contributes to the incidence of fires in other parts of the country, too, but to a much more limited extent, and the practice is generally interpreted as an antisocial act. Stringent legal sanctions against allowing fires to escape control undoubtedly encourage some persons interested in use of fire for land management purposes to surreptitiously start fires. Some local fire control personnel in California have suggested that migrants from the rural South may have been responsible for the introduction of "woods-burning" into certain limited areas of that state. Most incendiary fires in the West, however, are considered of malicious or pathological origin. At present, only accidental fires are subclassified in fire reports. Kaufman's suggestion that subclassification may be just as important for incendiary fires appears valid (1967). It is quite possible that a careful study of the behavior of those who start fires will lead to a new system of classification of fire origin for both deliberate and accidental fires.

Systematic studies of the fire-risk characteristics of Western forest users are even less plentiful than those of the South (Chandler and Davis, 1960; Christensen et al., 1969; Folkman, 1963, 1965; Folkman et al., 1965). In these studies, measures of fire prevention knowledge are related to forest use and to various demographic and socioeconomic characteristics (See Tables 2-5). In two of the studies,

TABLE 1. *Interviewees' Responses to the Question, "How Often Should the Woods Be Burned in Order To Provide the Best Grazing Conditions for Cattle?"*

	Number	Percentage
Annually	36	29.5
Every 2 Years	23	18.9
Every 3 Years or More	10	8.2
Qualified (Sometimes Yes, Sometimes No)	5	4.1
Never (No Longer Necessary)	34	27.8
Don't Know	11	9.0
No Information	3	2.5
TOTAL	122	100.0

Source: Jones et al., 1965.

some attempt was made to assess natural resource and fire-related attitudes.

Hermann (1960) reports an exploratory study concerning known fire law violators (See Table 6). Their attitudes differed from those of nonviolators, but the study did not establish whether enforcement action produced the difference or preexisting attitudes contributed to the violation.

The fire-reporting category "incendiary" may include a variety of types of fire starts, from an etiological point of view. The sharp dichotomy of fire starts into incendiary and accidental may be blurred by the recognition of this variety within the broad categories. The causes of fire starting of any type are not well understood. The characteristics of fire have made it a potent, fascinating, and fearful focus of folklore, ritual, and myth of virtually every primitive culture through the ages (Bachelard, 1964; Frazer, 1930). The literature suggests an almost universal interest among children, primarily boys. This sex bias gives some credence to the psychoanalytical linkage of

TABLE 2. *Fire Prevention Knowledge Score Related to Types of Wildland Activity—Butte County, California*

	Number Reporting Activity (N = 761)	Mean Score (Percentage correct)
Frequency of Wildland Use		
None	183	54
1-2 times	86	60
3-5 times	126	61
6-10 times	122	62
11 or more times	244	62
Work in Wildlands		
Frequently	65	65
Occassionally	62	63
Never	256	59
Camping		
In Butte County	116	64
Outside Butte County	236	61
Fishing	274	61
Hiking	291	62
Hunting	183	62
Picnicking	400	60
Sightseeing and Driving for Pleasure	627	60
Other Activities	138	63
TOTAL		58

Source: Adapted from Folkman, 1965.

TABLE 3. *Fire Prevention Knowledge Score Related to Types of Wildland Activity—Utah County, Utah[a]*

	Number Reporting Activity (N = 901)	Mean Score (Percentage correct)
Frequency of Wildland Use		
None	112	79
1-4 times	203	79
5-9 times	174	81
10-19 times	181	81
20-49 times	153	82
50-99 times	44	82
100-199 times	8	81
200 or more times	6	90
Work in Wildlands		
No	854	81
Yes	42	83
Camping	230	81
Fishing	382	96
Hiking	199	82
Hunting	331	96
Picnicking	500	81
Sightseeing and Driving for Pleasure	587	79
Other Activities	45	82
TOTAL		81

[a]Test used is identical to the one for the Butte County study.
Source: Adapted from Christiansen et al., 1969.

TABLE 4. *Response of Residents of Utah County, Utah, and Butte County, California, to the Statement, "Forest fire danger in this area is highly overrated" (Percentage)*

	Utah County (N = 901)	Butte County (N = 761)
Strongly Agree	1.1	2.0
Agree	5.3	5.4
Undecided	14.1	18.4
Disagree	65.7	56.2
Strongly Disagree	13.8	16.3
Don't Know, or No Answer	—[a]	1.7
TOTAL	100.0	100.0

[a]Tabulated with the "Undecided."
Source: Adapted from Christiansen et al., 1969.

TABLE 5.   Comparison of Persons with Extreme Levels of Wildland Activity and Fire Prevention Knowledge and Attitude Scores by Selected Socioeconomic Characteristics—Butte County, 1964 (Percentage)

| | Knowledge-Attitude Scores | | | | |
| | Greatest Wildland Activity[a] | | Least Wildland Activity[b] | | |
	Lowest quartile (N = 14) (1)	Highest quartile (N = 43) (2)	Lowest quartile (N = 42) (3)	Highest quartile (N = 10) (4)	All Respondents (N = 761) (5)
Age					
14-24	50.0	23.3	9.5	10.0	23.4
25-34	14.3	16.3	9.5	–	13.8
35-49	7.1	34.9	14.3	40.0	25.8
50-64	7.1	23.3	26.2	30.0	21.7
65 and over	21.5	2.3	38.1	20.0	15.2
Not reported	–	–	2.4	–	0.1
TOTAL	100.0	100.0	100.0	100.0	100.0
Sex					
Male	50.0	62.8	23.8	40.0	48.5
Female	50.0	37.2	76.2	60.0	51.5
Not reported	–	–	–	–	–
TOTAL	100.0	100.0	100.0	100.0	100.0
Marital Status					
Single	50.0	23.3	14.3	10.0	18.5
Married	50.0	74.4	52.4	80.0	68.5
Widowed, divorced, or separated	–	2.3	33.3	10.0	13.0
Not reported	–	–	–	–	–
TOTAL	100.0	100.0	100.0	100.0	100.0

TABLE 5. continued

	(1)	(2)	(3)	(4)	(5)
Race					
White	85.8	97.7	88.1	100.0	97.5
Negro	7.1	–	7.1	–	1.3
Other	7.1	2.3	4.8	–	1.2
Not reported	–	–	–	–	–
TOTAL	100.0	100.0	100.0	100.0	100.0
Years of Schooling Completed					
0-4	7.1	–	14.3	–	3.7
5-7	35.8	–	19.0	–	6.7
8	21.4	4.6	21.4	10.0	14.8
Some high school	28.6	20.9	23.8	20.0	25.8
High school graduate	–	42.0	14.3	20.0	23.1
Some college	7.1	18.6	2.4	20.0	17.6
College graduate	–	4.6	4.8	10.0	4.7
Post graduate	–	9.3	–	20.0	3.6
Not reported	–	–	–	–	–
TOTAL	100.0	100.0	100.0	100.0	100.0
Occupational Status					
Employed, full time	14.3	55.9	19.1	60.0	37.3
Employed, part time	21.4	16.3	7.1	10.0	15.3
Retired or disabled	7.1	4.6	35.7	–	13.1
Housewife	21.4	11.6	35.7	30.0	22.2
Student	35.8	11.6	2.4	–	11.8
Other	–	–	–	–	0.3
Not reported	–	–	–	–	–
TOTAL	100.0	100.0	100.0	100.0	100.0

TABLE 5. continued

	(1)	(2)	(3)	(4)	(5)
Occupation					
Professional, technical	—	9.3	—	20.0	6.3
Farmer, farm manager	—	2.3	—	10.0	2.4
Manager, official, proprietor	—	7.0	—	—	6.2
Clerical worker	7.1	11.7	2.4	—	8.8
Sales worker	—	7.0	—	—	4.3
Craftsman, forman	—	9.3	2.4	10.0	6.6
Operative	14.3	9.3	9.5	10.0	6.8
Service worker	—	4.6	9.5	20.0	9.1
Farm laborer	7.1	4.6	—	—	4.3
Laborer	7.1	9.3	2.4	—	4.9
Not employed, retired	64.4	21.0	73.8	30.0	39.8
Not reported	—	4.6	—	—	0.5
TOTAL	100.0	100.0	100.0	100.0	100.0
Percentage of Respondents Who Are Chief Income-earners of Household	28.6	55.8	50.0	50.0	49.4
Family Income					
Under $1,500	7.1	2.3	28.9	10.0	8.0
$1,500-$2,999	14.3	2.3	33.3	—	12.8
$3,000-$4,499	35.8	11.7	11.9	30.0	13.3
$4,500-$5,999	14.3	16.3	7.1	20.0	13.1
$6,000-$7,999	7.1	27.9	7.1	10.0	17.3
$8,000-$9,999	—	16.3	—	20.0	10.8
$10,000-$14,999	7.1	11.6	2.4	10.0	12.9
$15,000-$19,999	—	4.6	—	—	2.5
$20,000 and over	—	—	—	0.9	0.9
Not reported	14.3	7.0	9.5	—	8.4
TOTAL	100.0	100.0	100.0	100.0	100.0

[a]This group includes those in the highest third of the respondents reporting frequent wildland activity.
[b]This includes those in the lowest third reporting wildland activity.
Source: Folkman, 1965.

TABLE 6. *Attitudes of Fire Law Violators and Nonviolators in Southern California Toward Such Laws and their Enforcement (Percentage)*

	Violators (N = 42)	Nonviolators (N = 256)
Do you feel that the present fire prevention laws are known by most people?		
Yes	22	36
No	71	53
Don't know	7	11
TOTAL	100	100
Do you feel that present fire prevention laws are reasonable?		
Yes	48	80
No	34	16
Don't know	18	4
TOTAL	100	100
Do you think that most people who visit National Forests have enough information about laws or rules to avoid breaking them?		
Yes	31	58
No	53	31
Don't know	16	11
TOTAL	100	100
Have you ever been contacted by a Forest Ranger concerning a violation of some fire prevention law?		
Yes	94	17
No	6	83
TOTAL	100	100
(If yes) Do you feel that you were treated fairly?		
Yes	60	85
No	30	15
TOTAL	100	100
Do you feel that there should be:		
More fire prevention law enforcement?	36	87
Less fire prevention law enforcement?	46	7
No answer	18	6
TOTAL	100	100

Source: Adapted from Hermann, 1960.

fire fascination to male psychosexual development. It is also quite clear that fire, like sex play, is an object of the most general prohibition for children. There are no data on the relative frequency of fire play in different cultures.

The literature on fire setting is fragmentary, and most of it is of dubious validity. It consists mainly of isolated anecdotal reports based on very few cases, buttressed by psychoanalytical theorizing concerning individuals involved in repeated starting of fires (Kaufman et al., 1961; Nurcombe, 1964; Rothstein, 1963; Siegel, 1957; Sturup, 1955; Yarnell, 1940).

An examination of fire investigation reports shows that a small minority of children is identified with such multiple fire setting. However, it is this group of fire incendiarists (collectively accounting for a small proportion of the total fires) who have received the research attention that has been given to the subject.

A recent study (Siegelman and Folkman, 1971) found the following characteristics associated with such fire incendiarism: hyperactivity, aggression, psychosomatic difficulties, learning problems, behavior problems, and family traumas. The frustration engendered in attempting to function under these handicaps usually precipitated an acting out that frequently involved fire. A tentative typology identifies two different types of children: (1) the withdrawn, anxious child, with anger directed against himself, and (2) the restless child, subject to antisocial behavior, with anger directed outside himself. Fire setting means different things to these different types of children. To the first it may represent a cry for help, a plea for adult authority to help him deal with feelings too big and too dangerous for him to master by himself. To the other it may be a means of revenge, a way to further increase his ability to gain attention and, perhaps, the awed admiration of adults. Actually, both kinds of feelings are probably involved to a greater or lesser extent in any deliberate setting of fires.

Most fires, however, are not the result of such pathological behavior. In the great majority of cases, the fires are either accidentally started or, although deliberately set, their getting out of control is neither anticipated nor desired.

Research on the etiology of this most prevalent type of man-caused fires is essentially nonexistent. Findings from the studies of pathological cases may well have some relevance, but more insights as to the causation of accidental fires may be gleaned from the slightly more plentiful studies of other types of accidents.

Taking the lead from the poetic but sound dictum that "the child is father to the man," it would appear profitable to look for the origins of adult fire-related attitudes and behavior in the developing child. Reports of childhood accident studies suggest that a child's natural curiosity, sometimes coupled with an attempt to imitate the behavior of an adult or older sibling, may place him in a situation where his lack of knowledge of cause-and-effect relationships precludes his control or prediction of the consequences. The resulting fire incident thus becomes part of the fire record of the fire control agency. The number of similar actions, similarly motivated, which do not result in reportable fire accidents is unknown, but must be many times larger than the number reported.

At one time accident research gave considerable attention to the concept of "accident proneness." More recent research has questioned the validity of the concept, especially as it was sometimes defined in terms of a subconscious desire to have an accident (start a fire) (Haddon et al., 1964;385-444; Mellinger et al., 1965). Statistically different rates of accidents for different individuals are observed, but a more parsimonious explanation is that the differential represents failure to learn skills in coping with potentially dangerous situations, rather than subconscious pressures to inflict pain on self or others. Clinical cases have been reported by various psychiatrists of a neurotic tendency on the part of some individuals to inflict self-injury through deliberate accidents. However, it is questionable whether such evidence justifies the use of accident proneness to explain all, or even most, cases of high accident frequency. Since chance plays a part in many accidents, we would expect to find in any given period a certain proportion of the public suffering an inordinately high number of accidents *by chance alone.*

Studies of interpersonal relationships of children involved in accidents indicate that the family environment exerts an important influence upon accidents that occur, not only in that environment but also in other situations (Haddon et al., 1964:446, 483-490). Their findings reveal that a disturbed home environment renders an individual (especially a younger child) more susceptible to accidents away from home as well as at home. Accident occurrence in these studies seems to be related primarily to the protection role of the mother. Any factors (such as illness, outside work, or other preoccupations) which distract her, increase the accident vulnerability of her child. A high ratio of dependents to earners in the household, limited or no play area at home, and overcrowding were also reported as related to accident occurrence.

Ross (Haddon et al., 1964:496-503) reports a study which seeks to determine the extent to which traffic law violation might be classified as a "folk crime," a general term under which he would also include white collar crime as described by Sutherland. Folk crimes are defined by Ross as "crimes that are ignored or even condoned and that involve a lack of congruence between the new laws and established mores." Ross proposes this category in order to group together violations of laws that are introduced to regulate the novel kinds of behavior that an increasingly advanced technology and an increased division of labor generate. The data used in Ross's study were taken from a sample of a ten-year record of traffic law violations in a midwestern metropolitan area. The comparisons made of the violations of various occupational groups only indirectly relate to the hypothesis considered. The records are of unknown reliability and the important socioeconomic variable and other factors used, including whether or not an accident was actually reported, probably influenced the police action recorded.

Ross's study is merely exploratory, but the area is a potentially important one, deserving of more careful research. On the surface, the application of the concept may appear more apropos of the fire problem in the southeastern states, but the position of fire law enforcement and fire protection in the value system of the society and the individual elsewhere also needs to be considered. To what extent are fire law violations, like traffic law violations, not subject to social stigmatization—that is, in public opinion, not considered to involve "real" criminality? Debris burners, for example, who permit their fires to escape control often define themselves, and are so considered by their neighbors, as unfortunate victims of circumstances rather than lawbreakers (Folkman, 1968a). Similar results from the careless or indifferent behavior of young people, however, may frequently be defined as "juvenile delinquency."

Given the pervasive and rigid taboos against the use of fire by children, we might expect that much of the fire behavior of young people will be socially defined as delinquent. Since this is so, one might look to the theories and research of delinquency for some enlightenment concerning the increasing problem of forest fires caused by children and youths.

THE PROBLEM REEXAMINED

Forest fire problems arise from such varied behavior as the innocent play of a child to the deliberate, premeditated act of an arsonist; from the unthinking careless behavior of a novice camper to the compulsive acting out of a pathological personality; from the conditioned reflex action of a smoker discarding a match or cigarette butt to the violent expression of a social protester.

The lack of a unifying general theory applying to this variety of fire-relevant human behavior and the plethora of conceptual approaches conceivably related to the subject preclude following a single, straightforward line of attack upon the problem. Despite the breadth and complexity of the subject area, however, specific portions of it can be related to relevant theoretical contexts. By so relating our efforts to the mainstream of social theory, this research would assuredly be added to the increased understanding of human behavior that sociology is achieving. At the same time, a much more significant contribution may be expected to the solution of long-term problems of applied resource management without necessarily diminishing immediate positive applications.

In any initial studies, high priority must be given to identifying, characterizing, and categorizing various types of fire starters and fire situations. Given the difficulty of identifying most actual fire starters, much of the previous research effort has been directed to studying the population at risk. Because of the relatively unhampered movement of people in and out of the National Forests and similar wildland areas, only gross estimates are available of the numbers of forest users and of the uses they make of the forests. In attempts to define the population at risk, forest fire researchers, therefore, are grateful for the research on outdoor recreation which contains some work on the characteristics and activities of populations of wildland users, as well as some indication of the numbers involved. One of the most comprehensive surveys was prepared by the Outdoor Recreation Resources Review Commission on the basis of data collected by the Bureau of the Census. This was a nationwide survey of the outdoor recreation habits and preferences of Americans 12 years of age and over. Participation rates by activity and region are shown according to age, sex, place of residence, education, occupation, and race. Activity rates are also shown by state of health, physical impairment, and size of community. Activity preference and data on vacation trips and outings are expressed according to selected socioeconomic characteristics. Descriptive analyses of the results of the survey include socioeconomic factors associated with participation in 17 specific outdoor activities, expenditures on vacations, trips, and outings, and background factors associated with participation in certain groups of activities (Outdoor Recreation Resources, 1962c).

Other Outdoor Recreation Resources' reports (1962a, 1962b) contain analyses of their surveys of the social and economic characteristics of specific types of users of outdoor recreation resources.

A bibliography of recreation research by the U.S. Forest Service (1967) contains a number of similarly pertinent references. (See especially the work of King, Taves, Hathaway, Bultena, and Lucas of the North Central Forest Experiment Station; and Burch, Hendee, and Catton of the Pacific Northwest Forest and Range Experiment Station.)

Of necessity, the characterizing and categorizing of various types of high fire-risk persons and fire situations may continue to be the focus of much research. Efforts to make meaningful use of existing data from fire investigation reports in the study of identified fire starters should continue, while encouragement is given attempts to improve the system of investigating and reporting fires. Some desired studies, such as certain types of epidemiological research, must await accumulated data from improved investigation and reporting of fire causes.[2] We recognize that under the best of circumstances we will be in a similar position to that of those studying (other types of) criminal behavior: Only the "unsuccessful" individuals will be identified.

Our research must not rest on purely taxonomic types of studies, useful as they may be. It must investigate the cause of fires, study in depth the interaction of man and forest fuels as mediated by the physical, biological, and sociocultural environments within which the action occurs.

The use of observation techniques as suggested by Burch (1964) and as proposed in the study of depreciative behavior in public campgrounds by Campbell, Hendee, and Clark (1968) would appear particularly adaptable to the study of fire-related behavior.

Papers by Jacobs and Suchman (1961:3-15, 26-47) present methodological and/or conceptual discussions of accident research which appear to have rather direct applications to the study of fire accidents (unintentional fire starts or escapes).

Jacobs draws attention to the problems of dealing with a class of events characterized by relative rarity and a low level of predictability and controllability. He recognizes quite formidable problems of formal statistical inference.

The conceptional analysis by Suchman of the accident phenomenon "has led us to the conclusion that accidents are subject to the same form of causal analysis as would be used to explain any nonaccidental event—we view accidents as social events—and, as such, subject to the general model for studying social action or human behavior" (Jacobs et al., 1961:46-47). He sees accidents as falling at one end of the continuum of predictable—unpredictable and controllable—uncontrollable behavior. This permits the analysis of these events in terms of current social theories of human behavior.

---

[2]Some of the values, and deficiencies, of such a comprehensive data source may be grasped by considering the Nationalized Uniform Crime Reports published by the Federal Bureau of Investigation. The history of this accomplishment reveals some of the problems that might be expected in attempting a similar consolidation of fire reports. In fact, much still remains to be done in the FBI reports to obtain comprehensive and comparable statistics relating to juvenile and adult offenders, as well as data on the administration of criminal justice (Office of Statistical Standards, 1963:112-113).

Haddon, Suchman, and Klein stress that accident studies limited exclusively to single host, agent, or environmental variables tend to be inherently inadequate, since the pertinent parameters and their interrelationships may be entirely missed (Haddon et al., 1964d: 231-232). They cite a study by Haddon et al. (1964:232-249), concerning fatally injured adult pedestrians as an example of an attempt to deal with all of these pertinent parameters.

Bronfenbrenner (Jacobs et al., 1961:139) makes a similar point when he brings to task his fellow psychologists for the one-sidedness of much of their empirical research. He makes a plea for more naturalistic observation at this initial stage of accident research, following the pattern of the natural sciences where the issues of how to handle the problem of taxonomy and of systematic description of complex phenomena get major consideration. To apply his advice to the area of accidental fires, we would look for the particular combinations of properties of persons and situations that are associated with particular kinds of fire starts. The object of such research would be to seek the invariances of persons, events, and environmental contexts that raise the occurrence above the expected level. ". . . what is called for at this stage of inquiry is careful observation at a concrete level leading eventually to the development of a differentiated taxonomy appropriate for systematic, descriptive studies. Certainly this was the strategy that actually paid off in the investigation of disease; clinical observation led to a diversified nosology which in turn stimulated descriptive studies of the differing circumstances in which various disease syndromes developed. And finally, the observed invariances led to hypotheses about etiology and ultimately to methods of cure and prevention" (Jacobs 1961).

Children and youths are felt to warrant special attention in our studies. The study of children is especially important because (1) fire seems to have a universal and strong attraction for children; (2) childhood is the period during which lifetime patterns of behavior and feelings regarding fire and its use are developed; and (3) children are responsible for an increasing number of man-caused forest fire starts. (The California Division of Forestry reports that within its area of responsibility the proportion of man-caused forest fires attributed to children has increased steadily from 10.5 percent in 1954 to 23.5 percent in 1968. This increased incidence of children-caused fires is only partially related to increased numbers of children in the total population. One might speculate that such social factors as changing residential patterns, by means of which children are brought into proximity with high fire hazard environments; changing family patterns, with reduced parental supervision of children; and changing recreational patterns, involving greater use of high fire-hazard wildlands, may also be involved. The relative influence of these and other possible factors needs verification.)

Research involving children should proceed along two main tacks:(1) The early identification and treatment of incipient fire-prone children is an area that is showing promise. It is closely related to the more general problem of the educationally handicapped child, with the attendant overtones of emotional problems and minimal brain dysfunction. Treatment of the adult pyromaniac has proven singularly unrewarding, but treatment at the inception of the problem is more encouraging.(2) The study of the "normal" child and his development of abilities to avoid, or cope with, actual or potential fire situations is central to our understanding of the etiology of the widely prevalent "accidental fire" problem. This may be seen as an integral part of child development. There is also a direct tie to the behavioral approaches to accident research. Cross-cultural studies of child-rearing practices may be particularly rewarding in revealing societal weaknesses in developing fire-safe behavioral patterns and attitudes in our children.

There is limited direct evidence for linking adolescents and young adults with a disproportionate share of fire starts. However, their high level of wildland activity, and an apparently quite pervasive feeling of anomie and disaffection with their society suggests that they may represent a rather high risk segment of the general population which warrants special attention. Deviance theories and research, especially as related to juvenile delinquency, are seen as directly relevant to studies in this area. The broader subjects of social control and social changes are also related.

Kahn outlines the long and complex history of delinquency theories (Lazarsfeld et al., 1967:477-505). He points out that there have been changing emphases and perspectives. A clinical view of delinquency prevailed through the 1940s and well into the 1950s. "Whatever the social context, ... behavior must essentially be interpreted in psychological-motivational terms, and the roots of motivational dynamics were to be found in parent-child relationships as seen in the perspective of psychoanalytic theory." Glueck's well-known prediction instrument represents one of many research developments utilizing this theme (Lazarsfield et al., 1967:503-505).

During this same period "there was also a tradition of *interest* in social problems and in the concentration of delinquency in underprivileged areas, in poor housing, and so on."

Cohen's work, stressing the idea that delinquent subculture is the source of a considerable amount of antisocial behavior, is seen as marking a turning point in theoretical and applied emphasis. The perspective became one of viewing delinquency as the normal adaptive behavior in lower class culture. Others saw it as a transitional adolescent phenomenon. Kahn identifies two major groups of theories at this juncture: Sutherland, Shaw, McKay, and others "dealt with the learning of delinquent norms and behavior in specific environments," while Parsons, Merton, and others were concerned with anomie and the "dysfunction between culturally prescribed goals and socially organized access to them by legitimate means." Cloward and Ohlin took the next step by joining these two threads into their "opportunity theory," which has influenced the direction of recent action programs. These programs originated as delinquency prevention efforts, and evolved into youth development and, finally, community development programs.

None of these theories represent a complete and rounded explanation of all delinquency. The preoccupation of most theories with delinquency associated with poverty or social deprivation would seem to limit their applicability in explaining fire-related delinquency, which, in the main, seems to be more widely spread across the social spectrum. In terms of our immediate concern with identifying high-risk forest users, the latest "opportunity theory" of Cloward and Ohlin does not seem to have as much bearing as some of the earlier theories, although it may later prove particularly appropriate in devising effective action programs for combating the problem.

As a follow-up to the studies involving children and youths, similar studies of the fire-related behavior of normal adults should be made to determine how they learn, or fail to learn, to avoid, or cope with, actual or potential fire situations.

The intricate interrelationships of man, fire, and man's natural and social environments provide a stimulating and significant focus for sociological research. We have seen that such research, involving, as it must, institutional, interpersonal, and individual factors may be approached from several active theoretical positions and may range in scope from the epidemiological to case studies. Work in the area gives promise of making substantive contributions to sociology and related disciplines. At the same time the researcher, as a concerned citizen, has the satisfaction of attending to a pressing problem of social significance. Although fire has had a role in certain ecological systems, there are few circumstances today where an uncontrolled forest fire does not constitute a serious threat to important natural-resource values as well as to human life and property. In addition, studies of the fire-related behavior of forest-using publics have much in common with studies of such other depreciative behavior as vandalism, littering, and other assaults on our natural environment, and may be expected to contribute to the understanding of them.

REFERENCES

Bachelard, Gaston
   1964 The Psychoanalysis of Fire. Boston: Beacon Press.
Baird, Andrew W.
   1965 Attitudes and Characteristics of Forest Residents in Three Mississippi Counties. State College: Mississippi State University. Social Science Research Center Preliminary Report Number 8.
Baird, Andrew W., and M. L. Doolittle
   1966 Behavioral Aspects of Man-Caused Forest Fires: A Program of Research. State College: Mississippi State University. A paper presented at the 27th Annual Southern State Fire Control Conference and Southern Information and Education Chiefs' Meeting, Gatlinburg, Tennessee.
Becker, Howard S. (ed.)
   1964 The Other Side. New York: Free Press.
Burch, William R., Jr.
   1964 A New Look at an Old Friend—Observation as a Technique for Recreation Research. U.S. Forest Service, Pacific Northwest Forest and Range Experiment Station.
Campbell, Frederick L., John C. Hendee, and D. Clark
   1968 "Law and order in public parks." Parks and Recreation 3(12):28-31, 51-55.
Chandler, Craig C., and James B. Davis
   1960 What do People Know About Fire Prevention? U.S. Forest Service, Pacific Southwest Forest and Range Experiment Station, Miscellaneous Paper 50.
Christiansen, John R., William S. Folkman, J. Loraine Adams, and Pamela Hawkes
   1969 Forest-Fire Prevention Knowledge and Attitudes of Residents of Utah County, Utah, with Comparisons to Butte County, California. Social Science Research Bulletin 5. Provo: Brigham Young University.
Folkman, William S.
   1963 Levels and Sources of Forest Fire Prevention Knowledge of California Hunters. U.S. Forest Service Research Paper PSW-11. Pacific Southwest Forest and Range Experiment Station.
   1965 Residents of Butte County, California: Their Knowledge and Attitudes Regarding Forest Fire Prevention. U.S. Forest Service Research Paper PSW-25. Pacific Southwest Forest and Range Experiment Station.
   1966a "Forest fires as accidents: An epidemiological approach to fire prevention research." Proceedings of the 56th Western Forestry and Conservation Association Conference 1965:136-142.
   1966b "Children-with-Matches": Fires in the Angeles National Forest Area. U.S. Forest Service Research Note PSW-109. Pacific Southwest Forest and Range Experiment Station.
   1968a Problem Debris Burners in Western Oregon. Oregon State Forestry Department.
   1968b Research in Forest-Fire Prevention Oriented to the Child-Caused Fire Problem. Mimeograph of talk presented July 18, 1968, before the California State Board of Forestry in Sacramento, California.

Folkman, William S., Robert J. McLaren, and John R. Christiansen
    1968 Public Responsibility for Natural Resources . . . Attitude of Utah
          County, Utah Residents. U.S. Forest Service Research Note
          PSW-165. Pacific Southwest Forest and Range Experiment
          Station.
Frazer, J. G.
    1930 Myths of the Origin of Fire. New York: Macmillan
Haddon, William, Jr., Edward A. Suchman, and David Klein
    1964 Accident Research: Methods and Approaches. New York: Harper
          & Row.
Hansbrough, Thomas R.
    1961 A Sociological Analysis of Man-Caused Fires in Louisiana (un-
          published Ph.D. thesis). Baton Rouge: Louisiana State University.
Hermann, William W.
    1960 A Research Design for the Evaluation of Attitudinal Aspects of
          Fire Law Enformcement. School of Public Administration, Los
          Angeles: University of Southern California.
Jaco, E. Gartly (ed.)
    1958 Patients, Physicians, and Illness. New York: Free Press.
Jacobs, Herbert H., Edward A. Suchman, Bernard H. Fox et al.
    1961 Behavioral Approaches to Accident Research. New York: Associa-
          tion for the Aid of Crippled Children.
Jones, Arthur R., Jr., M. Lee Taylor, and Alvin L. Bertrand
    1965 Some Human Factors in Woods Burning. Agricultural Experiment
          Station Bulletin No. 601. Baton Rouge: Louisiana State Univer-
          sity.
Kaufman, Harold F.
    1939 Social Factors in the Reforestation of the Missouri Ozarks (un-
          published M.A. thesis). Columbia: University of Missouri.
    1967 Resident Forest Publics and Local Contacts Unpublished Problem
          Analysis. U.S. Forest Services, Southern Forest Experiment Station.
Kaufman, I., L. Heins, and D. B. Reiser
    1961 "A reevaluation of the psychodynamics of fire-setting." American
          Journal of Orthopsychiatry 21:123-136.
Lazarsfeld, Paul F., William H. Sewell, and Harold L. Wilensky
    1967 The Uses of Sociology. New York: Basic Books.
Mellinger, Glen D., David L. Sylvester, William R. Gaffey et al.
    1965 "A mathematical model with applications to a study of accident
          repeatedness among children." Journal of the American Statistical
          Association 60:1046-1059.
Nurcombe, B.
    1964 "Children who set fires." Medical Journal of Australia 1:579-584.
          Abstracted in the Digest of Neurology and Psychiatry 32:258.
Office of Statistical Standards, U.S. Bureau of the Budget
    1963 Statistical Services of the U.S. Government. Washington, D. C.:
          Government Printing Office.
Outdoor Recreation Resources Review Commission
    1962a Wilderness and Recreation—A Report on Resources, Values and
          Problems. Study Report 3, prepared by Wildland Research Center.
          Berkeley: University of California, Berkeley.
    1962b The Quality of Outdoor Recreation: As Evidenced by User
          Satisfaction. Study Report 5, prepared by the Department of
          Resource Development. East Lansing: Michigan State University.
    1962c National Recreation Survey. Study Report 19. Washington, D.C.:
          Government Printing Office.
Rothstein, R.
    1963 "Explorations of ego structures of fire-setting children." Archives
          of General Psychiatry 9(3):246-253.

Shea, John P., et al.
——1939 Man-Caused Forest Fires: The Psychologist Makes a Diagnosis. U.S.
Forest Service Mimeo Office Report, Washington, D.C.
1940 Getting at the Roots of Man-Caused Forest Fires. U.S. Soil
Conservation Service Fire Prevention Studies, series A, no. 2,
Washington, D.C.
Siegel, L.
1957 "Case study of the thirteen year old fire setter. A catalyst in the
growing pains of a residential treatment unit." American Journal
of Orthopsychiatry 27:396-410.
Siegelman, Ellen Y., and William S. Folkman
1971 Youthful Fire-Setters ... an Exploratory Study in Personality and
Background. U.S. Forest Service Research Note PSW-230. Pacific
Southwest Forest and Range Experiment Station.
Sturup, G. K.
1955 "The diagnosis and treatment of a pyromaniac." International
Journal of Social Psychiatry 1(10):54-59.
Suchman, Edward A., and Alfred L. Scherger
1960 Accident Proneness in Current Research in Childhood Accidents.
New York: Association for the Aid of Crippled Children.
Reprinted, with omissions, in Haddon, Suchman, and Klein
(1964), pp. 387-389.
U.S. Forest Service
1967 Forest Recreation Research: Bibliography of Forest Service
Outdoor Recreation Research Publications, 1942 through 1966.
U.S. Forest Service, Forest Recreation Research.
Weltner, George H.
1942 Wakulla-Vernon Study. U.S. Forest Service Region 8 (unpublished
office report). Atlanta, Georgia.
Yarnell, H.
1940 "Fire setting in children." American Journal of Orthopsychiatry
10:272-286.

SECTION II

Spatial Meanings: The Symbolic Organization of Physical Terrain

Man encounters a nonhuman environment filled with diversities. If it is to be understandable, the objects encountered must be defined with reference to the beliefs, values, and expectations which guide human behavior. Much of the variation observed in the encounters between man and natural resources, for example, can be explained by appeal to such variables. Why one man cuts down a tree while another venerates it does not lie in the tree itself, but in the subcultures shared with others of their species in a particular locale, in a particular historical era. In short, man is seldom neutral about the nonhuman environment. Since species survival remains locked into the relationship, it is hardly surprising that individual men should become passionate about their surroundings. The diversity of opinions about the nonhuman environment current among individual men thus reflects aspects inherent neither in the environment nor in biological man, but rather in cultures.

One of the most important aspects of culture is the definition of places or locales shared among men. The forests to the plainsman are foreboding and uninviting. Conversely, the plains to the woodsman are devoid of life and destitute of worth. It is culture, not objective genetic or habitat differences, which makes them so. For some reason man defines his habitats or locales as either desirable or undesirable. The definition of particular locales as sacred or secular is a common constituent meaning of all cultures. Robert Lee's study shows how the imputation of meanings to locales and places shapes

65

the social expectations and behavior of humans who live in them. The study also demonstrates that such meanings are not unitary in a society. Subcultural variations occur and their sources are many, including social class, ethnicity, region, and religion.

Apparently such meanings are not immutable, for they may change within the comparatively short span of a human generation. In part, such variations within a subculture may occur as an unintended consequence of behavior by man with reference to the nonhuman environment. For example, man may completely modify the topography of an area on the surface of the planet. Where once there was water, there may now be none. Where once trees, a desert. Where once a valley, now a lake or bog. But, though man may alter the appearance of the topography of a locale, the ease with which individuals may alter their definitions of it does not appear to be as flexible or, as Burdge and Ludtke demonstrate, as easily accomplished. Often such shifts in meanings generate feelings of apprehension and anxiety. Burdge and Ludtke demonstrate that only under specific conditions do individual men accord such changes legitimation. The implications of the study are far-reaching, for it suggests that concepts of spatial organization as a part of tradition themselves come to take on value. As a result, an appeal to reason is seldom effective in inducing acceptance of the action. Like much of any culture, the meanings attached to places are part of the traditions of a social group and, as such, are learned very early in life. They are part of a group's *Weltanschauung*. Being interconnected with other beliefs and values, they comprise the larger part of any culture, the nonrational. The nonrational can seldom be manipulated by rational means. Does this imply that the cultures of *Homo sapiens*, once evolved, are immutable?

Human exploitation of the nonhuman environment not only has consequences for land and water masses, air, and other species, but also has cultural consequences for the human participants. For example, as the Burdge-Ludtke study reports, a change in a locale or habitat brought about through the use of a technology may remove it as a possible dwelling place for the species. Yet adaptation to enforced migration occurs through the culture. Alternatives exist within it which permit the individual to survive even in the face of extreme disruption of daily life. Such occurrences also have consequences for the preservation of shared meanings of places, that is, the basis for attachment by individuals to other locales elsewhere may be similar. In some cases particular places may become sacred through the emergence of myth to "explain" the movement of groups and individuals away from it. It may provide status enhancement in the sense of individuals' feelings of self-sacrifice for the good of a larger group, the society. From a sociological point of view, it means the readjustment of the moral order: changes in social deference patterns, variations in work and nonwork relationships among the participants. Practices (customs) once appropriate become no longer appropriate to the same degree. Though the culture provides alternatives and, thus, increasing individual animal survival potentialities, the moral order as specific to the original habitat and its inhabitants usually faces major variation, if not obliteration, as a coherent whole. Seemingly, under these and other conditions, one of the consequences of man's exploitation of the nonhuman environment is the emergence of and fluctuation in human moral orders.

The Burdge-Ludtke study deals with people who are displaced from their traditional locales, but who remain within the generally shared cultural meanings of the larger social order. Knowlton documents the cycle of events and consequences when a technologically more powerful group seeks to replace one set of cultural meanings with its own. Though the history of the species is replete with such cases, he deals with one of current relevance. He illustrates how Spanish-American attitudes toward the land as an integral way of life are forcibly replaced by Anglo attitudes toward the land as a commodity whose primary value is its profit potential.

As Knowlton clearly demonstrates, the result is that environmental impoverishment is closely intertwined with social impoverishment. Of particular interest is his evidence that organizations designed to solve environmental problems often seem to accelerate human problems.

PAPER 4
The Social Definition of
Outdoor Recreational Places

ROBERT G. LEE

Concern about the quality of outdoor recreational environments most often focuses on the behavior of the participants. Commonsense interpretations attribute increasing problems to such causes as the population explosion, affluence, and a breakdown in moral standards. A great number of factors undoubtedly bear on the issue, some of which at first appear to be significant bases for corrective action. But if problems are to be solved, then decisions must rest on better information than that which tradition, opinion, and conjecture indicate is significant.

This study generates a theory of outdoor leisure behavior that is linked to more comprehensive theories of sociocultural organization. It suggests that outdoor recreational settings might best be understood in terms of the meanings assigned to them by particular sociocultural groups. This approach may be of interest to both social scientists and natural resource specialists concerned with the relationships between culture, social organization, and the nonhuman environment.

THEORETICAL CONCEPTS
Evaluation of Leisure Research

Recent evaluations of sociological theory dealing with play and leisure indicate that "It remains an unreached goal for sociologists to relate play and leisure to society" (Meyerson, 1970:66), because

This study was conducted while the author was employed as a research sociologist by the National Park Service, Office of Natural Science Studies, under the supervision of Dr. Neil H. Cheek, Jr.

The author also acknowledges the intellectual guidance of Professor William R. Burch, Jr., and thanks him for his critical reading of this manuscript.

"The sociology of leisure today is little else than a reporting of survey data on what selected samples of individuals do with the time in which they are not working and the correlation of these data with conventional demographic variables" (Berger, 1962:37). Contemporary empirical study of the sociology of leisure lacks sufficient conceptual analysis for linking data on leisure behavior to a theory of community or class or subculture.

To remedy this situation Bennett Berger (1962:45) suggests that the sociology of leisure be considered a part of a sociology of culture ". . . which attempts to discover the moral character of a style of life by studying the behavior of groups under conditions where that behavior is least constrained by exclusively instrumental considerations." Berger identifies two reasons for past difficulties with conceptualizing leisure. First, leisure traditionally was conceptualized as a kind of time, and was opposite in meaning to work, which was characterized as a kind of action. If, as Berger suggests, work and leisure are not of different orders of phenomena, then leisure must also be considered as a kind of action which can be distinguished from work. The second reason further clarifies the first by suggesting that the idea of free time ". . . belongs to a presociological age . . ." (Berger, 1962:38) in which time not spent working was considered free of normative constraints. As forms of social action, work and leisure must be distinguished by the kinds of cultural norms which order behavior and the degree to which these norms are of problematic concern to the individuals who share them.

Sociocultural Definition of the Environment

Numerous scholars indicate how perceptions of the nonhuman environment and man's relationship to it vary between cultures (Spoehr, 1956; Lynch, 1960). Each culture creates and maintains an orderly view of man and his relationship to himself, others, and nature.

The major lineaments with which a social order is identified and articulated within a given culture are usually such social characteristics as sex, age, kinship, ethnicity, personal identity, social status, and lifestyle. The physical environment is also important for maintaining orderly social relationships because it serves as a repository of meanings for symbolizing relationships (Werthman, 1968; Goodenough, 1951), and also provides a spatial field in which social life can be organized (Fortes and Evans-Pritchard, 1940; Evans-Pritchard, 1940; Suttles, 1968; Goffman, 1961).

When individuals encounter unfamiliar objects which do not immediately fit a preconceived scheme of order, they become fearful

(Riezler, 1944). But by comparing the unknown to the known new objects can be fitted into a scheme of order, and fear overcome. Culture can be understood as a system of related schemes of order that is shared by all the members of a society. Thus, the relationship between fear and knowledge is a primary factor in forming distinct social and subcultural groupings and their location in and conception of space.

Children and adults whose experiences have seldom penetrated the invisible walls of the urban ghetto may perceive natural wildland settings as disordered, frightening places. They have no place in their universe of discourse for assigning positive meanings to the natural features of outdoor settings. An account of a trip to the redwoods by a group of black teenage males illustrates this well.

> *Nothing in their prior experience had equipped them to cope with such natural phenomena. And so they translated the trees into objects with which they could deal and began talking about how they'd like to be Godzilla, the monster in the movie, so they "could climb up to the top and throw rocks at the people on the ground". . . . It became obvious . . . that they were frightened, frightened of the size of the trees, by the vegetation, by the strange smells and the darkness. This was not their scene, their turf, their familiar battleground (Jacobs, 1970).*

Experience and Concepts of "Place"

When the environmental experiences of a variety of cultures or subcultures are compared, one common phenomenon emerges as a prominent feature. This is the shared experience of particular physical spaces as "places" with peculiar qualitative characteristics (Briggs, 1968). Such spaces or areas are identified by those characteristics that somehow fit a scheme of order peculiar to a social group or groups. A conversation with a Mexican-American visitor to a state park illustrates this phenomenon:

> Researcher: *"Why did you choose to come to this park rather than some of the private developments nearby? What particular things about this park do you appreciate?"*

> Respondent: *"This is a family park. People like us with lots of kids come here to have a good time. There's lots of room and we don't need to worry about the kids. . . . We like it here because there are many kinds of people here . . . colored people, Chinese people, and Latin people like us . . . ."*

*Sometimes I meet these people that I have worked with on
jobs in the city. That man over there . . . we are old friends."
(He points to an elderly black man playing cards with his
family under a tree.)*

Much investigation has been directed at the kind of psychic
attachments that develop through using or imagining a specific
location (Lynch, 1960). Yet the psychological study of how
individuals and groups create "places" by attaching themselves to
spaces has skirted the related, but less obvious, sociological question
of how shared images of such places arise and ensure orderly group
life.

Kinds of Places

The type of use that organized groups make of physical spaces
is important in determining the definition of place they will share.
The number and kinds of places shared by groups will vary with the
cultural and social conditions of their existence, because patterns of
work, consumption, recreation, worship, and mobility will be
different.

Within urban settlements it is possible to identify several
general kinds of spaces by type of use: *residences* (including houses
and apartments), *neighborhoods* (the network of relationships
characteristic of the domestic level of interaction), and *districts*
(medium to large sections of cities which are identifiable by
characteristic uses, such as exclusive residences, industry, or business).
(A related classification of spaces could be identified for nonurban
settlements.) Within each kind of space individuals and groups define
significant places in and between which they live, move, and interact.

Outdoor Recreational Places

Recreational settings are significant places for groups within this
classification of spaces. But the character of a public recreational
place is largely determined by the social milieu in which it is situated.
Sherri Cavan (1966) described how the use of drinking establishments
varied with city districts. Outdoor recreational places, whether urban,
suburban, or rural, are also defined by the character of surrounding
places.

Outdoor recreational spaces can be categorized into four kinds
of places on the basis of their social milieu and of the residential
origin and image of place held by most visitors: *neighborhood,
district, regional,* and *remote* outdoor places. Neighborhood outdoor
places are situated in or near residential neighborhoods. Most visitors

reside in the neighborhood and conceive of the place as a part of the local community. District outdoor places may or may not be located in a residential neighborhood, but most visitors reside throughout a larger section of a city or other residential area that is conceived of as a distinct place. Regional outdoor places may or may not be located in residential neighborhoods or districts. They are mainly used by residents from an area extending throughout a cluster of towns, cities, or counties which share a common cultural identity. Such places are conceived of by visitors as part of the region. Remote outdoor places may or may not be located in neighborhoods, districts, or regions. They are often widely known for their unique features and attract visitors from the local region, other regions, states, or sometimes even foreign countries.

Particular outdoor recreational spaces may take on the characteristics of all four kinds of outdoor places. For example, Central Park in New York City attracts visitors from outside adjacent neighborhoods and districts. The definitions of place experienced by such visitors are usually formalized by rules of conduct associated with attractions such as museums, theaters, picnic grounds, and botanical gardens. In contrast, neighborhood and district visitors are likely to establish definitions of place that reflect the activities of local groups. Teenage hangouts, play areas, drinking areas, and gambling areas are examples of local definitions of place.

Those who live in rural and wildland areas are usually proportionally too few to play an important role in defining remote public outdoor places near their residences or communities. For this reason visitors are more likely to conform to definitions of place associated with activities and attractions, such as water sport areas, or establish idiosyncratic definitions of place that reflect the expectations of the sociocultural group with which they identify.

Toward a Sociocultural Theory of Leisure

At first one might expect the recreational meaning of outdoor places to be closely related to the everyday meanings of leisure. If commonsense interpretations of leisure as "free" time were true, then outdoor recreational areas might be considered "free" spaces where everyday normative constraints were relaxed or even lacking. But the idea that these are "free" spaces must, along with "free" time, be consigned to a presociological age. It remains to clarify the social features which best typify the normative order of outdoor recreational places.

Regularities in meaning and use cannot be adequately understood without discovering the interpretive status of salient outdoor objects and situations for given groups. Interpretive status is the degree to which the meaning or definition of objects must be negotiated in order that joint or collective action may occur (Denzin, 1969). Groups which share a scheme of order because of a common social position, subculture, or area of residence will more easily negotiate a definition and take an object for granted. Where consensual agreement does not exist then objects will remain problematic elements. Interaction with others and the nonhuman environment can be viewed as an ongoing learning process in which groups of individuals mutually agree upon the meaning of objects. By doing so they may pursue daily life with confidence that other individuals will usually act on the same assumptions, even in problematic situations (Garfinkel, 1963).

A theory relating leisure meanings and behavior to sociocultural background is suggested by this interpretation of social order. Outdoor leisure behavior, as with all forms of social action, is contingent upon a shared scheme of order. But leisure behavior is differentiated from more exclusively instrumental forms of social action by a reduction in the number and intensity of socially problematic elements. Note that only social objects are necessarily specified as problematic, as much outdoor leisure behavior occurs in rigorous physical environments such as wilderness areas.

PROCEDURE

A survey of parks and outdoor recreation areas was designed as a means for discovering new concepts and theory (Glaser and Strauss, 1967). Parallel observations of subcultural groups were made in similar geographic settings throughout a major urban region. A number of settings were selected from throughout the broad survey for intensive observation. The criterion for selecting particular settings was their theoretical relevance for stimulating the emergence of distinct and unifying concepts.[1] Requirements specified diversity of sociocultural conditions and natural environments. Income, ethnicity, and life style were selected as readily identifiable indicators of social and cultural conditions.[2] These indicators were thought to be fairly

---

[1] This selection process is usually referred to as "theoretical sampling," and has been defined as "... the process of data collection for generating theory whereby the analyst jointly collects, codes, and analyzes his data and decides what data to collect next and where to find them, in order to develop his theory as it emerges" (Glaser and Strauss, 1967:45).

[2] Census tract data and interviews with community service workers were used to classify neighborhoods by income and race. Neighborhoods with mean family income of $5,000 or below were termed *low income*, while those above

reliable for an exploratory study, but should be considered only provisional for purposes of more intensive research. More variation could be explained by identifying variables that better describe the rule structures typical of various sociocultural groups. But a premature definition of these variables would introduce greater uncertainty than the use of the easily observable indicators mentioned above.

I employed a combination of conversational interviews, behavioral observations, and documentary analyses (see Webb et al., 1966, for a discussion of multimethod analysis). For each carefully studied setting the researcher obtained unstructured interviews with the park or recreational staff, neighborhood officials, police, and park users. These were combined with observation of park users, giving particular attention to aspects in the use of space such as accessibility, rate and manner of movement, selection of locations for specific activities, and self-segregation on the basis of sociocultural background. Locational behavior was studied at both the macro (setting selection) and micro (site selection within a setting) levels. Observations were recorded in the form of field notes, maps, and photographs. Conversations were recorded in the field book during or as soon as possible following the encounter.

FINDINGS

Three features were discovered which typify the normative order of socially defined places in general, and are especially useful for understanding outdoor recreational places:

1. the mode of "belonging" or being "at home";
2. the cognitive structure or organization of the spatial environment; and
3. expectations of legitimate social control over the organization and use of space.

All three features were found to be shared cognitive elements in the environmental perspectives of sociocultural groups. They there-

(Footnote 2 *continued*)

$5,000 were termed *middle income* (no high-income neighborhood parks were sampled).

Ethnic and life-style variations were identified by direct observation of recreationists and conversations with informants and community workers. Life style was typified by the range of variation in the expression of a given cultural or subcultural pattern, as signified by dress, hair style, posture, gestures, and paraphernalia. It was less useful where cultural variation was less extreme.

The income class of recreationists was estimated by noting such indicators of income as clothing, recreational equipment, and motor vehicle, and, where verbal contact was possible, determining their occupation.

fore serve as theoretical constructs for typifying the interpretive status of outdoor places for such groups.

Neighborhood Outdoor Places

Neighborhood outdoor places are an integral part of the everyday lives of local inhabitants (Jacobs, 1961: 95). For this reason an understanding of local outdoor places presupposes knowledge of the meanings and uses of space for the neighborhood as a social unit. Sociocultural conditions obtaining in a neighborhood determine the form of expression for the mode of belonging, cognitive organization of space, and social control of space. The following illustrations clarify how this functions for neighborhood social life.

Fried and Gleicher (1962:313) suggest that the "ownership of real property" is closely related to the "middle class" sense of belonging, while a knowledge of local inhabitants, events, and situations is closely related to the sense of belonging in the urban "working class." This proposition raises the question of whether the "propertyless lower class" is as alienated from what they do not own as the "property-owning middle class." Are they better able and more willing to treat any property as common property? Is their shared scheme of order such that they do not require legal property rights to experience space as their "own"?

Parallel observations in neighborhoods with differing sociocultural conditions have led me to formulate this proposition in terms of two primary modes of belonging that are not necessarily mutually exclusive: belonging through *possession* and belonging through *knowledge*. The Oak Knoll District of Pacific City is a typical example. The north and west section of the Knoll is a white middle income residential neighborhood, while the south and east section is inhabited by low income blacks, most of whom reside in a public housing project owned and administered by the city. A playground and recreation center occupy the intermediate space near the hilltop. The middle income residents have formed a "Neighborhood Development Committee," which has the vigorous support of the local real-estate agent. This organization promotes the standing of the community as a residential area for professional and white collar workers. Middle income residents perceive the presence of low income black residents, especially young people, as a threat to public safety and property values. Children from the middle income neighborhood make little use of the playground and recreation center. Recreation directors report that middle income residents think these facilities are controlled by and managed for the low income residents, and therefore do not encourage their children to participate in the activities.

Living space in middle income neighborhoods is governed more by formalized rules of property ownership (Sommer, 1969:39-58) than by rules for negotiating mutual expectations on a personal basis. On Oak Knoll, residents of the low income neighborhood must possess sufficient knowledge of one another to predict everyday actions if they are to live with order and safety. Rules governing possession do not suffice. Strangers who enter the low income neighborhood are treated with suspicion until the reasons for their presence can be explained. Children from this neighborhood make more use of the outdoor spaces than do children from the middle income neighborhood.

The most important element in the *cognitive organization* of a place is its boundary, or what Kevin Lynch has termed its "edge" (1960:47, 62-66). Within the boundaries of a place people learn a set of expectations appropriate for specific actions. They overcome immediate uncertainties and fears, and take for granted, or deal habitually with, events, things, and people that are salient for their actions.[3] The edge of a place is particularly important to them because it signifies that they can no longer habitually rely on the same scheme of order if they penetrate it to explore the unfamiliar. In an unfamiliar place they become more conscious of their environment and themselves, as they must continually interpret things that do not fit the taken-for-granted scheme.

Fried and Gleicher (1962:312) relate the cognitive organization of space to the sense of belonging by suggesting that the "propertyless" class occupies "territorial" or locally bounded space, while the "property-owning," higher status classes occupy "selective" space in which "the boundary between the dwelling unit and the immediate environs is quite sharp and minimally permeable." In the highly individualized, mobile, and diverse life style of the "middle class," "distances are very readily transgressed; friends are dispersed in many directions; preferred places are frequently quite idiosyncratic. . . . few physical areas have widespread common usage and meaning." Space outside the dwelling unit, including hallways, streets, and open spaces, is "public" and "anonymous." Public space is

---

[3]This phenomenon imposes some frustrating constraints on the researcher who attempts to discover expectations peculiar to places. Most people "in" the place are not conscious enough "of" it to articulate its internal order. Candid respondents may describe boundaries, people, and events, but all too often their answers are shaped by their attempt to fit the questioner into their scheme of order so that his presence can be explained or exploited. For a splendid clarification of this situation see Schutz (1944). It was primarily for this reason that the combination of observation and interviewing was adopted for this study.

perceived as belonging to everyone, and as such belongs to "no one." It is often viewed as pathways between individualized significant places. In the more stable and homogeneous "working class" neighborhood, boundaries between dwelling units and public spaces are highly permeable. Residents often feel "at home" on the streets. Streets are not just paths, but have become bounded places to which residents feel they belong (see also Gans, 1962). Yet the subjectively defined geographical boundary does not extend far beyond the dwelling unit.

Observations in neighborhoods with differing sociocultural conditions have enabled me to further clarify the distinction between *territorial* and *selective* space in terms of the expectations associated with these two modes of assigning geographical boundaries. In lower-income neighborhoods "hanging" around street corners and storefronts, drinking, visiting, gambling, playing, dope peddling, and many other activities occur on the streets and in parks and are organized by distinct local definitions of place (Whyte, 1943; Liebow, 1967).

Local territorial definitions of place were observed in a small neighborhood park situated in a Chinese district of Pacific City. Community service workers report that the primary users of the park are propertyless low income residents, who use it as a place to join others for conversation, games of chance, or to observe local social life. Higher status residents use the park only as a pathway or a setting for local ceremonies. Territorial use varies both spatially and temporally. From daylight until 7:30 A.M. the park is used as a training ground for the Chinese martial arts. From 8 to 11 A.M. elderly men slowly gather on the upper level to play games and visit. Activity is greatest between 11 A.M. and later afternoon. Between midmorning and later afternoon mothers bring their small children to play in the children's playground, which is located at the northeast corner of the lower level of the park. When the weather is favorable they are joined in the late morning by elderly women who come to sit in the sun and visit. Adult women seldom use other sections of the park except as a pathway. At noon, Causasian white collar and construction workers occupy benches throughout the park to eat their lunch (reflecting their selective mode of spatial organization). A group with similar spatial orientations, the tourists, use the park as both an attraction and a pathway from midmorning until evening. In the late afternoon and early evening younger Chinese men, who had been working earlier in the day, come to visit and play games. Throughout the day both black and white Skid Row indigents wander about the park, begging from tourists, sleeping, and drinking.

Corresponding to the typical modes of belonging and organization of space are expectations governing the *social control* of space. In his insightful study of an urban slum, Gerald Suttles (1968:4) distinguishes between the conceptions of public morality shared by slum dwellers and those shared by members of the wider society. To the slum dweller public morality is a practical set of guidelines for conduct that exists mainly as a means of protection. To those from the wider society public morality is an ideal set of guidelines for conduct to which is attached much heartfelt sentiment. In observing diverse neighborhoods I have used this distinction to typify *practical* and *formal* modes of social control over physical space.

When the moral order of the largest Pacific City park came to be defined as deviant by higher status users because of its heavy use by street gangs, homosexuals, hippies, and drug addicts, the police tripled surveillance patrols and succeeded in creating a less deviant definition of place. Such tactics are particularly efficient and just in the eyes of higher status residents, because the law does not differ too greatly from shared expectations favoring formal means of social control.

In low income neighborhoods social life is not organized by formalized roles. Consequently, residents are suspicious of anyone appointed to look out for the interests of anyone else (Suttles, 1968:36). Policemen and other public officials are considered "no better or worse than anyone else as individuals," but cannot be expected to carry out more than minimal responsibilities.

Neighborhood outdoor places vary with the degree to which they are informally controlled or "belong to" a particular race, class, age, or sex grouping. In Pacific City the Cherry Street Boys are still a powerful force in the use and control of outdoor spaces in their district, as is illustrated by this selection from the author's field notes:

> "I sat on one of the benches at the west end of Washington Park, took out my newspaper and opened it on the bench beside me. Three Latin mothers with young children were seated at the playground on the east end of the park. Several 'hippies' lounged, read, or drank wine in the center of the park. Four Puerto Rican youths in their late teens or early twenties leaned against the trees and cars on the southwest corner. Soon a retired Italian man came and sat beside me on the center of the bench. We chatted. . . . One of the Puerto Ricans, with long, bushy hair, looked intently at me and walked straight over to my bench, taking the remaining seat on the

other side of the old man. The old man immediately got up, broke off his conversation in the middle of a sentence, and trotted over to the sidewalk where he chatted with another retired Italian.

"I soon became uncomfortable under the intrusive stares of my bench partner and wandered over to deposit my Coke bottle in the garbage can near the other three young men. They asked to see the sports page in the paper, and I was soon convincing them that I was not a 'pig.'

"Within half an hour a teenager with blonde hair and 'straight' life style approached and attempted to sell $400 of 'Reds' . . . ."

Sections of Washington Park are definitely under the control of the Cherry Street Boys and are used as a place to "hang" and deal in drugs. Rules governing the control of local outdoor space are practical rather than formal, and to be appropriately followed require knowledge of local residents and events.

These three features of neighborhood places which have been under discussion were also found useful for directing observations of sociocultural groups using recreational settings outside of their residential neighborhoods. The following illustrations demonstrate the utility of this means of typification.

District Outdoor Places

Definitions of place occurring on district recreational spaces are likely to reflect schemes of order typical of the district. Idiosyncratic behaviors are tolerated only if condoned by the larger community and police authorities. Park officials and community workers report that low income residents generally have less knowledge and make less use of district places than of neighborhood places. Many district parks were beyond the boundaries of the familiar world for a high proportion of residents in low income and ethnically distinct communities.

When asked why more Chinese did not use outdoor areas in Pacific City, a Chinese community worker responded:

"What areas? There are none!"

When reminded of a large park nearby he tersely replied:

"Garfield Park is not for Chinese. They cannot feel that it is their own. After all, it is only very recently that they have been permitted to use it. It belongs to the White American culture."

Blacks and other ethnic minorities were not as open in their criticism, but expressed similar reservations about using district, regional, and remote parks.

A high proportion of low income teenagers in Pacific City have never been beyond the borders of their distincts, and many more have never experienced a nonurban environment. Numerous transportation programs are now being implemented to provide disadvantaged youth with the opportunity to visit district, regional, and remote outdoor areas.

Most visitors to district parks on weekends and holidays are picnickers who select a micro-space in a pleasant setting for their activities. Their sense of belonging is linked to the possession of space rather than to an intimate knowledge of persons and control of larger territory. However, low income picnickers, usually ethnic minorities, show a greater tendency to gather in larger groups and define a common territory. Modes of spatial behavior typical of the neighborhood park are transferred to the district park and are used to identify it as a place where others with a similar sociocultural background are welcome. Among blacks the display rituals may include loud talk, music, bongo drummers, and a variety of gestures and postures (see also Suttles, 1968:124-130).

Regional Outdoor Places

When outdoor spaces draw visitors from regions they tend to take on pecularities of the scheme of order typical of the regional culture. Belonging through possession, selective organization, and formalized control is typical of both regional and remote places, as proportionally few low income groups or ethnic minorities visit these areas.

Public places defined by mobile higher income visitors are perceived as belonging to everyone, and thus, contrary to the perceptions of local low income residents, belong to no one in particular. Such places are often interpreted as "open" and "free" both by those who conform to higher status norms and by those who conform to counter- or alternate-culture norms. All three features of the higher status definition of place are evident in a typical response by a youth to the question of why he ignored the leash law on a public beach and permitted his large German shepherd to run about in the crowd:

> *"Nobody's going to make me tie up my dog. He's just as free as I am."*

When reminded of the regulations and the presence of small children nearby he replied:

"We are doing nothing wrong, so I'll only tie him up if they 'bust' me, and then I won't come here again. We just don't want to be hassled."

His definition of place was possessive, selective, and responsive only to formal social control.

Remote Outdoor Places

Definitions of place in remote outdoor settings are usually determined by the kind of attraction present and the visitors drawn to it. Individuals and groups have greater control over idiosyncratic definitions in remote settings than in any of the other outdoor places. Wilderness backpackers, rock climbers, and tent, pickup, and trailer campers are a few of the many kinds of users whose orientation toward outdoor spaces is typified by possession, selective organization, and formal social control.

An exception to this pattern was observed in certain fishing areas. Low income members of ethnic minorities, especially blacks, heavily fish district, regional, and remote lakes, and along the Pacific shoreline. This anomaly can be explained by a combination of traditional norms, economic requirements, and cultural tastes. Most ethnic and lower income fishermen express as much interest in the meat as in the sport, and many ethnic groups, specifically Orientals, require certain species of fish for traditional ceremonial meals.

Self-segration on the basis of counterculture life style is a new form of use engaged in primarily by highly mobile youth from middle or high income families, and most fully expressed in remote places. Countercultural membership is signified by mode of dress, hair style, posture, gestures, language, equipment, and activities. Outdoor space is perceived as belonging to everyone, and thus may legitimately be used for many activities usually considered illegal or immoral. Nude bathing, marijuana smoking, open sexual enjoyment, and loud rock music are a few of the many activities that can be maintained only in selective territories where surveillance by law enforcement officials is difficult or where the number of participants is too large to prevent effective social control.

Implications for social theory and planning are suggested by these observations. The question of how social meanings of the nonhuman environment ensure orderly group life is important to sociological theory dealing with both leisure and instrumental behavior. Observations indicate that man's relationship to the nonhuman environment can be typified by patterned expectations, norms, or rules, which ensure predictable behavior. By linking the expectations of sociocultural groups with recreational behavior in outdoor settings, a theory of outdoor leisure behavior has been suggested. This theory rejects the psychological interpretation that in their "free time" individuals may escape the borders of ordinary society with all its normative constraints by seeking refuge in outdoor areas where they may "be themselves" and feel "free." Instead, it presents the sociopsychological interpretation that individuals seek outdoor areas where they may share a scheme of order with others similar enough to themselves to be able to take for granted many everyday normative constraints. It is hypothesized that normative constraints are not necessarily relaxed during leisure behavior, but rather are at a very low level of awareness. Thus, outdoor leisure behavior is typified by a situation where a consensus exists regarding the status of socially problematic elements.

If a necessary condition for outdoor leisure activity is indeed not that normative constraints be reduced, but rather that socially problematic elements be reduced, then the solution of routine problems requires more specific information than is now available. Decision makers are obliged to reevaluate policies made at all levels in organizational hierarchies. Three practical problems illustrate the utility of this theory.

First, objectives for preserving open space and creating parks might be best formulated in terms of the social functions outdoor recreation serves for specific visitor populations. With whose expectations in mind are such areas reserved, designed, and managed? Do the planners consider how differing visitor definitions of place will affect intragroup and intergroup relationships? When should groups with differing expectations be separated by zoning for incompatible uses, and when should mutual understanding be encouraged as a form of social therapy?

Second, programs such as nature interpretation might be better utilized as a means of formally introducing users to an outdoor recreational culture. Whose scheme of order do interpreters use for introducing visitors to the rules of outdoor living? Should activities be designed to help overcome social differences by encouraging the development of a sense of group identity and mutual responsibility?

Finally, social controls might be designed to fit the moral order of specific user groups. Whose normative order should obtain on given recreational areas and should it be informally or formally enforced? What outdoor places and user groups require formal authoritarian controls to protect persons and property? Should park rangers, park policemen, or local law-enforcement officers perform such functions?

This study has demonstrated that areas reserved for outdoor recreation are not perceived as free spaces by all social groups. Such perceptions typify the views of those with higher mobility and income who take for granted the normative order they share. Policy makers usually identify with this group. It is therefore incumbent upon them to suspend their personal and organizational perspectives so that they may objectively consider the recreational needs of socio-cultural groups whose schemes of order differ from their own.

REFERENCES

Berger, Bennett M.
   1962 "The sociology of leisure: some suggestions." Industrial Relations 1 (February): 31-45.
Briggs, Asa
   1968 "The sense of place." Pp. 77-98 in Smithsonian Annual II, The Fitness of Man's Environment. New York: Harper & Row.
Cavan, Sherri
   1966 Liquor License. Chicago: Aldine.
Denzin, Norman K.
   1969 "Symbolic interactionism and ethnomethodology: A proposed synthesis." American Sociological Review 34 (December): 922-934.
Evans-Pritchard, E. E.
   1940 The Nuer. Oxford: Clarendon.
Fortes, Meyer, and E.E. Evans-Pritchard.
   1940 African Political Systems. London: Oxford University Press.
Fried, Marc, and Peggy Gleicher
   1962 "Some sources of residential satisfaction in an urban slum." Journal of the American Institute of Planners 27 (November): 305-315.
Gans, Herbert J.
   1962 The Urban Villagers. New York: Free Press.
Garfinkel, Harold
   1963 "A conception of, and experiments with, 'trust' as a condition of stable concerted actions." Pp. 187-238 in O. J. Harvey (ed.), Motivation and Social Interaction: Cognitive Determinants. New York: Ronald Press.
Glaser, Barney G., and Anselm L. Strauss
   1967 The Discovery of Grounded Theory. Chicago: Aldine.
Goffman, Erving
   1961 "The underlife of a public institution." Pp. 171-320 in Erving Goffman, Asylums. Garden City, N.Y.: Anchor.
Goodenough, Ward
   1951 Property, Kin, and Community on Truk. New Haven: Yale University Publications in Anthropology, No. 46.
Jacobs, Paul
   1970 "Godzilla in the Redwoods." Earth Times (July):10.
Jacobs, Jane
   1961 The Death and Life of Great American Cities. New York: Random House, Vintage Books.

Liebow, Elliott
    1967 Tally's Corner: A Study of Negro Streetcorner Men. Boston: Little,
       Brown.
Lynch, Kevin
    1960 The Image of The City. Cambridge, Mass.: M.I.T. Press.
Meyerson, Rolf
    1969 "The sociology of leisure in the United States: Introduction and
       bibliography, 1945-1965." Journal of Leisure Research 1 (Feb-
       ruary): 53-69.
    1970 "The charismatic and the playful in outdoor recreation." The
       Annals of the American Academy of Political and Social Science
       389 (May): 35-45.
Riezler, Kurt
    1944 "The social psychology of fear." American Journal of Sociology 49
       (May): 489-498.
Schutz, Alfred
    1944 "The stranger: an essay in social psychology." American Journal of
       Sociology 49 (May): 499-507.
Sommer, Robert
    1969 Personal Space. Englewood Cliffs, N.J.: Prentice-Hall.
Spoehr, Alexander
    1956 "Cultural differences in the interpretation of natural resources."
       Pp. 93-102 in William L. Thomas, Jr. (ed.), Man's Role in
       Changing the Face of the Earth. Chicago: University of Chicago
       Press.
Suttles, Gerald
    1968 The Social Order of the Slum. Chicago: University of Chicago
       Press.
Webb, Eugene J., Donald T. Campbell, R. D. Schwartz,
and L. Seechrest
    1966 Unobtrusive Measures: Nonreactive Research in the Social
       Sciences. Chicago: Rand McNally.
Werthman, Carl S.
    1968 "The social meaning of the physical environment" (unpublished
       Ph. D. dissertation). Berkeley: University of California.
Whyte, William F.
    1943 Street Corner Society. Chicago: University of Chicago Press.

PAPER 5

Social Separation Among Displaced Rural Families: The Case of Flood Control Reservoirs

RABEL J. BURDGE
RICHARD L. LUDTKE

Foremost among current demands of the urban community is the need for ample water supplies, abundant recreation facilities, and adequate flood control reservoirs. Whether the need be water projects, highways, or public recreation, the urban need for rural land is continuously forcing the displacement of large numbers of persons. As a result, many hundreds of rural persons must find new homes each year.

The focus of this paper is on how rural people anticipate forced moves. It illustrates, in the thesis of this book, differential meanings attached to places, to physical environments. Interfaces between environment and social behavior are made manifest. Indeed, this type of evidence indicates the necessity for sociologists to systematically deal with physical place meanings—environments—as a major variable.

NATURE OF THE MIGRATION RESEARCH PROBLEM

The unique aspect of the phenomenon under study is that return migration is precluded. In most types of forced migration there is at least some possibility of return. Expectations or hopes of return to one's home can serve tension management functions for most forced migrants, but this is not an alternative for involuntary flood control reservoir migrants.

The dissociative nature of migration (that is, separation from membership systems and locality situations) operates as a basic starting point for developing the present research design. Persons who experience migration are placed in a different situational context and

The work on which this paper is based was supported in part by funds provided by the United States Department of Interior, Office of Water Resources Research, as authorized under the Water Resources Research Act of 1964, Project No. A-020-KY.

are faced with the task of establishing themselves in a new social environment. Investigations by social scientists consistently support the basic proposition that migration produces mental stress and associated *psychoses.* Malzberg and Lee (1956) found considerably high frequencies of both functional and nonfunctional psychoses among migrants of all ages. In a more recent study Lee (1958) concluded that *migrants had higher rates of functional and nonfunctional psychoses than nonmigrants even though age, sex, and race were controlled.* A stronger generalization of the relationships between migration and mental illness was set forth by Abrahamson (1965), who suggests that *emotional disorder and general deteriorating health are associated with migration.* None of the research studies which were reviewed rejected the notion that migration was not a stress-producing activity.

For many types of migration it is possible to conceive that planning to move is an adjustive process in itself. However, in the case of involuntary migration, one can scarcely suggest that the move is an effort to gain better adjustment. Weinberg (1964) places involuntary migration in perspective by indicating that it is more stress-provoking than voluntary migration, and he generally acknowledges that a mental uprooting occurs even among many healthy, voluntary migrants.

For purposes of this study, stress produced as the result of anticipation of migration is the variable under examination. We assume that actual physical migration is not needed to produce stress. Much of stress-producing adjustment will have taken place long before the physical move.

The simple knowledge that one must move can be viewed as a crisis to the participants. Brown and Birley (1968) contend that being told of an impending change, such as a job transfer or forthcoming move, provides stress much in the same manner as the actual move. In effect the dissociative nature of migration is recognized in advance and produces a mental strain qualitatively parallel to that of the actual migration. Therefore, in the context of this study we see the stress produced through apprehension over moving as the key variable under consideration. Other factors investigated in this study will moderate the effects produced by a forced move. Thus, the definition of the premigration situation can be expected to vary among migrants, as would their postmigration adjustment.

RESPONSES TO RESERVOIR PROJECTS

Studies of attitudes toward watershed development, river basin development, and highway construction projects among affected persons have provided a list of variables that related to people's attitudes toward development projects (see Table 1). Empirical results suggest that socioeconomic status, vested interests, and knowledge of project would serve as explanatory variables in determining individual response to reservoir projects. People with more favorable attitudes toward reservoir projects would be of high socioeconomic standing, have vested interests served by the projects, and would have more knowledge of the projects. *Therefore, the contention of this study is that favorable attitudes towards reservoir projects will in turn serve to reduce the prospective migrant's apprehension over moving and contribute to his willingness to accept separation.* This hypothesis is derived from the review of literature summarized in Table 1. Other factors included in this summary are treated as control variables for purposes of this study. We have also introduced the variable identification with place.

TABLE 1.   *Factors in Previous Research Studies Related to Favorable Attitudes toward Water Resource Development and Public Development Projects*

	Factor
Researchers	
Dasgupta	1. High organizational involvement
	2. Nonfarm occupations
	3. Education
	4. Level of Living
	5. History of flood damage to property
	6. Knowledge of projects and purposes
Wilkenson	7. Community socioeconomic status
Photiadis	8. Tenure status of renter
	9. Age related negatively to favorable responses when the extremes were considered Photiadis also found support for numbers 3 and 6 above
Kraenzel	10. Perceptions of metropolitan dominance related negatively to favorable attitudes toward resource development
Hallberg and Flinchbaugh	11. Shortness of residence

Source: Dasgupta, Satadal, 1967: Attitudes of Local Residents Toward Watershed Development (State College: Mississippi State University). Wilkenson, Kenneth P., 1966: Local Action and Acceptance of Watershed Development (State College: Mississippi State University Water Resources Research Institute). Photiadis, John D., 1960: Attitudes Toward the Water Resources Development Program in Central South Dakota (Brookings: South Dakota State College). Kraenzel, Carl F., 1957: "The social consequences of river basin development," Law and Contemporary Problems (22): 221-236. Hallberg, M.C., and B. L. Flinchbaugh, 1967: Analysis of Factors Associated with Property Holder's Decision in Eminent Domain Proceedings (University Park: Pennsylvania State University).

Identification with Place—An Exploration

Identification with place is defined as an attachment to a particular home or geographical location.[1] This concept is concerned with attachments to physical places such as the "old farmstead," or the "family place." Persons who have an emotional attachment to a place by definition would experience difficulty in moving. It is suggested that strong identification with place would produce apprehension of moving and have a differential affect on migration plans.

METHODOLOGY
Model of Forced Migration

The model of forced migration tested in this study is shown below.

Vested interests served (X_1)

Knowledge of project (X_2)

Socioeconomic status (X_3)

Indentification with place (X_4)

Attitude toward → Apprehension → Separation
reservoir projects   over moving   plans
(X_7) (X_5, X_6) (X_8, X_9)

The variables, vested interests, knowledge of reservoir projects, socioeconomic status, and the degree of identification with place of affected persons are seen as producing differential attitudes toward reservoir projects. Different attitudes toward the project will produce differential apprehension over moving, which in turn will influence individual migration plans.

To test this model of forced migration, data were obtained in 1969 by means of personal interviews with persons living in two areas to be flooded by multipurpose reservoirs. One area was located in southeastern Ohio and the other in central Kentucky. The populations involved were predominantly rural, and in each location a small village was to be flooded. All adult members of each community were interviewed ($N = 261$). "Adult" was defined as a person over 18 years of age or living independent of parental support.

Vested Interests (X_1). In measuring vested interests, each respondent was asked to respond positively or negatively to a list of consequences which might have personal affects if the reservoir were built. Each respondent was allowed to add additional items to the list. The eight items were:

[1]This variable was suggested informally by Daniel O. Price of the University of Texas at Austin. The treatment of the variable and its measurements are, however, the sole responsibility of the authors.

1. The project will end periodic losses due to floods.
2. In general, how will selling your property affect you?
3. Water recreation facilities will be available in the area.
4. Land not taken for the reservoir will probably become more valuable.
5. Churches are going to be removed when the reservoir is built.
6. Schools will be changed by the reservoir (that is, re-districted).
7. Reservoirs may break up families (such as contact with cousins and so on).
8. Do you feel that at your age it is either good to move or difficult to move?

   To develop an ordinal measure, the benefits were scored +1, the detrimental consequences were scored -1, and those not applicable were scored 0. The items were then summed to yield the net vested interest score of each respondent and a constant of 10 was added to eliminate negative numbers. A test of reliability was not calculated for the vested interest scale because the open end items yielded nonstandard questions. Responses to a question on overall feeling of gain or loss correlated very highly (0.90) with the measure of vested interest.

   Knowledge (X_2). Knowledge of the reservoir project was measured by a twelve-item "test" based on the proceedings of the public hearings held at each site. The items were:

1. Can you tell me where the proposed dam will be built?
2. What counties have land that will be affected by the reservoir if it is built?
3. Is the proposed dam supposed to be used as a source of generating electric power?
4. Who will be building the dam, the federal government, the state or both together?
5. How many acres of land approximately will be flooded by the reservoir?
6. Will people who own land that borders the reservoir be able to build private beaches and boat-landing facilities?
7. Do you know how much it will cost to build such a reservoir?
8. Will everybody have open access to the reservoir for watering livestock or will other arrangements have to be made?

9. Who is responsible for the final decision as to whether or not to build these reservoirs?
10. What will happen to the cemeteries that are located in places that will be flooded?
11. Does the Army Corps of Engineers pay moving expenses for everyone affected?
12. What is done with the buildings purchased by the Corps of Engineers?

The knowledge scores were accumulated as one would an academic test, with credit for partial correct answers. For example, if a person could name two out of three counties affected he would receive a correct score on that item.

Socioeconomic Status (X_3). Sewell's (1943) socioeconomic scale was utilized as a measure of social status. This scale includes information on education, social participation, and the presence or absence of utilities and household appliances. The application of the Sewell scale was justified by the character of the study location. The study populations were in depressed economic areas and their material levels of living were comparable to Midwest farm populations of previous decades.

Identification with Place (X_4). The measure "identification with place" was designed to determine the extent to which people maintain affective attachments to their place of residence. The scale developed was a Likert-type twelve-item summated rating scale, using five response categories. The twelve items utilized to measure this variable were:

1. Of all the places I have been, I like this area best.
2. People like me just belong in a place like this.
3. This area is in my blood, it is really a part of me.
4. I don't really feel any strong attachment to this place.
5. Whenever I die, I would like to be buried in this area.
6. I've seen a lot of places that I would really prefer to live rather than staying here.
7. There might be things I would like to have, but this place is mine and I love it.
8. I think that I could be at home in any number of places away from here.
9. I've seen other places but this is the only place I could ever call home.

10. I think that our home is as good as another, so it doesn't make any difference where I live.
11. The memories I have of this home are the best memories I have.
12. I really feel that I'm a natural part of this place.

The coefficient of reliability was 0.99.

Apprehension (X_5, X_6). Apprehension of moving was measured with two Likert-type attitude scales. *Apprehension of leaving the present community* was a measure of the degree to which respondents were apprehensive in leaving present occupational and friendship ties. *Apprehension of new communities* was a measure of the difficulty in establishing occupational and friendship ties in new communities. The split-half reliability for these scales were 0.91 and 0.96 respectively using only items with t-scores significant at the 0.001 level. Each scale contained eight items. The eight items used to measure apprehension of leaving the present community were:

1. Just getting a chance in life will be a rewarding experience.
2. It is hard to leave all the businesses one has traded with for a long time.
3. A chance to leave rural life is pleasing.
4. It's hard to leave a place where you have spent most of your life.
5. Leaving a place where everyone knows all about you is a comfortable feeling.
6. All the ties one establishes make it difficult to leave the area.
7. The help one can always get from his neighbors is bound to be hard to leave.
8. The thought of losing contact with old friends is disturbing.

The eight items used to measure apprehension of new communities were:

1. Starting a new life in a new community is really a pleasant feeling.
2. Living in a strange neighborhood is pretty nerve wracking.
3. One feels as though he is all alone when he's among strangers.
4. Making a whole new set of friends is going to be an enjoyable experience.
5. Having all new people around is quite enjoyable.

6. The way everyone looks you over in a new town gets pretty irritating.
7. Not knowing what to expect from the people who live here makes one a little nervous.
8. It is easier to relax and be yourself when nobody knows who you are.

Water Resource Development (X_7). Attitudes toward water resource development were measured with a ten-item Likert-type scale, namely:

1. More dams are being built today than are necessary for flood control.
2. Money spent on building reservoirs exceeds the benefits that we get from them.
3. Local people should have more to say about flood control in their areas.
4. Reservoir construction often floods land that is worth more than the land it protects.
5. Reservoir construction nearly always improves the areas in which they are built.
6. Reservoirs should only be constructed where they won't take people's homes or good farm land.
7. Flood control projects always help more people than they hurt.
8. Fish and wildlife development alone provide good reasons for reservoir construction.
9. Since floods only occur once in a while, it is foolish to give up good farm land for reservoir construction.
10. Reservoir construction is a good investment for reducing flood losses in the long run.

This scale measures the degree of favorableness of respondents toward the construction of multipurpose reservoirs. The split-half coefficient of reliability for this scale was 0.98 using only items that had t-scores significant at the 0.001 level.

Separation (X_8, X_9). Two measures of social separation were used in this study. The first was *the presence or absence of expected contact with current neighbors after moving*. Questions determined the degree to which respondents expected to maintain friendships with present neighbors after moving. The second measure was *whether or not the respondents intended to move to communities of different population and cultural makeup*. In constructing these measures the researchers compared the present residences and the future residences (or expected residences) on population and cultural characteristics.

ANALYSIS DESIGN

Analysis in this study involves an application of Blalock's (1961) techniques for making casual inferences from nonexperimental data. This technique provides a methodological fit with models that entail a sequential process so that a chain-like series of phenomena produce a given result.

Blalock (1961:54) constructed his technique for casual inference on the basis of previous work in econometrics, using a recursive system. In recursive systems two-way causation is ruled out, yielding a pattern without reciprocal causation or feedback. This is an acknowledged simplification necessary for analysis, and no imputations are made that this is the definitive nature of social systems. There is no single dependent variable in a recursive system. It involves an initial variable, labeled the exogenous variable, caused by unknown factors outside the system. Using this exogenous variable as a starting point, the variables that follow sequentially may be dependent or independent. That is, they are caused by the preceding variables, making them dependent or casual (independent) for the variables that follow them. Only the concluding variable of the system is seen strictly in terms of being a dependent variable. For example, in the hypothetical four-variable model $(X_1 \rightarrow X_2 \rightarrow X_3 \rightarrow X_4)$, X_1 is exogenous (independent), determined by unkown factors outside the system. Variables X_2 and X_3 may be considered independent or dependent and X_4 considered strictly as a dependent variable. This is essentially the nature of the model used in this paper. Therefore, in the present study socioeconomic status, knowledge of projects, vested interests, and identification with place are seen as variables determined by forces beyond the scope of this investigation. Apprehension over moving and attitudes toward projects are seen as either dependent or independent variables and separation plans as dependent only.

Statistics

Since the data in this study are ordinal, the Goodman and Kruskal's (1954) measure for ordinal association, gamma, was used. Also, gamma as a proportional reduction of error statistic is analogous to the coefficient of determination (r^2) and as such can be similarly interpreted (Costner, 1965).

The principle partialling technique used in this study is the net partial coefficient for gamma (Davis, 1967). This net partial coefficient allows one to assess the net effect of one or more control variables, thus providing an advantage over the more traditional subgroup analysis.

Tests of significance were not used because the population was enumerated rather than sampled. In the absence of any standard criterion, four categories were arbitrarily constructed to describe the statistical relationship in this study. Relationships below 0.15 are considered substantively insignificant. Those between 0.15 to 0.29 are considered slight, relationships from 0.30 to 0.49 are considered moderate and any coefficient above 0.50 is described as strong. Generalization was to the model rather than to any finite populations. As such the relationships established in the model become the relevant factors in cooking generalizations about persons displaced by forced migration situations. Of course, the strength of the statistical relationships determines the credibility of the model.

RESULTS OF THE ANALYSIS
Apprehension over Moving

Apprehension is the variable through which other variables in this investigation produced their effects. Two measures of apprehension over moving were employed to tap conceptually different aspects of apprehension. These two dimensions were labeled apprehension of leaving the present community and apprehension of new communities. These dimensions of apprehension were not seen as identical, but some overlapping characteristics were present. That is, persons who were apprehensive over leaving their present communities may also be apprehensive over new places of residence, but theoretically the two types of apprehension were distinct. The two measures of apprehension were strongly associated (gamma = 0.61).

Separation

Two instruments were designed to tap two different aspects of social separation. These measures were expected separation from present neighborhood and friendship contacts and expected change in residence type (that is, from farm to nonfarm, small town to city, and so on). The two dimensions of separation were not statistically related to any appreciable degree (gamma = 0.13).

Both apprehension of leaving and apprehension of new communities were negatively associated with expected separation from present contacts, yielding moderate gammas of -0.40 and -0.42, respectively. These statistical results establish the association between apprehension and separation plans and support the obvious conclusion that persons who are most apprehensive about leaving friends, neighbors, and their communities to face new situations will not be favorable toward moving.

Attitudes toward Reservoir Projects

Based on the review of literature in Table 1, we suggest that the more favorable are persons' attitudes toward flood control projects, which force them to move, the less apprehensive they will be about moving and, as a consequence, the more likely to accept separation from their present community. Four tests of this hypothesis were made utilizing each of the two measures of apprehension (X_5, X_6) and separation (X_8, X_9). Figure 1 shows the

FIGURE 1. Attitudes Toward Reservoir Projects (X_7), Apprehension of Leaving (X_5), and Separation of Contact $(X_8)^a$

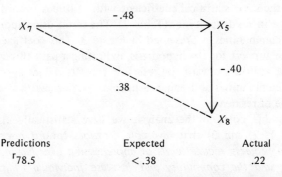

Predictions	Expected	Actual
$r_{78.5}$	$< .38$	$.22$

[a]Unless indicated otherwise, solid lines indicate theoretically predicted relationships in all figures throughout the remainder of this paper.

results involving people's apprehension of leaving their present communities and expected separation from current friends. These coefficients indicate moderate support for the relationship. Persons with favorable attitudes toward projects do experience less apprehension of leaving and consequently are more likely to accept separation from their present friends and relatives. Apprehension over leaving mediates the strength of positive attitudes toward the project as indicated by the partialling analysis results shown in Figure 2.

The results using apprehension of new communities as a measure of people's apprehension over moving show moderate support for the relationship, with people's attitudes toward projects, reducing their apprehension of new communities and increasing their willingness to accept separation from present contacts with neighbors, friends, and relatives (Figure 2).

When studying people's expectations of change in type of

FIGURE 2. Attitudes Toward Reservoir Projects (X_7), Apprehension of New Communities (X_6), and Separation of Contact (X_8)

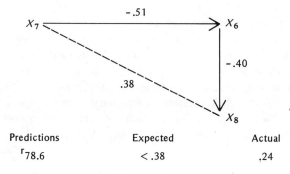

Predictions	Expected	Actual
$r_{78.6}$	< .38	,24

residence, the test using apprehension of leaving was excluded since it showed the same statistical coefficient with attitudes toward projects as change in residence type (Table 2). The result using apprehension of new communities is presented in Figure 3. This coefficient shows moderate support for the hypothesis, indicating a path through which favorable attitudes toward the reservoir projects reduce apprehension of new communities and enhance people's willingness to change to a new type of residence.

At this point in the analysis we have statistically established (Figures 1, 2, and 3) that *favorable attitudes toward reservoir-construction projects reduce levels of apprehension over leaving friends, relatives, and the community and increase individual willingness to move.* The next step is to study this relationship while introducing the four independent variables—vested interests (X_1), knowledge of the reservoir project (X_2), socioeconomic status (X_3), and identification with place (X_4).

FIGURE 3. Attitudes Toward Reservoir Projects (X_7), Apprehension of New Communities (X_6), and Change in Type of Residence (X_9)

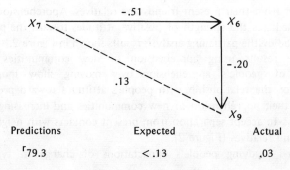

Predictions	Expected	Actual
$r_{79.3}$	< .13	,03

TABLE 2. *Matrix of Zero-Order Relationships Obtained Using the Goodman and Kruskal (1954) Measure for Ordinal Association, Gamma*

Variables	Independent			Independent or Dependent				Dependent	
	X_2	X_3	X_4	X_5	X_6	X_7	X_8	X_9	
X_1 Vested interests served	0.06	-0.10	-0.65	-0.05	-0.52	-0.73	-0.54	0.19	
X_2 Knowledge of project		0.45	0.13	0.14	-0.02	0.01	0.06	-0.20	
X_3 Socioeconomic status			0.14	0.20	-0.02	0.06	0.22	-0.09	
X_4 Identification with place				0.65	0.63	-0.50	-0.54	-0.30	
X_5 Apprehension of leaving					0.61	-0.48	-0.40	-0.12	
X_6 Apprehension of new communities						-0.51	-0.42	-0.20	
X_7 Attitudes toward reservior projects							0.38	0.13	
X_8 Separation of contact								0.13	
X_9 Change in type of residence									

Vested Interests (X_1)

Vested interests here refers to those personal interests that may either be served or damaged by the construction of reservoirs. Based on extensive research by other sociologists we suggest that *the more people expect to have their interests served by the reservoir project, the more favorable will be their attitudes toward the reservoir project and, as a consequence, will be less apprehensive over moving and will be more willing to move from their present community.*

The results of the statistical analysis shown in Figure 4 strongly support the hypothesis that those persons expecting to benefit from reservoir projects have more favorable attitudes toward the project. These favorable attitudes toward the project in turn appear to reduce people's apprehension over leaving and consequently they are more likely to move from their neighbors and friends. Examination of the predictions made for the partialling equations suggest that although a path exists conforming to the hypothesis, the measures involved in this test do not completely explain the influence of vested interests. The analysis in Figure 4 shows that vested interests retain an

FIGURE 4. Vested Interests Served (X_1), Attitudes Toward Reservoir Projects (X_7), Apprehension of Leaving (X_5), and Separation of Contact (X_8)

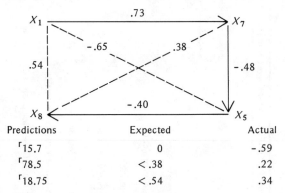

Predictions	Expected	Actual
$r_{15.7}$	0	-.59
$r_{78.5}$	< .38	.22
$r_{18.75}$	< .54	.34

apparent direct relationship with apprehension of leaving friends and relatives when the effects of attitudes toward projects are partialled out. Therefore, Figure 5 is presented which shows the direct and indirect contribution made to persons' apprehension over leaving by vested interests.

In Figure 6 we substitute apprehension of new communities (X_6) for apprehension of leaving (X_5). Again the analysis shows that

FIGURE 5. Reconstructed Alternative to the Model in Figure 4—Vested Interests Served (X_1), Attitudes Toward Reservoir Project (X_7), Apprehension of Leaving (X_5), and Separation of Contact (X_9)

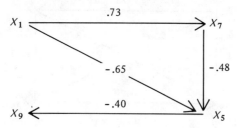

FIGURE 6. Vested Interests Served (X_1), Attitudes Toward Reservoir Projects (X_7), Apprehension of New Communities (X_6), and Separation of Contact (X_8)

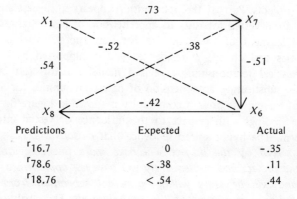

Predictions	Expected	Actual
$r_{16.7}$	0	-.35
$r_{78.6}$	< .38	.11
$r_{18.76}$	< .54	.44

vested interests have both a direct and indirect influence on apprehension of new communities. The reconstructed alternative is the same as shown in Figure 5.

The introduction of people's anticipated changes in type of residence, presented in Figure 7, supports the general hypothesis that if a person's vested interests are served by the reservoir he has less apprehension over moving. The sequential pattern hypothesized was also supported. On the basis of the statistical analysis we conclude that *persons expecting to have their interests served by the reservoir project will have more favorable attitudes toward the project and that those with favorable attitudes will experience less apprehension over moving.* It should be noted that vested interests explain the level of apprehension only partially through its influence on attitudes toward

FIGURE 7. Vested Interests Served (X_1), Attitudes Toward Reservoir Projects (X_7), Apprehension of New Communities (X_6), and Change in Type of Residence (X_9)

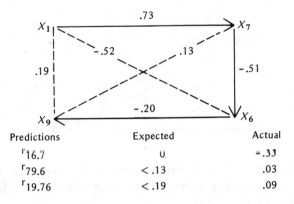

Predictions	Expected	Actual
$^r 16.7$	U.	=.33
$^r 79.6$	< .13	.03
$^r 19.76$	< .19	.09

reservoir projects. Part of this relationship appears to suggest a direct influence from vested interests to apprehension of new communities. The final segment of the sequence between apprehension of new communities and change in residence type is supported by only a slight statistical relationship. A revised model for this test of the hypothesis substituting apprehension of new communities for apprehension of leaving the present community is shown in Figure 8.

The findings with respect to the influence of vested interests are uniform. The hypothesized sequence that *persons who have their interests served by the project will have more favorable attitudes toward the project and consequently will have less apprehension over moving and will be more willing to accept separation from their friends and/or a new way of life, is supported.* The analysis also indicates that *vested interest is directly related to attitudes toward reservoir projects.* The strength of the associations in the foregoing

FIGURE 8. Vested Interests Served (X_1), Attitudes Toward Reservoir Projects (X_7), Apprehension of New Communities (X_6), and Change in Type of Residence (X_9)

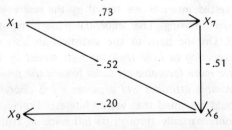

tests indicated that vested interests must be considered when seeking to explain people's migration plans under such involuntary conditions.

Knowledge of Projects (X_2)

Knowledge refers to the levels of information people have about reservoir construction and sale procedures used by the Corps of Engineers. The model designates knowledge as influencing separation through essentially the same variables as vested interests. Thus, we suggested the relationship that the more knowledge people have about the flood control projects affecting them, the more favorable will be their attitudes toward the projects and, as a consequence, the less apprehensive they will be over moving and the more likely they will be to accept separation from their present community.

However, based on the statistical analysis in this study the effects of knowledge of the project (X_2) upon separation from contacts with friends and relatives (X_8) appear to be negligible (0.06). The only sizable statistical relationship with knowledge of the project (X_2) was the slight relationship (-0.20) with change in type of residence (X_9). Therefore, we must conclude (although previous research on watershed development has indicated a correlation between knowledge of projects and attitude toward the projects) that in the case of total displacement of all persons, knowledge does not appear to be an important factor. Studies of information campaigns in other areas have shown that information alone was not sufficient to produce changes in attitudes (Hyman and Sheatsley, 1947).

Socioeconomic Status (X_3)

Socioeconomic status theoretically should relate indirectly to separation in the same manner predicted for vested interests and knowledge. We suggested that the higher people's socioeconomic status, the more favorable would be their attitudes toward the projects and, as a consequence, the less apprehensive they would be over moving and the greater their acceptance of separation from their present community.

Socioeconomic status is not related to attitudes toward projects with sufficient strength to be considered important (0.06). In view of this lack of substantive support for the hypothesis, we conclude that socioeconomic status does not operate through attitudes toward reservoir projects to affect separation. Socioeconomic status (X_3) related only slightly (0.22) to separation of contact with present community (X_8). Socioeconomic status (X_3) was related (0.45) to knowledge of projects (X_2). This simple relationship was supportive of other research studies shown in Table 1.

Identification with Place (X₄)

Identification with place is here defined as *an affective attachment to home and region.* This attachment is hypothesized as relating to separation and apprehension, with the effect on separation being through the intermediate variable apprehension. The basis for this hypothesis is conceptual, rather than supportive through previous research. We suggest that the more people identify with their present place of residence, the more apprehensive they will be over moving.

When using the measures apprehension of leaving and expected separation from present contacts, the variable identification with place is quite significant and highly supportive of the hypothesis (Figure 9). Identification with place relates strongly to apprehension

FIGURE 9. Identification with Place (X_4) Apprehension of Leaving (X_5), and Separation of Contact (X_8)

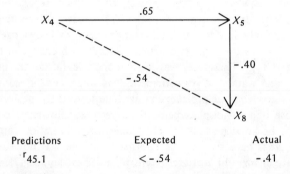

Predictions	Expected	Actual
$r_{45.1}$	$< -.54$	$-.41$

of leaving and in the predicted direction. That is, *the more people identify with their present places of residence the more apprehensive they will be of moving.*

The presence of a sequential pattern is also supported by the net partial. The relationship between identification with place and separation of contact is reduced by partialling out apprehension of leaving. This reduction indicates the presence of an indirect relationship between identification with place and separation of contact, but also suggests that this path explains only a portion of the influence of identification with place. The remaining portion may be explained by other paths.

Utilizing the measure, apprehension of new communities (X_6), yields results that basically parallel the above findings. Both the zero-order coefficients and the net partial in Figure 10 support the hypothesis that *the more people identify with their present places of residence the less likely they will be to leave their present friends and relatives.*

FIGURE 10.   Identification with Place (X_4), Apprehension of New Communities (X_6), and Separation of Contact (X_8)

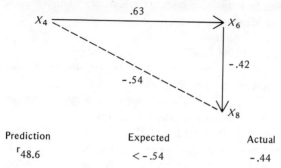

Prediction	Expected	Actual
$r_{48.6}$	$< -.54$	$-.44$

When expected change in residence is used, the variable identification with place continues to yield strong coefficients (Figure 11). The nature of the relationships is almost the same as with expected separation from present contacts with but one exception. Identification with place relates negatively to expected change in residence type. Both of these statistical relations support our original theoretical model. Identification with place also relates inversely to expected change in community type, and this relationship is not significantly reduced when the effect of apprehension of new communities is partialled out. This analysis indicates that identification with place contributes both directly and indirectly to expected change in type of residence.

Based on this analysis we suggested that identification with place is an important variable to consider in the explanation of social migration. *Persons who are strongly identified with their present homes and are required to move will attempt to retain both their present circle of associations and type of residence.* This finding

FIGURE 11.   Identification with Place (X_4), Apprehension of New Communities (X_6), and Change in Residence Type (X_9)

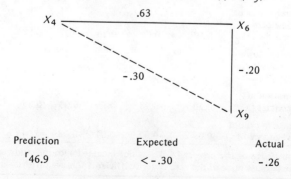

Prediction	Expected	Actual
$r_{46.9}$	$< -.30$	$-.26$

supports the inclusion of identification with place as a variable relevant in the explanation of forced migration. This variable might also be used in explaining people's reluctance to move under totally voluntary conditions.

CONTROLS FOR ALTERNATIVE VARIABLES

Controlling for additional variables not included in the study model involves the continued application of the net partial coefficient for gamma (Davis, 1967). The relationships on which the controls are exercised are those between the exogenous variables, X_1-X_4 (those independent of all the rest) and the intervening variables $(X_5$-$X_9)$ through which these exogenous variables operate. An initial examination of the zero-order coefficients was used to determine which controls were to be executed (Table 3).

Vested Interests (X_1)

Vested interests was found to be one of the more important determinants of people's attitudes toward flood control projects and

TABLE 3. Zero-Order Coefficients for Statistical Relationships Between Control Variables and Study Variables[a]

	Control Variables					
	Leisure orientation	Familism	Age	Sex	Group Move	Proclivity for change
Study Variables						
Vested interests served (X_1)	0.23	0.07	-0.49	0.05	-0.16	-0.35
Socioeconomic status (X_3)	0.21	0.01	0.09	0.08	-0.26	0.16
Identification with place (X_4)	-0.13	0.13	0.24	-0.14	0.29	-0.15
Apprehension of leaving (X_5)	-0.08	0.12	0.23	-0.05	0.11	0.17
Apprehension of new communities (X_6)	-0.10	0.02	0.10	-0.01	0.17	0.00
Attitudes toward reservoir projects (X_7)	0.03	0.08	-0.30	-0.01	-0.06	-0.56
Separation of contact (X_8)	0.20	-0.18	-0.24	0.03	0.65	0.13
Change in type of residence (X_9)	0.09	-0.02	-0.01	-0.03	-0.01	0.12

[a]Knowledge of the project (X_2) was not included with the study variables in this table because none of the zero-order coefficients was even slightly related.

subsequently affect individual apprehension and willingness to accept social separation. A strong relationship (0.73) was found between vested interests and attitudes toward projects (Table 2). This relationship is maintained under controls for age. When age is held constant, the resulting association is 0.69 which did not differ appreciably from the 0.73 found in the original test.

Socioeconomic Status (X_3)

Age is controlled in the relationship between socioeconomic status and apprehension of leaving (0.20) which produced no significant change in the relationship (0.18).

The relationship between socioeconomic status and separation of contact from friends and neighbors (gamma = 0.22) is examined using two controls. Age and the presence of plans for a group move are controlled sequentially, yielding gammas of 0.25 and 0.15, respectively. None of these coefficients indicates an appreciable change in the original relationship and permits us to retain the weak relationship between socioeconomic status and separation of contact from friends and relatives.

Identification with Place (X_4)

Identification with place provided strong relationships with both measures of apprehension. Using the measure apprehension of leaving, the original relationship (gamma= 0.65) was not affected by age. Controlling for age the resulting coefficient was again 0.65.

The original relationship between identification with place and apprehension of new communities (0.63) was not affected by controlling for the presence of plans for a group move. The resulting coefficient of this control was gamma = 0.60.

The result of introducing test factors in the relationship between identification with place and the measures of apprehension is indicative of support for the original relationships. The effect of identification with place on apprehension does not appear to have a direct causal effect.

SUMMARY

The major findings of this study may be summarized as follows:

1. Apprehension over moving relates inversely with people's willingness to separate themselves from their current friends and homes.
2. People with more favorable attitudes toward the projects are less apprehensive over moving and as a consequence are more

willing to engage in moves that require greater separation from their current friends and type of residence.

3. Vested interest proved to be an exceptionally powerful variable in support of the theory that attitudes affect social migration. Vested interests were found to relate to apprehension indirectly as the theory predicted, supporting the idea that those persons with vested interests served by the reservoir project were more willing to engage in moves that require greater separation from their current friends and types of residence.

4. Knowledge had a negligible effect on people's attitudes toward the reservoir project and did not contribute to the explanation of social migration.

5. The level of identification with place was found to relate consistently and strongly with apprehension and consequently produced indirect effects on social separation. Uniformly, the more intense the identification with place, the less inclined people were to move.

Of major interest in this study is the attitude of respondents toward reservoir projects. Previous research indicates that positive attitudes toward water resource development are characteristic of persons with high organization activity, high education and high SES, knowledge of flood control projects, not being a farmer, and negatively related to age. With the notable exception of socioeconomic status our study generally supports these findings and provides more information through the addition of social-psychological variables.

Attitudes toward water resource development related very strongly (0.73) with vested interests and correlated strongly negatively (-0.50) with identification with place. These results suggest that favorable attitudes toward reservoir projects are likely the result of having one's vested interests served. Persons who see personal benefit from water projects will naturally want the reservoir. This finding was further supported by the strong negative relationship between identification with place and attitude toward water resource development.

This study suggests a portrait of a person with favorable attitudes toward reservoirs to be one who is younger, less likely to change, has high vested interests in the reservoir project, and has an extremely low identification with his physical place of residence. Because of these factors the person is likely to be less apprehensive of leaving his present home and moving to a new community. Social status and knowledge of the reservoir project do not appear to make substantial contributions to determining favorable attitudes toward reservoirs.

In the thesis of this book the editors interpret this type of empirical evidence as illustrating part of the interface relationship between the two variables of physical environment and social behavior. It is widely perceived that men modify their physical environment, in this case by a reservoir. It is also shown here that physical environment—identification with place as the measure used here—modifies social behavior.

REFERENCES

Abrahamson, J. H.
  1965 "Emotional disorder, status inconsistency migration." The Milbank Memorial Fund Quarterly 64 (January): 23-48.
Becker, Catherine C.
  1971 "Factors associated with attitudes toward reservoir construction" (unpublished M.S. thesis). Lexington: University of Kentucky.
Belcher, John C.
  1951 "Evaluation and restandardization of Sewell's socioeconomic scale." Rural Sociology 16: 246-255.
Blalock, Hubert M.
  1961 Casual Inferences in Nonexperimental Research. Chapel Hill: University of North Carolina Press.
Brown, George W., and J. L. Birley
  1968 "Crisis and life changes and the onset of schizophrenia." Journal of Health and Social Behavior 9 (September): 195-203.
Burdge, Rabel J., and Richard L. Ludtke
  1970 Factors Affecting Relocation in Response to Reservoir Development. Water Resources Institute, Research Report No. 29. Lexington: University of Kentucky.
Costner, Herbert L.
  1965 "Criteria for measures of association." American Sociological Review 30: 341-353.
Dasgupta, Satadal
  1967 Attitudes of Local Residents Toward Watershed Development. Social Science Research Center in Cooperation with Water Resource Research Institute, Preliminary Report 18. State College: Mississippi State University.
  1968 "Sociology of watershed development." A paper presented at the Mississippi Water Resources Conference, Jackson, Mississippi.
Davis, James H.
  1967 "A partial coefficient for Goodman and Kruskal's gamma." Journal of the American Statistical Association 62 (March): 189-193.
Goodman, Leo, and William H. Kruskal
  1954 "Measures of association for cross classification." Journal of the American Statistical Association 59 (December): 732-754.
Hallberg, M. C., and B. L. Flinchbaugh
  1967 Analysis of Factors Associated with Property Holder's Decision in Eminent Domain Proceedings. Institute for Research on Land and Water Resources, University Park: Pennsylvania State University.
Hyman, Herbert R., and Raul B. Sheatsley
  1947 "Some reasons why information campaigns fail." Public Opinion Quarterly 11 (August): 413-423.

Kraenzel, Carl F.
    1957 "The social consequences of river basin development." Law and Contemporary Problems 22: 221-236.

Lee, Everett S.
    1958 "Migration and mental disease: New York State, 1949-1951." Pp. 141-163 in Selected Studies of Migration Since World War II. New York: Milbank Memorial Fund.

Ludtke, Richard L., and Rabel J. Burdge
    1970 Evaluation of the Social Impact of Reservoir Construction on the Residential Plans of Displaced Persons in Kentucky and Ohio. Water Resources Institute, Research Report No. 26. Lexington: University of Kentucky.

Malzberg, Benjamin, and Everett S. Lee
    1956 Migration and Mental Disease: A Study of First Admissions to Hospitals for Mental Disease, New York, 1936-1941. New York: Social Science Research Council

Photiadis, John D.
    1960 Attitudes Toward the Water Resources Development Program in Central South Dakota. Department of Rural Sociology Extension Service and Water Resources Commission, Preliminary Report No. 1. Brookings: South Dakota State University.

Sewell, William H.
    1943 "A short form of the farm family socioeconomic status scale." Rural Sociology 8: 161-170.

Weinberg, Abraham A.
    1964 "Mental health aspects of voluntary migration." Mental Hygiene 39 (July): 450-464.

Wilkenson, Kenneth P.
    1966 Local Action and Acceptance of Watershed Development. Water Resources Research Institute, State College: Mississippi State University.

Wilkenson, Kenneth P., and Lucy W. Cole
    1967 Sociological Factors in Watershed Development. Water Resources Research Institute, State College: Mississippi State University.

U.S. Army Corps of Engineers.
    1965 Pertinent Data and Plans Considered: Taylorsville Reservoir, Salt River, Kentucky. (January) Louisville, Ky.
    1967 Caesar Creek Dam and Reservior (June) Louisville, Ky.

PAPER 6

Culture Conflict and Natural Resources

CLARK S. KNOWLTON

One of the largest, oldest, and most important Spanish-speaking groups in the Southwest is found within a 250-mile radius of Santa Fe, New Mexico. Known as the Spanish Americans, they are the product of intermixture between seventeenth- and eighteenth-century Spanish settlers; Mexican Indians brought into New Mexico by the Spanish; local Indian groups such as the Pueblo, Navajo, and Apache; French-Canadian and American mountain men, trappers, and traders entering New Mexico in the nineteenth century; and European immigrants and American cowboys, merchants, miners, workers, farmers, and soldiers coming into the area in the late nineteenth and early twentieth centuries. The Spanish Americans, as long as they were in a numerical majority in New Mexico, demonstrated an amazing ability to absorb people of diverse ethnic and racial origins. Living in isolation from other European and Mexican settlements for almost two centuries, they developed a deeply rural, preliterate, peasant-type subsistence agriculture village culture, well adjusted to the natural environment of northern New Mexico.[1]

The Spanish Americans today inhabit the high mountain valleys of the southern Rockies which penetrate northern New Mexico in the form of a large forested peninsula riding high above the semiarid plains and deserts of the Southwest. Van Dresser (1964: 53-74) describes this peninsula as follows:

[1]No comprehensive social or economic history of the Spanish-American people has been written. Material on specific aspects of Spanish-American history and culture can be found in the following publications: Burma, 1954; Gonzales, 1969; Knowlton, 1961a, 1969b; Loomis and Leonard, 1941; McWilliams, 1968; and Saunders, 1954.

> *The resulting . . . peninsula of wooded or forested uplands covers about 13,000 square miles and ranges from slightly below 6,000 to almost 13,000 feet in elevation above sea level. It is thus a relatively verdant and well-watered oasis in the general semi-desert of the Southwest, although all except a few score square miles at the very highest elevation, which receive less than 30 inches of precipitation annually, are still semi-arid climatically. . . . What we might describe as the "hydrologically strategic" position of this region—the fact that it receives relatively high rainfall and snowpack in a generally semi-desert land—has always influenced the forms of human culture within and around it, and is especially significant today. A substantial proportion of the stable flows of three major basins—the Rio Grande, the Pecos, and the Canadian—originate here, and much of the economic life of New Mexico and adjacent portions of Oklahoma, Texas, and even Mexico is dependent on these flows.*

Northern New Mexico resembles Switzerland in topography, climate, and natural resources. Switzerland is one of the more prosperous nations in Europe. Northern New Mexico, like Switzerland a region of high mountain uplands, is in severe contrast, an economically distressed region. After one hundred years of American occupation, conditions of human existence among the Spanish Americans of northern New Mexico are but little better than those in many rural sections of Latin America (Knowlton, 1964; Maloney, 1964: Sanchez, 1967).

The Spanish-American inhabitants of northern New Mexico are afflicted by high rates of tuberculosis and other poverty-related diseases such as anemia, malnutrition, low per capita income, high indices of unemployment and welfare, almost nonexistent medical services, few all-weather paved roads, low quality school systems, and a seeming inability of county, state, and federal government agencies to resolve the difficult economic and social problems of the region (Burma and Williams, n.d.; Knowlton, 1961).

Such depressed social and economic conditions are not unique to northern New Mexico. They can be found in other rural sections of the United States such as Appalachia, the lower South, and the cut-over lands of the upper Midwest. In northern New Mexico, these conditions are intensified and complicated by complex muted ethnic and racial antagonisms between Indians, Spanish Americans, and Anglo Americans, unresolved culture conflicts, language barriers, failing government institutions, and by the deeply rooted memories of past mistreatments (Hollon, 1961; Lamar, 1966; and Steiner, 1969). Without a knowledge of Spanish-American settlement patterns, social systems, and the impact of American occupation upon the Spanish-American rural village people, it is difficult to understand the causes of poverty in this region, the cynical attitudes of the Spanish Americans toward government, and the failures of government programs among them (Cordova and Oberg, 1943: 56-201; Lamar, 1966: 56-82; Ulibarri, 1958; and Walter, 1944).

This presentation will illustrate the ways in which environmental and human problems are intertwined. Material will first be presented on traditional Spanish-American land settlement patterns and social systems. This will be followed by a discussion of the impact of American political, legal, and economic systems upon the Spanish Americans. Finally there will be an examination as to how agencies established to conserve natural resources become major contributors to the economic impoverishment of the Spanish Americans.

LAND SETTLEMENT PATTERNS

The Spanish ancestors of the Spanish Americans first settled in the Rio Grande Valley from Belen in the south to Espanola and Taos in the north. As population increased and Indian pressures permitted, they gradually expanded during the seventeenth and eighteenth centuries into the mountain valleys of the Southern Rockies and then down the rivers flowing from the mountains into the eastern and southern plains and plateaus (Keleher, 1929, 1945; Leonard, 1953). By the middle of the nineteenth century, the Spanish-American settlements began to expand into the plains of eastern New Mexico, southeastern Colorado, and western Texas and Oklahoma, as the Commanches and Kiowas relaxed their hold. The Spanish Americans soon encountered the westward-moving cattle frontier of the Texans in the Staked plains. The eastward-moving Spanish American frontier was quickly rolled back in a cloud of violence by the better-armed and more aggressive Texans. Since then the Spanish Americans have continuously retreated toward the mountains, forced back by the land-hungry Anglo-American ranchers (Baca, 1954: 1-8, 17, 60-68; Haley, 1953: 18-37).

The majority of the Spanish Americans until the 1940s lived in numerous small self-sufficient farm villages, supporting themselves and their families through subsistence agriculture, livestock raising, handicrafts, hunting, and barter with the Indians before the Indians were corraled on reservations. As communications were and are poor, roads virtually absent until the last few years, and danger from Indian assaults quite real before the last decade of the nineteenth century, the village people were isolated from contacts with other villages for long periods of time. The village inhabitants were forced to depend upon their own resources (Calkins, 1935; Edmundson, 1957; Maes, 1941; Walter, 1939).

The numerous village communities among the Spanish Americans became socially and economically independent, self-contained, small social worlds. The extended patriarchal families (Gonzales, 1969: 84-88; Ulibarri, 1958: 26-36; Knowlton, 1965) in the larger villages were linked by marriage and the compadrazgo system.[2] Small villages often were inhabited by members of a single large family. Among the village inhabitants, little sense of identification existed with any social grouping larger than the village, such as ethnic group, minority group, state, or nation, until very recently. The village community included not only the village and its inhabitants but all of the land owned or traditionally used by village people. The inhabitants of neighboring villages were mistrusted, and foreigners were viewed with considerable suspicion. As Burma (1954: 7-8) noted, few people before World War II ever left their villages in spite of the economic sacrifices involved.

The majority of the Spanish-American villages were founded upon community land grants. These grants were, for the most part, granted by the Spanish and Mexican governments to groups of village families requesting land to settle a new village. Upon receiving the grant, the family groups jointly chose a village site, selected house lots, erected a church, built a communal irrigation system, and divided among themselves the plots of irrigated land. Each village family usually owned its own house lot and irrigated farm lands. The rest of the land grant was held in communal ownership. Every village family could use the resources of the communal lands. Poor families in the village that had lost their private farm lands existed by grazing

[2]The compadrazgo is a Roman Catholic religious and social mechanism that is used to strengthen relationships between two friendly families, to establish a patron-client relationship with a more powerful family, and to intensify relationships between related families. A child baptized in the Roman Catholic Church should have two adult sponsors, one of each sex, selected by the child's parents and approved of by the priest. The sponsors are responsible for the religious and physical care of the child if something happens to the parents. The child has the same type of obligations to his sponsors as though they were his parents, and the sponsors as though the child were their own. The child's parents call each other compadre among the men and comadre among the women, co-father and co-mother. Compadres and comadres should support and assist each other as though they were brothers and sisters. The relationship in Spanish-American villages unifies village families into a network of reciprocal cooperative relationships (Mintz and Wolf, 1953: 1-28).

livestock, hunting, and cutting timber and firewood from the village common, known as the ejido. Privately owned lands could be sold, preferably to members of the village, but the ejido by traditional custom could not be alienated from the inhabitants of the village. Grant boundaries were apt to be rather vague (Calkins, 1935; Leonard, 1943).

Two other types of land grants common in New Mexico were the sitio and the proprietary. The sitio grants were large extensions of land granted to ranchers to establish livestock ranches. Proprietary grants, on the other hand, were given to important and prominent persons to thicken the zones of settlement or to establish villages and ranches at strategic locations. The recipients of proprietary grants promised, in exchange for the land, to secure settlers, build a church, put in an irrigation system and provide military protection. Proprietary and sitio grants over several generations often came to resemble village communities, as all children inherit equally among the Spanish Americans. For the most part, the rural farming villages predominated in the mountain heartland of the Spanish Americans in northern New Mexico and along the rivers and streams flowing from the mountains. Sitio grants, although found throughout New Mexico, were more common on the plains and in regions where ranching was economically more feasible than farming (Perrigo, 1960: 78-80).

The large landowners during the Spanish and Mexican periods in New Mexico dominated the economic and political affairs of the territory. Possessing unlimited access to land and owning large herds of livestock, they drew their labor from three sources: (1) indebted Spanish-American landless workers, known as peons, who could not leave the employment of their employers as long as they owed him money—having to buy their necessities from the store owned by the rancher, they were seldom out of debt (sons inherited the debts of their fathers); (2) captured or purchased Indian slaves who gradually were absorbed into the ranks of the peons; and (3) free workers from neighboring villages. The relationship between the peon and his employer was contractual in nature. The landowner provided employment and support for his peons and their families, took care of them in times of illness and accident, led them to battle against Indian raiders, and protected them from abuse by other landowners or by the law enforcement officers. In return, the employer received absolute obedience from his peons in political and economic matters (Lamar, 1966: 27-28).

Powerful and wealthy ranchers could secure the political support of the neighboring village population through economic and political favors and even to some degree through intimidation, but the villages nestled on their land grants were seldom dependent economically upon the ranchers. If the rancher refused to grant privileges and favors to the village people, he would quickly lose their support. The numerous villages located in the more remote mountain valleys where ranching was not feasible were seldom molested or deeply influenced by the powerful landowning families. On the northwestern frontier facing the Ute and Navajo Indians few large ranchers could survive the constant Indian raiding. Villages here were inhabited by independent frontiersmen who paid little attention to the wishes of Spanish, Mexican, or American governors. It is in these villages that the tides of unrest against the Anglo Americans have always run the strongest (Swadesh, 1966; Kluckhohn, 1961: 180-191; Knowlton, 1962, Burma, 1954: 12 13).

Leadership within the villages rested in the hands of the more powerful and wealthy family heads able to grant economic and political favors to village families. Known as the village patron, he mediated between the village and outside political authorities. He judged village disputes, organized military resistance against Indian raiders, financed religious celebrations, supported the village church, called the men of the village together to labor on the irrigation system, and in general enforced village values. Those who refused to accept his decisions might have to flee the village. He was not, however, a dictator. His decisions had to rest upon village customs, and his power depended upon the consensus of the village population. If, for one reason or another, he lost the tacit support of the village people, he would inevitably be challenged by another family head who in many cases was a relative. The position of the village patron was not an inherited one and depended as much upon personality and ability to embody village mores as upon wealth and power. A village patron was expected to use his position to increase his wealth and political power, but he had to do so discreetly and not at the expense of his fellow villagers (Swadesh, 1966; Kluckhohn, 1961; Knowlton, 1962; Burma, 1954).

The subsistence farming village communities, based securely on their land grants and unified by the interlocking mechanisms of the patriarchal extended family, the compadrazgo, the folk Catholicism, the patron system, and the almost mystical identification of the village people with their villages were most resistant to acculturation, assimilation, and Anglo-American dominance. Each village tended to become a closed social and economic world of its own, suspicious and hostile toward the outside. As long as the villages retained their land base, they were able to maintain a relative independence for a long period of time from the economic, political, and legal institutions imposed upon them by the Anglo-American conquest.

Once the land base was eroded away, the village world collapsed. Today, it lives on as a golden memory in the minds of the embittered rural Spanish-American people as an Eden from which they were ejected by Anglo Americans and as a paradise to which they long to return (Calkins, 1935; Leonard, 1943; Knowlton, 1969a).

IMPACT OF THE AMERICAN CONQUEST

Much of the profound bitterness and cynicism of the Spanish Americans toward American political, legal, and economic systems can be traced back to the circumstances of the American occupation of New Mexico in 1847. The Spanish Americans believe that the occupying American generals made certain promises in the name of the American government to respect and to protect their land-holdings, and their personal and civil rights. These promises were later formalized in the Treaty of Guadalupe Hidalgo that ended the state of war between the United States and Mexico. The Spanish Americans are convinced that they were misled by the American generals and the American government. They are persuaded that they were robbed of their lands and treated with violence by Anglo Americans in defiance of the solemn promises made to the Spanish Americans to obtain their compliance with the American occupation of the territory.[3]

[3]The Treaty of Guadalupe Hidalgo that ended the state of war between the United States and Mexico was officially announced on July 4, 1848. The treaty articles that guaranteed the property and liberties of the inhabitants of New Mexico are as follows: Article Eight, titled "Rights of Mexicans Established in Territories Ceded to the United States," reads "Mexicans now established in territories previously belonging to Mexico, and which remain for the future within the limits of the United States, as defined by the present treaty, shall be free to continue where they now reside, or remove at any time to the Mexican republic, retaining the property which they possess in the said territories, or disposing thereof, and removing the proceeds wherever they please, without their being subjected, on this account, to any contribution, tax, or charge whatever. . . . In the said territories, property of every kind now belonging to Mexicans not established there, shall be inviolably respected. The present owners, the heirs of these and all Mexicans who may hereafter acquire said property by contact shall enjoy with respect to it guarantees equally ample as if the same belonged to citizens of the United States."

Article Nine, "How Mexicans Remaining in Ceded Territories May Become Citizens of the United States," reads "Mexicans who, in the territories aforesaid, shall not preserve the character of citizens of the Mexican Republic, conformably with what is stipulated in the preceding article, and be admitted at the proper time (to be judged of by the Congress of the United States) to the enjoyment of all the rights of citizens of the United States, according to the principles of the Constitution; and in the meantime shall be maintained and protected in the free enjoyment of their liberty and property, and secured in the free exercise of their religion without restriction."

See "Treaty of Peace Between the United States and Mexico" (Zimmerman, 1966: 362-380).

General Stephen W. Kearny, the commander of the American army that took possession of New Mexico, told the inhabitants of Las Vegas, New Mexico, the first settlement of any consequence of his route to Santa Fe on August 15, 1846, "We come amongst you as friends, not as enemies, as protectors, not as conquerors. We come among you for your benefit, not for your injury."[4] Entering Santa Fe on August 18, 1846, he reiterated his message to the assembled inhabitants. "We come as friends to better your condition and make you a part of the Republic of the United States. We do not mean to murder you or rob you of your property. Your families shall be free of molestation, your women secure from violence. My soldiers shall take nothing from you but what they pay for." (Twitchell, 1963b: 250-266).

Leaving for California soon after with most of his troops, General Kearny appointed a resident American trader, Charles Bent, as acting governor and Colonel Alexander W. Doniphan as military commander. The colonel suffered no illusions about the feelings of the Spanish Americans. He pointed out: "A people conquered but yesterday could have no friendly feeling for their conquerors, who have taken possession of their country—changed its laws and appointed new officers, principally foreigners" (Beck, 1962: 134). Colonel Doniphan was shortly ordered to march to Chihuahua, Mexico, to join the American invasion forces. He was replaced by Colonel Sterling Price who apparently was unable to maintain discipline among his troops.

The behavior of the American military intensified Spanish-American unrest and resentment. An American living in New Mexico at the time called the American troops, "a degenerate military mob, violators of law and order, heaping daily insults and injury upon the people. Price's lack of military education and his apparent inability to control either officers or men has produced among the New Mexicans the strongest feelings of distrust and hatred and a desire to rebel exists among the inhabitants" (Emmet, 1965: 53-54). An Englishman, traveling in New Mexico shortly after the American occupation,

[4]On the morning of August 15, 1846, General Stephen W. Kearny, commander of the American army occupying New Mexico said to the inhabitants of Las Vegas, New Mexico, "Henceforth, I absolve you from all allegience to the Mexican government.... I am your governor. I shall not expect you to take up arms and follow me to fight your own people who oppose me; but I now tell you, that those who remain peaceably at home, attending to their crops and their herds, shall be protected by me in their property, their persons and their religion.... My government... will keep off the Indians, protect you in your persons and property..." (Twitchell, 1963a: 250-266).

"found all over New Mexico . . . the most bitter feelings and most determined hostility against the Americans who certainly in Santa Fe and elsewhere have not been very anxious to conciliate the people, but, by their bullying and overbearing demeanor towards them, have in great measure been the cause of the hatred" (Ruxton, 1965: 180).

Growing Spanish-American and Indian bitterness and resentment generated by the behavior of American soldiers, the belief among some Spanish-American leaders that the small number of American troops could not maintain control of New Mexico, a sense of shame and humiliation at the lack of resistance to the American army, and perhaps a lingering sense of Mexican patriotism led to a widespread Spanish-American revolt in which the Taos Indians participated. A number of Americans including Charles Bent, the acting governor, were killed in Taos, Mora, and Las Vegas. The rebellion was put down and its participants severely punished for rebelling against the occupying power (Lamar, 1966: 67-70).

Mrs. Thomas Boggs (Denver Post, January 11, 1890), the stepdaughter of the slain governor, related years later how the Indian rebels from Taos were treated by the American soldiers:

> *I well remember how severely the soldiers punished the offenders. One favorite pastime was to harness six Indians to an army ambulance and then at a signal put them on the run from the Pueblo (the Indian pueblo), to Taos. They would reach us exhausted, the crack of the driver's whip heralding their approach, with blood streaming from their unprotected backs and legs, one ambulance being followed by another and another, racing as they came on. And when the soldiers tired of this sport, their unfortunate captives ended their miserable existence at the end of a rope.*

Spanish Americans were treated little better. The communities of Mora and Las Vegas were almost totally destroyed by American soldiers, and many of their inhabitants were hanged (Twitchell, 1963a: 134-146).

The Spanish-American rebellion and its aftermath intensified the feelings of hostility and mistrust between Spanish Americans and Anglo Americans in New Mexico that to some degree have persevered from that time to the present. The behavior of American troops toward the Spanish Americans deteriorated after the revolt. A New York Tribune newspaper reporter (Emmet, 1965: 67-68) wrote from Santa Fe on June 12, 1847 to his paper about the behavior of American troops in the city:

> *It is with feelings of profound sadness that we are obliged to record the disgraceful proceedings of our troops under Col. Price at Santa Fe. Their conduct has been characterized by the grossest insubordination; they plunder at their pleasure the defenseless Mexican and give to his complaints no answer save contumelious reproaches and disgraceful blows. . . . They cheat and browbeat the natives by day and when night comes, blown with insolence and wine, they resort to the fandangoes and give full scope to their unbridled passions.*

Spanish-American resentment and hostility toward their American conquerors did not diminish after the unsuccessful revolt. Although many wealthy Spanish-American ranchers and merchants accommodated themselves to the new political order, the majority of the Spanish-American people remained as alienated from their American conquerors as before. Rev. W. C. Kaphart, an early Protestant missionary resident in Santa Fe (Grant, 1934: 154-155), commented on June 27, 1851 about the Spanish-American attitudes:

> *This is a conquered people and, like all such, I have reason to believe that they secretly hate the Americans and would at any time gladly avail themselves of an opportunity to throw off the yoke. . . . We live upon a volcano which, but for the continual parade of arms, would burst out almost any moment. There is but little room to doubt that there are many dissatisfied Mexicans who would at any time form a coalition with the savages against us, did they believe that thus combined they would be strong enough to rout an army. The conduct of many Americans toward the Mexican population is calculated greatly to increase that feeling. In all their intercourse with them, they put on airs of superiority and treat the Mexicans as a degraded and inferior people, feeling secure in the protection of our military force.*

The 530-some-odd Americans living in New Mexico in the 1850s were most reluctant to accept the Spanish Americans, then called Mexicans, as equal citizens of a common country. A group of resident American merchants (Emmet, 1965: 105) expressed their sentiments quite freely in a petition submitted to the President of the United States expressing their opposition to ending military government in New Mexico. They stated that:

> *We are fully convinced that there is no hope for the improvement of our territory unless Americans rule it, and that the spirit of Mexican rule must be corrupt and disgraceful in a territory of the United States.*

The invasion of New Mexico by Texan forces in 1861 during the Civil War did much to reconcile the Spanish Americans to American rule. No matter how much the Spanish Americans disliked the Americans they detested the Texans even more. After the destruction of their supplies, the Confederate troops who had occupied in sequence Las Cruces, Albuquerque, and Santa Fe were forced to fall back to El Paso. The Americans, short of troops, were forced to recruit and to arm three thousand Spanish-American volunteers under Spanish-American field officers who participated in Civil War campaigns in the Southwest (Hall, 1960: 23, 27; Colton, 1959: 25).

CAUSES OF LAND LOSS
AMONG THE SPANISH AMERICANS

Since 1854, the Spanish Americans have lost, according to one estimate, in the upper Rio Grande Valley alone well over two million acres of privately owned lands and 1.7 million acres of communal lands to Anglo Americans, one million acres to the state government, and even larger acreages to the Federal government (Cordova and Oberg, 1943: 61-62). Similar losses have occurred in other sections of northern New Mexico. The erosion of Spanish-American landholdings still continues. The loss of a land base is primarily responsible for the collapse of the Spanish-American rural village economy. It is perhaps the major causal factor of the poverty among the village people. The lost land has become the focus of the resentments, the hostilities, the dreams, and the ambitions of present generations of Spanish Americans. These emotions have generated a growing demand among the Spanish Americans for the return of the land (Knowlton, 1969a).

Among Anglo Americans little sense of identity with or attachment to the land has ever existed. Land has always been regarded as a commodity to be exploited like any other commodity for the profit that it might yield. Privately owned land has been valued more highly than publicly owned land. The private land-owner, in his search for wealth, has had the legal right to use the land as he desired with little concern for the future or for the welfare of his neighbors. The Anglo American, thus, has always been a transient, exhausting one section of land before moving on to the other, lured by the eternal dream of making enough money to enable him to retire to a better, more desirable place in which to live (Otteson, 1963: 307-335; Whitaker and Ackerman, 1951: 12-14). As Murphy (1967: 7) puts it:

> *English settlers brought to the frontier ideas which*
> *precluded the sort of accomodation with nature and the native*

peoples that marked Spanish settlements from Florida to California, or the sort of self-contained agrarian economy descriptive of most of the French settlements. To the English immigrants, all of North America was a vast preserve of resources waiting to be processed.

In contrast, the Spanish Americans had a very close sense of identity with the land. A peasant-type people, they believed that the land was essential for human life. Every family head had a natural right to secure enough land to support his family. Although the right of private property existed, communally owned property was just as important. The concept that a man could own or monopolize large sections of land when landless families existed was and is morally repugnant to the Spanish-American village people. Every child in a Spanish-American family, regardless of sex or age, has equal rights of inheritance. Spanish Americans even today struggle hard to preserve their landholdings. If the land is lost, the village people grieve as though they had lost family members. The sense of deprivation is handed down from one generation to another. Today, Spanish-American families that lost their land over fifty years ago still feel the loss as sharply as though it had happened but yesterday. There is no reconciliation to the loss of the land over the generations (Atencio, 1964).

So deeply engrained among Anglo Americans of the nineteenth century was the concept of private landownership that they found it almost impossible to comprehend or to accept the fact that the major areas of the village land grants were owned jointly by the inhabitants of the village and not by any single village family. The ejido or communal lands belonged to the village as a community. Every family had the right to use these lands.[5] Anglo-American lawyers persuaded Anglo-American courts to adopt the legal fiction that the village communal lands belonged to the body heirs of those who had originally petitioned for the grants. Such a concept was completely foreign and alien to Spanish-American customs. Once the courts had been persuaded to accept this fictitious concept, shrewd Anglo-American lawyers were able to get the naive Spanish-American

[5]The American courts rejected the concept of communal lands on the Spanish-American land grants, as witnessed by the following statement from a decision of the United Court of Private Land Claims: "The idea that we desire to incorporate in the decree is that what is known as the agricultural lands, the valley land as we discover in these two valleys shall be confirmed, but that what is ordinarily known as pasture lands and commons will not be included in the decree "—this confirms the title of the Santa Cruz Land Grantees *(New Mexican,* September 5, 1899; see also Calkins, 1937a, and Mosk, 1942).

descendents of the original settlers to sign their names to bits of paper for a few dollars in which, without knowing it, they signed away portions of the communal lands.[6] Spanish-American informants claim that their fathers and grandfathers never realized what they were signing and that even if they had, they still had no power or right under Spanish-American customs to sign away any portion of the communal lands to which they but had rights as members of the village (Brayer, 1949: 16-19; Keleher, 1962: 10-16).

Conflicting methods defining legal title caused serious land conflicts in New Mexico. A valid land title according to Anglo-American usage, is one in which the sequence of ownership from the first owner to the current owner can be legally traced. If the sequence of owners and the legal transfer of the land from one owner to another is not perfect, the title is apt to be defective. In contrast, among the Spanish Americans, title to the land was, and is, based more upon custom and tradition than upon written documents. If families and villages have used land for several generations without being challenged, the land is defined as belonging to them by their neighbors (Moynihan, 1968: 15-347; Knowlton, 1967).

Land conflicts could have been reduced and the landholdings of the Spanish Americans protected if the American government had accepted as authentic all Spanish-American landholdings recognized as legal by the Spanish and Mexican governments rather than requiring each land claimant to prove legal ownership in American courts of law or by negotiating with the Surveyor General or the Federal Land Offices in New Mexico. Another method of legalizing and recognizing Spanish and Mexican land titles would have been the formation of the committee composed of men familiar with conditions in New Mexico to pass upon the land claims with the government carrying the burden of legal research, boundary surveys and judicial hearings. As neither of these two methods were adopted, the Spanish-American landowners, the majority of them poor, illiterate, village people, were caught in the toils of a legal system based upon the adversary principle in which they found it impossible to protect their landholdings.[7]

[6]The stories about lawyers and their Spanish-American agents persuading village people to sign documents in English in return for a few dollars and thus signing away land rights are extremely common both among the Spanish Americans and lawyers. Today Spanish Americans are so suspicious that very few are willing to sign anything without consulting people of confidence. The entire state and federal court systems are in bad repute among the Spanish-American people of northern New Mexico.

[7]The incredibly complicated legal system of the litigious Anglo American still baffles the Spanish-American village people. They have a terrible fear of the state and federal courts and will often abandon property when the title is challenged rather than go to court.

As Governor Ross of New Mexico observed in his testimony of January 11, 1888 (*New Mexican,* January 12, 1888) before the U.S. House Committee on Territories:

> *Under the Spanish and Mexican governments for many generations there was little need of intervention by governments or courts for the more perfect definition of the rights of grantees or claimants upon the public lands. Their grants were held under special concessions to individuals or to communities or by virtue of general laws for colonization for town building and by right of possession. Few of them had muniments of title beyond a condition permit from the Crown of Spain or an act of the Mexican Congress. They needed no legislation, no adjudication by the courts, their titles were perfect to all intents and purposes. Their ownership was universally recognized, and the indefinite nature and lack of minute description of boundaries was of small moment in a country whose population was sparse that there were ample room for all and land was practically valueless. There were little or no public records, practically no courts. Isolated as the people of New Mexico were, fifteen hundred miles from civilization on the east, a thousand miles from the brethren of Mexico in the south and west, and hemmed in by an impenetrable cordon of savages on all sides . . . .it is not strange that a degree of laxity in the preservation of records and in the administration of equity and a confusion and demoralization something startling to the American mind should have come to prevail.*

Although the Spanish and Mexican governments did provide written land deeds to the recipients of land grants, these documents, over the years, among an illiterate village people living in a frontier environment, tended to vanish. Original copies of the deeds were preserved in Spanish and Mexican archives in Santa Fe, the capital of the territory, but these archives were partially destroyed by early American territorial governors (Horn, 1963: 135-149). From the date of the destruction to the present, the Spanish Americans have believed that the destruction was performed deliberately to destroy the official copies of land grant deeds.[8]

The government of the United States, through the Treaty of Guadalupe Hidalgo at the close of the Mexican War in 1847, had

---

[8]Adolph F. Bandelier, a pioneer anthropologist in the Southwest, recorded in his journal on August 25, 1880, the following item: "Padre Eguillon, very strong concerning the wanton destruction of the archives under Governor Pyle (Pile), says it was done on purpose to destroy Mexican claims" (Lane and Riley, 1966: 73).

obligated itself to protect the property and civil rights of the Spanish-speaking population of the Southwest. However, it was not until 1854 that Congress finally bestirred itself to consider the matter of property titles in New Mexico. By that time, the Spanish Americans were already being victimized. A Catholic Sister of Charity, living in New Mexico at the time, observed (Segale, 1949: 194-195):

> *In the early years of Anglo settlement in New Mexico, the unsuspicious and naive Spanish Americans were victimized on every hand. When the men from the states came out west to dispossess the poor natives of their lands, they used many subterfuges. One was to offer the owner of the land a handful of silver coins for the small service of making a mark on a paper. The mark was a cross which was accepted as a signature and by which the unsuspecting natives deeded away their lands. By this means, many a poor family was robbed of all its possessions.*

By congressional enactment on July 22, 1954, Congress reserved for itself the right to pass on the validity of land grant titles. By the same Act, Congress established the Office of Surveyor General of New Mexico to provide Congress with information on the history, the boundaries, the physical characteristics, and the validity of land grant titles in New Mexico and then recommend to Congress, through the Secretary of Interior, acceptance or rejection of each land grant title. Because of inadequate staff and funds, corruption, unfamiliarity with Spanish and Mexican law, Spanish-American land tenure customs, and the sheer number of land grants, the Surveyor General was never able to properly process the numerous land grant claims.[9] Congress accepted some of its recommendations and rejected others. As Twitchell (1912: 467) stated:

> *No claimant could secure congressional affirmation of his title unless he was able to spend a long period of time in Washington and was abundantly equipped with funds to*

[9]For good analysis of the frauds associated with the early Surveyor Generals of New Mexico, see Julian, 1887. Keheler, in discussing the work of the office observes: "The Surveyor General was given a task entirely beyond the ability of any one man. Surveyor General after Surveyor General struggled with the flood of land grant claims that were filed in his office. Claims were approved or disapproved and reports were submitted to the Secretary of Interior who in turn submitted reports to Congress. The Congress of the United States was not equipped with the machinery required to cope with the land grant problems. Some claims were confirmed out of hand after a hurried study by members of a committee. Other claims languished indefinitely, receiving no attention" (Keheler, 1964: 7).

organize a lobby to smooth the passage of a private act confirming his land claim.

The isolated, illiterate, rural Spanish-American village people, speaking very little English, unfamiliar with the functions of Congress, the structure of the American government and the intricate labyrinth of Anglo-American legal and political practices, and lacking funds to employ lawyers, were at the mercy of Anglo-American land speculators and claimants who possessed the funds and the political influence to smooth the passage of favorable legislation through Congress. Keleher (1962: 105) summarized the result of the Congressional action as follows:

> *The Alcalde [Spanish word for mayor], on the roof top in Las Vegas, New Mexico, must have grinned broadly as General Kearny spoke of protecting the people against the Indians and protecting them in their property rights. The fine promises Kearny made in Las Vegas were for the most part repudiated in Washington. Ignorance, stupidity, traditional red tape, an occasional bit of fraud, all had a place in federal government dealings with New Mexico. General Kearny had promised the people of New Mexico security in their property; and the Treaty of Guadalupe Hidalgo signed in 1848 promised the same thing. The government of the United States, however, failed to adequately execute that treaty. . . . The belief prevailed at the signing of the Treaty of Guadalupe Hidalgo that if the government of the United States should claim any part of the territory as public domain, it would, at its own cost and expense, find out what it might be entitled to, and in doing this, necessarily ascertain the boundaries of private estates, whether called land grants or small homesteads. The Congress of the United States required all claimants of lands under Spanish or Mexican grants to pay for their own surveys, to undertake and carry forward long, burdensome, and expensive procedures and litigation to perfect their titles. Litigation required the services of lawyers and lawyers were quick to learn that they could exact important interests in land grants for professional work. Government officials, at times in the office of the Surveyor General of New Mexico, in the Commission of the General Land Office in Washington were not adverse to whittling down acreage, to throwing out entirely genuine land grants, on the pretext that they were fictitious and fraudulent. Mexican citizens soon found their estates in jeopardy. Many of*

them became pauperized as the result of the failure of the
United States of America to back up in good faith the
assurances extended in the Treaty of Guadalupe Hidalgo.

As transportation and communication facilities between New
Mexico and other American states and territories improved after the
Civil War, and dangers of Indian attacks diminished, the westward
moving Anglo-American frontier engulfed New Mexico in the 1870s
(Lamar, 1966: 67-70). Military veterans of northern and southern
armies, soldiers, merchants, prospectors, trappers, politicians, cattlemen, and lawyers migrated to New Mexico in search of economic
opportunities. As Larson (1962: 161-200) wrote:

> *Of all who came, the group which was to play one of the*
> *most important roles influencing the course of New Mexico's*
> *fight for statehood proved to be lawyers, lawyers of varying*
> *capabilities. . . . Many of the lawyers were quick to see what a*
> *vast fortune could be built up in so rich a country. They*
> *looked with unrestrained ambition upon the obscure titles of*
> *ownership to thousands of acres in the territory. The original*
> *owners of the land had received their titles under the Spanish*
> *and the Mexico rule which preceded the Treaty of Guadalupe*
> *Hidalgo. . . . Now with many of the titles to these grants*
> *clouded in doubt after generations during which more and more*
> *members of the original family lived on the land, the American*
> *lawyers saw that they could use their legal skills to acquire a*
> *great deal of the land for themselves. Their success in this*
> *endeavor as well as in various other economic enterprises*
> *undertaken over the years was amazing. Because of the*
> *constant and close cooperation of these lawyers, their oppo-*
> *nents soon labeled them as members of a ring.*

The ring mentioned above was known as the Santa Fe Ring.
Composed of a group of Anglo-American lawyers loosely grouped
around an important Santa Fe law firm, the ring soon came to
include important Republican and Democratic county, territorial,
state and national political leaders, prominent government appointees
and office holders, businessmen and bankers, newspaper editors,
ranchers, and men in many diverse political and business positions.
Based in Santa Fe, the ring had component rings in every county in
New Mexico. From the late 1870s to the 1900s, the ring played an
important role in almost every economic and political event in New
Mexico (Lamar, 1966: 136-170, 185-198). Men opposed to the ring

did not prosper and some died violent deaths.[10] Within a few years of its founding, the leaders of the ring had acquired, through legal and political manipulations, title to vast acreages of land that once belonged to the Spanish-American villages and landowners.[11]

The Santa Fe Ring was described by an Anglo-American governor of the territory of New Mexico (Larson, 1962: 161-200) in the following words:

> *From the Land Grant Ring grew others, as the opportunities for speculation and plunder were developed. Cattle Rings, Public Land Stealing Rings, Mining Rings, Treasury Rings, and Rings of almost every description grew up, till the affairs of the territory came to be run almost exclusively in the interest and for the benefit of combinations organized and headed by a few long-headed ambitious and unscrupulous Americans. . . . Thus the Santa Fe Ring became to all intents and purposes a closed corporation, and the syndicate it represented and controlled, came to be and has for many years been known as the Santa Fe Ring, a great combination which included all the lesser rings and dictated at will the legislation and general conduct of the affairs of the territory, with branches here and there in the lesser towns, but all subservient to the Central Head.*

Many poor Spanish-American village inhabitants lacked funds to finance land cases through the complicated legal American system from the local district court to the U.S. Supreme Court. When their land claims were challenged, many Spanish Americans, in sheer frustration, abandoned their holdings. Other villagers paid off their lawyers in land. Groups of lawyers, in collusion, brought suits against village land titles. Other lawyers, parties to the collusion, would agree to defend the village claims for sections of the land as a fee. Whether the village won or lost the land claim was not significant to the

---

[10]No history of the Santa Fe Ring has ever been written. Many men in commenting about the activities of the ring to the writer stated that it was commonly believed in New Mexico that members of the ring endeavored to buy off opponents whenever possible. If this could not be done, then efforts were made to frighten the persons and, finally, if this did not work, the most deadly and threatening enemies might be killed.

[11]Thomas B. Catron (Lamar, 1966: 149-150), the most important leader of the Santa Fe Ring, had acquired by 1898 the following portions of major land grants in New Mexico: portion of the Tierra Amarilla Grant; 50,000 acres of the Mora Grant; 80,000 acres of the Beck Grant; two-thirds of the 78,000 acres of the Espiritu Santo Grant; one-half of the 21,500 acres of the Juana Lopez Grant; 24,000 acres of the Piedras Lumbre Grant; 11,000 acres of the Cabaldon Grant; and 15,000 acres of the Baca Grant.

lawyers involved, as in either case they split the lands among themselves.[12]

During most of the territorial period, only two federal land offices were opened in New Mexico. As no land titles derived from the public domain were considered legal unless registered at these offices, unregistered land was legally defined as belonging to the public domain and open to settlement (Keleher, 1962: 86-87). Few Spanish-American village people knew about the existence of the land offices or the legal requirement that they had to register their village lands with the land offices. Anglo-American lawyers and politicians familiar with the requirements, and often in collusion with the personnel of the land office, were able to know which land grants were registered and which were not. They were thus able to register title to the unregistered land grants whose Spanish-American inhabitants thus lost legal titles to their lands.[13]

Finally, Congress, in response to the growing furor over the New Mexican land grants, established on March 3, 1891, a Court of Private Land Claims to "untangle the greatest land embroglio in American history" (Lamar, 1966: 192). The court, composed of five federal judges drawn from outside of New Mexico, a federal attorney, and such court officials as clerks and translators, met regularly in New Mexico to hear land-grant cases until June 30, 1904. The court operated on the adversary principle. Land-grant claimants had to hire attorneys, secure witnesses, and present evidence favoring their claims. These claims were challanged by the court attorney who at times carried his opposition to the U.S. Supreme Court (Session Laws: 51st Congress, 2nd session, 854-862).

Thus, the vital question of Spanish-American land ownership was decided in an Anglo-American court whose Anglo-American

[12]Collusion between opposing lawyers on land-grant cases were reported by village people to be quite common around the Las Vegas, New Mexico area. The Anton Chico Land Grant near Santa Fe was said to have been a victim of this type of collusion.

[13]Governor L. Bradford Prince on December 28, 1892 said in his message to the state legislature of New Mexico: "In my last message, I endeavored to point out the dangerous character of the act to quiet titles. The object of this law is not objectionable, but it can be abused in such a way as to defraud hundreds of land owners or unknown heirs, and then serving them by publication in some obscure newspaper or one published at a great distance from their residence, and in a language which they do not understand. I have heard of one case in which a party who had bought the interest of a single heir in a grant which had a multitude of owners thus employed this law and those interested never knew or heard of any suit until after a decree had been entered depriving them of their right. (New Mexican, December 28, 1892).

judges were quite unfamiliar with Spanish-American land tenure customs and traditions. Court decisions were based upon the most rigorous interpretation of Spanish, Mexican, and American land laws. One observer noted that two-thirds of all Spanish-American land claims were rejected by the court. The land grants whose titles were rejected became part of the public domain opened to general settlement (Keleher, 1945: 86-87).

The Spanish Americans lost large acreages of land to Anglo-American cattlemen through violence. The Spanish Americans, in comparison with the Anglo Americans of the frontier period, were a peaceful people. They had an abhorrence to the taking of human lives. Unable to secure many firearms before the coming of the Americans, the Spanish Americans were forced to defend themselves against the Indians with Indian weapons, such as lances and bows and arrows. They were virtually helpless before the invasion of New Mexico by the Mexican-hating Texas cattlemen moving into New Mexico in the late 1870s and 1880s as the Commanche barrier was overcome. The Texans treated the Spanish Americans but little better than they did the Indians. "Killing a Mexican was like killing an enemy in the independent war that apparently each Texan waged, and since it was a conflict with historic scores (the Alamo) to settle, the killing carried a sort of immunity with it" (Hale, 1959: 137).

The Spanish Americans were never able to secure protection from Anglo-American violence from either local, state, or federal law enforcement officers. When cases were brought into court, the judges, juries, and lawyers were threatened and browbeaten by Anglo-American ranchers. They were at the mercy of lawless bands of Anglo Americans, primarily Texans, who gradually occupied the range lands of New Mexico, killing Spanish Americans, destroying their crops, rustling their livestock, and driving them off their lands.

The Spanish-American village people, living in a slow-changing almost static subsistence agricultural economy were and still are unfamiliar with the principles of credit, the operations of financial and commodity markets, the laws of supply and demand, and the economic fluctuations of the American economic system imposed upon them by military conquest.

The Spanish Americans had imposed upon them a county and state system of government that was far more cumbersome, complex, and expensive than any form of government that they experienced under Spanish and Mexican rule. The American system with its many highly paid employees, its ever-increasing number of agencies and departments, and its costly judicial, legislative, and executive divisions, placed staggering financial burdens upon the Spanish

Americans, who were the majority of the population of New Mexico down to the 1940s. To finance this top-heavy government structure the Anglo Americans imported the fixed land-tax concept from the more humid east. Such a tax system that placed fixed annual charges payable in cash upon a subsistence agricultural system in which money was scarce, located in a semiarid area, marked by chronic drought cycles and crop failures, had a most serious and harmful impact upon the Spanish-American village economic systems.[14]

Fraud and corruption in the administration of the land tax made its impact even harsher. The landholdings of the Spanish-American village people have generally paid a higher land tax per acre than the more productive acres of Anglo-American ranchers. Many Spanish Americans paid their land tax to county officials who did not record the payment or issued a fraudulent receipt. It was not unknown for county officials to raise the land tax so high that the poor village people could not pay it and then pick up choice bits of real estate at tax foreclosure sales. The tax rates were then lowered. Furthermore, few Spanish Americans were able to secure the indulgence of county officials to lax payment of land taxes so generously extended to more influential landowners and businessmen.[15]

From the 1880s to the 1920s, the Spanish Americans lost access to the natural resources of northern New Mexico. The agricultural, mineral, grazing, water, and timber resources of their former landholdings passed into the hands of private Anglo-American owners, frequently absentee owners, the state government and the national government. The accelerating loss forced increasing numbers of Spanish Americans into the migrant stream. Leaving their homes early in the spring, they returned late in the fall. During their absence, their families cultivated their diminishing acres of farm

---

[14]Keleher (1929), in commenting upon the burden of taxes on the Spanish Americans, states: "Taxes have been a staggering burden for all of the land grants in New Mexico. . . . The grants were burdened with taxes . . . the issuance of patents by our government resulted in litigation because the rights were vested in a hundred or perhaps a thousand or more heirs of the original grantee. The individual grantee owning perhaps a thousandth part of the whole or less, declined or was unable to pay his proportionate share of the tax levied against the grant as an entirety."

[15]Another New Mexican historian in analyzing the operations of the land tax says: "Buying up tax titles is also recommended for acquiring land. Often many owners of a grant are unable to pay taxes on their commonly held grazing lands assessed at perhaps a dollar and a half an acre. The state takes over the land for delinquent taxes and resells the whole grant for thirty-five or forty cents an acre. Having influence, the new owner than gets the assessed valuation reduced to fifty cents an acre" (Ferguson, 1933: 260).

lands. Although many villagers did migrate to the mining camps and the growing urban centers, and some found employment on the railroads, the majority of the villagers, even though they knew that they could improve their economic conditions by migration, preferred to live in their native villages.

The migrant stream was dammed up by the depression of the 1930s (Sanchez, 1967: 64; Calkins, 1937b). Unable to find work in the harvest field, the migrants were forced to remain at home. They were joined there by their unemployed urban relatives who returned to their native villages. The resources of the patriarchal extended families and traditional village mutual aid managed to preserve the village people from extreme destitution. Available land resources were farmed intensively in the early 1930s by archaic farming methods. Then the prolonged drought cycle of the middle 1930s, with its long series of failing harvests, brought the village economic systems to the ground. The village people were saved from hunger by the varied programs of the New Deal (Calkins, 1936).

The depressed economic conditions in northern New Mexico are the result, for the most part, of the complex interplay of economic, political, and cultural factors unleashed in New Mexico by the 100 years or more of American occupation. Poverty in this region has not been caused by Spanish-American racial, cultural, or emotional characteristics. It is rather the end product of American colonization of New Mexico. The Spanish Americans were trapped in a spider's web of alien economic, political, and legal systems imposed upon them that ignored Spanish-American traditions, customs, needs, and aspirations. Small groups of Anglo-American lawyers, politicians, businessmen and their Spanish-American dependents were able to enrich themselves through the manipulation of these systems at the expense of the Spanish Americans. They have acquired ownership, often absentee, of the agricultural, mineral, grazing, water, and timber resources of the lands that once belonged to the Spanish Americans.

CAUSES OF FAILURE OF FEDERAL
GOVERNMENT PROGRAMS IN NORTHERN NEW MEXICO

Since the end of World War II, federal agencies in northern New Mexico have sporadically grappled with the existence of poverty among the Spanish Americans. Few government programs have really benefited the Spanish Americans, and many programs have done them serious economic damage. One of the most important factors responsible for the failure of government programs is the inability of government agencies to establish effective communication with the Spanish Americans. The agencies make little effort to recognize that the Spanish Americans are different in culture, language, values, aspirations, and definition of social and economic problems from Anglo Americans. Government personnel until very recently received little training in the history, culture, socioeconomic problems and needs of the Spanish-American people. As a result, few government personnel can work effectively with Spanish Americans. In turn, the Spanish Americans tend to be puzzled, angered, and embittered by the failure of government agencies to show respect for the Spanish language and for Spanish-American culture, and by a tendency to patronize the Spanish Americans. Relationships between Spanish Americans and government agencies have deteriorated to where the Spanish Americans consider both the state and federal governments to be their major enemies directly responsible for their economic plight.[16] Few minority groups in the United States are as cynical and hostile toward the pretensions of the American political, legal, and economic systems as are the Spanish Americans.[17]

Anglo-American administrators seldom realize how strange and alien traditional American concepts about initiating, organizing, and managing local government programs are to the Spanish Americans. Most government programs require that local programs must be administered by local boards who hire directors to manage their programs or to advise government agencies in program administration. Such boards and local councils are usually required to meet regularly, conduct their deliberation by Robert's Rules of Order and follow a written agenda publicized in advance. Members of the Board are expected to debate issues in public and to resolve conflicts by majority vote. Once the vote is taken, minority representatives on the board are expected to acquiesce in the result and support the majority opinion.[18]

Spanish Americans are confused by such a process. They love public meetings and enjoy abundant tides of florid oratory, but they are most reluctant to take a public stand on an issue or to debate a

[16]A former governor of New Mexico, David Cargo, is reported to have said: "If you could pave the roads with broken promises we would have black-topped all northern New Mexico years ago" (Albuquerque Journal, June 15, 1967).

[17]Governor Cargo also stated in testimony before a federal district court in Las Cruces, New Mexico that the Spanish Americans view government "as being a natural antagonist who never helps them out" (Albuquerque Journal, November 9, 1967).

[18]Social psychologists, sociologists, and anthropologists could find a fertile field for research in the social interaction between Anglo Americans, Indians, blacks, and Mexicans in public meetings involving community issues. Each group reacts in distinctive ways that often block communication because other groups do not understand the patterns of behavior involved.

point with fellow Spanish Americans. They would rather discuss issues informally in a long series of small private meetings, listen to the opinions of persons whom they trust, and try to reach a consensus of viewpoints before an issue is put to the vote. Decisions reached at these meetings must subtly incorporate different Spanish-American points of view. Until this is done, the views of the majority are never binding on the minority. Anglo-American participants find Spanish-American meetings to be baffling. Written agendas are never followed. The discussion seems rambling and irrelevant to the issues at hand. Motions are tabled for no apparent reason. Decisions once made seem to always fall apart and then suddenly an agreement emerges with full board support without any apparent public debate.

Anglo Americans are also chronically unable to locate the real leaders of Spanish-American villages. They assume that better educated, English-speaking Spanish Americans who have achieved some financial success must be village leaders. It is very hard for them to realize that among the rural Spanish-American village people, education, the ability to speak English, and financial success do not automatically qualify a person for village leadership. Such people are often in flight from traditional Spanish-American culture and values. They tend to seek out Anglo Americans for companionship and improvement of their social status. In the past, many of them have been used by Anglo Americans to exploit the village people. The real leaders of the village tend to be influential men, willing and able to assist their fellow villagers, and who exemplify traditional village values in their personal lives. They are often men who have little education and do not necessarily speak English.[19]

The chronic power struggles between agencies within a single government department and between government departments for Spanish-American loyalty resembles conflicts between Christian denominations for control of mission territories. Many village people dependent upon agency employment are corrupted by such conflicts without understanding the issues at stake. Villages are factionalized and programs sabotaged. Many agency administrators at peace with each other do not know what is going on in the field or else tacitly encourage the quiet but vicious warfare waged by their field staffs that not only threatens the unity and integrity of the Spanish-Amer-

---

[19]Spanish-American village inhabitants are incredibly suspicious of strange well-educated English-speaking Spanish Americans. In many instances they would prefer to communicate with an Anglo American. All too often the better educated Spanish Americans have been employed by non-Spanish-speaking Anglo Americans as intermediaries with the village people.

ican villages but also undermines Spanish-American loyalty to the government itself.[20]

CONSERVING RESOURCES AND LOSING A PEOPLE

One of the most tragic aspects of the operations of the federal government in New Mexico is the very harmful impact that many well-meaning programs, sponsored with highest motives by the Bureau of Reclamation, the U.S. Corps of Army Engineers, and the Forest Service, have had and are still having upon the lives of the Spanish-American population of the state. If the engineers and administrators had ever considered the socioeconomic and cultural characteristics of Spanish-American village economics and cultural aspirations in their planning, the harsh negative impact could have been minimized. The narrow segmented engineering and economist approach, so characteristic of government departments in New Mexico, was largely responsible for the damage. Almost every problem involving government action in the Southwest is far more complicated than the simple approach of engineers and economists might indicate. Virtually every situation has its cultural and social components that must be considered as well as the financial costs and problems of engineering. If the former are not considered, the government agencies may end up doing more harm than good.[21]

The majority of farmers along the Rio Grande River before the 1920s were Spanish-American subsistence farmers earning their living by farming small plots of irrigated land along the river and grazing livestock on the plateaus overlooking the river. As they lost their grazing lands to the Anglo Americans, they became even more dependent upon their small farms. The Bureau of Reclamation during

[20]The author once served as chairman of the San Miguel Area Redevelopment Committee from 1960 to 1962, the county in which the university at which the author taught was located. The committee held hearings and listened to many village people discuss what in their opinion were the more important causes of poverty in their communities. The committee was told by many villagers in 1961 that extension agents and field workers of the Extension Division and the Rural Area Development Program were strongly criticizing the Area Redevelopment Program and urging the village people not to participate. As committee chairman, the author at once protested to the head of the Extension Program in New Mexico who stated that he knew nothing about the attacks of his field staff on the work of the committee.

[21]In private conversations with several field staff members, the author was told that the U.S. Corps of Army Engineers would be glad to build large dams on any stream in New Mexico if the land affected could bear the cost, but the Corps would not build a sequence of small dams just to improve the irrigation facilities of the Spanish-American villages lining the streams.

the 1900s organized an irrigation district including El Paso, Texas, and Las Cruces, New Mexico. Several dams including the Elephant, Butte, and Caballo were built to store water for irrigation. The Bureau of Reclamation, to reimburse the federal government for its expenses, placed an annual charge upon each acre within the district. The large majority of Spanish-American farmers, unable to pay the cash charges, lost their lands through court action by the officers of the Irrigation Districts. The lands were taken over by commercial Anglo-American farmers who could not survive in the Rio Grande Valley without heavy government subsidies—subsidies never paid to the Spanish-American subsistence farmers.[22]

At the urging of the Albuquerque city fathers, troubled by the chronic floods of the Rio Grande River, the Corps of Engineers designed and organized the Middle Rio Grande Conservancy District to control flooding in the area. The District embraced not only the city of Albuquerque but also a number of neighboring Spanish-American villages. Once again annual cash charges were affixed to each acre within the district. Hundreds of subsistence farming Spanish-American farmers unable to pay these charges lost their lands through foreclosure. Similar conditions came into existence on the Canadian River flowing from northern New Mexico into Oklahoma and Texas. The Corps of Army Engineers built dams on the river to control flooding and to provide water for municipal use by the Anglo-American communities along the river. Once again, the Corps neglected to consider the water rights or welfare of the numerous Spanish-American villages on the headwaters of the Canadian. Many of these villages had to be abandoned because the villagers had lost the water rights which were taken from them without compensation.[23]

[22]Johansen (1948) in his analysis of Spanish-American villages in southern New Mexico says: "The tendency toward a more highly commercialized type of farming which developed with the coming of the irrigation project, The Caballo-Elephant Butte Dam Project, between 1910 and 1920 was to a large extent the imposition of a heavy financial burden which was in turn due to the cost of the irrigation project. After the completion of the dam construction, water costs were so high that it became necessary to change to more efficient farming methods. This change might have been justified on economic grounds, but from the standpoint of sociological consequences, it left much to be desired. Many small Spanish-American farm owners lost their land. Instead of being farm owners, they became either farm tenants or laborers" (Johansen, 1948: 25-26).

[23]The impact of the Middle Rio Grande Conservancy District, a flood control district organized by the U.S. Corps of Army Engineers in the Albuquerque, New Mexico area embracing the landholdings of neighboring Spanish-American villages, is seen in the following quotation: "These activities

The United States Forest Service is the most hated government agency in all of northern New Mexico among the Spanish Americans. Because of growing hostility toward the Forest Service, its personnel have had to move away from Spanish-American villages. Forest Rangers have been threatened and numerous fires set in the national forests. One Spanish-American commentator described Spanish-American attitudes toward the Forest Service as follows (Atencio, 1967: 36):

> *It is not uncommon for the native population to see the forest ranger in his olive drab uniform as an American occupation trooper guarding the spoils of the Mexican-American war. The injustices of the past are manifested in the attitudes of the northern New Mexico commoner. There is an enemy in those hills. It is the forest ranger.*

When the Spanish-American village people lost their land grants to the Anglo Americans in northern New Mexico, the new Anglo-American owners let the Spanish-American village people graze some livestock, secure firewood, and cut minor amounts of timber in order to avoid difficulties with the villagers. When the National Forests were set up in northern New Mexico in the 1900s, the long-existing rights of the Spanish Americans to use the land was not recognized by the Forest Service. The surveyors of the forest boundaries were rather careless and managed, by accident or design, to include considerable amounts of Spanish-American lands within the forest boundaries.[24]

Until World War II the National Forest personnel in New Mexico were sympathetic toward the Spanish Americans. Recognizing the poverty of the people, they permitted the Spanish Americans to utilize the resources of the national forests quite freely. But these rangers retired; they were replaced by forest rangers who knew very

---

(Footnote 23 *continued*)
(flood control projects) are admired as developing the land. And according to the prevalent ethic, land must be developed no matter what becomes of the people. The arch example to the effect of such procedures is in the Middle Rio Grande Valley where an elaborate job of engineering and of financing resulted in a dam on the tributary Chama River, and a network of drainage canals covering the valley for a hundred miles. There was also a network of debt which resulted in the loss of hundreds of small (Spanish-American) farms" (Ferguson, 1940: 261-262).

[24]This situation was admitted by several Forest-Service personnel in private discussions in New Mexico about the rising hostility of the Spanish Americans toward the National Forest Service in 1968. Gonzales states: "The creation of the National Forests starting in 1900 had a tremendous effect upon the villages, some of which found themselves completely surrounded by federalized lands" (Gonzales, 1969: 122).

little about the Spanish Americans and were not particularly concerned about them. During the late 1950s and early 1960s, the policies of the Forest Service, once oriented toward meeting the needs of the local Spanish Americans for grazing lands, changed drastically and harshly without any consideration for the poverty or the lack of grazing land of the local village Spanish Americans. The philosophy of multiple use and the principle of rational utilization and development of the national forests for the greatest financial return to the government were given priority (Gonzales, 1969: 122).

Spanish Americans in northern New Mexico holding grazing permits on the Kit Carson National Forest—the national forest located in the heart of the Spanish-American area in nothern New Mexico—were required to fence in their grazing allotments at their own expense. As few Spanish Americans possessed the financial resources to erect an animal-proof fence, their livestock were apt to stray into other allotments and were thus in danger of being impounded and sold. People had their permits transferred from the section of the national forest that they had traditionally used, land that once belonged to the land grants of their villages, to forest lands that once belonged to other villages. Village people are most reluctant to trespass on such lands.[25]

The precarious Spanish-American village economies soon suffered even more serious blows from the Forest Service. The inhabitants of the villages located around and in the national forests had lost most of their original range to the Forest Service and to nearby Anglo-American ranchers. Without any source of outside employment, they were forced to depend upon their tiny plots of irrigated farm lands and upon their permits from the Forest Service to graze small herds of livestock. Although they were living in poverty, they were able to remain in their native villages. For reasons known only to the Forest Service personnel, the Forest Service suddenly banned the grazing of village work horses while permitting the grazing of Anglo-American owned riding horses. Spanish-American farmers unable to buy farm machinery and lacking any alternative source of grazing were in danger of being forced out of agriculture. At the same time, the grazing of all milk cattle was banned. Almost every Spanish-American family in these villages had grazing permits for several head of poor-quality milk cattle whose milk they

[25]Wolff (1950) in analyzing social change in a northern New Mexican village says: "The most far-reaching event was the establishment of the National Forest early in this century. It eliminated sheep and goats by pre-empting grazing lands and pasture; thus indirectly eliminating spinning, weaving, and related skills."

converted to cheese and butter for domestic use and for sale (New Mexican, June 18, 22, July 9, September 17, 1967; Albuquerque Tribune, June 22, 1967).

The village people tried desperately to persuade the Forest Service, without success, to revise its regulations. Forest Service personnel refused to meet with the village people. Communications to the Forest Service went unanswered or were answered in English, a language strange to many village people. The majority of the Spanish Americans involved came to believe that the Forest Service intended to drive the Spanish Americans off the National Forest and replace them with large Anglo-American commercial operators.[26] Unable to continue in agriculture, the village inhabitants were faced with the grim dilemma of either migrating to the cities in search of work or selling their small farms and going on welfare. In bitter anger, after having sought the help of both state and federal agencies and political leaders fruitlessly, they turned to militant organizations for assistance. Fires began to burn in the national forests, and forest property was damaged.[27]

The Forest Service, when pressed for an explanation of the new regulations, alleged that they were necessary to prevent overgrazing. It was hard, however, to understand why Spanish-American work horses would overgraze more than Anglo-American riding horses. The Spanish Americans lost whatever faith they had had in the integrity of the Forest Service. Many of them are angrily aware that the National Forest spends far more for the construction of picnic and camping grounds, improvement of hiking trails, rehabilitation of wild-life habitat, and roads for timber extraction for the convenience of Anglo-American businessmen and tourists than they do for the improvement of grazing resources so vital to the meager economy of the Spanish-American village people. Anger and unrest among the rural Spanish Americans is increasing to such a high level that

[26]The incredible ineptness of the Forest Service personnel in their treatment of the Spanish Americans verges close to arrogance. Spanish-American village people tried to discuss their problems with forest supervisors but could not get to them. Forest Service personnel were invited to meetings of Spanish Americans but failed to attend. No effort was ever made to communicate with the Spanish-American village inhabitants. Changes in grazing policies were made, and the local people were required to obey them upon penalties of losing their grazing permits.

[27]The leaders of one Spanish-American community wrote as follows: "The U.S. Forest Service is limiting grazing permits to an unreasonable degree. Our U.S. Department of Agriculture is encouraging all farmers and ranchers to raise more livestock, to stay on the farms and ranches. On the other hand, one of its departments, the U.S. Forest Service, is telling them to get out and get out fast" (Mora, 1961).

violence has already broken out and the lives of forest personnel and the continuance of the National Forests are in danger from vindictive Spanish Americans.[28]

The Department of Agriculture and the Office of Economic Opportunity are perhaps the two government departments most active in northern New Mexico. Both departments have agencies and programs that have penetrated into most sections of the region. The procedures and goals of the Department of Agriculture resemble those of other standard government departments so that the same criticisms made of the Department of Agriculture can be made of the Departments of Commerce, Labor, and Interior. Although the Office of Economic Opportunity began as a "swinging" government agency more in tune with the aspirations and life styles of the poor, it has settled down by now into a more stable, demure existence, calmly awaiting what seems to be its demise. Perhaps an analysis of its operations may have some value, as its component parts are in the process of being assigned to the old-line government departments.

Although the primary function of the Department of Agriculture is to improve the welfare of the rural population of the United States, the programs sponsored by the department agencies in northern New Mexico have benefited but one small segment of the population, the large commercial rancher and farmer who is usually an Anglo American. The needs, economic problems, aspirations, and social and economic problems of the small subsistence Spanish-American rancher, farmer, and migrant worker have been almost totally ignored by the agencies of the Department of Agriculture. The majority of the small Spanish-American landowners do not have the acreage, the credit rating, the commodity production, or the income level necessary to qualify for participation in Department of Agriculture programs.[29]

The economic position of the majority of Spanish-American rural people who do qualify is so precarious that participation in Department of Agriculture programs usually increases their debt load without substantially improving their economic position. By strengthening the competitive position of the larger commercial farmer and

[28]For example, in 1968, $240,753 was proposed for range and revegetation by the Forest Service in New Mexico while $1,235,823 was budgeted for recreation (Atencio, 1967: 8).

[29]The author served as chairman of the San Miguel Area Redevelopment Committee from 1959 to 1961 and as Chairman of the Regional Development Association of northern New Mexico from 1961 to 1962. During this period, he was involved in almost constant discussions with government agencies, village leaders, and individual Spanish Americans and ranchers. The data on which this discussion rests comes from his own personal experiences.

rancher in northern New Mexico—through loans and grants to improve his farming techniques, to expand his acreage, to permit him to buy larger and more improved farm machinery, to insure his crops against hail, to level his land, to practice soil conservation, and by introducing strains of hybrid crops into the area that require large amounts of expensive fertilizer—the Department of Agriculture has been responsible for worsening the competitive position of the small Spanish-American farmer. The economic value of the land and the costs of farming have risen so high that the small subsistence Spanish-American farmer can hardly remain in agriculture.

The information arm of the Department of Agriculture is the extension service. County extension agents are responsible for acquainting the farmer with the varied programs of the department, for providing personal advice about farming problems, and for arranging demonstrations to show new farming methods, materials, and machinery to the farm population. They organize 4-H programs for the farm youth and the Home Demonstration agents carry out home enrichment programs with farm wives and girls. County governments bear the burden of financing the county extension program. Poor counties, such as those in northern New Mexico whose inhabitants need the service of the extension agent the most, have few extension agents (Mirelez, 1967). The problem is compounded by the fact that extension agents prefer to live in the bigger communities as most of their activities are carried out among the larger commercial farmers and among the rural people who live close into town. Very few agents work with the migrant workers or with the small subsistence farmer. Many remote villages seldom see an extension agent (Mirelez, 1967).

Large numbers of Spanish-American subsistence farmers are struggling to remain in their small rural villages even though they live in extreme poverty. They do not want to migrate to the slums of the larger cities. They operate small irrigated farms of from five to 25 acres. They run small herds of livestock on the national forests. They see Anglo-American farmers and ranchers flourishing on lands that once belonged to them. Their cash income is minimal. They grow corn, chili beans, vegetables, and fruits for home consumption. Many still travel in the migrant stream. The quality of their small independent school districts is extremely low. Dropout rates are extremely high. Almost no health services, except those few administered by the state Department of Public Health, exist in the villages. Roads are extremely bad. Although they pay state and federal taxes, no state or federal agency seems very interested in their welfare (Van Dresser, 1962).

As the majority of Spanish Americans still live in rural areas in northern New Mexico, the extreme conditions of poverty that afflict them are a serious indictment of the Department of Agriculture. There seems to be no real reason why the Spanish Americans cannot be stabilized in northern New Mexico rather than permitted to drift into urban areas, adding to the serious social and population problems staggering our metropolitan centers. If the Department of Agriculture were to utilize the village as the major unit of planning and program design, rather than individuals, their programs would be more successful. If the Department of Agriculture were to assist the village people to organize communal farming cooperatives to own land, machinery, and livestock, they would appeal to the deeply rooted communal tendencies of the Spanish Americans. If the state and federal governments were to assist the village people to modernize their antiquated irrigation systems, agricultural production would sharply increase. If some agency of the Department of Agriculture were to sponsor the development of cheaply operated and cheaply maintained farm machinery specially designed for small farmers, the Spanish Americans could mechanize their operations. If the state of New Mexico would assist in the financing, which it has so far refused to do, of an agricultural experiment station specially designed to develop varieties of crops adjusted to the short growing season of northern New Mexico, the Spanish Americans would get the same type of technical assistance given by other experiment stations to Anglo-American farmers in southern and central New Mexico. If state and federal governments were to provide the same kinds of technical assistance and sponsorship to the dying handicraft traditions of the Spanish Americans as they do to the Indian tribes of the Southwest, the rural village people could develop supplemental sources of income. If the U.S. Forest Service were to operate the national forests of New Mexico to best serve the interests of the local people who are so dependent upon them, the future of the national forests in the region would be more predictable. If some agency of the Department of Agriculture were to develop a land purchase program to restore the land base of the villages, the confidence of the village people in the American political, legal, and economic systems would be strengthened. And finally, if the Spanish Americans were given assistance to develop light industry utilizing the natural resources of northern New Mexico, perhaps northern New Mexico might come to resemble Switzerland more than it does the poorer areas of Latin America.

At the present time, the mood of the rural Spanish-American village people in northern New Mexico is shifting perceptibly toward more militant solutions to their social and economic problems. A widespread somber disillusionment toward the Office of Economic Opportunity is spreading. The Spanish Americans had really believed that the Office would eliminate poverty. In spite of the many constructive programs developed that benefited many individuals and families, widespread poverty still remains. The faith in its government of a deeply loyal but cynical minority is eroding very fast. Violence broke out in connection with National Forest Service in 1967, and the possibilities of additional violence remain very high. The programs sponsored by the War Against Poverty agencies did break through the shell of protection apathy in nothern New Mexico. The apathy is now turning to bitterness, and bitterness is moving many Spanish Americans toward violence. Many Spanish Americans, trained in the skills of community organization and leadership by the Office of Economic Opportunity, are spearheading the formation of militant groups. The most significant reason for the failure of government programs in northern New Mexico is that they have addressed themselves to the symptoms of the poverty syndrome and not to its basic causes. Until the Spanish Americans secure access to the natural resources of the land settled by their ancestors, poverty cannot be eliminated in the region or the dangers of violence averted.

REFERENCES

Atencio, Tomas C.
  1964 "The human dimensions in land use and land displacement in northern New Mexico Villages." Pp. 44–52 in Clark S. Knowlton (ed.), Indian and Spanish American Ajustments to Arid and Semi-Arid Environments. Lubbock, Texas: Texas Technological Press for the Committee on Desert and Arid Zones Reasearch.
  1967 "The forest service and the Spanish-surname American." pp. 35-38 in Testimony Presented at the Cabinet Committee Hearings of Mexican-American Affairs, El Paso, Texas, October 26-28, 1967. Washington, D.C.: Inter-Agency Committee on Mexican-American Affairs.
Baca, Fabiola Cabeza de
  1954 We Fed Them Cactus. Albuquerque: University of New Mexico Press.
Beck, Warren A.
  1962 New Mexico: A History of Four Centuries. Norman: University of Oklahoma Press.
Brayer, Herbert O.
  1949 William Blackmore: The Spanish-American Land Grants of New Mexico and Colorado: A Case Study in the Economic History of the West, 1863-1873. Denver: Bradford Robinson.
Burma, John H.
  1954 Spanish-Speaking Groups in the United States. Durham: Duke University Press.
Burma, John H., and David E. Williams
  n.d. An Economic, Social, and Educational Survey of Rio Arriba County. Prepared for Northern New Mexico College.

Calkins, Hugh C.
   1935 Tewa Basin, vol. 2, The Spanish-American Villages. Albuquerque: Southwest Region, Soil Conservation Series, U.S. Department of Agriculture.
   1936 Reconnaissance Survey of Human Dependency on Resources in the Rio Grande Watershed. Albuquerque: Southwest Region, Soil Conservation Series, U.S. Department of Agriculture.
   1937a Notes on Community Land Grants in New Mexico. Albuquerque: Southwest Region, Soil Conservation Series, U.S. Department of Agriculture.
   1937b Village Dependency on Migratory Labor in the Upper Rio Grande. Albuquerque: Southwest Region, Soil Conservation Series, U.S. Department of Agriculture.
Colton, Ray C.
   1959 The Civil War in the Western Territory. Norman: University of Oklahoma Press.
Cordova, Andrew, and Kalervo Oberg
   1943 Man and Resources in the Middle Rio Grande Valley. Albuquerque: University of New Mexico Press.
Culley, John H.
   1940 Cattle, Horses, and Men. Los Angeles: The Ward Ritchie Press.
Edmundson, Munro
   1957 Los Manitos. Middle American Research Institute, New Orleans: Tulane University.
Emmet, Chris
   1965 Fort Union and the Winning of the Southwest. Norman: University of Oklahoma Press.
Ferguson, Erna
   1933 Our Southwest. New York: Knopf.
Ferguson, Harvey
   1933 Rio Grande. New York: Knopf.
Fogel, Walter
   1967 Mexican Americans in Southwest Labor Markets. Mexican-American Study Project, Los Angeles: University of California.
Franke & Cornell, Planning Consultants
   1962 Overall Economic Development Program Provisional Rio Arriba County, New Mexico. Prepared for the U.S. Department of Commerce, Santa Fe, N.M.
Gonzales, Nancie L.
   1969 The Spanish Americans of New Mexico. Albuquerque: University of New Mexico Press.
Grant, Blanche C.
   1934 When Old Trails Were New. New York: Press of the Pioneers.
Hale, Will
   1959 Twenty-four Years of Cowman and Ranchman in Southern Texas and Old Mexico. Norman: University of Oklahoma Press.
Haley, J. Evetts
   1953 The XIT Ranch of Texas and the Early Days of the Llano Estacado. Norman: University of Oklahoma Press.
Hall, Martin H.
   1960 Sibley's New Mexico Campaign. Austin: University of Texas Press.
Hollon, E. Eugene
   1961 The Southwest: Old and New. New York: Knopf.
Horn, Calvin
   1963 New Mexico's Troubled Years. Albuquerque: Horn and Wallace.
Johansen, Sigurd
   1948 Rural Social Organization in a Spanish-American Culture Area. Albuquerque: University of New Mexico Press.

Julian, George W.
  1887 "Land-stealing in New Mexico." North American Review 145 (July): 17-31.
Keleher, William A.
  1929 "Law of the New Mexican land grant." New Mexico Historical Review 4 (October): 350-371.
  1945 The Fabulous Frontier. Santa Fe: Rydal Press.
  1962 The Fabulous Frontier. (rev. ed.). Albuquerque: University of New Mexico Press.
  1964 Maxwell Land Grant. New York: Argosy-Antiquarian.
Kluckhohn, Florence R.
  1961 "The Spanish Americans of Atrisco." Pp. 175-191 in Florence R. Kluckhohn and Fred L. Strodtbeck, Variations in Value Orientations. New York: Harper & Row.
Knowlton, Clark S.
  1961a "The Spanish Americans in New Mexico." Sociology and Social Research 45 (July): 448-454.
  1961b A Preliminary Overall Economic Development Plan for San Miguel County. Prepared for the U.S. Department of Commerce.
  1962 "Patron-peon pattern among the Spanish Americans of New Mexico." Social Forces 40 (October): 12-17.
  1964 "One approach to the economic and social problems of northern New Mexico." New Mexico Business 17 (September): 3-22.
  1965 "Changes in the structure and roles of Spanish-American families in northern New Mexico." Proceedings of the Southwestern Sociological Society 15 (April): 38-48.
  1967 "Land grant problems among the state's Spanish Americans." New Mexico Business 20 (June): 1-13.
  1969a "Changing Spanish-American villages of northern New Mexico." Sociology and Social Research 53 (July): 455-474.
  1969b "Tijerina, hero of the militants." Texas Observer 61 (March 28): 1-4.
Lane, Charles H., and Carroll L. Riley
  1966 The Southwestern Journals of Adolph F. Bandelier, 1880-1882. Albuquerque: University of New Mexico Press and School of American Research, Museum of New Mexico Press.
Lamar, Howard R.
  1966 The Far Southwest, 1846-1912. New Haven: Yale University Press.
Larson, Robert W.
  1962 "Statehood for New Mexico, 1888-1912." New Mexico Historical Review 37 (July): 161-200.
Leonard, Olen E.
  1943 The Role of the Land Grant in the Social Organization and Social Processes of a Spanish-American Village in New Mexico. Ann Arbor, Mich.: J. W. Edwards.
Loomis, Charles P., and Olen E. Leonard
  1941 Culture of a Contemporary Rural Community. Washington, D.C.: Bureau of Agricultural Economics, U.S. Department of Agriculture.
Loomis, Charles P.
  1942a "Wartime migration from the rural Spanish-speaking villages of New Mexico." Rural Sociology 7 (December): 384-395.
  1942b "Skilled Spanish-American war industry workers from New Mexico." Applied Anthropology 2 (October, November, December): 33-39.

Maes, Ernest E.
1941 "The world and the people of Cundiyo." Land Policy Review 55 (March): 8-14.

Maloney, Thomas J.
1964 "Recent demographic and economic changes in northern New Mexico." New Mexico Business 17 (September): 2-14.

McWilliams, Carey
1968 North From Mexico. New York: Greenwood Press.

Mintz, Sidney W., and Eric R. Wolf
1953 "An analysis of ritual co-parenthood, compadrazgo." Southwestern Journal of Anthropology 9 (Spring): 1-28.

Mirelez, Pete M.
1967 "The extension service in the Southwest." Pp. 5-7 in Testimony Presented at the Cabinet Committee Hearings on Mexican-American Affairs, El Paso, Texas, October 26-28, 1967. Washington, D.C.: Inter-Agency Committee on Mexican-American Affairs.

Mora County
1961 Report of the Community of Chacon, A.R.A.-R.A.D. Provisional Plan, Mora County. Submitted to the U.S. Department of Commerce.

Mosk, Sanford M.
1942 "Influence of tradition on agriculture in New Mexico." Pp. 34-51 in papers presented at the second annual meetings of the Economic History Association, September 4-5, 1942, Williamstown, Massachusetts.

Moynihan, Cornelius J.
1968 Introduction to the Law of Real Property. New York: Bender.

Murphy, Earl F.
1967 Governing Nature. Chicago: Quadrangle Books.

Otteson, Howard S. (ed.)
1963 Land Use Policy and Problems in the United States. Lincoln: University of Nebraska Press.

Parish, William J.
1961 The Charles Ilfeld Company. Cambridge: Harvard University Press.

Perrigo, Lynn I.
1960 Texas and Our Spanish Southwest. Dallas, Tex.: Banks Upshaw.

Ruxton, George F.
1965 Ruxton of the Rockies. LeRoy R. Hafen, ed. Norman: University of Oklahoma Press.

Sanchez, George I.
1967 Forgotten People. Albuquerque, N.M.: Horn & Wallace.

Saunders, Lyle
1944 Cultural Differences and Medical Care. New York: Russell Sage Foundation.

Segale, Sister Blandina
1948 At the End of the Santa Fe Trail. Milwaukee, Wis.: Bruce Publishing.

Shannon, Lyle, and Elaine N. Krass
1966 The Economic Absorption and Cultural Integration of Immigrant Workers. Department of Sociology and Anthropology, Iowa City: The University of Iowa.

Steiner, Stan
1969 La Raza: The Mexican Americans. New York: Harper & Row.

Swadesh, Frances L.
1966 Hispanic Americans of the Ute Frontier from the Chamas Valley to the San Juan Basin, 1694-1960. (Ph.D. dissertation), Boulder: University of Colorado.

Twitchell, Ralph E.
> 1912 The Leading Facts of New Mexico History, vol. 2, Cedar Rapids: Torch Press.
> 1963a The History of the Military Occupation of the Territory of New Mexico from 1846 to 1851 by the Government of the United States. Chicago: Rio Grande Press.
> 1963b Old Santa Fe. Chicago: Rio Grande Press.

Ulibarri, Horacio
> 1958 The Effect of Cultural Differences in the Education of Spanish Americans. Albuquerque: University of New Mexico Press.

Van Dresser, Peter
> 1962 Development Potentials of the Northern New Mexico Uplands. A Reconnaissance Report Prepared for the Technical Panel of the Regional Development Association of Northern New Mexico.
> 1964 "The bio-economic community: reflections on a development philosophy for semi-arid environment." Pp. 53-74 in Clark S. Knowlton (ed.), Indian and Spanish-American Adjustments to Arid and Semi-Arid Environments. Lubbock, Texas: Texas Technological Press for the Committee on Desert and Arid Zones Research.

Walter, Paul A.
> 1938 A Study of Isolation and Social Change in Three Spanish-Speaking Villages in New Mexico (Ph. D. dissertation), New Haven, Conn.: Yale University

Whitaker, F., and Edward A. Ackerman
> 1951 American Resources. New York: Harcourt Brace Jovanovich.

Wolff, Kurt H.
> 1950 "Culture change in Lomas: a preliminary research report." Ohio Journal of Science 50 (March): 53-59.

Zimmerman, Albert A. (ed.)
> 1966 New Mexico Statutes, 1953. Indianapolis, Ind.: Allen Smith.

SECTION III

Nature as a Component of the Community Moral Order

As the previous section illustrated, changes may arise with respect to the meanings of places or locales, as when man is forced physically to vacate a habitat because of variations in rainfall, or because of man-induced variations such as flooding of a previously nonflooded area, or because of the forcible replacement of one set of meanings by another. The persistence of the moral order shared among the human participants in such cases is problematic. But moral orders may vary, while the human groupings remain in the same approximate locale or habitat. For example, new meanings may arise with respect to the utilization of the nonhuman environment among individuals still resident in the locale. Heffernan and Welch provide a study in which such was the case. It is clear from the studies of innovation, including the Haas, Boggs, and Bonner study which follows, that, irrespective of the manner in which a change in the moral order occurs, the extent to which it becomes widely accepted among those sharing the same universe of discourse will vary. Heffernan and Welch demonstrate that the acceptance of new meanings with reference to a specific locale may act as an adaptive mechanism for the social grouping involved. The extent to which new meanings become a substitute for previously held definitions may depend upon the comparative impact upon existing social deference and allocation systems in the group. In short, where new meanings may be incorporated into the moral order without disrupting the social organization of the group, then culture provides an adaptive mechanism for the group as a whole.

Within a grouping such as a community in a particular locale, there may also occur variation among individual members as to the acknowledged support of a new moral order. For many social-structural reasons (for example: status, communication linkages, and so on) as well as idiosyncratic reasons, not all individuals will equally support the new meanings. One of the interesting aspects of human social systems is the extent to which behavior may vary and still be accorded legitimacy within a moral order. It is only when a flagrant act occurs which is recognizable to many as not tolerable that a group applies negative sanctions. Since behavior is always interpreted with references to the moral order, outrageous behavior is often tolerated, provided that the participants do not openly disavow the legitimacy of the moral order. However, to the extent that behavior does not violate or cannot be construed as violating the moral order, the nonacceptance of the new meanings may still produce social isolates within a group. This may be maladaptive for both the group and the individuals. For example, if the new meanings are particularly salient to the structure of the society and the persistence of the moral order, then failure to accord such support, even without actual negative behavior, once known to others may result in isolation. Usually mechanisms such as ostracism come into operation in such situations. In this sense, it is social beliefs which operate to differentiate and exclude individuals, thus reducing individual adaptation potentials shared among other species. For example, social stratification systems based upon individual possession of a territory places certain animals into "surplus" positions, thus threatening their chances of survival. Notice that culture in one case subsumes what is behavioral in another species. Thus, exclusion of individuals from communities and particular locales or habitats may enhance group adaptation to the nonhuman environment while reducing individual animal survival potential.

Another facet of the process is shown in the Heffernan and Welch study. If beliefs about the world are not supported, but no behavior occurs demonstrating such, then individuals may remain in the group. Culture as an adaptive mechanism may enable the retention of culturally deviant individuals in behaviorally homogeneous units. Indeed, as Kai Erikson has argued, a certain level of deviation may be necessary to maintain the normative order. However, the presence of isolates in a group always provides the potential for the formation of new communities once they begin to coalesce, either within the community or outside after exclusion. Clearly as new communities arise, new definitions of the nonhuman environment will also arise. As this happens, practices among men, with respect to the same aspect of the nonhuman environment, will differ.

Everyday practices and meanings of the nonhuman environment in specific locales may also be changed through new practices and meanings not previously a part of the culture. Haas, Bonner, and Boggs present a study of this intriguing phenomenon. Whenever new practices and meanings arise from outside of a community, they may or may not become part of the existing moral order. As was not the case in the previous examples discussed, we are now concerned with additions to shared definitions and meanings, not the substitution of new for old. In short, culture is always crescive. The Haas, Bonner, and Boggs study shows that events involving meanings about the nonhuman environment which are not already embedded in the social organization may have comparatively little consequence in an existing social order (for example, a stratification system) even though individuals may express support for the new meanings. Apparently individuals may even evaluate a new technology and incorporate such into personally held cognitive structures. But until new objects, technologies, and so forth can be incorporated into a moral order, the actions and behavior occurring on the basis of individually perceived and desired matters do not provide a sufficiently secure base for purposeful action on a broader scale. Thus, culture as an adaptive mechanism provides opportunities which are open-ended to a point, but not entirely so. (If this line of thought is correct then it may provide some insight into the apparent anomaly that the mass media were not particularly important in either the Haas, Bonner and Boggs study or the Burdge-Ludtke study. Despite the oft-repeated notion that the mass media are opinion molders, it may be that such function is structurally improbable.)

Forster's study provides some insight into the way ecological and cultural features may combine to condition a community's acceptance or resistance to innovation. Though economic arrangements external to Hawaii altered traditional feudal institutions of land tenure to those of private property and shifted crop production from subsistence to production for a cash market, there were many variations in local community adaptation. Like Knowlton's study (in Section II) the indigenous peoples lost their lands and a new ecological distribution took place. However, in Hawaii a plantation system rather than a freehold system prevailed. The plantation system imported massive numbers of landless field workers, primarily from China and Japan. But the plantation system was not ecologically viable throughout Hawaii or the individual islands. Thus, different sets of cultural meanings often existed in close jutaposition, though both reflected the impact of culture contact.

In the two villages studied by Forster, one tended to be organized hierarchically and to remain ethnically segregated while the other exhibited an ethnically integrated, egalitarian social form. Of most interest is the influence such different adaptive strategies had upon the prevailing moral order of the two communities. In the hierarchical community, suspicion and fear of the outside world prevailed, while in the egalitarian community openness and ambition were the predominant beliefs and values. In this sense, certain habitat features may combine with certain moral-order characteristics of a local community to provide either a closed or an open approach in adjusting to the innovations from dominant and external forms of change.

PAPER 7

Science, Technology, and the Public: The Case of Planned Weather Modification

J. EUGENE HAAS
KEITH S. BOGGS
E. J. BONNER

Man and his works exist within a thin envelope called the atmosphere. The characteristics of that atmosphere vary by area of the earth, by season, and from day to day. From the human perspective the atmosphere is both benign and harmful; it is also capricious.

Damage from dramatic atmospheric events such as high wind, rain, flood, hail, and blizzards probably exceeds half a billion dollars yearly in the United States. To that figure we need to add additional millions in losses from drought and freezing. But the atmosphere also provides sustenance for man, both directly, as in the case of protection from solar radiation, and indirectly, as in the case of moisture for the production of food. In addition the atmosphere makes a significant contribution to the aesthetic needs of man. Multicolored sunsets and snow-laden trees are usually valued positively.

But if it is obvious that the atmosphere has an impact on social life, it is also becoming obvious that man is inadvertently affecting the atmosphere. Man-made deserts affect rainfall patterns as do man-made asphalt jungles. Man's use of the "sewer in the sky" is apparently doing more than creating visual pollution (esthetic degradation). Evidence is mounting that patterns of precipitation, both rain and snow, are being altered as a result of "unplanned" air pollution.

Man is not only changing the atmosphere, but some of those changes are rebounding to his own detriment. Serious health problems apparently are no longer limited to rare instances of severe smog episodes in urban areas. Dramatic increases in respiratory diseases seem to be related to our increasing propensity to pollute.

Since the dawn of civilization man has attempted to cope with perceived atmospheric hazards by devising protective technologies: houses, clothing, dams, levees, drainage systems, drought-resistant crops and suntan lotion. In the United States we have developed a 400 million dollar a year weather information service intended to allow us to schedule our activities so as to maximize profits and convenience while minimizing losses and inconvenience. And we are currently developing "sky technologies" so that we can selectively increase rain and snow fall, disperse unwanted fog, reduce hurricane winds, decrease the size of hail stones and prevent unwanted lightening strikes. We have used smudge pots to manipulate air temperature for a long time.

THE INCREASING NEED FOR WATER

Water has been in short supply in some areas of the United States for many decades. In most of those areas, however, the population has been sparse. Now the burgeoning population growth in the Southwest and in some other areas is bringing fresh, insistent demands that new approaches be used to produce additional water supplies. Earth-bound water technologies (dams, reservoirs, transmountain tunnels) no longer seem adequate to meet the projected needs for water (White, 1969). The per capita consumption of water is increasing at the same time that semiarid regions of the country are experiencing rapid population growth. And no serious attempts are being made to deter population increases in those areas already having a water deficit. It is generally assumed that the only viable solution is to search for more water.

Where will the water come from? One approach, long popular in California, is to transport water from areas to the north that have a water "surplus." A more recent dream envisions huge pipelines bringing water from Canada to the semiarid United States Southwest. To be successful, this transportation approach requires high expenditures, the solutions to some technological problems and, above all, complex legal and international considerations. An alternative, or perhaps supplemental, source being advocated is to tap the "rivers in the sky" through cloud seeding in order to increase precipitation in the river basins upstream from the Southwest. Precipitation augmentation, as the approach is called, will require some additional development of the technology and the acceptance of the application of that technology by the general public (or at least by the most powerful interest groups in the affected regions) before it becomes a feasible alternative.

We turn now to a consideration of how this cloud-seeding technology has been developed and the apparent social consequences of attempted application.

FROM THE PRACTICE OF MAGIC
TO SCIENTIFIC RESPECTABILITY

In the 1930s Bergeron and Findeisen developed a theoretical basis for the artificial modification of clouds. In 1946 Schaefer demonstrated that solid CO_2 (dry ice) dropped into supercooled clouds rapidly transforms the droplets into ice crystals, and in 1947 Vonnegut demonstrated a similar effect using silver iodide (AgI) particles. These and other experiments under the guidance of Irving Langmuir attracted the attention of the Department of Defense, which subsequently supported Project Cirrus, a five-year series of field experiments conducted by the General Electric Company (Fleagle, 1968).

Commercial cloud seeding got off the ground in the late 1940s. Enthusiastic acceptance by relevant publics (for example, ranchers, orchardists and public utility companies) developed in part from the claims growing out of the Project Cirrus experiments. This acceptance and the search for economic gain provided the impetus for an annual investment of three to five million dollars by the early 1950s. Ten percent of the land area of the United States was undergoing commercial cloud-seeding operations during that peak period (Maunder, 1970: 41).

Then the roof fell in. Disillusioned investors began to have second thoughts. The claims of commercial operators were widely questioned by interested nonscientists. Commercial operations were sharply reduced.

Skepticism among atmospheric scientists about the effectiveness of cloud-seeding for precipitation augmentation remained high despite the 1957 report of the President's Advisory Committee on Weather Control. The committee concluded that seeding could produce an average 10 to 15 percent increase in precipitation in mountainous areas of the western United States in winter. A 1964 National Academy of Sciences Committee on Atmospheric Sciences report concluded that it had *not* been demonstrated that precipitation from winter orographic storms can be increased significantly by cloud seeding (National Academy of Sciences-National Research Council, 1964).

The tide of scientific opinion apparently turned in the mid 1960s, however. While still cautious in conclusions presented,

National Science Foundation (1966) and National Academy of Sciences (1966) reports provided support for the view that experimental cloud seeding efforts should be continued. By 1967 the Bureau of Reclamation had 26 different contractors at work on various phases of Project Skywater (U.S. Department of the Interior, 1967). In 1968 the American Meteorological Society sponsored the First National Conference on Weather Modification. The most recent National Science Foundation annual report on weather modification shows that federal agencies are spending $11,301,457 in support of 65 weather modification projects (National Science Foundation, 1968b).

By late 1970 the Bureau of Reclamation had launched a large-scale cloud-seeding effort in the San Juan Mountains area of Colorado. The experiment is designed to operate for five years. Bureau spokesmen were announcing that the cloud seeding would produce 15 percent increase in snowpack in the affected areas, even though seeding would be conducted on only half of the "seedable" days.

TESTING THE TECHNOLOGY

During the 1960s a few social scientists and administrators began to raise questions about the probable social, economic, legal, and ecological consequences of planned weather modification efforts (Sewell, 1966; National Science Foundation, 1968a). But less than 3 percent of the national weather modification budget was used for research on such matters (National Science Foundation, 1968b).

As has been indicated, most of the funds needed for research and development on cloud-seeding technology come from various federal agencies. As is often the case, the expert knowledge and opinion of the relevant scientific fraternity were a major determinant of the decisions on research funding during the decade of the 1960s. During the last half of that decade federal support for research in the atmospheric sciences began to taper off, as was the case for many other nonmilitary programs. This budget tightening was used as a justification for nonsupport of research on the social, economic, legal, and ecological implications of cloud seeding. A typical expression of this dominant view among atmospheric scientists was "There are still many conceptual and technical problems that must be solved before cloud-seeding technology is ready for the operational phase. First we must know whether operational programs are feasible. If our research and development efforts show that they are feasible, *then* it will be appropriate to support research on the assessment of 'side effects,' i.e., social, economic, legal and ecological consequences."

Since many of the federal officials administering funds for the atmospheric sciences are themselves atmospheric scientists, this view generally prevailed. The funding in the National Science Foundation Weather Modification Program was a partial exception to this wait-and-see attitude. In all fairness it should be noted, however, that social scientists, legal scholars, and ecologists requesting research support were not numerous during this period. They were not pounding on the doors of federal research funding agencies.

During fiscal year 1971, however, the Bureau of Reclamation's Atmospheric Water Resources Program appeared to be leading a new trend toward an increasing interest in supporting research on ecological, legal, social, and economic considerations. Approximately 6 percent of the program's research budget was committed to the support of such research. And for the first time the National Center for Atmospheric Research and the National Oceanic and Atmospheric Administration supported field research on social, ecological, and economic implications of weather modification programs.

Meanwhile, cloud-seeding technology was being field tested in many areas of the United States. The research groups conducting the field experiments varied widely in their approach to potential public reaction. Where possible, federally owned land was used for locating the equipment for the research effort. But in most cases the target areas, areas where the cloud seeding could be expected to produce an effect, included privately owned land. Thus, the weather modifiers always had some concern for what they called "the people problem."

Some researchers tended to be secretive. They gave out information about field experiments only when it appeared to them to be absolutely necessary. In a few instances the researchers planned and carried out a fairly extensive "public information" campaign in an effort to forestall potential negative reaction. Most research groups, however, took a flexible ad hoc approach. Advance planning was largely absent. If a news reporter contacted the head researcher for an interview, his questions were answered and the dissemination of the information was allowed to follow the normal course. This or some similar "passive" approach was most typical.

But regardless of the variation in approach to the release of information about the experiment there was a uniform view of the decision process. The researchers assumed that *they alone* had the right to decide where the cloud seeding would be conducted. The idea that the citizens living in the target area might vote on the matter in a public referendum was never seriously considered. It was simply assumed that scientific criteria relevant to success of the experiment were the only significant criteria.

This perspective of the atmospheric scientists should not be surprising. In fact, there is no established or institutionalized mechanism for such decision making. Past precedent supported the "right" of the atmospheric scientist to conduct his work as he sees fit. Thus, the typical researcher was only concerned with the possibility that someone might mount a concerted protest effort which could force him to change locations or stop the experiment entirely.

Perhaps surprisingly, vehement protests developed in only a relatively few areas of the country. In Pennsylvania the protestors organized the Tri-State Natural Weather Association after a group of orchardists had hired a commercial firm to seed clouds to reduce hail damage. The association continues to be active and apparently influential more than five years after the "cloud seeders were run out of town." Less extensive protests developed in the Kalispell, Montana area, northern California, Florida, southwest Colorado, and western New York. In the Montana, Florida and Colorado incidents, local newspaper editorials seemed to have been significant catalysts.

At the end of the decade there was no indication that atmospheric scientists were having second thoughts about the decision process. While there continued to be some mild concern about potential negative public response to weather modification field experiments, no proposals for altering the decision-making process were being considered.

A FIRST LOOK AT SOCIAL IMPLICATIONS

In 1968 we had an opportunity to begin comparative studies of selected social consequences of planned weather modification experiments.[1] In an effort to maximize comparability of social context we selected three rural areas of the United States, western New York, Montana, and Utah, where we knew that snow modification experiments would be started in the winter of 1968-1969. The characteristics of these settings were as follows:

1. There would be a field experiment conducted by scientists, not commercial operators.
2. The experiments would be supported by public funds.
3. The experiments would take place over private property, at least in part.

[1]The research effort, still in progress, is supported by the National Science Foundation, Weather Modification Program, under Grant No. 18724.

4. There was no standardized mechanism for informing relevant individuals or organizations regarding the plans for the experiment.
5. The experiments would be conducted in a medium generally understood to be a public or common property: the atmosphere.
6. There was no institutionalized mechanism for ascertaining citizen approval or rejection.
7. There was no established precedent regarding who should and should not benefit from the change, if any, in the weather.
8. There was no institutionalized procedure for compensation if damage should occur.
9. The results of the cloud seeding, at least during the first winter, would be inherently ambiguous.
10. Weather modification efforts had not been carried out in these areas previously.

Prior to any announcement of the planned experiments we selected communities within the target areas, areas that would be affected if any weather change were to occur, and matched communities outside the target areas to serve as controls. During the summer and fall of 1968, intensive, semistructured interviews were conducted with a representative sample of adults in each community. The household was the basic unit of analysis. The same respondents were reinterviewed in midwinter while the experiments were underway and again in the spring after the first experimental season was over.

Included in the interviews were questions designed to elicit information regarding the respondents' views of: (1) scientific experiments in general; (2) weather modification experiments in general; (3) weather modification experimentation in the local area; (4) information regarding characteristics of respondent's nuclear family; (5) demographic characteristics of the respondent; (6) respondent's involvement with friendship groups and community organizations; (7) exposure to mass media; (8) use of broadcast and printed weather information; and (9) data on numerous other variables thought to be potentially related to the respondent's acceptance or rejection of the innovation.

Concurrent with the interview phase of the project, studies of the communities' power structures were made. Initially, using a reputational approach, persons who had been influential in prior community controversies were identified. Each of these "community influentials" was contacted and interviewed. Information about their views of the planned experiments and the possibility of any community action in response to the experiments was elicited. Case histories of each area concentrating on any controversy that developed were maintained.

Periodic interviews with representatives of the experimental agencies were also obtained. Records of any changes in public information programs or actual experimental procedures were kept. All interaction between the agencies and any groups in the community was monitored. A special effort was made to contact all local interest groups which were potential protest or support organizations for the experiments, and an attempt was made to keep close track of their reactions during the experimental period.

Monitoring of all mass media was undertaken so as to assess the effects of publicity on the fate of each experiment.

WHO ACCEPTS THE NEW TECHNOLOGY?

Acceptance of a new technology usually requires some positive action by the individual. He changes his buying pattern, as when the farmer buys hybrid seed for the first time, or changes his behavior, as when the physician prescribes or administers a new drug in place of the one previously used. The typical process of accepting an innovation, then, entails some modification in behavior while the rejector simply continues in his customary ways (Katz, et al., 1963).

For the average citizen the new technology of weather modification does not necessarily require a change in behavior, at least not in the early stages of cloud-seeding experimentation. Later, if the experiment should significantly alter the weather (for example, produce above normal snowfall) both the acceptor and the rejector may have to make adjustments in behavior, but the adjustments may well be the same for both.

In this study, therefore, acceptance simply means that the respondent has indicated in an interview setting that he approves of the concept of cloud-seeding experimentation.[2] He need not take any other action although he may decide to do so subsequently. He may, for example, urge his congressman or senator to vote for continued funding for the weather modification program. Likewise, the person rejecting the new technology need only express his disapproval when queried by the interviewer. Subsequently, he too may decide to act

[2]Even though this innovation has an object component associated with it, for the citizen in the area the decision to accept or reject is essentially a symbolic one. In Rogers' terms it is an individual-symbolic-optional decision (Rogers and Shoemaker, 1970).

out his disapproval by complaining to the experimenters or to public officials.

The effectiveness of the new technology in a given location during a single season is still very much open to question. This is the justification for conducting the experiment in the first place. If the outcome were known with a high degree of certainty, there would be no need to carry out the field experiment. The year-to-year natural variation in weather events is so great that, even if at the end of a season the citizen learns that precipitation has been 25 percent greater or 20 percent less than the long-term average, there is no way to determine with any certainty that variation from the mean was in fact produced by the cloud-seeding effort. Similar and even greater variation has occurred in a number of other seasons when there was no field experiment in progress.

This inherent ambiguity of outcome should be kept in mind in interpreting our findings. While a comparable element of ambiguity may be present in the adoption of other innovations, the degree of ambiguity may be considerably less. The farmer who adopts hybrid seed can compare his bushels-per-acre outcome with his experience in previous years and with the yield which his nonadopting neighbors got during the same season. The physician can compare the results from the newly adopted drug with previous results. Thus, for most other adoptions there is a more stable basis for comparison of outcome.

Factors Associated with Initial Acceptance

After an examination of relevant models dealing with the acceptance of innovations, Bonner (1970) applied to our data a paradigm originally developed by Suchman (1967). While Suchman's model was designed to treat innovations in the health field, the factors enumerated appear to be sufficiently general for application to many other technologies.

In his words, using the model

> would lead us to analyze the individual factors present in the host which determine his "exposure" to the innovation and his "susceptibility" to its promises, the social factors present in the environment which influences his perception and interpretation of the innovation as "acceptable, appropriate and desirable" from the point of view of his social group referents, and the agent or attribute factors present in the innovation itself and the way it is introduced that affects his "image" of [its effectiveness or appeal] (Suchman, 1967: 199).

He classifies these factors as follows:

   A. *Personal Readiness Factors (Tendencies of the host)*
      1. *Recognition of seriousness of the problem*
         The individual must be aware of the problem being attacked by the desired measure and believe that it is an important one.
      2. *Acceptance of personal vulnerability*
         The individual must feel personally threatened by the problem and believe that he is in danger.
      3. *Predisposition to take action*
         The individual must be favorably disposed toward the desired action or change. His attitudinal set must be positive.
      4. *Motivation to act*
         The desired action must offer the promise of need satisfaction or reward, i.e., reduction of sense of personal vulnerability.
      5. *Ability to act*
         The individual must be in a position to take the desired action, physically and psychologically.
      6. *Knowledge of desired action*
         The individual must know how to act. He must be aware of and know the desired measure of what he is expected to do.
      7. *Belief in desired action*
         The individual must be convinced that the action or measure offers an effective solution to the problem, or at least, one worth trying.

   B. *Social Control Factors (Influences of the environment)*
      1. *Social pressure to act*
         The individual must feel that members of his social group approve of the desired action and are, in fact, acting themselves.
      2. *Incorporation into role performance*
         The individual must define the desired act as expected and appropriate for fulfilling his role obligations.
      3. *Acceptability of the action*
         The act must be consonant with the existing values and customary behavior patterns of the individual and his group.

   C. *Situational or Action Factors (Attributes of the agent)*

1. *Effectiveness of the action*
   The action or measure must produce the desired effect or the promised solution.
2. *Pleasure of the action*
   The action must offer more pleasure than pain. It cannot create too much discomfort or interference with what the individual likes to do.
3. *Effort of the action*
   The action or measure must be convenient and accessible without too much effort. It must fit into the individual's regular routine as much as possible.
4. *Previous experience*
   The individual must have had positive previous experiences with the desired action or measure, or, at least, not negative ones.
5. *Favorable environment*
   The action or measure must be presented in an environment or situation favorable to its completion or use.
6. *Attractiveness*
   The action or measure must be offered in an attractive 'package' or image (Suchman, 1967: 207-208).

In this study a factor is designated "positive" if the proportion of initial "acceptors" responding favorably to it was significantly larger than the proportion of "nonacceptors" so responding. According to the model, if more of these factors are positive than negative, the innovation will be accepted by a majority of the respondent sample. Each factor was given the same weight.

In the preexperiment interviews no difference was found between the experimental and control communities in level of acceptance and, therefore, the data from respondents of all communities have been combined for purposes of testing the model.

We found eight positive factors. They are recognition of seriousness, motivation to act, knowledge of the action, belief in proposed action, informal social pressure, incorporation into role performance, acceptability of the action, and pleasure of the action. Five of the factors were not related to the acceptance of the innovation in this study. They are acceptance of vulnerability, ability to act, effort of the action, previous experiences, and attractiveness. Inadequate data preclude the assessment of the relationship for two factors: effectiveness of the action and favorable environment. The results of one factor, predisposition to action, are too ambiguous to draw a meaningful conclusion. Thus, firm conclusions can be reached for thirteen factors, eight positive and five negative or nonsignificant. Hence the data, taken as a whole, indicate that the model does predict successfully for the total sample, since the majority expressed acceptance of the weather modification experiment.

To examine further the usefulness of the model in predicting acceptance of the innovation, each respondent was assigned an acceptance score—one point for each of the factors for which he had a positive response, and zero for a negative response. The points were summed for each person with a possible range from 0 to 14. If the model is correct, respondents with a score of eight or above should accept the innovation and those with scores of less than eight should reject it. The data support this hypothesis. Respondents with high scores were more apt to accept the innovation and the relationship was significant at the 0.001 level.

If the two factors for which we lack adequate data are treated as negative factors (every respondent assigned a score of zero for both) the individual's total score will not change, but the number of factors that constitute a majority changes from eight to nine. When this is done, the relation between the assigned factor acceptance score and approval of the innovation continues to be significant at the 0.001 level (Bonner, 1970: 84-86). Thus, the model permits prediction of initial acceptance successfully for the group as a whole and for individual members.

Changes in Acceptance over Time

Other studies have shown changes in attitude toward a new technology at various stages of the adoption process (Rogers, 1962). We also noted changes during the course of the three interview periods

TABLE 1. *Expressed Acceptance of Weather Modification by Interview Phase, All Communities*

| | Interview Phase | | | | | |
| | Preexperiment | | Midexperiment | | Postexperiment | |
	N	%	N	%	N	%
Local Experiment						
Accept	109	45	125	65	136	69
Reject	79	32	25	13	31	15
Uncertain	52	21	42	21	29	14
In General, with Area Unspecified						
Accept	216	89	156	78	163	82
Reject	10	4	21	10	15	7
Uncertain	15	6	21	10	19	9

(see Table 1). Given the fact that planned weather modification is relatively new and, therefore, is not widely known, we anticipated that information received during the first year via the mass media would be associated with whatever attitude change that might occur. As will be shown later the mass media did not produce such an anticipated change in attitude.

The attitude change model discussed below is based on two questions which were put to the respondents in all three interviews: acceptance or rejection of the *local* weather modification experiment; and acceptance or rejection of weather modification efforts in general, area unspecified. In general we found that the level of acceptance of the local experiment increased as time passed, and level of acceptance, area unspecified, decreased. With these changes, the two expressed attitudes tended to converge, become more similar. We attempted, therefore, to develop a model which would encompass both of these change trends.

It is reasonable when a person usually seems to hold compatible opinions on related issues. It is intriguing when this is not the case. Discrepancies between various attitudes, opinions, and behavior, and the processes involved in coping with and reducing this kind of cognitive incongruity have been the subject of a voluminous body of social-psychological research (Zajonc, 1968: 359ff.). The predominant theoretical work is Festinger's theory of cognitive dissonance (1957). It is known that persons experiencing this state will frequently change their opinions so as to minimize the resulting psychological discomfort and that they will change in predictable ways. It is also a sociological commonplace that membership in groups involves strong pressures to conform to whole interrelated patterns of behavior and attitudes. It is clear that in the development of opinions, individuals attempt to arrive at positions that minimize divergencies between both cognitive sets of ideas about things and conceptions of how significant others also feel about those things. In the model developed it is assumed that dissonance between various opinions on issues held by an individual and divergence between personal and group opinions are both important determinants in the process of opinion formation on new issues.

The basic assumption of the model proposed is that persons try to be consistent in their attitudes, opinions, and behavior. Whenever they are inconsistent, psychological discomfort results and an attempt will be made to lessen this discomfort. At any point in time an individual may be in one of two states, consonance or dissonance, the former being the circumstances of consistency between related cognitions and the latter being the state of inconsistency.

As we have noted, one of the crucial elements in regard to any issue is the relationship between the individual's opinion and the opinion supported by membership reference groups. An individual's opinion can also be categorized as either congruent or noncongruent with group opinion. Thus the following paradigm (see Table 2) makes it possible to locate any person's position on an issue in respect to other related opinions he holds and the relationship between his opinion and group opinion (Eckhardt and Hendershot, 1967).

TABLE 2. Dissonance/Congruence Typology

Relationship to Group Opinion	Relationship to Other Individual Opinions	
	Consonant	Dissonant
Congruent	Consonant/Congruent (1)	Dissonant/Congruent (3)
Noncongruent	Consonant/Noncongruent (2)	Dissonant/Noncongruent (4)

An examination of this paradigm will show that individuals in various states may be distinguished according to the number of divergent factors in respect to a held opinion.

The first state (consonant/congruent) is characterized by *no* divergent factors; the second state (consonant/noncongruent) has one factor divergent; the third state (dissonant/congruent) has one factor divergent; and the fourth state (dissonant/noncongruent) has two factors divergent.

Since there are two issues involved, each person can be assigned two separate labels. For example, if public opinion was consistent on the two issues, a respondent who was dissonant in his own opinions would be classified as a dissonant/noncongruent on one of the issues and dissonant/congruent on the other. Seven such combinations are possible. Table 3 summarizes these possibilities given varying relationships between public opinion on the two questions.

If we assume equal weights for the salience of each opinion and for the relationship with the group, we can make predictions about the relative frequency of attitude change for each state and the direction of change.

Change will occur most frequently for persons in the dissonant/noncongruent state and least frequently among persons in the consonant/congruent state. Change rates for persons in the other two states will be somewhere between these extremes. Furthermore, we would anticipate that persons who do change will alter their views in a manner that will move them into more stable states. Hence, among dissonant/noncongruents we expect change in the attitude that is most divergent from other attitudes and most divergent from the

TABLE 3.   *Possible Dissonance/Congruence Combinations with Local and General Weather Modification Questions*

Personal Dissonance	Consistency of Majority Public Opinion	Possible Classifications
Consonant	Consistent	1. Consonant/Congruent (Local) Consonant/Congruent (General)
	Not consistent	2. Consonant/Congruent (Local) Consonant/Noncongruent (General)
		3. Consonant/Noncongruent (Local) Consonant/Congruent (General)
Dissonant	Consistent	4. Dissonant/Congruent (Local) Dissonant/Noncongruent (General)
		5. Dissonant/Noncongruent (Local) Dissonant/Noncongruent (General)
	Not consistent	6. Dissonant/Congruent (Local) Dissonant/Congruent (General)
		7. Dissonant/Noncongruent (Local) Dissonant/Noncongruent (General)

majority group (community) opinion. In the two middle states, consonant/noncongruent and dissonant/congruent, we would expect equal frequencies of change. Whatever differences exist in this respect are probably a consequence of an invalidity of our assumption of equal salience. We would expect no change at all in the consonant/congruent state.

The first step in analysis consisted of categorizing each respondent according to the paradigm each time he was interviewed.[3] Table 4 presents these classifications for both issues at the preexperiment and postexperiment time periods. Clearly, over time, respondents who were initially in highly unstable states did change

[3]Only respondents whose answers were unambiguous were included in analysis. If a respondent answered "I don't know" or "I'm not sure" to any question, this circumstance was considered as ambiguous and no categorization was attempted. Respondents who answered both questions "definitely" or "probably yes" or "definitely" or "probably no" were defined as consonant. Subjects who said "definitely" or "probably yes" to one question and "definitely" or "probably no" to the other were defined as dissonant. Similarly, the distinction between congruence and noncongruence was made within each separate community. Respondents were classified as congruent when they agreed with the local majority and noncongruent when they disagreed with this majority. Again, ambiguous situations were deleted from analyses. In two communities there was no clear majority opinion during the preexperiment phase. These respondents were deleted from all pre- to midexperiment analyses.

TABLE 4. *Distribution Within Dissonance/Congruence States During Pre- and Postexperiment Phases*

	Preexperiment		Postexperiment	
	N	%	N	%
	Local[a]			
Consonant/Congruent	44	61	96	84
Consonant/Noncongruent	10	13	11	9
Dissonant/Congruent	9	12	1	1
Dissonant/Noncongruent	9	12	6	5
	General[b]			
Consonant/Congruent	52	72	95	89
Consonant/Noncongruent	2	2	12	5
Dissonant/Congruent	18	25	6	4
Dissonant/Noncongruent	0	0	1	1

[a]x^2 = 27.02, df = 3, p $<$ 0.001 (Chi-square not corrected for expected frequencies less than 5.)
[b]x^2 = 14.19, df = 2, p $<$ 0.001 (Dissonant/congruent and dissonant/noncongruent were combined for chi-square computation.)

their positions and tended to move into more stable states. Tables 5 and 6 show the same kind of pattern, tracing the movement of respondents from one state to another, from the preexperiment to midexperiment and midexperiment to postexperiment time periods. Predicted movement would always be to the left of the main diagonal in these tables. In general, movement tended to be in the predicted direction. Summing across the two tables, 48 respondents moved to more stable states and 25 to less stable states. But 30 of the movers were

TABLE 5. *Changes in Dissonance/Congruence States from Preexperiment to Midexperiment Phase*

	Midexperiment Phase			
	Consonant/Congruent	Consonant/Noncongruent	Dissonant/Congruent	Dissonant/Noncongruent
Local, Preexperiment Phase				
Consonant/Congruent	43	0	1	0
Consonant/Noncongruent	6	3	0	1
Dissonant/Congruent	6	1	0	2
Dissonant/Noncongruent	6	1	0	2
General, Preexperiment Phase				
Consonant/Congruent	49	1	1	1
Consonant/Noncongruent	0	2	0	0
Dissonant/Congruent	12	2	4	0
Dissonant/Noncongruent	0	0	0	0

TABLE 6. *Changes in Dissonance/Congruence States from Midexperiment to Postexperiment Phase*

	Postexperiment Phase			
	Conso-nant/Con-gruent	Conso-nant/Non-congruent	Disso-nant/Con-gruent	Disso-nant/Non-congruent
Local, Midexperiment Phase				
Consonant/Congruent	90	4	0	3
Consonant/Noncongruent	2	6	1	1
Dissonant/Congruent	1	1	0	0
Dissonant/Noncongruent	3	0	0	2
General, Midexperiment Phase				
Consonant/Congruent	90	4	3	0
Consonant/Noncongruent	2	6	1	1
Dissonant/Congruent	2	1	2	0
Dissonant/Noncongruent	1	1	0	0

in the two extreme states and, therefore, had only unidirectional possibilities for movement. Consonant/congruents can only move to less stable states and dissonant/noncongruents can only move to more stable states. If these 30 are subtracted from the totals, 36 "correct" movers remain and only seven "incorrect" movers. Hence, among the respondents who had a "choice," about five times as many moved into more stable states as moved to less stable states.

Tables 7 and 8 show similar support for the predictions concerning the amount of attitude change occurring in the various

TABLE 7. *Summary of Attitude Change Among Dissonance/Congruence States, Pre- to Midexperiment Phase*

	Midexperiment Phase			
	Stable		Change	
	N	%	N	%
Local, Preexperiment Phase[a]				
Consonant/Congruent	44	100	0	0
Consonant/Noncongruent	8	80	2	20
Dissonant/Congruent	3	33	6	66
Dissonant/Noncongruent	3	33	6	66
General Preexperiment Phase[b]				
Consonant/Congruent	50	95	2	4
Consonant/Noncongruent	2	100	0	0
Dissonant/Congruent	15	83	3	17
Dissonant/Noncongruent	0	0	0	0

[a]$x^2 = 31.03$, df = 1, $p < 0.001$ (Consonant/noncongruent, dissonant/congruent and dissonant/noncongruent were combined for chi-square computation.)
[b]Expected frequencies were too small for chi-square computation. An approximation of the exact probability test showed $p \approx 0.10$.

TABLE 8. *Summary of Attitude Change Among Dissonance/Congruence States, Mid- to Postexperiment Phase*

	Postexperiment Phase			
	Stable		Change	
	N	%	N	%
Local, Midexperiment Phase[a]				
Consonant/Congruent	93	96	4	4
Consonant/Noncongruent	6	60	4	40
Dissonant/Congruent	1	50	1	50
Dissonant/Noncongruent	3	60	2	40
General, Midexperiment Phase[b]				
Consonant/Congruent	96	99	1	1
Consonant/Noncongruent	6	60	4	40
Dissonant/Congruent	4	80	1	20
Dissonant/Noncongruent	0	0	2	100

[a] $x^2 = 8.65$, df = 1, p < 0.01 (Consonant/noncongruent, dissonant/congruent and dissonant/noncongruent were combined for chi-square computation. Yules correction for small expected frequencies was employed.)

[b] $x^2 = 17.64$, df = 1, p < 0.001 (Consonant/noncongruent, dissonant/congruent and dissonant/noncongruent were combined for chi-square computation. Yules correction for small expected frequencies was employed.)

states. While small frequencies in some of the categories make comparisons between the less stable cases difficult, the differences between the most stable state and other states are highly significant. Attitude change occurred far less frequently among consonant/congruents than among persons in other states. Table 9 groups these data by category irrespective of the issue or the time at which change occurred, making a more precise comparison of ranking possible. The order is as predicted for the two extreme states and the two states predicted to be in the middle do fall between the extremes. Generally, least change occurred in the attitudes of respondents classified as consonant/congruent and most change occurred among the dissonant/noncongruent group. Consonant/noncongruents and dissonant/congruents fell between these two extremes. Hence, the model accurately predicted change in attitudes toward the local experiment and for weather modification efforts in general.

TABLE 9. *Summary of Attitude Change Among Dissonance/Congruence States, All Phases*

	Stable		Change		
	N	%	N	%	Rank
Consonant/Congruent	283	98	7	2	1
Consonant/Noncongruent	22	69	10	31	2
Dissonant/Congruent	23	68	11	32	3
Dissonant/Noncongruent	6	35	11	65	4

It is probably reasonable to assume that experiments in the future will be conducted in areas where our assumption of equal salience for all the factors involved will prove wrong. In such instances these differential saliences will have to be included in the model.

There are at least two factors which could operate as intervening variables to make the dissonance/congruence process model less effective as a predictor of attitude change: (1) really significant mass-media information input; and (2) the development of polarization of attitudes. In the communities we studied, neither factor was operative and thus the attitude leveling process could proceed unimpeded.

Nevertheless, this model worked extremely well with the data at hand and we conclude that change in these attitudes is adequately explained through the use of this dissonance/congruence resolution process model.

THE ROLE OF THE MASS MEDIA

During the period in which a new technology is being introduced in an area the mass media can be a mechanism for informing the public of the characteristics of the innovation. The media also have the potential of influencing acceptance by selective and pejorative news reporting and through the expression of editorial opinion.

We used two general sources of data on the extent and content of mass-media coverage of the cloud-seeding experiments: the reports of community respondents and our own direct monitoring of mass media coverage. During the midexperiment and postexperiment interviews, community respondents reported to us on what they remembered seeing, hearing, or reading about the experiment. In the instances where radio and television reports were mentioned we contacted the sources directly to obtain details on what was broadcast. In addition we subscribed directly to all newspapers reportedly read occasionally or frequently by the respondents, and those were examined for all mentions of planned weather modification whether local or national, past or current. There were no reports of information on weather modification in any of the magazines read by the respondents.

Our monitoring of mass media coverage showed that the most extensive reporting occurred in New York and the least in Utah. The respondent reports of information received via the mass media showed the same rank order. Only in New York did a majority report receiving *any* information about the experiment.

We attempted to ascertain the extent to which reported receipt of information through the mass media was associated with changes in expressed attitude toward local weather modification experiments. Several modes of analysis, including a within-states design, were utilized but the findings were the same in every case. There is no discernible relation in these cases between the amount of information received and respondents' attitude changes. This lack of association holds for all the time period comparisons; pre- to postexperiment period, pre- to midexperiment period and mid- to postexperiment period. The number of persons reporting the receipt of information which the respondent defined as *critical* of the weather modification experiment was too small to permit meaningful analysis.

THE DECISION PROCESS

As part of our standard preexperiment interview each respondent was asked "If scientists wanted to experiment with cloud seeding in this community, *who* should decide whether or not they may do it?" Of those expressing a preference, 85 percent thought that local residents or local public officials should make the decision, while 10 percent preferred state or federal governmental officials and only 4 percent wanted the decision made by scientists. This is not an expression of antiscience bias, however, because these same respondents believe (80 percent) that "scientific experiments in general usually produce useful results— produce things that are helpful to man."

During the midexperiment interview respondents were asked who should make the decision concerning whether or not the cloud-seeding experiment *should* continue. They were also asked who they thought *would* actually make that decision. Table 10 summarizes their responses.

TABLE 10. *Community Respondents' View of Who Should and Who Will Make Decision To Continue Local Cloud-seeding Experiment (Percentage)*

	Should	Will
Decision To Be Made By:		
Local residents	34.7	12.1
Those affected	18.9	6.0
Local governmental officials	3.6	3.0
State and federal officials	13.0	19.0
Government and courts, general	9.0	18.3
Experimenters, scientists	9.2	15.7
Other	3.6	3.0
Don't know	8.0	22.9

It is clear that a majority want the decision on continuing the experiment to be made at the local level but they also recognize that it won't be made there. This discrepancy between the preferred and the real may be tolerated so long as the cloud-seeding effort is perceived to be an experimental program. Citizen or interest group action may be more likely in situations where the effort is defined as a continuing operational program, such as is being considered for the Upper Colorado River Basin.

Let us review briefly some of the major factors in the decision process. Rain and snow augmentation efforts, hail and hurricane suppression, and the dispersal of supercooled fog are the major weather modification efforts to be considered for the immediate future.

Clearly there are scientific and technical considerations which call for the involvement of relevant specialists. Cloud seeding is effective only under certain conditions and in certain areas. It is also obvious that persons living in the immediate areas affected by the weather modification efforts have a stake in the outcome. Some of these people are *directly* affected, as when the size of hail stones is reduced or the amount of rain or snow is increased or decreased. Some are *indirectly* affected, as when the weather changes produce a change in the local economy (for example, tourism increases or decreases). Furthermore, within the same area there will be gainers, losers, and possibly those for whom the weather modification has little or no consequence. Some persons will be inconvenienced, others will not.

In addition, there are those who live downstream and downwind. Some may benefit, others may lose. Added snowpack may produce cheaper water downstream but there is also the prospect of damaging floods should unusual weather conditions produce very rapid runoff.

Thus, for rain, snow, and hail programs one can conceive of the target area and the related downstream and downwind areas as constituting a specific "weather modification region" that could be delimited geographically. One could argue that *all* citizens residing in the region and *all* business concerns operating in the region should have a voice in the decision process. A region may include parts of several states and in some instances another country. Delimiting a "hurricane modification region" is a much more complex problem since it could conceivably include the entire Gulf and Atlantic coasts.

If we limit our consideration to weather modification efforts supported by public funds, then all citizens regardless of region have a stake in the decision process.

What is the range of decisions that must be considered?

1. What types of modification efforts are technically feasible at any point in time?
2. Where is it feasible to use them?
3. Of those technically feasible, which ones are economically justifiable?
4. In which areas are they justified?
5. What social, legal (Taubenfeld, 1970), and ecological criteria shall be used in considering proposed efforts?
6. Who should establish these criteria?
7. Who should apply the criteria to any proposed effort?
8. Assuming a decision has been made to establish an operational program, what safety and convenience criteria shall be applied? (For example, if the snowpack in any season exceeds 300 percent of normal, should cloud seeding be stopped for the season?)
9. What mechanism should be used to handle damage claims (Taubenfeld, 1970)?
10. Should those who benefit most pay a relatively larger share of the cost of the modification program?

These and related decisions will be made in the next decade or two. It is likely that they will be made through acts of Congress and through administrators of federal agencies. Undoubtedly congressional committees and the administrators will seek the advice of scientific and technical experts in making the decisions. It is less likely that those who will be most directly affected by weather modification will have any direct influence on the decision outcome.

It would seem the better part of wisdom to begin now to examine carefully the alternative decision-making models. In other federally funded programs the concept of "resident participation" in decision making is being tried and it is probably worth serious consideration in the weather modification arena also. Pilot programs utilizing several different decision-making mechanisms should be seriously considered. Satisfactory solutions may be difficult to achieve, but it appears that weather modification is here to stay and, therefore, social scientists face an interesting challenge.

REFERENCES

Bonner, E. J.
  1970 Response to Weather Modification: A Test of a Model of Innovation Acceptance (unpublished Ph. D. dissertation). Boulder: University of Colorado.

Eckhardt, K. W., and G. Hendershot
   1967 "Dissonance-congruence and public opinion." American Journal of Sociology 73 (September): 226-234.
Festinger, Leon
   1957 A Theory of Cognitive Dissonance. New York: Harper & Row.
Fleagle, R. D. (ed.)
   1968 Weather Modification: Science and Public Policy. Seattle: University of Washington Press.
Katz, Elihu, Martin L. Levin, and Herbert Hamilton
   1963 "Traditions of research in the diffusion of innovations." American Sociological Review 28 (April): 240-241.
Maunder, W. J.
   1970 The Value of Weather. London: Methuen.
National Academy of Sciences-National Research Council
   1964 Scientific Problems of Weather Modification. Washington, D.C.: National Academy of Sciences.
   1966 Weather and Climate Modification: Problems and Prospects, publication no. 1350, vols. I-II. Washington, D.C.: National Academy of Sciences.
National Science Foundation
   1966 Weather and Climate Modification. Report of the Special Commission on Weather Modification, report no. 66-3. Washington, D.C.: National Science Foundation.
   1968a Human Dimensions of the Atmosphere. Washington, D.C.: National Science Foundation.
   1968b Weather Modification, Tenth Annual Report. Washington, D.C.: National Science Foundation.
President's Advisory Committee on Weather Control
   1957 Final Report, I. Washington, D.C.: Government Printing Office.
Rogers, Everett M.
   1962 Diffusion of Innovations. New York: Free Press.
Rogers, Everett M., and F. F. Shoemaker
   1970 Communication of Innovations: A Cross-Cultural Approach. New York: Free Press.
Sewell, W. R. Derrick (ed.)
   1966 Human Dimensions of Weather Modification, Department of Geography Research Paper 105. Chicago: University of Chicago.
Suchman, Edward A.
   1967 "Preventive health behavior: a model for research on community health campaigns." Journal of Health and Social Behavior 8:197-209.
Taubenfeld, Howard J. (ed.)
   1970 Controlling The Weather. New York: Dunellen.
U.S. Department of the Interior, Bureau of Reclamation,
Office of Atmospheric Water Resources
   1968 Project Skywater, 1967 Annual Report, vol. I. Washington, D.C.: Department of the Interior.
White, Gilbert F.
   1969 Strategies of American Water Management. Ann Arbor: University of Michigan Press.
Zajonc, Robert B.
   1968 "Cognitive theories in social psychology" Pp. 320-411 in Gardner Lindzey and Elliot Aronson (eds.), The Handbook of Social Psychology. Reading, Mass.: Addison-Wesley.

PAPER 8
Latent Deviancy and
Social Interaction:
The Willful Destruction
of Natural Resources

WILLIAM D. HEFFERNAN

G. DALE WELCH

The increasing concern for natural resources is accompanied by an increased number of laws regarding the conservation of such resources. Many current laws designed to protect our natural resources, however, are being violated. Evidence indicates that in portions of many southern states the deliberate burning of the woods, which is in violation of the law, continues at a relatively high rate. The laws of Louisiana state that anyone who intentionally damages the property of another by the use of fire, without the consent of the owner, is guilty of arson and is subject to penalties ranging up to $5,000 (Louisiana Forestry Commission, 1968).

Although a knowledge of the sociological conditions related to deviancy in rural areas would undoubtedly increase our understanding of factors related to woods burning, a review of the studies concerning social disorganization reveals that few studies have been done on deviancy in rural areas. Most of the studies which have been done are concerned with differences in rates and types of crime between rural and urban areas. Lagey (1957) has suggested that the limited number of rural social disorganization studies may be a reflection of a long-held belief that the primary group relationships which predominate in rural societies are instrumental in forcing compliance with the norms.

The purpose of the present study is to determine (1) if rural adults who support norms which favor woods burning interact intensively among themselves; (2) if persons supporting such deviant

The research from which the data were taken was supported by the Louisiana Agricultural Experiment Station and the Southern Forest Experimental Station. Appreciation is also expressed to James L. McCartney, Alvin L. Bertrand, and personnel in the Louisiana Forestry Commission for their assistance.

174

norms are integrated as well into the community as persons not supporting such norms; or (3) whether they are social isolates. Although the study is concerned with norms regarding the burning of woods, the theoretical framework will be drawn from studies done of rural delinquency, and the implications of the study will not be confined to deviancy concerning natural resources.

PREVIOUS STUDIES IN RURAL AREAS

In criticizing studies of delinquency which are largely urban in nature Ferdinand (1964) notes that our knowledge about the relationship of sex and family organization to delinquency is more complete than our knowledge of the relationship between delinquency and social class and "community unsolidarity." Useem and Waldner also note the lack of concern with community factors. They conclude that "most studies focus on crime as a function of urbanization with little analysis of the dynamic forces at work in rural society producing criminality" (1942:185).

Lentz (1956) concludes that there is considerable evidence which suggests that urban theories of deviant behavior do not explain rural delinquency. Some insight into possible differences between rural and urban delinquency with regard to social organization is suggested by Lagey (1957). He suggests that the urban delinquent receives support for his norms because he is integrated into a group, while the rural offender is one who lacks integration and suffers from anomie. "In the one instance, the youth is a delinquent because of associations and the other, he is a delinquent because of isolation" (Lagey, 1957:233). Studies by Clinard (1944), Useem and Waldner (1942), and Wilks (1967) provide further empirical support suggesting that rural youth are not involved in gangs and commit fewer criminal acts with accomplices.

The overall hypothesis which guides this particular study is that adults in rural areas who support a set of norms which is in conflict with those held by the majority of the population will be more socially isolated than those individuals who support norms compatible with the majority. Specifically, the following two hypotheses are tested: (1) intensive interaction does not take place among persons supporting norms which are in conflict with those held by the majority of the population; and (2) those persons supporting norms in conflict with the majority have fewer informal ties, hold memberships in few formal voluntary organizations, and are less influential in the community than those persons who support the dominant norms of the neighborhood. The set of norms examined concern the deliberate setting of fire to the woods.[1]

METHODOLOGY

In the fall of 1967, 259 heads of household were interviewed. This comprised all of the persons who could be identified as heads of household of a particular ward in western Louisiana.[2] The ward was selected for study because it was identified by the Louisiana Forestry Commission as having one of the highest fire rates in Louisiana.

Although social deviation has been defined as failure to conform to customary norms of society, deviant behavior has traditionally been operationally defined as apprehension by formal agencies of control. This method implies that one must then look back upon an individual's life and attempt to isolate variables to see how they fit into the person's present behavior pattern. Certainly such a procedure has merit. However, the question arises whether this method measures deviancy or whether it measures one's inability to escape the formal agencies of control.

The method of attempting to determine deviancy used in this analysis is that of examining the norms supported by the persons living in a community. In this way, persons who support norms which are in conflict with the norms of the majority of the persons in the community can be identified. It must be granted that the second method has a serious shortcoming in addition to the difficulty involved in empirically determining norms. Just because an individual supports norms which are contrary to the majority does not mean that he will engage in behavior defined as deviant. He may support deviant norms privately, but the informal and formal pressures may very well be great enough to prevent him from engaging in deviant behavior. On the other hand, by identifying the persons who support deviant norms, we can discover what Williams (1965) discusses as stresses in the social system occurring at either the group or individual level.

---

[1]The authors use the term "woods fire" rather than "forest fire" since this is the term usually used by the local people. In addition, woods fire usually refers to fires which burn along the ground, in which case the authors understand that mature trees are not harmed. Such fires, however, started on another persons property constitute a criminal act and have the potential of "getting out of control" and destroying all forms of plant and animal life in their path.

[2]A ward is a political unit. Since within this political boundary the largest concentration of homes numbered about 12 which were grouped around a general store and service station, the area would be considered rural. The ward does not include all the necessary institutions and since the people did not appear to have a psychological identity with this particular area studied, it would not be considered a community.

The latter method does not identify deviant behavior per se, but it does indicate the potential source for deviant behavior, or what is referred to in this paper as latent deviancy.[3]

Williams (1965) says that norms always carry some descriptive or prescriptive quality or some one of the many qualitatively different kinds of shoulds or oughts. He further notes that there is enormous variation in the kind of normative emphasis. This may range, for example, from the conformity accompanying fashions and fads to the deeply ingrained taboos and ethical precepts. In the present study the respondents were shown three statements designed to indicate the norms they supported regarding setting fire to the woods. The three statements are: (1) persons who intentionally set woods fires on other people's land should be prosecuted as criminals, (2) firing the woods is an established custom that ought not be regulated by law, and (3) it is all right for an individual who has cattle which graze on land owned by an absentee landlord to burn the woods to improve the grazing, if the landlord does nothing with his woods. The respondents were asked whether they agreed, disagreed or had no opinion regarding each statement.

From Table 1 it can be seen that 10 percent of the population disagreed with the first statement, 11 percent agreed with the second statement, and 14 percent agreed with the third statement. Said another way, at least 80 percent of the population concurred with each of the statements.

When comparing the responses to the three statements, it was found that six respondents differed from the majority on each of the three items. In addition, three respondents indicated at least one deviant response and at least one neutral response without conforming on a single item. These nine respondents were grouped into a category labeled "latent deviants" (see Table 2). On the other hand, 170 respondents (65 percent) concurred on each of the three statements. These persons were placed in the category of "conformists," since they supported norms which conformed to the laws of the larger society. Four respondents had to be omitted from the analysis since they did not respond to the three statements.[4] The

[3]Our use of "latent" in this paper follows the common usage: lying hidden and underdeveloped in a person. It should not be interpreted in the functionalist tradition as elaborated by Merton.

[4]Two of the four respondents were widows; one was 75 years of age and the other 85. A third respondent, who did not answer this set of questions, was a widower of 84. The remaining respondent was a 45-year-old father. He owned 10 acres, had a nonfarm job and a yearly income of almost $5,000. Using another source of information, the authors predict that he would have been classified a latent deviant.

TABLE 1. *Responses to the Three Normative Statements*

	Agree		Neutral		Disagree		No Response		TOTAL	
	N	%	N	%	N	%	N	%	N	%
1. Persons who intentionally set woods fires on other people's land should be prosecuted as criminals.	220	85	4	2	27	10	8	3	259	100
2. Firing the woods is an established custom that ought not be regulated by law.	28	11	9	4	215	83	7	3	259	100
3. It is all right for an individual who has cattle which graze on land owned by an absentee landlord to burn the woods to improve the grazing if the landlord does nothing with his woods.	35	14	8	3	207	80	9	4	259	100

TABLE 2. *The Number and Percentage of Persons Categorized as Conformists, Marginals, and Latent Deviants*

	N	%
Conformist	170	66
Marginals	76	29
Latent Deviants	9	3
No Response	4	2
TOTAL	259	100

remaining 76 respondents (29 percent) differed from the majority or were neutral on some items but conformed with the majority on at least one item. They were placed in the category called "marginals." Any detailed analysis of this marginal category would require subcategories based on responses to each of the three statements since it is not a homogeneous category. The response to one statement might be more highly related to the behavior being examined than would the same response to another statement. Given that only 76 respondents are classified as marginals, further divisions would again involve the use of small numbers. The reason for including the marginals in this analysis is because of the question of reliability when using the small number of latent deviants. We assume that the reliability of our findings are increased if the marginals are characterized by a position between that characterizing latent deviants and that characterizing conformists. Again, let it be said that latent deviance does not refer to behavior since we have no measure of whether supporting these norms is related to the behavior of setting fire to the woods.

Having determined those persons who supported deviant norms, we had only to determine if intense interaction existed among the latent deviants when testing the first hypothesis. Interaction was measured by asking the respondents: "Whom do you visit with most? To this question most respondents listed two or three persons by name. Data in Table 3 indicate that only one of the nine deviants listed another deviant as a person with whom he visited most. That is, of the 16 persons living in the area studied whom the latent deviants said they visited most, only one was a latent deviant. Four persons listed by the latent deviants were marginals and the remainder were conformists. The data indicate that latent deviants do not interact intensively among themselves.

While the first hypothesis suggests that latent deviants do not interact intensively with other latent deviants in the area studied, the second hypothesis is concerned with comparing the community interaction of the latent deviants to that of the conformists. Because we predicted that latent deviants were isolates, we hypothesized that they would list fewer persons outside their neighborhood as persons whom they visited most. On the other hand, one might argue just the opposite. Because latent deviants do not interact with other latent deviants within the area studied, one might suspect that such persons interact with other persons outside the local area who support the same deviant norms.

We determined the residence of persons with whom the respondents visited most by asking the respondent to indicate

TABLE 3. *Category of Persons With Whom Deviants, Marginals, and Conformists Visit Most*

	Deviants		Marginals		Conformists		TOTAL[a]	
	N	%	N	%	N	%	N	%
Deviants	1	6	4	25	11	69	16	100
Marginals	2	3	24	38	45	59	71	100
Conformists	16	9	37	21	126	70	179	100

[a]Only those persons listed by the respondent who were heads-of-household in the area studied could be included in this analysis.

TABLE 4.   *Place of Residence of Those Visited Most by Conformists, Marginals, and Deviants*

	Residence of Persons Visited Most										
	Outside of parish		Elsewhere in parish		In a contiguous community		In this community		In this neighborhood		TOTAL	
	N	%	N	%	N	%	N	%	N	%	N	%
Deviants	0	0	0	0	1	5	5	0	20	95	21	100
Marginals	22	13	20	11	10	6	49	28	74	42	175[a]	100
Conformists	32	11	31	9	18	5	105	30	158	45	351[b]	100

[a]One person did not give place of residence.
[b]Seven persons (2 percent) did not give place of residence.

whether each person they visited lived in this neighborhood, this community, a contiguous community, elsewhere in the parish, elsewhere in Louisiana or out of the state.

The data in Table 4 support the hypothesis that latent deviants, as compared to conformists, are isolates with regard to visiting persons outside their neighborhood. Of the 21 persons listed as being visited most by latent deviants, only one person (5 percent) lived outside the neighborhood, and this person was the mother of a latent deviant. On the other hand, over half (56 percent) of the persons visited most by conformists were said to live beyond the neighborhood boundaries. Thus we conclude that the latent deviants are less integrated into the larger community than conformists. The findings which indicate no difference between marginals and conformists regarding place of residence of persons visited cause one to be cautious in accepting the above conclusion.

Another measure of social integration involved determining whether those persons listed as "being visited most" reciprocated. That is, did the persons identified as being visited most by the respondent also indicate that they visited the respondent the most? Since we predicted that the latent deviants are isolates, we hypothesized that fewer persons visited by latent deviants would reciprocate than those visited by conformists.

If one assumes that a relationship is more intense if both individuals list the other person as one with whom he visits most, the measure has value in determining intensiveness of interaction. However, we suggest that this measure might also be viewed as a measure of frequency of interaction. When person A, who does not interact with many persons, lists those with whom he visits most, he may indicate B. However, when B, who interacts with many persons, lists those persons with whom he visits most, he may list several persons with whom he visits more than A.

Data in Table 5 support the hypothesis that, compared to conformists, fewer persons listed as being visited most by latent deviants reciprocated. Nineteen percent of the persons listed by deviants as persons visited most reciprocated. Twice as many (39 percent) of the persons listed by the conformists reciprocated, while 23 percent of the persons visited most by the marginals gave the marginal's name when they were asked whom they visited most.

Having examined informal participation, the analysis now turns to participation in formal voluntary organizations. Participation in formal voluntary organizations was measured by asking the respondent whether he was a member of voluntary organizations. The data reported in Table 6 indicate the number of organizational memberships for each organization type. For example, if a respondent was a member of a men's organization and a family organization both affiliated with a particular church, he would be credited with two memberships in a church organization.

TABLE 5. *Proportion of Those Visited Most Who Reciprocated for Deviants, Marginals, and Conformists*

	Reciprocal		Nonreciprocal		TOTAL	
	N	%	N	%	N	%
Deviants	3	19	13	81	16	100
Marginals	17	23	56	77	73	100
Conformists	49	39	77	61	126	100

TABLE 6. *Membership per Person in Formal Voluntary Organizations by Latent Deviants, Marginals, and Conformists*

	Latent Deviants		Marginals		Conformists	
	N	Membership per person	N	Membership per person	N	Membership per person
Church-related Organization	1	0.11	21	0.28	80	0.47
Fraternal Organization	2	0.22	14	0.18	50	0.29
Agriculture Organization	0	0.00	13	0.17	51	0.30
Farm Bureau	0		6		22	
Breeders Association	0		3		10	
Watermelon Association	0		3		11	
Cattlemen's Association	0		1		8	

Data in Table 6 support the hypothesis that latent deviants are members of fewer formal voluntary organizations than conformists. Although latent deviants hold fewer memberships in each of the three types of organizations than conformists, the difference between latent deviants and conformists is greatest for farm organizations. In the case of church-related organizations the latent deviants have approximately one membership for every 10 persons compared to one membership for every two persons for the conformists. Only two latent deviants out of nine were members of a fraternal organization, and no latent deviant held a membership in a farm organization. This compares to about three memberships in fraternal organizations for every 10 conformists and about one membership in a farm organization for every two conformists. With the exception of fraternal organizations, the category of marginals was characterized as midway between latent deviants and conformists.

Another way of examining membership in formal voluntary organizations is to determine the percent of the latent deviants and conformists who were members of at least one organization. The data in Table 7 indicate that two-thirds (65 percent) of the marginals held a membership in a voluntary organization and one-third (33 percent) of the latent deviants were members of an organization. It should be noted that in addition to the data regarding membership in church-related organizations, fraternal organizations and farm organizations, data in Table 7 include memberships in civic organizations and other organizations listed by the respondents. The number of memberships in the latter two categories was too small to allow any additional analysis.

The final measure used to compare how well the latent deviants are integrated into the community, relative to the conformists, involves examining the community leadership pattern. Each respondent was asked: "To whom in this community do most people turn for advice on general community affairs?" and "Which persons in this community are the most powerful in terms of bringing about action they desire in the community or in terms of preventing actions

TABLE 7. *Percentage with a Membership in at least One Formal Voluntary Organization by Latent Deviants, Marginals, and Conformists*

| | Member of an Organization | | | | | |
| | Yes | | No | | TOTAL | |
	N	%	N	%	N	%
Latent Deviants	3	33	6	67	9	100
Marginals	34	45	42	55	76	100
Conformists	111	65	59	35	170	100

they do not support?" We attempted to get each respondent to list three or four names for each of the above questions. The number of times that each person in the community was identified by a respondent as being a good source of advice was tabulated. The same procedure was used for determining the number of times a person was listed as a powerful person in the community. Although the persons listed as a good source of advice by each respondent often differed from the persons he suggested as powerful persons in the community, a comparison of the persons appearing on both lists revealed a high degree of similarity.

Differences exist between the frequency with which given persons were identified as good sources of advice and as powerful persons in the community. When the data were grouped into the three categories of 0 to 2, 3 to 9, and 10 or more, however, no differences were observed between the measures used to determine if persons are a good source of advice and if persons are powerful. Since no differences exist, we reported only the information concerning the powerful persons in the community.

Data in Table 8 indicate that of the persons involved in our study are, only six were listed by 10 or more respondents as being powerful individuals in the community. These six persons were conformists. Fifteen conformists (9 percent) were listed by three to nine persons as being powerful compared to only three (4 percent) of the marginals. No latent deviants were listed by more than two persons as being powerful in the community. Data not reported in the table indicate that two latent deviants were listed by a respondent as being most powerful. The evidence again provides support for the hypothesis that persons not supporting the norms concerning woods burning which are supported by the majority of the population are not as well integrated into the organization of the community as are the conformists.

TABLE 8. *Percentage of Latent Deviants, Marginals, and Conformists Who Were Listed as Powerful Persons*

| | Frequency of Being Identified as Powerful | | | | | | | |
| | 0-2 | | 3-9 | | 10 or more | | TOTAL | |
	N	%	N	%	N	%	N	%
Latent Deviants	9	100	0	0	0	0	9	100
Marginals	73	96	3	4	0	0	76	100
Conformists	149	87	15	9	6	4	170	100

DISCUSSION

This study of rural adults supports the studies done of rural delinquents which suggest that rural deviancy is not the result of association with other deviants. Data collected from adults in this rural area support the general hypothesis that persons supporting norms which are in conflict with the norms supported by the majority do not interact intensively with one another.

The second general hypothesis predicting that latent deviants participate less in informal and formal associations was also tested and supported. Since a predicted difference between latent deviants and conformists was observed regarding visiting outside the neighborhood, reciprocal visiting patterns, and formal participation and community leadership, we conclude that a relationship does exist between supporting the norms supported by the majority and social integration. Compared with the conformists, the latent deviants are isolates.

Although survey type data were used in the analysis, the study represents a case study and, thus, the findings need to be tested in other populations and for other forms of deviant behavior. The limited number of latent deviants obviously presents a problem in drawing any conclusions. A researcher attempting to increase the number of latent deviants, however, faces a dilemma. If he attempts to increase the number of deviants in the population by redefining deviancy, he must recognize that a deviant act is not as "deviant" if a large proportion of the population supports it. On the other hand, if he attempts to increase the size of the rural population studied he faces the problem that geographic and time limits prevent a potential for interacting between all persons in the area. In addition, the employment of the sociogram analysis becomes exceedingly difficult as the population size is increased.

Given the small number of latent deviants, many of the differences noted were not great even though all hypotheses were supported. On the other hand, latent deviancy was based entirely on norms regarding woods burning. This is important when woods burning is viewed in its historical context. It appears that over the years a change in the norms regarding woods burning has taken place in this particular community. Apparently the norms that were once supported by the majority are now the norms supported by the latent deviants. From the information we have obtained, it appears that woods burning was accepted behavior and was supported by the norms of the community only a couple of decades ago. One would not, therefore, expect great social sanctions to be applied to such deviant behavior. Because it was assumed that woods burning would receive mild (if any) sanctions compared to other deviant acts, the finding that informal and formal participation are related in a predictable direction to norms favoring woods burning is almost surprising. One is left asking the question: Would the relationship be even higher if one examined norms supporting deviant acts which carried stronger social sanctions? A closely related question is: How are different types of crime related to social organization?

Because woods burning was an historically acceptable practice in the area, the latent deviants might also be considered social laggards. One could predict that because these persons are somewhat isolated, they are not aware of the changing norms regarding woods burning. Data in Table 9, however, indicate that little difference exists between latent deviants, marginals, and conformists with regard to the mean age, income, education, and years lived in the community. In addition, the latent deviants represented a wide range on the four characteristics. The age of the latent deviants ranged from 23 to 79, their years of schooling from 4 to 13, their years of residency in the community from 5 to 53, and their annual income from $1,250 to $9,500. Not only do the data fail to indicate that all the latent deviants are older persons who lived in the community when woods burning was acceptable, the data also indicate that characteristics such as age, income and education, which students of deviant behavior have found to be related to deviancy, are not highly related to latent deviancy regarding woods burning.

The finding that latent deviants appear to be relatively isolated may be viewed as consistent with Williams' (1965) proposition that clashes in subcultures often may become intrapersonality conflicts as the subcultures interpenetrate. Perhaps the reason latent deviants have somewhat withdrawn from informal and formal participation can be explained on the basis of the internal conflict and frustration they

TABLE 9. *Income, Education, Age, and Years Lived in Community for Deviants, Marginals, and Conformists*

	Income[a]		Education		Age		Years in Community	
	N		N		N		N	
Conformists	167	$3700	162	9.3	167	54.2	159	29.1
Marginals	75	$3600	76	8.3	76	50.7	75	26.3
Deviants	9	$4500	8	8.0	9	48.8	9	28.0

[a]Represents approximate mean total family income since it was computed from grouped data.

experience. This conflict and frustration may be a form of cognitive dissonance. Festinger (1967) has suggested that one way of reducing dissonance is to withdraw from the dissonant situations so that none of the elements are salient. If we assume that the latent deviants are aware that the norms they support regarding woods burning are not compatible with the norms of others in the community, we may conclude that they experience conflict and frustration when they interact with others. Thus, they may withdraw from both informal and formal participation so that they are not being continually reminded of the inconsistency between the norms they support and the norms supported by others.

Certainly Lagey's comment (1957) "In view of the paucity of research on rural delinquency, . . . study in this field is necessarily exploratory" is even more appropriately applied to a study of adult deviancy in rural areas. The study undoubtedly raises more questions than it answers. The implications of this study seem to be, however, that in designing programs to encourage the conservation of natural resources in this area, one must be concerned not with changing the laws or attitudes of the majority, but rather one must attempt to change the attitudes of a small number of somewhat isolated individuals. A problem in reaching these persons arises since they do not interact with each other, which would provide an informal association through which an attempt might be made to reach them, as in the case of some urban youth programs. In addition, the usual channels of formal and informal communication operating in the community, which have been of major interest to students of diffusion research, appear to have limited usefulness in reaching the somewhat isolated latent deviants.

REFERENCES

Clinard, Marshall B.
    1944 "Rural criminal offenders." American Journal of Sociology 50 (July):38-45.
Cohen, Albert K.
    1955 Delinquent Boys: The Culture of the Gang. New York: Free Press.
Ferdinand, Theodore N.
    1964 "The offense pattern and family structures of urban, village and rural delinquency." Journal of Criminal Law, Criminology and Police Science 55(March): 86-93.
Festinger, Leon
    1957 A Theory of Cognitive Dissonance. New York: Harper & Row.
Louisiana Forestry Commission
    1968 Forest Laws of Louisana. Baton Rouge, Louisiana.
Lagey, Joseph C.
    1957 "The ecology of juvenile delinquency in the small city and the rural hinterland." Rural Sociology 22(June): 230-234.

Lentz, William P.
    1956 "Rural urban differentials and juvenile delinquency." Journal of
        Criminal Law, Criminology and Police Science   47(October):
        331-339.
Useem, John, and Marie Waldner
    1942 "Patterns of crime in a rural South Dakota county." Rural
        Sociology 7(June):175-185.
Wilks, Judith A.
    1967 "Ecological correlates of crime and delinquency." Pp. 138-156 in
        Task Force Report: Crime and Its Impact—An Assessment, The
        President's Commission on Law Enforcement and Administration
        of Justice. Washington, D.C.: Government Printing Office.
Williams, Robin M., Jr.
    1965 American Society. New York: Knopf.

PAPER 9

Land, Social Organization, and Change

JOHN FORSTER

For centuries the relation of man to his physical environment has fascinated writers and scholars. In the works of a number of Greek and Roman writers physical environment is used to explain differences in the behavior of different peoples, both collectively and individually.[1] Such a view persisted in scholarship for a long time, and in fact Emile Durkheim (1951) considered, and rejected, environmental explanations in his study of suicide.

This explanatory use of physical environment has been rejected in the social sciences and, indeed, the phrase "environmental determinism" carries a strongly pejorative connotation. However, other forms of determinism have taken its place, and on the aggregate level "culture" is used to "explain" the behavior of people. That is, explanatory weight is placed upon custom, tradition, and historically patterned social forms.

Such an explanatory principle will not, of course, serve as it cannot account for the "culture" it seeks to explain other than by reference to preexisting "cultures" (from which the one to be explained must be assumed to be derived), and, by assumption, without the intervention of other factors (for example, physical environment).

This is not intended to dismiss the importance of historical continuity in human societies, but rather to stress that social scientists frequently speak as if "culture," "society," or "social organization" existed *in vacuuo*.

In a sense, the reason for the lack of attention to physical environment is obvious. We feel less directly dependent upon it. In

---

[1]For example, Hippocrates on Airs, Waters and Places or Tacitus in his descriptions of the early Germans.

preliterate societies with simple technology the relation of man to his physical surroundings was close, and it influenced every aspect of his behavior. With increases in technological sophistication, what we have come to call "mastery of the environment," the effect of physical conditions has been mediated and tempered, often to such an extent that we feel ourselves untouched by environmental factors.

From this I wish to make two observations. The first is perhaps already trite; namely, we have discovered in the last few years that our "physical mastery" is still in fact a delicate balance with natural forces and conditions, a balance we can ignore no more readily than can a primitive nomad.

Second, as an explanatory factor, environment is still indeed a relevant consideration, provided that we appreciate the limits of the concept. To understand the behavior of Australian aborigines in relation to their environment in the days before contact, it was necessary only to look at their immediate physical surroundings. To comprehend the behavior of a modern community, environment must be construed in a much wider sense. Technological innovation dictates that the manner of adaptation to physical conditions is governed by factors quite extraneous to the immediate situation.

This increase in scale means not only that technological innovations introduced from outside a given situation are relevant to a group's adjustment, but also that adaptive changes, even in far distant societies, may disrupt the adaptation of a particular group to its environment.

In studies of man and his environment, the relation of forms of production to the environment (including available resources) along with the interplay of new technology and resources (or in an older usage with the idea of "open" and "closed" resources) are familiar, (Aabakkuk, 1962).

Less clear in the literature is the relationship between environment and forms of production to social organization.[2] We are aware of the limitations of environment and of production on forms of social life, but both environment and production are seen as setting limits rather than determining outcomes. Most studies by social scientists concerned with these problems have stayed fairly close to the level of community or region and have attempted to relate man and his way of life quite directly to his physical environment and his forms of economic activity within this network of community or region. Such analysis is a valid method of proceeding, provided that the unit under examination is to a great

---

[2]Here the writings of Marx are renowned, but also such recent works as Wittfogel (1957).

extent autonomous. More typically in the modern case, external economic factors are interposed between man and his immediate environment.

The growing impact of international economic arrangements makes it clear that there are few cases where the condition of autonomy can be said to hold and, in fact, in the past we have often assumed that this condition held where it did not.

Throughout the nineteenth century, in the Pacific, forces quite external to the islands served to determine the relation of man to his environment within the possible limits imposed by the physical setting. The outcome, a symbiosis which was moderately satisfactory to those directly or indirectly concerned, included a variety of forms of social organization which came to be supported and maintained as part of the life style through sets of beliefs and attitudes.

I wish to suggest that these social forms persist even when the supporting conditions are altered. In the Pacific the alteration of international economic arrangements is now placing older social forms under stress by requiring new kinds of environmental adaptation.

This complex of relationships can be explored by examining two communities in Hawaii.

FROM CONTACT TO 1840

On the island of Maui, in Hawaii, there are two small communities located on the south coast of the island in an area called the Hana district. This district has always been, and remains to the present, rather isolated from the rest of the island. Like all the high islands of the Pacific, Maui has a high central core of mountains and a narrow coastal rim caused by erosion and by lava flow. The Hana district is on a strip of the coastline about thirty miles in length at a point where the coastal rim is very narrow.

Historically the district was important because it was fairly heavily populated and was the closest point of land to the big island of Hawaii. For these reasons it was frequently the center of warfare and thus important in Hawaiian folk history (Beckwith, 1940). In the years after the discovery of the islands by Captain Cook in 1776, Hana appears to have been quite isolated from European contacts. It was not until 1820 that there is evidence of direct European contact with the district. However, by that date indirect influences had been extensive, including the influence of Christianity and the establishment of a school by the Hawaiian Chief.

Prior to contact with Europeans, land in Hawaii was the property of a chief. He held the land and allocated its supervision to his followers who, in turn, gave land use rights to tenants. The system was close to our conception of feudalism (Malo, 1951:52-62). (Such an organization was in marked contrast to most of Polynesia where land ownership was invested in extended families.) During the first half of the nineteenth century land ownership in the Hana district appears to have been unaffected by European influence.

During this period the district was uniform in its usage of land resources. The native people lived from the sea and from the growing of taro. Taro may be grown in one of two ways: wet or dry. In the case of wet taro, the root is planted and cultivated in small fields with raised banks to hold irrigation water, much in the manner of rice paddies except that the units of cultivation are generally smaller. In the case of dry taro, the root is planted in the ground and absorbs moisture without irrigation.

Like most island areas, Hawaii is marked for its variations in microclimates and, depending upon the specific conditions in a locality, the technique of taro growing varies.

In the southern end of the Hana district in a community known as Puuiki, taro was traditionally grown dry. Puuiki lies at a point in the district where the coastal rim is widest, perhaps a mile, and here in precontact days the local population was spread across the arable land from the coast to the foot of the mountain.

Twenty-five miles to the north lies Keanae, a small village on a lava outflow which projects about a half mile into the sea and is perhaps a mile wide at the widest point. In normal circumstances such an area is, of course, quite useless; but, according to local legend, some centuries ago a chief organized a large labor force to carry top soil to his lava outcrop and then, through careful irrigation and building of terraced retaining walls, this most unpromising area was turned into a fertile spot (Handy, 1940). So, unlike the area around Puuiki, Keanae has a high population density on a small but fertile peninsula. Surrounded by ocean on three sides, the community is backed by a steep cliff face. Here taro is grown in small enclosed fields where the shoots are started under water controlled by a complex of irrigation canals.

These economic practices in the two communities remained virtually unchanged throughout the early years of European contact and on toward the middle of the last century.

THE PERIOD OF EXPERIMENTATION: 1840-1850

From the mid-1830s a group of Europeans began to settle in Hawaii, mainly in Honolulu and far away from the Hana district. These people were most often missionaries or missionaries' children, or people on their way to the northwestern United States. (In those days ships carrying people bound for the West Coast frequently sailed to Hawaii in order to catch the trade winds into the coast. Bishop, a very famous figure in Hawaiian history, arrived in this way (Kent, 1965).

Despite all the remarks which have been made about people going to Hawaii to do good and then doing very well, these men were an interesting group. They were supporters of the Hawaiian monarchy and, as well as looking to their own interests they appeared to have shown some altruism in assisting the monarchy to resist the encroachment of outside powers and to find some basis on which to build an economy for the islands. To this end they formed scientific societies, experimented widely with potential crops, and explored possible markets. At various times through the late 1830s and 1840s, cocoa, cotton, rubber, coffee, and other crops were raised on parts of the island (Kent, 1965:40, 108-121).

As is well known, the solution to their problem was found in sugar. In 1848 a sugar plantation was started near Puuiki, the first in the Islands. In subsequent years sugar became the basis of the island economy and it remained so until quite recently (Lind, 1938).

During this same period, the 1840s to the 1850s, the great *mahele* (or land division) effected the transition from the feudal land-tenure system previously described to private ownership. A common Hawaiian family, by placing a claim, could receive a fee-simple grant of the land on which it lived. These grants, known as *kuleanas,* numbered not quite 10,000 and came to about 30,000 acres. At this time the native population numbered about 85,000. It was hoped that through the possession of his own land the Hawaiian could learn initiative, industry, thrift, and other qualities which he had no doubt possessed before the disintegration of his culture but had, according to the prevailing view, lost. While the *mahele* did make possible the development of the sugar-plantation agriculture—mostly of course in the hands of the Europeans and Americans—and also provided large-landed estates for the *alii* (or chiefs) and their descendants down to the present, it did little for the Hawaiian commoners (Lind, 1938; Kuykendall). Like all situations involving natives, it is unlikely that the meaning of private ownership or that the potential value of land was understood, and very quickly throughout the islands Hawaiians were dispossessed through purchase, barter, or other means.

AFTER 1850

The implications of the sugar industry for the village of Puuiki are probably obvious and simply repeat the general story of Hawaiian history. In very brief form, Puiiki's experiences were as follows.

The Hawaiians quickly became dispossessed of their land and a new ecological distribution came into existence for the community, with Hawaiian settlement centered on the shore. The hinterland back to the foot of the mountain became devoted entirely to the raising of sugar.

At first the Hawaiians were offered employment on the Hana Sugar Plantation, but by and large they did not take advantage of the opportunity. When they did, they appear to have been only moderately successful. The reasons for this seem fairly obvious in the circumstances as there remained for those in the district a fairly satisfactory life which could be conducted on their own terms and in their own style. Employment in the rigorous and continuous labor of plantation work was clearly a secondary choice.

In this setting the Hana Sugar Company had little option but to seek labor elsewhere. This it did in a manner that is very well known. At first it brought labor when it could from other islands in the Pacific, a solution which proved quite unsatisfactory because most of the imported Polynesian laborers quickly died of what we would call childhood diseases. Later, on the same plantation, came the Chinese, followed by the Portuguese, the Japanese, and the Filipinos (Lind, 1938).

In this setting, while the Hawaiians were not necessarily employed directly by the plantation, they were very clearly entirely under its influence. Such plantations in the early days tended to be monopolistic within their sphere of influence. In the case of Hana this was as true as anywhere else; the plantation owned the means of communication, the shops, and all the other ancillary services which supported the plantation community. Furthermore, such plantations tended to be paternalistic in their attitude (Lind, 1938). While slavery might well have been the most happy solution for the Hawaiian sugar plantations during their period of development, it was a possibility which could never be carried out in the climate of the times. However, the plantations did exercise extraordinary control over their employees. A few examples may suffice. Plantations provided homes for the employees and did not permit them to own anything other than the possessions in their homes. They could not own land, nor could they grow anything that was in competition with the plantation, nor in most cases were they permitted to keep animals. Workers lives were dominated by the plantation bell (and later whistle), which determined their time of rising, their time of going to bed, and the frequency and timing in their church attendance. In order to leave the plantation, permission was necessary, and in order to return permission was also necessary. This type of paternalism, which dominated the area of Puuiki for a great many years, from

1848 until about 1945 (in another form to be described later), clearly had a variety of consequences for those who lived under its influence.

In the village of Keanae the history of development was markedly different. As I have described, this area was made up of small irrigation plots in which wet taro was grown. Beginning about 1850 many of the earliest plantation workers, who were Chinese, began to violate their contracts. Most of them were unable to return directly to China or to leave the island, but they did find another solution; many small isolated communities, like Keanae, became their homes. They came to communities where, very quickly, they established themselves with the Hawaiians on friendly terms and not only married into the community but made a considerable impact on the local technology. For example, in Keanae, the earliest Chinese had married a local woman within a year and had changed the agricultural practices of the village from taro growing to rice growing.

What I have described of the taro patches makes it clear that they were equally usable for the growing of rice, and this, of course, is what happened. By the middle of the 1850s Keanae was a center of rice growing. This pattern of rice growing persisted in Keanae through the nineteenth century until 1927 when, in competition with California-grown rice, Keanae reverted back to the growing of taro and has based its economy on this to the present.

To complete this brief sketch of local history it is necessary to look at the postwar period. During World War II considerable pressure was placed upon the Hawaiian sugar plantations to mechanize their activities because of the labor shortage and the problems of bringing in plantation workers. The sugar plantation near Puuiki was unable to cope with mechanization. As I indicated earlier, the amount of land available for the plantation was not great and it was rolling foothill country, too rugged for large scale mechanical equipment. Thus, at the end of the war the plantation, which had been supported by subsidies during the war, went out of business. The land thereafter was used for ranching and later, up to the present, as a tourist resort.

In Keanae, on the other hand, the pattern which had been previously created persisted, not only through the war but after the war, and even now the community operates much as it has over the last century.

SOCIAL ORGANIZATION

We have, in very brief terms, recounted the history of these communities. However, the comments have almost exclusively been concerned with the economic base. What is perhaps even more interesting is the fact that these two communities developed substantial differences not only in the form of social organization, but also in the attitudes and feelings which people had about their communities and about the world at large.

First, on the level of organization: In the case of Puuiki, as already suggested, the Hawaiians were by force of circumstance attached to the plantation even if they were not directly working for it. Plantation social organization is hierarchical in form and in the case of Hawaii the various strata in the organization tended to be related to race. That is, the ownership, and management of the plantations were in the hands of Europeans, the supervision of field labor tended, on the other hand, to be in the hands of the Portuguese, Russians, French, and others, while field labor itself was performed at various times by the Chinese, Japanese, and Filipinos. (As one follows the history of plantations, one can see the movement of these various ethnic groups up through the system.) This ethnic stratification combined with the authority vested in the plantation meant that communication between the various strata was frequently limited, not only in work itself but in social activity. For example, in the organization of plantation communities, the arrangement of housing was normally along ethnic lines: there was a Japanese village, a Chinese village, and so on—arranged in such a manner that social intercourse between the groups was minimal.

This brief sketch of the plantation community stresses three significant characteristics: (1) the ethnic stratification of the community, (2) the monopolistic character of plantation, and (3) the paternalism of plantation organization.

In contrast to this experience of the plantation village, Keanae had quite a different organization during the period 1848 to 1945. In this community the arrival of Chinese settlers, who quickly integrated themselves into the community in every sense and who provided not only a new crop but a new set of agricultural techniques, created a situation which was open, egalitarian, and essentially cooperative in character. Throughout most of this period the crops grown in Keanae (rice most of the time and taro after 1927) were grown by individual families but marketed cooperatively.

PERCEPTIONS OF SOCIAL REALITY

What is most interesting about these two communities is less their divergent history than the manner in which the experiences of each were explained, justified, rationalized and mythologized.

In Puuiki, the average level of education for the Hawaiians was less-than-completed elementary school. Most of the Hawaiians who lived in Puuiki never left the district and had no desire to do so. Those who had been away for a visit appeared in most cases to have quickly returned, convinced of the wisdom of their choice.

Among the reasons for this attitude was the view held by most people in the community that the world was closed to Hawaiians. As they saw it, there were few opportunities for them either on the island of Maui or in the world outside. Because they were Hawaiians, they felt disadvantaged and that no matter how hard they tried, they could never really be successful.[3]

Such views were supported by a variety of frequently recounted stories about people who had left Puuiki and had unfortunate experiences in the world outside. Such stories stressed the limits of opportunity, the existence of discrimination towards Hawaiians, and the notion that the world really was run by persons who were either Europeans or Chinese.

In Keanae there was also a set of behaviors reinforced by folklore but, in this case, it had a very different orientation. In this setting families went to extraordinary lengths to educate their children and to encourage them to go away from home on the grounds that there were no opportunities available for them in the little village of Keanae. An extreme case of this was shown by one family who had sent their daughter to Honolulu twice, and on each occasion she had returned to the comforts of home. On the third occasion her parents took her to the airport, bought her a one-way ticket to Honolulu, and told her on no account ever to come back. She was told that if she wished to see her parents to let them know and they would go to her. Such a view was in extreme contrast to the behavior in the village of Puuiki. Furthermore, in Keanae these attitudes were supported and maintained by constant recounting of local histories in which the hero was always some young village boy of Hawaiian or Hawaiian-Chinese ancestry who had left the village and was now a millionare somewhere in Honolulu or in the States. In several cases these stories were true and could be authenticated. But true or not, what seemed important was their constant repetition and the frequency with which folk heroes, as they might be called, were held up as examples to the young people of the community.

[3]It is interesting to note that while the ethnic composition of both communities was the same—that is, 92 percent Hawaiian and part Hawaiian, and that persons of mixed ancestry, Chinese-Hawaiian, were most numerous in both—in Puuiki residents thought of themselves as Hawaiian, in Keanae as Chinese.

To account for such differences between two communities which were, in the middle of the twentieth century, virtually identical in ethnic composition, and which were in fact only 25 miles apart, seems difficult, to say the least. One suggested explanation might be selective migration between the two villages. But it appears evident that experience over three or four generations in the nineteenth and early twentieth centuries had, at least for a time, a very profound effect upon the attitudes and beliefs of the local residents.

The divergent results of these experiences were not determined by geographic factors but unquestionably by local topography, and microclimate placed limits on the options available under the press of external economic forces, with consequences which ramified through a number of generations.

THE PACIFIC

At the time this study was made in the late 1950s, I was interested in it primarily as a piece of local history. In the intervening years, as my knowledge of the Pacific at large has increased, I am impressed with the implications that such a minute study may have on a broader scale. However, I would not like to pursue the argument beyond the region in which I feel myself competent, namely the Pacific. For about 190 years this region has been the scene of European exploration, settlement, and in some cases exploitation. In many respects the experience of other islands has been very close to that of Hawaii and, even in some detail, close to my description of the Hana district.

During the nineteenth century the various island groups of Polynesia established an adaptation, both economic and political, to the larger land masses of America and Europe. This adaptation involved certain assumptions about the nature of economic change and predictions of the value of certain commodities. In Hawaii this adaptation is clear. In New Zealand, by contrast, the adaptation was to the production of wool and, later, butter and lamb for the British market. In other islands the adaptation has been slightly different. For all of the island areas the adaptation proved to be adequate, and many of them indeed enjoyed higher standards of living in the early part of the century than they do at the present time.

With World War II, the basis of the nineteenth-century adaptation has collapsed, partly because of the war and partly because of the rate of technological innovation which has been taking place since then. Innovation has made many of the commodities produced, and many of the functions the islands served, irrelevant or obsolete. (At the same time, and again for technological reasons, the population increase in Polynesia has been very marked, while out-migration has become more difficult because potential receiving countries have increased their requirements for the level of technical skill for entry into their labor forces.)

Thus, very briefly stated, the islands of Polynesia have entered a period when their future appears uncertain. The adaptation which was made to nineteenth-century circumstances and to the available land resources has ceased to be viable. And in each case, whether Hawaii, New Zealand, or other small islands, attitudes, beliefs, and assumptions about the world at large have become the basis of resistance to change, just as in the case of Hana. While the world outside the islands has been radically altered in the last 25 to 30 years, the perceptions of reality held by the islanders have frequently remained largely unaltered. It therefore becomes interesting to speculate on this resistance to change, on how long it is likely to last, and on what sorts of circumstances could bring about a rapid modification.

One thing appears clear: when the realities of a situation change but perceptions of that reality remain unchanged, there is a basis for a considerable amount of personal unhappiness and collective difficulty.

The limited example I have used for purposes of illustration has, I think, a variety of implications.

At the present time much energy is directed to problems of social development. This means that those involved are dealing with that intricate complex of relationships between man, his technology, the limits of the physical setting, the social organization which exists, and the broad international economic and political environment within which development must take place.[4]

It is easy to ignore the complex changes which must come about in the life of a people, particularly given the persistence of social forces and their culturally embedded justifications. Further, the general international environment is frequently ignored and directions for development are encouraged which may be satisfactory at a particular time but are predictably inadequate within a few years.[5]

---

[4]Such complex issues are becoming more clear in recent studies of social history. One of the more remarkable of these is by Thompson (1966).

[5]A current illustration of the problem has been the encouragement given to many developing countries to invest in the production of heavy machinery. Having done so they find that (1) many countries have followed the same path, (2) demand has diminished, and (3) international trade barriers in developed countries make marketing very difficult.

Finally, I would like to suggest that the study of physical environment has much to offer sociologists. For the most part they have separated themselves from geography and related fields and spent their energies at the level of social reality. Hopefully, one consequence of our present concern with environment may be a new and closer alliance between sociology and those fields which have a more direct concern with physical reality.

REFERENCES

Aabakkuk, H. J.
   1962 American and British Technology in the Nineteenth Century. Cambridge: Harvard University Press.
Beckwith, Martha
   1940 Hawaiian Mythology. New Haven: Yale University Press.
Durkheim, Emile
   1951 Suicide. New York: Free Press.
Handy, E. S. C.
   1940 "The Hawaiian planter, his methods and areas of cultivation," 2 vols. Bishop Museum Bulletin 161. 1:110.
Kent, H. W.
   1965 Charles Reed Bishop. Palo Alto: Pacific Books.
Kuykendall, R. S.
   1966 The Hawaiian Kingdom, vol. 1, 1778-1894. Honolulu: University of Hawaii Press.
Lind, A. W.
   1938 An Island Community. Chicago: University of Chicago Press.
Malo, David
   1951 Hawaiian Antiquities (Moolelo Hawaii). Honolulu: Bishop Museum.
Thompson, E. P.
   1966 The Making of the English Working Classes. New York: Knopf.
Wittfogel, K.
   1957 Oriental Despotism. New Haven: Yale University Press.

SECTION IV
The Societal System: Variations in Response to Nature

Man's response to the nonhuman environment is mediated by a moral order which influences individual perceptions in ways beyond those directly available via individual sensory modalities. Culture literally does not allow humans to believe their own individual senses except in extremes. Thus, Dillman and Christensen report that there appears to be no direct relationship between the presence of particulate matter in the air and the perception of air pollution as a problem by residents of an area. It seems that the method by which individual concern about the "problem" becomes reflected in a willingness to act, to change matters, depends upon social processes involving communication linkages characteristic of a particular human habitat. Thus, human response to the nonhuman environment, even including the water being consumed and the air being breathed, is not only mediated by a culture, but is constrained by the dynamics of social organization. Characteristic patterns of social organization, inherent to a subculture, mitigate human-nonhuman environmental perceptions, definitions of the situation and actions.

The late comparative psychologist, Schneirla, demonstrated that within all animal societies there exists differing levels of social organization. Each possesses its own dynamics, though often populated with individual animals simultaneously behaving on other levels. It appears that the emergence and response to nonhuman environments, apparent at the societal level of human groupings, is dependent upon processes several steps removed from such environments *per se* but inherent in the human environment (for example, traditional patterns of communication, allocation of symbolic resources, and so on). For example, the study by McEvoy suggests that the stratification patterns of a society in terms of life styles is probably more important to the understanding of the emergence of a public concern about "environmental issues" than any single variable alone (such as social class). In short, as the Gale study (in Section V) also demonstrates, the transformation of an "ecological problem" into a "social problem" is a complex process. Until certain cultural conditions are present among humans in a society, "social action" does not appear. Not the least among these is a shared conception of what is, or what is not, "ecological" and "social." Means' study reminds us of the inherited cultural traditions which complicate the emergence of new definitions within existing sociocultural structures. But a fuller understanding of them, obtainable through history, provides increased precision in predictions within a particular social order when such particulars are set within a broader theoretical framework. The lessons of history, so called, are few and do not speak for themselves in a scientific sense unless placed into a more generalized analytical framework. For the problem of history is to record what has been, while science is oriented to what will be. Note that each is a part of the culture of man and, as such, has consequences for his approach to the nonhuman environment.

PAPER 10
Public Opinion and Planned Changes in Social Behavior: The Ecological Crisis

RICHARD L. MEANS

It has been said that the American mind swings widely between moods of Calvinism and anarchism. Perhaps it is true that both traditions have been a viable force in our history. When discussing social issues we seem to alternate regularly between emphasizing social and environmental determinism (behaviorism) or the opposite, stressing individualism and autonomy (existentialism). In either case, social issues come and go in kaleidoscopic fashion, alternating between public mood and scientific fad and creating in the bargain a new genre of social literature: social criticism. At the moment biological and evolutionary concerns seem to have a new lease on life; and the current word evoking the most social and political discussion is "ecology" (Means, 1969; Anderson, 1970; Burch, 1971).

One reason is, of course, a realization that man is deeply involved in the natural world—inevitably intertwined with the world of air, and water, of land, and trees, and space. Countless articles and editorials, political speeches, and private associations make us conscious of our natural environment and what has happened and is happening to it. The real question is how do we perceive these problems, what is our response, and into what framework do we cast this issue?

The Calvinistic mood plays on the role of natural processes, searching for a determinate scientific sequence of cause and effect, and calls for more technical scientific knowledge to enable us to clean up the pollution, recycle our wastes, and protect the beauties of the landscape. The anarchistic mood stresses the role of individual decision, of deed and misdeed, of freedom and autonomy both to act and to react to man's depredations. Both views contain important elements of truth. Yet, if carried to extremes, they lead to misplaced rhetoric—in the one case to a popular debunking of our industrial society; in the other, to a cry for more research and more technological understanding.

Thus, we will not concentrate on either the technical facts or the political imputations of special responsibility assigned to the various persons or groups for the abuses of nature. Others have already attempted this. Rather we shall, in a general way, discuss some of the cultural restraints which prevent many people from agreeing to the proposition that man's relationship to the natural world *is* a social problem in the United States.

There are several broad sociological and cultural factors that have been influential in limiting or restraining our understanding of the intimate relationship between our civilization and nature. These are cultural assumptions that seem to be widely shared by the majority of Americans. It is only recently that these factors may have begun to change. And only as these factors change, or are reanalyzed and reinterpreted, will we be able to create a new social policy capable of controlling our relationship to the natural world.

ABUNDANCE OF NATURAL RESOURCES

First, and perhaps foremost, is the tremendous natural wealth of the United States. It has been literally true that the abundance of the U.S. environment—forest, river, natural resources, even in some cases wildlife—has been almost inexhaustible (Jones, 1964; Nye, 1966). There are, of course, specific cases where resources have been decimated. Yet rivers and lakes were often restocked, special areas were set aside as state and national forests and parks, some wildlife was preserved, and reforestation was generally successful.

Whether or not all this was enough or was planned adequately for the future is always a key question. In the case of minerals and other resources, substitutes were found, or new extraction processes were developed, or a new source of supply was discovered (such as the Canadian oil fields). Thus the estimates of supply, even with a growing U.S. population, have had a tendency to expand.

It is important to note that the mode of thought is such that the resources of nature, both physical and biological, are usually conceptualized as objects to be weighed, measured, counted. They are considered as either in short or plentiful supply. The question of the quality of these resources, their action as variables and as processes connected with man's life, his health, his longevity, his peace of mind are issues infrequently discussed or appreciated. The point is that the general tendency in our culture is to assess man's relationship to nature in quantitative terms—on the basis of production statistics, board feet, metric tons, gallons of liquid, and so on—*not* in qualitative terms.

ATTITUDE TOWARD POPULATION GROWTH

A second factor, and probably one of the most important factors constraining our thoughts about nature, is our traditional public attitude toward increasing population growth. The truth is that until the end of World War II, U.S. demographers were predicting a decline in the rate of population growth. Very few demographers foresaw the rapid population growth in America in the 1950s. And if they did, they didn't foresee it as a continual trend. After the war, the birth rate shot up and stayed high until the middle 1960s. During this period, although some demographers were concerned with mounting population pressure in the United States (Day and Day, 1964), most population experts focused their attention on India and Latin America, assuming that overpopulation was a problem outside of U.S. borders and not significantly important to the American scene.

Although our crude birth rates declined slightly in the middle 1960s, we still face a rather large population gain in the next few decades. This is due to a combination of factors—including a low death rate and a large percentage of young people—most of them planning to marry (we have one of the highest marriage rates in the world). It is quite likely that we shall add another 100 million to the population in the next 50 years (Erlich and Erlich, 1970). This will mean tremendous pressure on living space, educational facilities, transportation, and, not least of all, obviously increased loads placed on sewage disposals, waste removal, and so on. And if we continue at the current rate of per capita consumption, there are some who are predicting that we shall be inundated under an avalanche of debris and junk spun off by our technological society (Stewart, 1968).

There is also the fact that since economists had been concerned with a depression after the war, the baby boom of the 1950s was interpreted in terms of Keynesian economics and population growth was understood to be a good thing. This idea still seems to be widely accepted. All the new mouths to feed, children to clothe, to send to school, and eventually to grow up and drive cars, purchase homes, and add to the labor force of the nation—meant for many minds, an increased consumer demand and in turn an economic influence for sustained growth. There were a few thinkers who were quite skeptical of this economic optimism—for instance, John Kenneth Galbraith; but since many people gave their attention (if interested in politics) to the Cold War or to the problems of civil rights, the impact of population growth was, until quite recently, somewhat obscured, and usually thought of as very desirable.

Even today it is not so much the force of demographic opinion but the immediate success of our social system that allows us to be sanguine and to carry on in a business-as-usual attitude, when dealing with the environment in America.

CITY VERSUS RURAL CONCEPTS OF LIFE

A third cultural tendency that has enabled us to rather ignore the man-nature problem in the United States has been the way in which we dichotomize experience between city and rural living (Huth, 1957; Marx, 1967; Shepard, 1967). This is reflected not only in the themes of our literature—for example, pastoral images versus city or urban images of life (White and White, 1964)—but also in more basic ways. For example, the U.S. census draws important distinctions between rural and urban areas; social science departments have separate courses in rural and urban sociology; divisions of government are divided on this basis (the Department of Agriculture versus the Department of Housing and Urban Development). For administrative (and historical) reasons, this makes a great deal of sense; but it may also reflect a basic social metaphysics or view of the world that is both wrong and pernicious.

There is a tendency to think of nature (the physical and biological world) as truly manifesting itself only in a rural environment while the world of the city, on the other hand, is thought of as separating man from nature. Somehow the city seems to transcend the environment; it separates man from the grim realities of the biological world of peasant or aboriginal culture where man traditionally struggled for survival against the natural world. The city represents the epitome of civilization, of contrivance, and manufacture, and is the result of man's labor and brains; whereas the forest, and even agricultural land, seem to affect man directly. But when carried to extremes, such divisions of thought are really cultural perceptions and imposed networks of interpretation on the phenomenal world, and do not necessarily reflect existing reality. There is no reason why a shift in perspective might not enable us to recognize areas of experience and life where city man is just as much a part of nature in an intimate and connected way as his rural counterpart (Kieran, 1959).

The environmental conditions of the city are indeed very important, as any health officer or epidemologist could well explain. Just because man lives in the city, the problems of waste disposal, the periodic circulation of oxygen and carbon dioxide, the relationship of land and space to human behavior are not one bit lessened. These processes may be actually *more* concentrated in cities. Cities reinforce or heighten natural processes by concentrating the energy and speeding up the cycles of man-nature relations. Diseases may not only spread faster, but the probability of mutations of various organisms—ranging from viruses to men—are increased both by the concentration of mutagenic agents and by the mere number of genetic possibilities open to alteration. Furthermore, in relation to man, medical and hospital facilities in urban areas may generally mean that sublethal changes in the genetic structure of a city's population may survive longer than in typical rural populations. Biologically speaking, cities undergo constant and rapid change in the human population, due in part to the intimate connection between special urban environments and man. How, then, can one arbitrarily say that urban life separates man more drastically from his environment than does rural life. In fact, the very essence of the evolutionary process, on the human level, is concentrated in the bioenvironment of the city (Dubos, 1965; Lerner, 1968). For it is through the intermingling of genetic pools (ethnic and religious), in the act of conception, that perhaps makes possible a speeding up of human evolution and adaptation.

There is also a teeming natural environment in the urban setting that is often missed because it is not, in the ecological sense, very well understood. It isn't just the trees in the park and the flowers on the mall that make up this environment; it runs all the way from microorganisms and animals to plants and even birds that thrive only in city environments. And, of course, changes in meteorological conditions and air, due to discharges of various industrial gases and automotive exhausts, are another factor of considerable importance (for example, the increasing problem of the concentration of lead from automobile exhausts) (Esposito, 1970).

It can be argued that pristine nature simply sits there; by definition it is that which is untouched by man and thus neither created nor contaminated by him. If nature is restricted to this definition, then, of course, there is a sense in which nature is not *in* the city. The arguments for this point are varied. But I think such a definition of nature has never been very satisfactory. As Alfred North Whitehead (1955: 85) once wrote: "Nature is plastic. . . . It is a false dichotomy to think of nature *and* man. Mankind is that fact *in* nature which exhibits in its most intense form the plasticity of nature." We often do distort the realities of nature in the city environment because we all too often think in a categorical way—sharply separating urban man from the natural world.

We should recognize that nature is a process-dynamic—and an everchanging mosaic of relations between species and environmental conditions. In addition, much of the natural environment in cities is radically affected by man, but the consequences of these effects are sometimes directly outside his immediate control (for example, long-run changes in climate).

The unaffected, untouched aspect of nature (removed from man) no longer exists—if it ever did. The cycling of radioactive materials in the atmosphere (and their subsequent absorption by plant and animal tissue) as well as the worldwide distribution of pesticide residues make the notion of a totally pure, untouched nature untrue (Woodwell, 1967).

Nature knows no city limits and spreads its wings across the urban frontier. In the last analysis, we are tied, rock-like, to our existence as a human species.

As the human ecologist, Amos Hawley, recognized a number of years ago in *Human Ecology* (1950: 35):

> *The multiplication of human wants and human techniques for their satisfaction which has been such a prominent feature of man's recent past has seemed to implicate men more thoroughly than ever in his environment.*

The idea that man in the city is radically removed from the laws of nature and almost totally separated from nature (the ecosystem) is a myth. Worse—it is the wrong kind of myth, untrue and misleading. Thus it is a myth without foundation, a myth that has passed its time; it is superstition.

SOCIAL MOBILITY

Another cultural factor contributing to the resistance against changing our traditional attitudes toward the use of nature is America's social mobility—movement of status or social position as well as spatial movement from place to place. We are a very fluid, dynamic society.

It is of interest that Richard Hofstadter, in a discussion (1968: 158-159) of Frederick Jackson Turner's frontier hypothesis, stresses that one aspect of the situation Turner did not adequately consider was the amount of social mobility in the United States. Turner argued that the existence of a western frontier, open land, and plentiful resources deeply influenced the American character and our culture (Hofstadter and Lipset, 1968). In summing up Turner's complicated thesis, Hofstadter writes: "I think we must get away from the immediate post-Darwinian frame of mind with its simple categories of man and environment, and consider the whole process of movement in terms of institutions, habits and ideas" (1968: 159). Hofstadter goes on to say:

> *We must sacrifice some of the romance of the frontier to our sense of the great American bonanza. We must give up—at least for the moment—the attractive figure of the omnicompetent pioneer with his rifle and his ax as our central actor, and accept the fact that the American farmer was a little capitalist, often by necessity a rather speculative one, operating in the new and uncertain Western world. . . . (1968: 158)*

This vision of the frontier farmer is, I think, essentially correct; it is for this reason that the *activities* of such men (whose emphasis was on using land for profit, and building, and constructing at the cost of cutting down timber, or spoiling the landscape) is the key to understanding the past reigning social myths concerning nature.

But as Hofstadter says, the whole frontier process may be considered as a "special instance of the much more general process of constant movement and migration" (1968). He points to the fact that America was built through a series of migrations (also see Hansen, 1961) that literally transported millions of people from their homeplace. And, in addition, a continual disruption of homes is still quite characteristic of the culture. The influences of this process on the American character is a question of continuing interest to historians and social critics (Potter, 1954; Smelser and Lipset, 1964).

What has this to do with man's attitudes toward nature in the contemporary world? If Hodstadter is right—that is, that general mobility was one of the social factors influencing American frontier attitudes—then the question might be raised (since the frontier is now closed) to what extent do social and spatial mobility influence our general attitudes toward nature, and to what extent in the direction of frontier conditions—that is, as exploitive, manipulative, and pragmatic?

The fundamental distruptive process involved in mobility may be the lack of a development of a sense of place. Man is a creature of habit, and he lives in *both* a complicated physical environment and a complicated social environment (Lynch, 1960; Hall, 1966; Sommer, 1969).

A sense of place may be important in several ways. It may be functional in terms of ease of movement (both spatially and socially) within a bounded area, and it also creates a sense of security, of familiarity, and habit that are rewarding to many people. It may also make possible an expansion of one's human experiences; for example, knowing the variety of places within a setting—rural or urban—may allow a person to change his setting in such a way as to minimize boredom. Furthermore, since changes in nature are often relatively slow—for example, the displacement of terrain, the effects of air pollution, the growth of new trees—then one has to have *time* (a sense of continuity) to perceive these changes. If one does not have time, then one may simply miss these perceptions of change.

It is difficult to prove empirically what the true effects of high rates of mobility are, but we should not be surprised if on closer analysis we discover, as Hofstadter has suggested, that one of the effects (at least historically) has been to exaggerate man's separateness from the natural world. And, indeed, since a high rate of social mobility seems to be a structural characteristic of our society—with its strong emphasis on economic change and measuring success by wealth—then a particular definition of man's actual dependency upon nature is likely to hold sway over others.

THE DOMINANCE OF ANALYTICAL THINKING

Another cultural tendency that may make it more difficult for us to assess our traditional attitudes toward nature is the fact that the dominant mode of scientific thinking has been analytical (Simpson, 1964; Dobzhansky, 1967). This is true not only in physics and chemistry, but also, to some extent, in the social sciences. By analytical I mean the tendency to reduce problems (sometimes organizations) to the simplest underlying principles or structures. In short, to *reduce* them usually to one cause or characteristic that is seen as essential for explanation. This is a powerful form of thought and an essential component of scientific thinking. It is the first step in developing inductive reasoning. Reductionism as the dominant style (or normative rule) for all rational, scientific thought may be highly dogmatic and restrictive as a major style of thought.

It may be, however, that another mode of thought—what we might call synthetic or compositional—is just as important to scientific understanding.

Compositional thinking has been influenced by evolutionary studies and animal behavioral studies; for example, the work of the psychologist Theodore C. Schneirla on the concept "levels of organization." This concept presupposes a hierarchical ordering of nature in terms of structure and function. Certain species reach the level of a "psychosocial" form of organization—that is, they have the ability to act on the basis of an integration of past experience—they are not just reacting to immediate stimuli. This is true of man. The conditions of nature, the history and evolution of the higher animals pass through various stages that create the basis or substructure on which higher levels of organization function. The point is, one cannot understand the more complex organization structures (the life of man or primates) just by reducing them to the lowest or earliest stages (Buckley, 1967; Von Bertalanffy, 1967). Understanding the lower stages *is* important, but new types of form or new relations actually mean *new* entities. Thus each level requires its own techniques for study (Kaplan, 1964). And the understanding of the underlying mechanisms of one level does not enable one to predict phenomena on a higher level.

It may be that the synthetic mode of thought is not widely taught and not appreciated enough in academic or intellectual circles. No matter what the case may be—and this in itself is a subject for research—there is no doubt that in science, especially in the field of biology, there are differences in style of thought between the analytical and the compositional approaches. It is not, however, really a question of either/or, as most biologists would recognize. It is rather a matter of emphasis.

The point is that if the dominant style of thought in science is understood as limited to reductionisms, and if, in turn, the scientist becomes a public hero and his assumed thought habits are accepted by the general population (probably in a rather crude way), then it is much more difficult to develop an understanding of nature as relating culture and social organization to natural processes.

Even if more and more Americans are concerned about man's proper relationship to the natural environment, there are cultural factors at work which make change problematic. The above-mentioned factors are just a few among many. Yet we need some awareness of the cultural restraints that seem to work against direct understanding of environmental problems. We might, of course, simply assume that an answer lies in a total and sweeping repudiation of industrial society, or, on the other hand, in some magical ability of technology to come to our aid. Neither answer is likely to prevail. Thus, some insight into the range of possibilities for redefinition of our environmental crisis is needed.

REFERENCES

Anderson, Walt
    1970 Politics and Environment: A Reader in Ecological Politics. Pacific Palisades, California: Goodyear Publishing.
Buckley, Walter
    1967 Sociology and Modern Systems Theory. Englewood Cliffs, N.J.: Prentice-Hall.
Burch, William R., Jr.
    1971 Daydreams and Nightmares: A Sociological Essay on the American Environment. New York: Harper & Row.
Day, Lincoln H., and Alice T. Day
    1964 Too many Americans. New York: Dell.

Dobzhansky, Theodosius
    1967 The Biology of Ultimate Concern. New York: World Publishing.
Dubos, René
    1965 Man Adapting. New Haven: Yale University Press.
Erlich, Paul R., and Anne H. Erlich
    1970 Population, Resources, Environment: Issues in Human Ecology.
        San Francisco: W. H. Freeman.
Esposito, John C.
    1970 Vanishing Air. New York: Grossman.
Hall, Edward T.
    1966 The Hidden Dimension. Garden City, N.Y.: Doubleday.
Hansen, Marcus Lee
    1961 The Atlantic Migration. New York: Harper & Row.
Hawley, Amos
    1950 Human Ecology. New York: Ronald Press.
Hofstadter, Richard
    1968 The Progressive Historians: Turner, Beard and Parrington. New York:
        Knopf.
Hofstadter, Richard, and Seymour M. Lipset (eds.)
    1968 Turner and The Sociology of the Frontier. New York: Basic
        Books.
Huth, Hans
    1957 Nature and America: Three Centuries of Changing Attitudes.
        Berkeley: University of California Press.
Jones, Howard Mumford
    1964 O Strange New World: American Culture in the Formative Years.
        New York: Viking Press.
Kaplan, Abraham
    1964 The Conduct of Inquiry. San Francisco: Chandler.
Kieran, John
    1959 A Natural History of New York City. New York: Houghton
        Mifflin.
Lerner, Michael I.
    1968 Heredity, Evolution, and Society. San Francisco: W. H. Freeman.
Lynch, Kevin
    1960 The Image of The City. Cambridge, Mass.: M.I.T. Press.
Marx, Leo
    1967 The Machine and the Garden. New York: Oxford University Press.
Means, Richard L.
    1969 "The New Conservation." Natural History 78(August-September):
        16-25.
Nye, Russell B.
    1966 "The American view of nature." Pp. 256-304 in The Almost
        Chosen People: Essays in the History of Ideas. East Lansing:
        Michigan State University Press.
Potter, David M.
    1954 People of Plenty: Economic Abundance and the American
        Character. Chicago: University of Chicago Press.
Shepard, Paul
    1967 Man in the Landscape. New York: Knopf.
Simpson, George Gaylord
    1964 This View of Life. New York: Harcourt Brace Jovanovich.
Smelser, Niel J., and Seymour M. Lipset (eds.)
    1964 Social Structure and Mobility in Economic Development. Chicago:
        Aldine.
Sommer, Robert
    1969 Personal Space: The Behavioral Basis of Design. Englewood Cliffs,
        N.J.: Prentice-Hall.

Stewart, George R.
   1968 Not So Rich As You Think. Boston: Houghton Mifflin.
Von Bertalantty, Ludwig
   1967 Robots, Men and Minds. New York: Braziller.
White, Morton, and Lucia White
   1964 The Intellectual Versus the City. New York: New World Library.
Whitehead, Alfred North
   1955 Adventure of Ideas. New York: New World Library.
Woodwell, George
   1967 "Toxic substances and ecological cycles." Scientific American (March):24-31.

PAPER 11

The American Concern
with Environment

JAMES McEVOY III

A sizable segment of the American public has had, since the founding of the colonies, definite attitudes and opinions toward the natural environment. These have, of course, varied in content and in their implications for behavior. But other than a small body of historical evidence and anecdotal data there is little basis for attempting an assessment of the public's views on environmental questions over the entire span of U.S. history. It is, however, possible to derive from this evidence some conclusions about the public's orientation to its environment and to isolate the major points of conflict within the society over questions of alteration and exploitation of the environment during the past three hunderd years. Clarence Glacken (1967) and Roderick Nash (1967) for example, have explored in detail the role that the natural environment and wilderness have played in Western and American culture. Other writers have also attacked the problem of the meaning of nature, wilderness, and the environment to Americans throughout the history of the country (Huth, 1967; McCloskey, 1966; Smith, 1967; Marx, 1964; Nash, 1967:237-240).

No brief summary of these scholars' analyses of elite and mass opinion can do more than isolate some of the conceptually and analytically important organizing concepts around which Americans' attitudes and behavior toward their environment have, in the past, been directed. However, it will be useful to us in our studies of contemporary public opinion to have in mind two of the prominent orientations that Americans have shared toward their environment in order that current empirical data—at both the mass and elite levels—can be organized and interpreted within the various historical traditions which have influenced its formation, content, and expression.

214

Historical evidence suggests that one early and prominent orientation to the natural environment was fear, and with this was linked the desire to conquer and control nature for man's ends. Nash, for example, points to the Puritans (the first immigrant Americans to attribute spiritual importance to the wilderness and undisturbed natural environments), who gave "transcendent importance . . . to conquering wilderness." This view did not end with the decline of puritanism but persisted throughout the seventeenth and eighteenth centuries during the westward expansion of the country (Nash, 1967:38-43). Indeed, it is still common today. This orientation to the environment I term *transformational*, and it includes not only the agrarian pastoralism which motivated the Puritan settlers and their westward-migrating descendants, but also the view of the natural environment which embraces the value of maximum economic return from the exploitation of natural resources. A similar dimension of environmental orientation was isolated by Florence Kluckhohn and Fred Strodtbeck in their studies of the values of five different, but geographically contiguous, communities in the Southwest (1961:1-48, 362-366). These authors identified control and mastery over nature and the environment as one of three important orientations of individuals and collectivities to their surroundings.

The contemporary significance of this orientation should be obvious. If we have a population of persons whose beliefs about the environment are governed by a transformational orientation to it, we can then expect little resistance to large-scale environmental altera- tions such as those produced by massive water storage and diversion projects, electrical transmission systems, extensive forest utilization and mining. Kluckhohn and Strodtbeck identify "mastery-over- nature . . . [as] the dominant orientation of most Americans. Natural forces of all kinds are to be overcome and put to the use of human beings. . . . The view in general is that it is a part of man's duty to overcome obstacles; hence there is the great emphasis upon technology" (1961:13).

Transformationists argue over the esthetic consequences of various types and degrees of development and, more importantly within this tradition, have debated policies of exploitation vs. wise and multiple use of renewable and nonrenewable natural resources. Nevertheless, although a grouping of this sort greatly simplifies and glosses over differences in emphasis and direction among its "members," it makes sense because of what we know of public opinion—namely, that we can often detect only the grossest, broad-gauge conceptualizations of issue areas among much of the mass public and this is particularly true of the assessment of values and value orientations among the public.

Arrayed against the transformational orientation to the environment that has been and apparently remains dominant in the United States is an opposing view, often termed preservationist, which developed in the early part of the nineteenth century (Nash, 1967:96-107). Arising out of fundamental changes in man's conception of nature, the promulgation of this view became the goal of the American wilderness movement. Its spokesmen, John James Audubon, James Fenimore Cooper, Thomas Cole, Francis Parkman and John Muir, were responding to the destruction of forests and wild areas by an unplanned and sprawling civilization which, after 1850, was to be predominantly urban and industrial. The ideology of this early movement was organized around the goal of preserving, in their natural state, tracts of wilderness for the spiritual, esthetic, tradition-evoking and scientific values these men and their followers argued were inherent in undisturbed nature.

Formally embodied within voluntary organizations such as the Sierra Club, the ideology of preservationism—with its implications for restriction and cessation of industrial expansion—has gradually gathered support among segments of the elite and mass public and is now a major element in the ideology of the ecology movement of the late 1960s and early 1970s (Lee, 1970). In some cases, however, preservationism has gone far beyond the wilderness-saving goals of its founders and in its more radical forms serves as a basis for a critique of growth economics in particular and capitalism in general (Lee, 1970).

. Finally, a new and emergent position which attempts to harmonize development with natural forms and environmental quality has found support in the planning professions and among some developers. To what extent this view is simply an evolutionary modification of traditional transformational thinking remains to be seen.

The tracing of these and similar themes through U.S. intellectual and social history is, however, not our task here. These positions are outlined merely to suggest that our specific analysis of the environmental and ecology movements and our assessments of opinion and awareness of environmental values, goals, and problems held and perceived by the public should be sensitive to the presence of these conflicting value structures which divide Americans' thinking on environmental issues. They will be an important focus of the debate over the means of maintaining the environmental and ecological integrity of American society in the next thirty years.

RISING CONCERN FOR THE ENVIRONMENT

During the past fifty years there evidently have been surges and declines in the public's concern about and interest in problems of

America's natural environment. A previous high point of interest probably occurred during the Pinchot-Muir era (1898-1913) when events such as the conflict over Hetch Hetchy, the expansion of the national forest reserves, and the White House Governors' Conference attracted and were in part a function of public concern for conservation and wilderness preservation. Two World Wars and the Depression evidently deflected public interest to the point where Grant McConnell, writing in *The Western Political Quarterly* in 1954, could say that the organized conservation movement was ". . . small, divided, and frequently uncertain," and, presumably, attracted little public attention (McConnell, 1954). However, a dramatic change in the posture of the public toward the environment and conservation has occurred in the seventeen years since McConnell's review.

In order to assess the extent of this change we will briefly examine some evidence drawn from periodical circulation figures, then consider some probable cause of the rates of growth of this concern, then move to a discussion and analysis of a national cross-section sample survey dealing with the American public's present levels of concern for the environment, finally giving some brief consideration to the environmental values of the American public.

One index of public interest in an issue can be derived from studies of periodical content. While a measure of this type does not reflect an entire population's behavior with respect to issues, it is, nevertheless, a rough index of what the media-attentive segment of the mass public is consuming and may, therefore, be considered to have a reciprocal effect on public opinion. That is, it not only reflects the media-attentive public's interests but also serves to activate concern about an issue among this and very possibly other segments of the population. As we know from earlier studies the portion of the mass public that consumes written media is considerably more active in attempts to influence policy than are non- or low media consumers. Such persons are a relatively high status group and therefore may have a greater effect upon national policy than their mere numbers would suggest.

Figure 1 depicts patterns of periodical content during the period 1953-1969. It is a compilation of the content of nonresource and resource periodicals which, from time to time, carry articles about environmental issues. The categories selected for environmental articles appear in *Guide to Periodical Literature* and include "Natural Resources," "Smog," "Sewage," "Air Pollution," "Water Pollution," "Oil Pollution," and "Noise Pollution" *(Guide to Periodical Literature 1953-1969).*

FIGURE 1. Growth Rates (in Frequency) of Articles Concerning Environmental Issues in Selected Periodicals and Number of Periodicals (U.S. only) Containing Environmental Articles—1953 to 1969

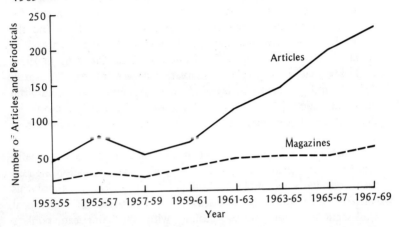

There has been a striking increase in the number of environmentally oriented articles appearing in U.S. periodicals during the years examined (1953-1969). The most obvious characteristic of the curve is its nearly monotonic linear progression from the period 1957-1959 when 68 articles appeared to the most current period, 1967-1969, when 226 articles were published, an increase of more than 330 percent. The overall increase for the 16-year period was slightly greater than 470 percent, from 48 to 226 articles.

An interesting question that emerges from these data is: what environmental values are of particular importance in this expansion of media attention to problems of this kind? Unfortunately, the scope of our research does not permit an extensive content analysis of all of this literature. However, Russell (1970) reviewed some of the themes expressed within resource-oriented periodicals in the period 1953-1970.

Russell selected three publications on the basis of ratings by professionals in the fields of conservation, education and forestry. From an original list of nine, the publications selected for their "breadth of subject matter and degree of influence" (1970:17-22) include *Outdoor America, National Audubon,* and *American Forests.* A total of 371 articles randomly sampled from a time-stratified universe of all articles in the period 1953-1969 formed the basis for a thematic analysis of types of changes in environmental values, issues, and concerns as reflected in these three publications during this period.

What is perhaps most interesting in this analysis is a review of the specific content of articles which advanced and declined in importance in these periodicals between two comparison periods, 1954-1960 and 1963-1969. Most prominent among these shifts in emphasis was the emerging concern with problems of the urban environment. In this case twelve times as many articles on this problem occurred in the seven-year period 1963-1969 as occurred in the seven years from 1954-1960. Typically, urban environmental problems involve specific issues such as open space, smog and other forms of air pollution, population growth and density, planning, and the like. There was also a substantial (65 percent) increase in concern with outdoor recreation, particularly centered on the need for more outdoor recreation facilities. Another area with a very large (4 : 1)[1] increase in media attention dealt with environmental problems created by industrialization. Other areas which attracted more attention in the recent period included legislation (8 : 5), conservation education (8 : 5), and threatened animal species.

Declining in importance in the same time frames were natural history (2 : 1), rural environmental problems (5 : 4), research (7 : 5), general news (7 : 5), and biographical, personal-tribute types of articles.

The general trend of these data is obvious: these media reflect and are anticipating the environmental problems introduced into the society through the joint effects of large-scale urbanization, population growth, and industrialization. They are transmitting information and opinion about both general and specific instances of these problems. As we shall see later, many of these problems are of direct concern to the public generally, not merely to the small segment of it reached by these particular periodicals.

Two other types of analysis of these articles were also employed by Russell: thematic analysis and a comparative study of authors between the two time clusters. The articles' themes suggested a growing concern with the total environment; that is, they reflected more frequently advocated federal intervention to solve environmental problems. The later period also produced more emphasis on conservation education, and this theme was manifested as a concern for the extension of this kind of education—both in quality and in quantity—to a greater proportion of the American public. Finally, it is interesting to note that the professional and occupational roles of

---

[1]Ratios refer to rates of appearance by type of article, between the two time periods examined. The first number refers to the 1954-1960 period, the latter number to the period 1960-1969.

contributors to these three journals has shifted markedly. In the period 1954-1960 less than 3 percent of (N = 133) identified authors were from non-resource-oriented professions and less than 2 percent were from business, government, or education. By the end of 1969, these two categories of authorship accounted for almost 25 percent (N = 160) of the articles in which it was possible to identify authorship. This finding suggests that not only are environmental problems of growing concern to the public at large, but also there is a growing dispersion of environmental awareness and concern among elite sectors outside of the resource and environmental sciences.

In addition to this growth in media attention, some limited time-series survey data on two specific environmental problems—air pollution and water pollution show that public concern over these two environmental quality issues is in fact rising sharply. In 1965 13 percent of the public indicated that they felt the water pollution problem was "very serious." By 1968 this had increased to 27 percent. The same general trend over concern with air pollution is evident: 10 percent classifying it as a "very serious" problem in 1965 and 25 percent giving the same response only three years later (Davies, 1970:79-80).

Before turning to a discussion of factors which may be responsible for this increasing attention to environmental problems, let us look briefly at another index of public concern about the environment—membership growth rates in conservation and environmental preservation organizations. Figure 2 depicts the growth rates of four of these groups, two predominantly of the western states in their membership bases and two predominantly eastern. As this figure shows, growth in membership in these organizations has been spectacular. In the past 20 years, for example, the Sierra Club went from a small, San Francisco Bay Area-based organization of less than 8,000 people to a national organization of more than 115,000 members (as of this writing). (Figure 2 shows the membership for 1969.) Other groups have done almost as well as the bulk of their growth has come in the five-year period 1965-1969.

In short, there has been a recent and sharp membership increase in the voluntary organizations which are most active in implementing preservationist environmental policies. It is probable that the growth rates we have observed are not indicators of ideological polarization within relatively elite sectors of the public but are, rather, one indication of increasing concern for and a desire to improve Americans' natural and urban environments. Thus, they are an additional indicator of public concern and may indicate that the organized environmental "issue public" is rapidly gaining strength in the United States today.

FIGURE 2. Growth Rates (in Absolute Numbers of Members) of Four Conservation Organizations—The Sierra Club, Wilderness Society, Audubon Society, and Save the Redwoods League—1950 to 1969[a]

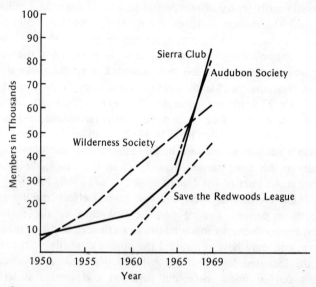

[a]Data supplied by the organizations.

If, as the indicators we have reviewed suggest, public concern for the environment has increased, it seems appropriate to review three probable causes of this rising level of public attention to and arousal over environmental problems.

First, and very probably most important, has been the increase of media attention to problems of smog, water pollution, population growth, and so forth. Such attention cannot help but have affected the public's perception of these problems. And as we will see later, the media-attentive segment of the society (that is, the higher socioeconomic groups) is substantially more concerned about these problems than others. While not entirely the result of their levels of media attention, these groups' concern probably reflects the relatively greater impact that the media has had on them since environmental issues became the focus of media attention in 1966. In addition to the effect of media attention in increasing the public's level of attention to and concern with the environment, however, the existence of two distinct trends in the society may also have had a strong impact. The first of these is the probable increase in Americans' personal exposure to their natural environments. The second is the clear and demonstrable deterioration in quality of many aspects of the natural rural and especially urban, environment.

Let us look briefly at changes in exposure to the environment indicated by visitation rates to state and federal parks. In the case of state parks, the rate of visitation in the 18-year period 1950-1968 increased almost 350 percent. The national parks had an ever greater increase in visits (entry of one person to a park) from 33.2 million in 1950 to 150.8 million in 1968 or a gain of more than 450 percent. All these rates are, of course, substantially greater than the simple increase of population. At the same time, land areas and the number of facilities in these areas have not expanded at anything like the rate of use. National parkland areas increased by almost 6 million acres—from 22.9 million acres to 29.1 million acres, or about 30 percent. State park areas had more substantial increases—from 4.7 million acres to 7.4 million acres in 1967, or about 75 percent. There was also a substantial increase in the absolute number of state park facilities in this same period, from 1,725 in 1950 to 3,202 in 1967 (*Statistical Abstract of the United States,* 1967, 1968, 1969).

These events may have had two general effects on the public. First, those persons coming for the first time to the parks and forests, encountering in many instances a crowded and semiurbanized environment, may have contrasted the potential beauty of these areas with the localized squalor and concluded that, indeed, America was running out of open space and parkland and what was left was overcrowded. As we shall see, this hypothesis receives some support in our survey data where three-quarters of the population express a desire to preserve more land for national parks, game reserves, and the like.

Furthermore, these rates of visitation, in conjunction with immense increases in the general mobility of the population, have provided much of the population with an opportunity to contrast directly one environment with another. As in all such cases, judgments—favorable or unfavorable—are more readily made, and the increasing opportunity for environmental contrast implied by these data may well have resulted in both increased environmental awareness and increased concern.

Second, as measured by a number of indicators, America's physical environment is changing—many feel for the worse. One simple indicator of this change is the density of the population which rose from 44.2 persons per square mile in 1940 to 60.1 in 1960 to an estimated 70 per square mile in 1970. But many other changes, in the form of increasing rates of urbanization, air pollution (which is now evidently declining), water pollution, urbanization of former relatively natural areas, increasing automobile density and traffic volume, and growing urban noise levels are but a few of the objective environmental problems which may have stimulated public concern. These factors and changes in the society are loudly lamented and are of grave concern to conservationists, preservationists, and ecologists. As we will see, the problems—if not their basic sources—are also of substantial concern to the American mass public.

In the fall of 1968, the Survey Research Center at the University of Michigan conducted a national cross-section sample survey as part of its ongoing series of studies of Americans' political and economic behavior. As part of the survey, respondents were asked to indicate what they believed to be the three most important problems facing the United States today. Generalized concern with the environment evidently ranked below other problems in the public's mind at that time. In fact, only 25 of more than 1,500 respondents gave answers to those questions that could be interpreted as expressive of environmental concern.[2] Issues such as the war in Vietnam, race relations, and student unrest were, at that time, far more salient for the public than the problems of the environment. Less than a year later a Gallup survey found some 51 percent of the adult public expressing "deep concern" over the problem of destruction of the natural environment.[3] It is unfortunate that we cannot draw any but the slimmest of inferences from a comparison of these two surveys. Presenting an individual with an open-ended question is a far better method of tapping what is on his mind than asking him how concerned he is about X or Y when X or Y have been selected by the researcher as problems he thinks ought to concern a respondent. This finding in conjunction with the Gallup data from a year later suggests that there may well have been a broad shift in primary-issue concerns among the public from 1968 to 1969. Indeed, as a survey conducted for the President's Commission on Obscenity and Pornography by Abelson in 1970 shows, this evidently has occurred to some extent (1971). Employing an open-ended, major-problems question very similar to that used by the Survey Research Center, Abelson found that "pollution and misuse of resources" was mentioned by 19 percent of the respondents as a major problem "facing the country today." It was exceeded in concern by the war (54 percent), breakdown of law and order (20 percent), and drugs (20 percent). Due to sampling error inherent in

[2]This is an unfortunate result because it prohibits the analysis of environmental concern through the only comprehensive national survey available at this time. A discussion of the inadequacy of data for analysis of public opinion concludes this paper.
[3]I would like to thank Mr. Thomas Kimball, director of the National Wildlife Federation, for the data reported in this section of the paper.

such surveys it is probably appropriate to treat the latter three problem areas as equivalent in concern to the public's views on pollution and misuse of resources. An additional 4 percent of this sample mentioned overpopulation as a major problem (Ogden, 1970).

These data indicate a rise in primary public concern over problems of the environment from a point where less than 2 percent of the population expressed concern to a point where 23 percent of the public now considers the environmental or population control issues as major problems facing the country—an increase by a factor of 11 since 1968.

WHO IS CONCERNED ABOUT THE ENVIRONMENT?

In January 1969 the Gallup Organization asked a national cross section of 1503 American adults a series of questions concerning their opinions about problems of the natural environment. This survey, sponsored by the National Wildlife Federation, was the first and, as far as I know, the only national survey thus far to assess public concern for a comprehensive set of environmental problems. The survey began with the following question:

> "You may have heard or read claims that our natural sur-
> roundings are being spoiled by air pollution, soil erosion, des-
> truction of wildlife and so forth. How concerned are you about
> this—deeply concerned, somewhat concerned, or not very con-
> cerned?

The distribution of responses to this question stratified over six demographic variables is reported in Table 1.

What do these data suggest? First of all, men are more concerned about the environment than women. This finding is not surprising given the well-known fact that men are typically more aware of and concerned about political and social issues than are women.

Surprisingly, given the high rate of participation of youth in events such as Earth Day, there is little substantial difference in level of concern by age with the exception of a 9 percentage point difference between the 21-34 age group and the over-50 age group in the proportion of these groups that are "not very concerned" about the problems raised in the question. The younger group has a smaller proportion of unconcerned members than the older group.

Education and family income, as we would expect, both show an effect on the level of expressed concern. College-educated respondents were more likely to be concerned than any other group, 62 percent of them saying that they were "deeply concerned" and

TABLE 1. *Distribution of Responses to a National Survey of Public Concern over Environmental Problems (Percentage)*

	Deeply con- cerned	Some- what con- cerned	Not very con- cerned	No opin- ion	TOTAL	Number of Inter- views
National Results	51	35	13	2	100	1503
By Sex						
Men	56	31	10	3	100	744
Women	46	38	14	2	100	759
By Age						
21-34 years	51	41	7	1	100	403
35-49 years	50	38	10	2	100	476
50-years and older	52	28	16	4	100	605
(Undesignated—19)						
By Education						
College	62	32	6	—[a]	100	395
High school	52	37	10	1	100	748
Grade school	39	34	20	7	100	352
(Undesignated—8)						
By Annual Family Income						
$10,000 and over	58	34	8	0	100	449
$7,000-$9,999	53	38	8	1	100	336
$5,00-$6,999	55	35	8	2	100	237
Under $5,000	41	34	20	5	100	463
(Undesignated—18)						
By Size of Community						
1 million and over	51	36	8	5	100	277
250,000-999,999	52	35	11	2	100	296
50,000-249,000	55	35	9	1	100	235
2,500-49,999	52	31	16	1	100	233
Under 2,500	46	37	14	3	100	462
By Region of Country						
East	46	38	12	4	100	425
Midwest	56	34	9	1	100	400
South	44	36	16	4	100	428
West	59	31	10	—[a]	100	250

Level of Environmental Concern

[a]Less than half of one percent.

only 6 percent expressing little concern. The same general effect is observed in the data on the family income but it is by no means as strong a predictor of environmental concern as education, with only the lowest income group differing importantly from the other three in the proportion of its members at the highest level of concern. In general, the higher the socioeconomic status of the respondent, the more likely he is to express high concern and conversely, the lower his socioeconomic status, the more likely he is to be unconcerned about these matters. This is a finding that confirms our expectations and findings from previous social research. There is, however, one important implication that may be drawn from this finding. That is, unlike many contemporary social issues such as race, welfare and poverty and, to some extent, the continuing war in Vietnam, the environmentally concerned segment of the society is relatively powerful in terms of its access to the economic and political resources of our democracy. Thus, if this segment's disproportionate level of concern continues to increase, there is a relatively good probability that its values and preferences will be reflected in political decisions, which in turn will affect the environment.

The other two variables in Table 1 are also of interest. Environmental concern is substantially greater in <u>urban</u> areas and it is markedly greater in the <u>Western</u> United States. In some ways this is a confusing result because if the concern is generated by urbanization (as it appears in part to be), we ought to find high levels of concern in areas of high urbanization, particularly the East. Further tabulations will perhaps clarify this.

SPECIFIC ENVIRONMENTAL CONCERNS OF THE PUBLIC

The respondents were presented with a list of seven environmental problems and asked to indicate which one of them they felt was most important.

Two problems—air (36 percent mentioned) and water pollution (32 percent mentioned)—are of principal concern to the American public at this time. Each of these is at least four times more likely to be named as any of the remaining four problem areas. However, simply because pesticides (7 percent), open space (6 percent), wildlife preservation (5 percent), and soil erosion (4 percent) did not receive as much attention as air and water pollution it should not be assumed that they are therefore unimportant to the public. This question is merely a measure of primary concern and it is quite possible and likely that many respondents who are most sensitive to water pollution, for example, may be nearly as disturbed by air pollution, erosion, and the preservation of open space.

Some differences in concern emerge when responses to this question are stratified with various demographic variables. Women are more likely to be concerned with air pollution and its associated effects than men. In Los Angeles, during "smog alerts," young children are often kept inside and this may be an added burden to their mothers. In Detroit, Swan has studied an area in which 22 *tons* per square mile of particulate matter settle to the ground *each month,* or more than 250 tons of such material each year (1970:9). The program such a vast quantity of particulate matter causes for the average housewife may easily be imagined.

There is also a substantial effect of age on the type of environmental concern expressed by this sample. Young people are substantially more concerned about air pollution than older persons and are 10 percentage points higher in concern over air than water pollution. Older people, on the other hand, are four times as likely as the younger group to express primary concern over pesticides. Among the older group (over 50) concern for air and water pollution as the primary problem is equal (31 percent). Stratification by educational level and income show few important differences other than the generally higher level of concern expressed among persons with more money and education. However, to this author at least, it is somewhat surprising that the college-educated segment of the society fails to locate its concerns more often in areas of pollution such as pesticides, erosion, and open space preservation. These are areas in which technological and political solutions such as those available for air and water pollution are by no means well developed and which will, in all probability, have a greater long-term effect on the biosphere and ecosystem than the more readily solved problems of air and water pollution. It is also interesting in this respect that only 7 percent of the group primarily concerned with pesticides as the major environmental problem thought we should stop using pesticides, while 26 percent felt that "new and improved" pesticides were the answer. Ecosystem awareness, then, seems somewhat deficient both in the best-educated subset of our sample and among those most concerned about the serious pollution by pesticides.

We find some interesting differences among specific environmental concerns of the public when we examine the size of the communities in which our respondents live. There is a generally linear increase in concern for air pollution as the size of the respondent's community of residence increases. Concern in metropolitan areas of 1 million or more persons is more than twice as great as it is in areas of less than 2,500 persons. The opposite is true of water pollution, but the curve is not linear. Persons in areas of less than 1 million population are, on the average, about 11 percentage points above those in the largest areas in their level of concern over water pollution. These findings are very much in line with what we might expect and what we have learned from other surveys of air pollution. That is, as exposure to air pollution increases (as it does in the United States with increasing urbanization), opposition and objections to it increase. A number of local studies by deGroot and Samuels (1962), Smith, (1967), Scheuneman and Zeidberg (1964), and Medalia and Finkner (1965) all support this basic and obvious finding. It seems appropriate to suggest that rural residents' greater relative concern with water pollution is found both in their comparative freedom from air pollution and in the probability that they will be exposed more than city dwellers to polluted rivers, lakes, and streams.

Finally, there are some distinct regional differences in the distribution of Americans' concern about their environment, and the problem we encountered in our discussion of the public's basic level of concern and the apparent discrepancy between concern and community size seems somewhat clearer on looking at these regional response patterns. Concern over air pollution is strongest in the two areas of the country with especially serious problems of this type (excepting Chicago which has very high rates of all types of air pollution)—the West (essentially, the Los Angeles and San Francisco Bay Area SMSAs), and the East (Boston, New York, Philadelphia, and Washington, D.C., SMSAs). But Westerners are somewhat less concerned than others about water pollution, largely, we suspect, because they have not as yet been exposed to this problem on a scale comparable to that in other regions of the country.

We have seen, in this section, that the public has focused its primary environmental concern on two problems—air and water pollution—and has given less importance to problems of pesticide use, preservation of open spaces and wildlife, and soil erosion. Observed differences in concern have been shown to be associated with sex, where women are more concerned than men about air pollution. Substantially greater concern for air pollution over any other problem was manifested by young people, and older citizens were more likely than any other group to express primary concern over pesticides. The size of a respondent's community was also associated with his concerns about air and water pollution, with metropolitan residents in areas of more than 1,000,000 people most concerned about air pollution and respondents living in cities of less than 50,000 persons most concerned about water pollution. Regional differences associated with air and water pollution were also noted with air pollution of most concern in the East and West; water pollution was of less importance in the West than in other areas.

In the next section we will move to a discussion of what solutions—technological or political—the public believes appropriate to solve two of the six problem areas we have discussed.

SOLUTIONS FAVORED BY THE AMERICAN
PUBLIC TO TWO MAJOR ENVIRONMENTAL PROBLEMS

After each respondent indicated what environmental problem he felt was most pressing he was asked, in open-ended format, "In your opinion what can be done to correct this problem?" He could give as many solutions as he wished.

These responses are worth examination because they point to the relative importance of technological, political, and value change solutions in the public's thinking and suggest which kinds of solutions may or may not be well received.

In the case of air pollution, industrial emissions and their control appear to rank first in importance to the public, with a total of 35 percent of the subset of the sample giving responses which indicated a focus on industry. Auto exhaust emission control was next with 30 percent of this group favoring this as the most efficacious means of eliminating air pollution. Only 10 percent of the responses focused on legislation directly although the solutions posed to this problem by the public appear to require legal sanction before they could be implemented.

Water pollution is seen as much more of an industrial problem than is air pollution, and legislation and legal solutions are also more attractive to the public most concerned with this particular problem. Only 17 percent of this group recognized the need to keep sewage out of the water—a major source of water pollution, largely the result of inadequate and overloaded sewage treatment systems owned by municipalities.

One result that did *not* appear in either of these queries was, I believe, particularly significant. Very few or none of the respondents suggested reducing air pollution by introducing economies of scale such as mass transit or by reducing industrial output. In the case of water pollution few, if any, of the respondents suggested that population control or limitation of industrial output might be partial solutions to this problem. Technical and legal solutions are seen as sufficient for handling these difficulties. In short, there is little indication in these free responses that the American public is seriously entertaining changes in its expansionist, growth-oriented value system—a topic to which we will turn our attention in the concluding section of this paper.

Two other areas of inquiry in this survey provide us with additional information about the public's attitudes and values with respect to the environment. The first of these concerns setting aside more public land for conservation purposes. The question read as follows:

*"Are you in favor of setting aside more public land for con-
servation purposes such as national parks, wildlife refuges, bird
sanctuaries, and so forth, or not?"*

Table 2 presents the responses to this question stratified by a series of demographic variables. Essentially, the patterns which we observed in our previous discussion of the public's general concern for the environment apply here as well. A desire to set aside land for conservation purposes is positively associated with education and income, and in this case there is a relatively strong effect of age—the younger group substantially higher (14 percentage points) in support of land preservation than the older group. There is, somewhat curiously, no systematic increase in a desire for land reserve as size of community increases, only a rather sharp dropoff in support in areas of less than 2500 residents. This, of course, is what we might expect given the probable availability of open space lands in these rural or quasi-rural communities. Regional differences appear to reflect similar differences; for example, the South, with the greatest number of small towns, is less likely to produce residents favoring land reserve than the East with the greatest percentage of large metropolitan areas.

One fact that should be stressed, however, is the generally strong public support that exists for the issue raised in this question. The younger segment of the population is, in particular, anxious to reserve public lands for the purposes specified in the question.

The final issue, and perhaps the one with the most potential impact on the American environment, is the degree to which the public favors population control. The question asked by Gallup is not a particularly good one in some respects because it is diffuse and unspecific in time period but, on the other hand, this may be an advantage in tapping the general orientation of the public to this matter.

*'It has been said that it will, at some time, be necessary to
limit the human population (number of people) if our present
living standards are to be maintained. Do you think this will be
necessary or not?"*

TABLE 2. *Attitude Toward Reserving Public Lands For Conservation Purposes (Percentage)*

	Yes	No	Don't know	TOTAL	Number of Interviews
National Results	75	19	6	100	1503
By Sex					
Men	76	19	5	100	744
Women	74	19	7	100	759
By Age					
21-34 years	83	13	4	100	403
35-49 years	76	18	6	100	476
50-years and older	69	24	7	100	605
(Undesignated—19)					
By Education					
College	82	15	3	100	395
High School	78	18	4	100	748
Grade School	64	26	10	100	352
(Undesignated—8)					
By Annual Family Income					
$10,000 and over	81	16	3	100	449
$7,000-$9,999	81	15	4	100	336
$5,000-$6,999	75	18	7	100	237
Under $5,000	66	25	9	100	463
(Undesignated—18)					
By Size of Community					
1 million and over	79	15	6	100	277
250,000-999,999	78	17	5	100	296
50,000-249,999	80	16	4	100	235
2,500-49,999	78	19	3	100	233
Under 2,500	66	25	9	100	462
By Region of Country					
East	82	12	6	100	425
Midwest	76	20	4	100	400
South	68	24	8	100	428
West	75	21	4	100	250

Source: Gallup, 1969.

Support for population limitation, like other measures of environmental preservation, comes from the young, well-educated, and relatively high-income segment of the population. In addition there is a substantial increase in support as the size of a respondent's community increases, but even in the areas of greatest population density in the United States (places of more than 1,000,000 persons) the proportion of respondents favoring limitation is only 50 percent.

Education and age again appear to have the greatest effects, with 60 percent of the college educated favoring limitation, compared with only 29 percent of those with a grade school education having the same opinion. Thirty-six percent of persons over 50 supported limitation while 55 percent of those under 35 gave the same response. In this respect these data argue for increasing support for population limitation among those in the society with the most potential for reproduction. Rates of acquisition of higher education are, of course, dramatically increasing. In 1947, for example, only 5.4 percent of the population over 25 years of age completed four years or more of college; by 1967 the percentage had increased to 14.6, a threefold increase in twenty years. In addition, the median age distribution of the population is declining in the United States, from 30.7 years in 1950 to 28.8 years in 1967.[4]

A number of other national surveys have also focused on factors likely to influence population control. Judith Blake, for example, has focused her attention on the causes of the recent decline in the United States crude birth rate. Her discussion (of 15 national surveys) points out the need for more time-series data on marriage intentions and age preference at marriage, as well as family-size goals. Her data suggest that at the aggregate level there was essentially no change in the desired family size between 1963 and 1966. However, she found that one of the trends revealed in the Gallup data we have been discussing was also present in her data—that younger men and women are very slightly more likely to have lower family-size goals than older persons. This effect was particularly strong among Catholics, where the mean ideal family size of females declined from 4.3 percent in 1961, based on an age range of 14-23, to 3.7 percent in 1966 based on an age range of 21 or older (1967). Her data are, of course, substantially older than the ones we have been discussing and, unfortunately, she does not report tabulations of her surveys by educational and income levels. Nevertheless, if we assume that one substantial behavioral response to environmental problems is the voluntary natural reduction of population growth, there are trends in both survey data and vital statistics which suggest that inhibiting growth mechanisms are now forming in the American public. Unfortunately, due to the absolute size and absolute rate of increase of the population at this time, far more direct means of population control will have to be established

[4]Bureau of the Census, U.S. Department of Commerce. Projections for the U.S. population in the year 2000 are as follows: Series A: 361.4 million; Series B: 336.0 million; Series C: 307.8 million; Series D: 282.6 million. Statistical Abstract of the United States (1969:7, 23, 111).

and implemented in the United States if population stabilization is to become a reality.

TAXATION AND CONCERN

A final question from the survey concerns the public's willingness to pay taxes to improve its natural surroundings. While this is a hypothetical situation posed to the respondents in the sample, data on water-bond-issue voting patterns suggest that the public is, in fact, often willing to pay for increased environmental quality and this parallels the result that emerges from the survey (League of Women Voters Ed. Fund, 1966).

A large majority (73 percent) of the population said that it would be willing to pay some additional sum of taxes each year for the specific purpose of "improv[ing] our natural surroundings." Only 9 percent rejected the idea totally but 18 percent said they did not know if they would be willing to do so or not.

The general effects of the demographic variables we have observed thus far are present in this measure. There is, however, a very strong effect of income on this variable with, as one might suspect, a strong positive relationship between ability to pay (having a larger income) and willingness to pay for this particular public good. Persons with incomes of $10,000 or more are ten times as likely as those with incomes of $5000 or less to express a willingness to pay "a large amount such as $100.00 or more" for environmental improvement, and they are almost three times as willing to pay a "moderate amount such as $50.00" as the lower income group. Again, however, we see the relatively strong effect of education, with a college education being the best predictor of the willingness to pay a relatively large amount in additional taxes.

Note, however, that we saw earlier that 86 percent of the population (Table 1) expressed strong or some concern over the environment. It is quite clear that while there is a strong positive association between concern and willingness to pay for improvement, the relationship is by no means perfect. Further, while 51 percent of the public expressed strong concern about environmental problems only 4 percent are willing to pay $100 or more in taxes and only 18 percent are willing to pay $50 to improve it. Thus, while aroused and apparently willing to increase its taxes, the public has clearly not reached the point where it is willing to make substantial financial sacrifices in order to insure improvement of the natural environment.

In part, we may speculate that these results are present because of the public's expectations that enforcement of antipollution laws against industrial polluters and the prospect of technological solutions to many (in particular, air and water pollution) environmental problems may not necessitate substantial tax increases. Unfortunately, our survey data do not permit examination of this issue in great detail.

ENVIRONMENTAL VALUES AND A COMMENT ON THE ADEQUACY OF DATA AVAILABLE TO DECISION MAKERS

From this limited analysis, some information about the environmental values of Americans can be drawn.

First of all, Americans *are* concerned about the quality of their environment. This fact is underlined both by the rapid growth of environment and conservation organizations and by the high levels of concern, accompanied by a willingness to increase tax loads as we have seen in the survey data analyzed previously. Americans want their environmental problems solved, and they support, in general, technological, legal, and financial solutions to these problems.

Foremost among the problems of concern to the public is air pollution, followed closely by water pollution.

The public tends to respond most strongly to those specific environmental problems which affect it most directly. Thus we see regional location and city size having a substantial effect on the distribution of opinion about matters such as open space, air and water pollution, and the acquisition of land for purposes of conservation.

There is very broad public support for increasing the amount of public land devoted to conservation in the form of national parks, wildlife refuges, and the like.

Substantial minorities of the population are seriously concerned about the preservation of open space, the use of pesticides, wildlife preservation, and soil erosion.

A near majority of the population sees eventual control of population growth as a necessity.

In general, it is the more affluent, better educated, and younger segment of the population that is most concerned about problems of the environment—although this group by no means has a monopoly on concern. These facts, however, suggest that the political power, both real and potential, available to this segment of the society is relatively great and that environmental preservation, reclamation, and protection is dominantly a middle class concern.

On the other hand, the data we have examined tell us very little about possible value and attitude changes in the general orientations to the environment with which we began our discussion: transformationalism and preservationism. Nor do they inform us directly of the degree to which the public believes that environmental preservation can be realized in a society with unchecked population and industrial growth. They tell us nothing about the linkage of political beliefs with attitudes toward the environment and, because the analysis was necessarily conducted with a small number of variables from tables supplied to the author, we have been unable to discern anything but gross surface relationships between the variables we have examined.

Professor Gilbert White, in his comprehensive essay on "The Formation and Role of Public Attitudes" (1966:105-127), points to a number of different sources from which information about the public's values can be obtained and to a number of different methodologies that are appropriate to each of them. Among these are content analysis of speeches, textbooks, and newspapers, analysis of social criticism, specialized forms of opinion research, and the like. Dean Daniel M. Ogden, in a discussion of "Environmental Values and Water Project Planning" (1970), also points out that, using these techniques and others, values can be specified such as man hours spent in recreational activities. Thus, there are available to decision makers a number of techniques through which measurements of environmental values might be made.

Unfortunately, one extremely serious gap in our information about public attitudes is illustrated in this paper: namely, the dearth of adequate, national cross-section sample survey data, including trend analyses, from which it would be possible to specify, in considerable detail, the values of the public with respect to the environment and their origin and linkage with various attributes of the population. Until such data are available, and until far more money and time are expended by resource managers, planners, and sociologists on the collection of pertinent data—including survey data—resource decisions and the public's environmental values will continue to be inadequately integrated.

REFERENCES

Blake, Judith
    1967 "Family size in the 1960s—a baffling fad?" Eugenics Quarterly
        14(1):60-74.
Davies, J. C.
    1970 The Politics of Pollution. Opinion Research Corporation 1965,
        1966, 1967. New York: Pegasus Press.
deGroot, I., and S. Samuels
    1962 People and Air Pollution: A Study of Attitudes in Buffalo, New
        York. Buffalo: New York State Department of Health, Air
        Pollution Control Board.

Glacken, Clarence J.
1967 Traces on the Rhodian Shore. Berkeley: University of California Press.

Gallup, George
1969 "Attitudes Towards Conservation," National Wildlife Federation.

Huth, Hans
1967 Nature and the American: Three Centuries of Changing Attitudes. Berkeley: University of California Press.

Kluckhohn, Florence R., and Fred L. Strodtbeck
1961 Variations in Value Orientations. New York: Harper & Row.

League of Women Voters Education Fund
1966 The Big Water Fight. Brattleboro, Vt.: Stephen Greene Press.

Lee, Robert G.
1970 World Savers or Realm Savers? The Dilemma of the Successful Eco-activist. School of Forestry and Conservation, Berkeley: University of California.

Marx, Leo
1964 The Machine in the Garden: Technology and the Pastoral Ideal in America. New York: Oxford University Press.

McCloskey, Michael
1966 "The Wilderness Act of 1964: its background and meaning." Oregon Law Review 45(4):288-321.

McConnell, Grant
1954 "The conservation movement—past and present." The Western Political Quarterly 7:463.

Medalia, N. Z., and A. L. Finkner
1965 Community Perception of Air Quality: An Opinion Study in Clarkston, Washington. Cincinnati, Ohio: U.S. Public Health Service Publication No. 99(10).

Nash, Roderick
1967 Wilderness and the American Mind. New Haven: Yale University Press.

Ogden, Daniel M., Jr.
1970 Environmental Values and Water Project Planning. Paper presented at the Arkansas-White-Red Inter-Agency Committee Meeting (summer).

President's Commission on Obscenity and Pornography
1971 Report. Washington, D.C.: Government Printing Office.

Russell, Cynthia
1970 The Evolution of the Nature Magazine: A Case Study of Three Publications: Outdoor America, National Audubon, American Forests, 1954-1969 (unpublished M.A. thesis). Ann Arbor: University of Michigan.

Smith, Henry Nash
1967 Virgin Land: The American West as Symbol and Myth. New York: Random House.

Smith W. S., J. J. Scheuneman, and L. D. Zeidberg
1964 "Public reaction to air pollution in Nashville, Tennessee." Journal of the Air Pollution Control Association 14:445-448.

Swan, James A
1970 Response to Air Pollution: A Study of Attitudes and Coping Strategies of High School Youth. Ann Arbor: University of Michigan, School of Natural Resources.

White, Gilbert F.
1966 "The formation and role of public attitudes." In Henry Jarrett (ed.), Environmental Quality in a Growing Economy: Essays from the Sixth Resources for the Future Forum. Washington, D.C.: Johns Hopkins University Press.

PAPER 12

The Public Value for Pollution Control

DON A. DILLMAN
JAMES A. CHRISTENSON

Protection of the environment against the continuing encroachment of our affluent society confronts us as a major public issue. Large-scale programs will be needed if environmental pollution is to be controlled and such programs are costly. In our society these programs are more likely to come about if significant and enduring shifts in public sentiment occur in the direction of an increased willingness to accept the costs which are involved. The costs might include, for example, increased prices for consumer goods, increased taxes, restrictions of certain personal freedoms, and discontinued use of technological innovations which pollute the environment.

The choice is not simply whether to control or not to control pollution. The resources necessary to combat pollution tend to be ones used for other purposes. A decision to allocate more funds for environmental protection is likely to mean less for other areas of concern. To individuals this may mean less money to spend for clothing, housing, and leisure. At the institutional level, this may mean less money for health and medical care, poverty programs, and law enforcement.

Changes in the allocation of public funds which would have to be made in order to facilitate pollution control, suggest that an assessment of public sentiment should involve more than a description of attitudes. An assessment is needed of the hierarchical nature of people's preferences for the allocation of personal and public resources. In short, the significant question is not simply whether or not people are concerned, but where protection of the

The research upon which this paper is based was done under project 0031, Citizen Preferences for the Allocation of Public Resources, Agricultural Research Center, College of Agriculture, Washington State University, Pullman, Washington.

environment *ranks* in their value hierarchy. This approach should provide knowledge of the extent to which pollution control efforts are desired, and insight into areas of concern in which less funds might be spent in order to transfer resources to the area of pollution control.

This chapter presents results from a study which has been conceptualized in such a manner that conclusions can be made about the relative position of pollution control in people's value hierarchies. Few studies of this type have been conducted. Several studies (Breslow, 1956; de Groot and Samuels, 1958; Smith, Scheuneman, and Zeidberg, 1964; Medalia and Finker, 1965; Schusky, 1965; Crowe, 1968; Rankin, 1969) have reported on the public's awareness and concern about air pollution. However, little effort was made to provide a rank ordering of air pollution in relation to other areas of concern. Even in cases where concern about community problems has been assessed in hierarchical terms (cf. Harris, 1970), the results cannot be equated, conceptually, with preferences for the allocation of public resources. Mueller (1963) conducted a study with objectives similar to the present study. However, it was limited to the then-current fiscal programs of the federal government and did not include environmental protection or pollution control. A Gallup poll conducted in 1969 found that 52 percent of the public felt that "We are spending too little to improve our environment" (National Wildlife, 1970:18). In terms of the percentage of those who felt that more money should be spent, environmental protection ranked below education, veterans benefits, and natural resources. The research reported here differs somewhat in technique from the Gallup study, but comparisons can be made. Of more importance, however, is the expansion of preferences for the allocation of resources to include all levels of government, and the presentation of a much more detailed analysis in accounting for the variation in the public value for pollution control.

PUBLIC VALUES

The conceptual focus of this study is on public values. The various ways in which the concept "value" has been used in past research suggests a need to clarify its use and to define "public values."

Value is a concept central to the explanation of human behavior. Simply, it is "a conception of the desirable."[1] Value is not

---

[1]Kluckhohn comments that "the only general agreement (on the use of the term) is that values somehow have to do with normative as opposed to existential propositions" (1951:390). A discussion of the various approaches for

to be equated with behavior. A person's values serve as standards against which he judges his behavior. One of the characteristics of value is its abstractness. A particular value will encompass a number of more specific objects and concerns (Nye, 1967). One who places a high value on pollution control is more likely to refrain from emptying garbage into rivers and lakes, to use lead-free gasoline, and to support antipollution legislation (other things being equal) than one who does not hold that value.

The values which are inferred depend upon how a person is asked to express them. Our approach is to ask persons to select among alternatives presented in symbolic form (words). Hence we are concerned with conceived values (Morris, 1964; Catton, 1966). In this framework, value is not placed in an object per se, but describes a desired relationship between an actor and a state of affairs and/or a symbolically represented object.

Some objects or actions may be valued because they are valuable in producing a desired outcome (instrumental values), whereas other objects or actions may be valued as ends in themselves (terminal or intrinsic values) (Nye, 1967; Rokeach, 1968). It is probably for instrumental reasons that the expenditure of resources by the government to control pollution is valued. A decrease in pollution is seen as leading to the preservation of life and other desirable ends. The above specification of the values under study as "public" ones, is intended as signification of the instrumental nature of the allocation of public funds.

Values are similar to attitudes. Confusion in usage of the terms is such that a distinction should be made. Attitudes also imply a "conception of the desirable," but are less general in nature, having specific empirical referents. While it is considered appropriate to speak of one's *value* for pollution control, how one feels concerning the desirability of a proposed program to ban the sale of nonreturnable bottles, is considered an *attitude*.

A second distinction concerning "values" centers on its hierarchical nature (Nye, 1967). A person may hold a higher value for education than for protection of the environment. Attitude is not generally employed in the sense of ranking one set of phenonema as higher or stronger than another set of phenonema. One reason for

(Footnote 1 *continued*)
conceptualizing value and a defense of the alternative accepted here, while important, would not contribute greatly to the purpose of this chapter, so are not included. The conceptualization utilized here draws considerably from the works of Kluckhohn (1951), Catton (1966), Nye (1967), Morris (1964), and Rokeach (1968).

studying values rather than attitudes is that the knowledge of the hierarchical nature of one's concept of the desirable should better help us to predict behavior in situations where resources are scarce. Although a person may hold very strong positive attitudes toward the accomplishment of many things, the usual situation demands that some concerns be given priority over others in the allocation of available resources.

Within our sociological frame of reference the attempt to account for one's public value for pollution control takes, as its starting point, position in the social structure. Values are learned through the socialization process, which is likely to be different depending upon one's statuses and roles in groups that define his position in the societal social structure. Shared values serve as one of the bases by which group loyalties are maintained and group distinctions articulated. Apart from these group affiliations one's public value may also be influenced by his physical and biological surroundings. Such influences do tend to be directed and reshaped by the contingencies of position in the social structure, however. In this paper the attempt to account for the public value for pollution control includes concepts indicating position in the social structure—socioeconomic status, age, and political orientation and identification. The influences of selected aspects of the surrounding environment—actual level of pollution and perceived extent to which pollution is seen as a local problem—are also considered.

RESEARCH METHODS

The public values studied are those of residents in the State of Washington.[2] It is relevant to note that considerable heterogeneity exists in the characteristics of Washington residents. For example, Washington contains three standard metropolitan statistical areas in which approximately 2 million people reside. Approximately 56.8 percent of the state's population live in four contiguous counties comprising little more than 7 percent of the total land area (and much of this land is so mountainous it can't be used for dwellings). In contrast, other sections of the state are quite rural, dependent upon agriculture and/or forestry as the major sources of economic income. Thirteen of Washington's 39 counties contain no town over 5,000 population.

[2]A detailed description of the procedures utilized in this study is presented in a forthcoming Washington State University Agricultural Experiment Station bulletin.

A systematic sample of 4,500 respondents was drawn using the telephone listings for every community in the state. Possible biases resulting from this procedure include (1) the omission of residents with unlisted phone numbers who are likely to be of middle and upper income status, and (2) the omission of persons without phones who are likely to be of lower income status. However, it should be noted that 93 percent of the households had telephone service in 1967 (U.S. Department of Commerce 1969:511). A proportional sample (corresponding to the population of counties in the state) was drawn utilizing 1970 projected estimates (State of Washington, 1968).

Data were collected by means of mail questionnaires between June 10th and September 8th, 1970. Recipients were instructed that the head of the household should provide the information requested. Eighty-two percent of the questionnaires were completed by men. Of the original 4,500 potential respondents, 363 respondents were deleted for reasons of being deceased, physically incapable of completing the questionnaire, having moved from the community with no forwarding address, or having moved out of the state. Of the remaining 4,137 potential respondents, 3,101 (75 percent) returned usuable questionnaires. This rather high response rate was due largely to the use of personalized techniques in conjunction with an intensive follow-up. The latter included three follow–up communications, the last being a certified letter with a replacement questionnaire. It was necessary for the recipient to sign for receipt of the certified letter.

At the time of this writing 1970 census data were not yet available, so the sample respondents could not be compared with the state's population to see if their characteristics differed. Another test for bias introduced by nonresponse was made, however. The responses of those returning their questionnaires after each of the four mailouts were compared. If those who failed to return their questionnaires until the later mailouts had different responses than those who returned theirs immediately, it would provide one basis (although a very limited one) for expecting that the public values of nonrespondents might differ from those of respondents. Differences in the public value for pollution control among those returning questionnaires after each of the four mailouts were not statistically significant ($X^2 = 11.8$; $p = 0.6905$; $d.f. = 15$; $N = 3025$).

FINDINGS

The findings are presented in two parts: first, a description of the overall public value hierarchy; second, an analysis of the factors hypothesized to account for variation in the value held for pollution

TABLE 1.   Percentage of Respondents Who Favor Spending Less, the Same, or

		Government
	(1) Yes	(2) Most important
Value Area		
1. Crime prevention and control	75.7	21.8
2. Pollution control	69.0	15.4
3. Job training and development of employment opportunities for the unemployed	51.5	8.9
4. Protection of forests and other areas for public enjoyment	50.7	1.4
5. Retirement benefits	49.0	6.5
6. Health and medical care	48.3	16.7
7. Public education	41.0	10.4
8. Help for those in poverty	39.5	6.4
9. Urban renewal and slum clearance	34.2	1.6
10. Veteran benefits	32.1	1.8
11. National defense	15.9	4.0
12. Assistance to agriculture	15.9	0.9
13. Space exploration	8.7	0.5
14. Assistance to cultural arts	6.9	0.0
15. Aid to foreign countries	1.3	0.1

[a]This table is based on responses to 3101 questionnaires. The actual number upon which each percentage is based differs slightly from that number because of a small number of nonresponses for individual questions.

control. The analysis is based on responses to a series of four questions.[3]

Public Value Hierarchy

Over two-thirds of the respondents indicated a desire for the government to spend more money on pollution control (Table 1). Of the 15 areas, only one area of concern (crime prevention and control) received a higher percentage than did pollution control. These two areas of concern tended to stand apart from all others. Only about

[3]The questions, in the order asked, are as follows:
1. Government spends public funds in many areas, some of which are listed on this page. This money comes from various federal, state, and local taxes. For each of the areas listed below, please indicate whether you would favor government spending less money, the same amount, or more money than is now being spent.

More Money in Fifteen Areas (N = 3101)[a]

Should Spend More			Government Should Spend Less	
(3) One of four most important	(4) Will accept increased taxes	(5) Yes	(6) First area to spend less	(7) One of four to spend less
58.8	31.3	2.0	0.0	1.1
52.4	28.4	4.5	0.1	2.3
33.6	15.9	11.4	0.3	6.3
25.9	10.0	4.1	0.1	2.3
28.6	12.6	8.3	0.3	4.1
38.8	21.5	9.2	0.5	3.9
30.0	17.6	13.4	1.1	6.7
25.5	13.4	19.1	1.0	10.5
14.8	5.7	21.3	0.8	12.7
13.2	4.5	10.1	0.6	5.7
11.5	6.0	36.1	7.0	28.2
5.8	1.8	41.4	3.7	32.4
4.7	2.3	63.5	20.7	57.8
1.2	0.5	56.6	13.0	49.8
1.2	0.4	87.2	45.7	83.5

one-half of the respondents felt that more money should be spent in other areas. Over one-half of the respondents felt that pollution control was one of the four most important areas of concern (Table 1, Column 2). Fifteen percent felt that it was the most important

(Footnote 3 *continued*)

2. Consider only those areas for which you answered *more* on the previous page. If it were possible for the government to spend more money in only some of these areas, to which areas should priority be given? Please rank the four most important areas by placing the number of the area, as indicated on the opposite page, on the blanks below.

3. For how many of the areas which you have just ranked above would you still favor spending more money if your federal income taxes had to be raised to get the money?

4. Consider only those areas for which you answered *less* on the opposite page. If the government were to spend less money in only some of these areas, in which areas should expenditure cuts be made first, second, third, and fourth? Please rank the four areas in which expenditure cuts should be made.

area of concern (Table 1, Column 3). The tendency for pollution control and crime prevention and control to stand apart from others as top-ranked areas was carried through in all the measures of importance. Although less than one-third of the respondents indicated a willingness to have their taxes increased in order to control pollution, this too was higher than for any other area except crime prevention and control (Table 1, Column 4). Although pollution control is not the highest area of concern, there is strong consensus among the respondents that it is highly valued.

Areas for which consensus tended to exist for the reduction in expenditures, and areas from which funds might therefore be secured for pollution control, included aid to foreign countries, assistance to cultural arts, and space exploration (Table 1, Column 5). These were the only areas for which at least one-half of the respondents favored a cut in expenditures. However, hardly any public funds are presently allocated to one of them, assistance to cultural arts. Less than 5 percent of the federal budget was allocated to the other two areas in 1968 (U.S. Government Printing Office). The trend in recent years has been one of decline in support both for aid to foreign countries and for space exploration. Thus, the possibilities of releasing large amounts of money from these three areas for pollution control efforts seem quite remote.

A definite tendency exists for persons to want more rather than less funds to be spent in most areas. A greater percent of the respondents want more rather than less money spent in 10 of the 15 areas. The mean number of areas for which respondents wanted more money spent was 5.5 as compared to 4.0 for which they desired that less be spent. However, it should be noted that less than a third of the respondents were willing to have federal income taxes raised to finance increases in any area of concern (Table 1, Column 4).

Public Value Index

An index of the extent to which pollution control is valued was developed and is the dependent variable in the analyses which follow. This public value index was constructed from responses to the questions already cited (footnote 3). The index consists of six ordered categories.[4]

In the statistical analysis of what factors are related to the public value index, two measures of association are used: Goodman

---

[4]The six ordered categories are as follows:
1. One of the four most important areas to spend more money and willing to pay increased taxes on it.

and Kruskal's gamma and Kendal's Tau C.[5] Both are nonparametric measures of ordinal association. Both are PRE measures (proportional reduction of error). This enables one to interpret values intermediate between -1 and +1 and thus is superior to those based on Chi-square because of the intuitive meaning that can be given to the actual value based upon probabilistic interpretations.

Gamma may be interpreted as the differences between the conditional probabilities of like and unlike order, given no ties. Tied pairs play no part in the definition of gamma. They are discarded as pairs for which order on at least one variable is indeterminate. Gamma may be applied to cross tabulations of any size (Mueller et al., 1970:279-292).

Kendall's Tau C is very similar to gamma except for the interpretation of ties. Tau C can be readily used when there are very large numbers of ties (Blalock, 1960:321-324). One advantage of gamma over Tau C is that gamma is not limited by marginal frequencies.

Actual Pollution Level and Local Concern

It is hypothesized that the actual level of pollution will affect a person's public value for pollution control. The greater the pollution level, the higher the expected value. However, measuring the pollution level is, at best, difficult. There are many types of pollution to consider, including air, water, visual, and noise. Each of these involves subtypes. For example, air pollution may be composed of particulates as well as different types of gases. Both particulates and gases differ in quantity and quality. Monitoring stations, which measure the levels of the various types of pollutants, do not exist in some parts of the state and do not operate uniformly in other parts. Even if the stations did operate on a uniform basis throughout the

(Footnote 4 *continued*)

2. One of four most important areas to spend more money, but not willing to pay increased taxes for it.

3. Should spend more money but not one of the four most important areas.

4. Should spend *same* amount of money as presently spent.

5. Should spend less money, but not one of the first four areas to cut expenditures.

6. Should spend less money, one of the first four areas to cut expenditures.

[5]Tabulation and statistical processing was conducted by the NWAY program which originated at the Campus Facility Computation Center, Stanford University, Stanford, California 94305. References for gamma and Tau C include Blalock (1960:321-324) Hays (1963:655-656) and Mueller, Schuessler, and Costner, (1970:279-292).

state, the problem of quantifying the existence of the types and subtypes of pollutants to construct an overall index of pollution levels would remain.

Indicators of pollution levels accepted for this study include (1) density of population and (2) city population, that is, the population of the town or city which a person identifies as his "community" (regardless of whether he resides within its city limits). The assumption is made that an increase in the concentration of people and the industries on which these people are dependent for jobs, are associated with increases in pollution levels.

Trends for the relationship between each of the indicators of the actual pollution level and the Value Index are in the expected direction, but the associations are very slight (Table 2). Neither indicator accounts for much of the variation in the value index. This suggests that either the variable is rather unimportant or the indicators do not really measure the actual level of pollution. In order to provide insight into which of the alternative interpretations is valid, the responses to questions about concern for pollution in the local community were examined.

TABLE 2. *Relationship Between Actual Pollution Levels and Index of Public Value for Pollution Control (Percentage)*

Indicators of Actual Pollution Level	N	Public Value for Pollution Control					
		1 (high)	2	3	4	5	6 (low)
Population Density of County (per square mile)							
0 to 24	222	25.2	24.7	19.8	23.9	4.1	2.3
25 to 49	587	24.0	25.6	19.3	26.2	2.6	2.4
50 to 149	362	25.1	24.9	20.4	26.5	1.9	1.1
150+	1864	31.5	23.2	15.5	25.2	2.6	1.9
		Gamma = -0.07 p = 0.1400					
		Tau C = -0.04 p = 0.0001					
City Population[a]							
Less than 5,000	576	23.1	25.5	16.8	29.2	3.1	2.3
5,000 to 19,999	518	28.2	23.4	18.0	25.9	1.9	2.7
20,000 to 99,999	670	29.9	27.6	16.9	22.1	2.5	1.0
100,000+	1266	31.4	21.7	16.9	25.3	2.8	2.0
		Gamma = -0.05 p = 0.1074					
		Tau C = -0.04 p = 0.0007					

[a]These classifications are based on 1968 population estimates provided by the State of Washington Office of Program Planning and Fiscal Management (no date given).

Respondents were asked to rank 14 different potential community problems according to whether each was *no*, a *slight*, a *moderate*, or a *serious* problem in their own community. One of the potential problems was air pollution; a second was water pollution. It was found that the greater the extent to which individuals saw either type of pollution as a problem in their local communities, the higher their value index (Table 3). Differences tended to be rather large. For example, those who perceived either type of pollution as a serious problem were from three to four times as likely to rank in the lower half of the value index (that is, to rank numerically from four to six) as those who saw either as no problem. All statistical tests were highly significant.

An examination of the relationships between the indicators of actual pollution level and concern for the two types of pollution as community problems provides some insight into the validity of these indicators. The assumption may be made that concern over pollution as a local problem is greatest where a higher pollution level exists. Support for this assumption in the case of air pollution is provided

TABLE 3.   Relationship Between Extent to Which Pollution Seen as Problem in Local Community and Index of Public Value for Pollution Control (Percentage)

Extent to Which Pollution Is a Problem in Local Community[a]	N	Public Value for Pollution Control					
		1 (high)	2	3	4	5	6 (low)
Air Pollution							
None	491	19.1	18.5	16.5	35.2	5.7	4.9
Slight	975	22.4	24.1	18.3	30.3	2.6	2.5
Moderate	961	33.0	25.2	14.9	24.1	1.7	1.1
Serious	584	41.4	26.8	18.8	11.8	1.2	0.0
		Gamma = -0.27	p = 0.0000				
		Tau C = -0.20	p = 0.0000				
Water Pollution							
None	444	17.3	24.1	15.8	32.7	5.0	5.2
Slight	915	24.6	22.0	15.5	33.1	2.7	2.1
Moderate	1090	31.4	24.4	16.2	24.9	1.8	1.3
Serious	540	41.5	27.0	21.3	8.7	1.3	0.2
		Gamma = -0.25	p = 0.0000				
		Tau C = -0.18	p = 0.0000				

[a]The question asked was as follows: "Listed below are some problems faced by many communities in the United States. Please indicate to what extent you think each of the items on this list are problems in *your community* for which a solution is needed."

Respondents were asked to identify their community using this definition: "The town or city in or near which you reside and depend upon most for supplies and services, and the rural area around it."

by several studies which are summarized by de Groot (1967). De Groot concluded that within limited geographic areas the major determinant of concern is the actual level of pollution prevalent in the area of residence (1967:680). If this assumption is true, then the absence of a positive association between the indicators of pollution levels and pollution as a community problem would strongly suggest the inadequacy of the indicators for the actual levels of pollution. Table 4 indicates that a strong positive association does exist, especially in relation to the concern about air pollution; the greater the density of the population, the greater the concern about pollution as a community problem. This suggests that the lack of association between the indicators for the actual level of pollution and the public value index is not due to the inadequacy of the indicators.

There appears to be a ready explanation for the existence of (1) a strong association between the indicators for the actual level of pollution and concern about air and water pollution in the local community; (2) a second strong association between the concern about air and water pollution in the local community and the public value index; but (3) a lack of association between the indicators for the actual level of pollution and the public value index. This is largely due to an internal characteristic of the association.

The extent of the association between concern for each kind of pollution and the public value index was examined for each level of city size and population density. The associations remained strong for each of the 16 individual relationships (Table 5). Hence, the association between local concern about pollution and the public value index holds for all levels of actual pollution. However, there is a tendency for those with a given level of concern to be more likely to exhibit a high value index if they live in a locality where the actual level of pollution is low. Thus, if a person remains unconcerned about pollution as a community problem when confronted with high levels of pollution in his community, he is more likely to hold a low public value for control of pollution than the unconcerned person who faces low levels of pollution in his community. Similarly, the person who is concerned about pollution in his local community is somewhat more likely to hold a high value for pollution control if he lives in a community with a low level of actual pollution. This trend is somewhat more marked in the case of air pollution than for water pollution.

These findings suggest the importance of studying variables other than the actual level of pollution and concern about pollution in the community in order to account for the variation in the public

TABLE 4. Relationship Between Actual Pollution Level and Extent to Which Pollution Is Seen as a Problem in Local Community (Percentage)

Indicators of Actual Pollution Level	N^a	Extent to Which Pollution Is a Problem in Socal Community							
		Air Pollution				Water Pollution			
		None	Slight	Moderate	Serious	None	Slight	Moderate	Serious
Population Density of County (per square mile)									
0 to 24	215	38.1	46.1	11.6	4.2	32.0	36.1	24.5	7.4
25 to 49	588	26.2	43.9	22.8	7.1	17.0	35.1	33.9	13.9
50 to 149	360	20.0	32.5	28.3	19.2	14.3	31.3	32.1	22.4
150+	1865	10.1	27.0	37.8	25.2	12.6	28.4	39.4	19.7
		Gamma = 0.44 p = 0.0000				Gamma = 0.19 p = 0.0000			
		Tau C = 0.25 p = 0.0000				Tau C = 0.11 p = 0.0000			
City Population									
Less than 5,000	573	40.7	40.3	14.1	4.9	30.0	35.1	24.4	10.5
5,000 to 19,999	517	21.3	43.7	25.9	9.1	17.5	37.9	33.0	11.6
20,000 to 99,999	669	14.5	37.1	32.4	16.0	11.1	30.2	37.5	21.2
100,000+	1264	4.1	21.7	42.1	32.1	9.2	25.7	42.7	22.3
		Gamma = 0.54 p = 0.0000				Gamma = 0.29 p = 0.0000			
		Tau C = 0.38 p = 0.0000				Tau C = 0.20 p = 0.0000			

[a]The listed numbers are for relationships involving air pollution. The numbers for relationships involving water pollution were slightly different in some cases due to nonresponses, but in all cases by less than 2 percent of the air pollution number.

TABLE 5. Relationship Between Extent of Concern for Pollution in Local Communities and Index of Public Value for Pollution Control, Controlling in Each Case for Density or City Population[a]

County Population Density Controlled							
Extent of Concern for Pollution in Local Community	150+		50 to 149		25 to 49		0 to 24	
	Public Value Index		Public Value Index		Public Value Index		Public Value Index	
	High	Low	High	Low	High	Low	High	Low
Air Pollution								
High	77.3	22.6	77.0	22.9	84.4	15.5	88.2	11.7
Low	58.4	41.5	64.3	35.6	62.1	37.8	67.4	32.5
	Gamma = -0.30		Gamma = -0.19		Gamma = -0.29		Gamma = -0.19	
Water Pollution								
High	77.9	22.0	75.8	24.1	78.8	21.1	81.1	18.8
Low	59.4	40.5	63.5	36.4	59.8	40.1	65.0	34.9
	Gamma = -0.27		Gamma = -0.22		Gamma = -0.28		Gamma = -0.14	

City Population Controlled							
	100,000+		20,000 to 99,999		5,000 to 19,999		Less than 5,000	
Air Pollution								
High	75.8	24.1	83.1	16.8	82.0	17.9	79.8	20.1
Low	52.7	47.1	66.4	33.5	62.4	37.5	62.3	37.6
	Gamma = -0.37		Gamma = -0.23		Gamma = -0.26		Gamma = -0.26	
Water Pollution								
High	76.5	23.4	80.1	19.8	80.0	20.0	76.5	23.5
Low	58.0	41.9	66.4	33.5	60.4	39.5	59.4	40.5
	Gamma = -0.29		Gamma = -0.23		Gamma = -0.27		Gamma = -0.18	

[a]For purposes of presentation, categories have been combined as follows. Extent of concern in local community: High = serious and moderate; Low = slight and none. Public value index: High = 1-3; Low = 4-6. The categories for city population and density are the same as in previous tables. Gammas were calculated on the basis of the original categorizations.

value index. They also point toward the possible effect of the mass media in successfully inducing people to be concerned about pollution in spite of pollution being perceived as a minor problem in their own local community. In any event, it is apparent that the public value for pollution control is not unique to those residing in more densely populated areas, which are presumably more polluted, but is widely shared.

Socioeconomic Status

A recent national poll found that those most willing to pay the price of stopping air and water pollution were the young adults, the well educated, and the affluent (National Wildlife, 1970). This finding might well be expected inasmuch as persons with these characteristics are probably best able to afford the costs of pollution control. The willingness of the young to support pollution control may stem from their concern about the livability of their environment in later life. The type of person represented here is also one whose job is probably less threatened by possible pollution control efforts. It might also be expected that these persons are more attuned to the rather complex arguments about ecological balance, depletion of resources, photochemical reactions in the atmosphere, and accumulation of toxic substances through food chains.

Our findings tend to support the Wildlife Federation study. The three indicators of socioeconomic status were each significantly associated with the public value index (Table 6). An examination of the frequency distributions suggests that the most pronounced differences exist with respect to education. Each additional increment of education is accompanied by a positive change in the public value index.

The association between occupation and the public value index is not as strong or as consistent. A pronounced difference exists between the highest skill category (officials and professionals) and the three middle categories (operatives, craftsmen, foremen; clerical, sales, service; and proprietors, managers). Another major difference exists between the three middle categories and the lowest skill category (laborers). Although not included in the five skill categories because of difficulties in classification, it should be noted that the homemakers and farmers are the least likely to rank high on the public value index, while the students are the most likely.

The association between the third indicator of socioeconomic status (income) and the public value index is even less strong. The public value index tends to increase with income, but only until it reaches the $10,000-$12,000 category. There appear to be no differences between persons in this category and those in the two higher categories.

A possible reason for the existence of the relatively strong associations for each of the above indicators is the effect of age. A total of 711 persons in the sample were 60 years of age or older. These persons can be expected to be located in disproportionate numbers in the lower categories for each of the indicators. Age itself is strongly associated with the public value index (Table 7). The older

TABLE 6.   Relationship Between Socioeconomic Status and Index of Public Value for Pollution Control (Percentage)

Indicators of Socioeconomic Status	N	Public Value Index for Pollution Control					
		1 (high)	2	3	4	5	6 (low)
Highest Level of Education							
1. Some grade school	68	8.8	13.2	23.5	42.7	5.9	5.9
2. Some high school	689	19.7	25.4	21.6	27.3	3.5	2.5
3. Completed high school	799	24.3	25.2	16.5	29.3	2.3	2.5
4. Some college	782	31.0	26.5	16.6	22.5	2.3	1.2
5. Completed college	326	37.7	22.4	12.0	24.2	1.8	1.8
6. Some graduate work	148	43.2	21.6	13.5	17.6	3.4	0.7
7. A graduate degree	211	52.8	16.1	13.6	15.1	0.9	0.9

Gamma = -0.20   p = 0.0000
Tau C   = -0.15   p = 0.0000

Occupational Skill Level							
Students[a]	50	56.0	24.0	10.0	10.0	0.0	0.0
Homemakers[a]	138	15.2	28.9	21.0	28.3	2.2	4.4
Farm (owners, managers)[a]	150	12.4	26.7	17.1	33.3	7.6	2.9
1. Laborers	262	15.6	23.3	24.9	30.4	2.5	3.5
2. Operatives, crafts, foremen	926	26.7	24.1	18.1	26.9	2.0	1.6
3. Clerical, sales, service	544	25.8	26.6	16.2	28.1	2.0	1.3
4. Proprietors, managers	351	25.6	23.3	19.3	24.8	4.0	2.9
5. Officials, professionals	679	45.0	21.7	12.2	18.6	1.3	1.2

Gamma = -0.17   p = 0.0000
Tau C   = -0.12   p = 0.0000

1969 Family Income							
1. Less than $7,000	723	18.8	26.3	23.5	26.4	2.5	2.5
2. $7,000 to $9,999	680	29.0	21.0	15.0	30.0	2.7	2.4
3. 10,000 to 12,999	668	34.1	25.9	13.9	22.2	2.1	1.8
4. 13,000 to 19,999	626	34.5	24.6	15.8	21.7	1.6	1.8
5. $20,000+	254	34.3	21.7	14.2	25.2	3.9	0.8

Gamma -0.12   p = 0.0057
Tau C   = -0.09   p = 0.0000

[a]Not included in calculation of Gamma or Tau C.

the person is, the lower his rank on the public value index. To check for the possible effect of age on the associations involving the indicators of socioeconomic status, the responses of all persons over 60 years of age were omitted and the tests of significance recalculated. The gamma and Tau C coefficients for education and occupation each increased by margins of 0.01 to 0.03. For income, a decrease of 0.01 for each coefficient was registered. Thus, it can be concluded that the associations between the socioeconomic indicators

TABLE 7. Relationship Between Age and Public Value Index for Pollution Control (Percentage)

	N	Public Value Index for Pollution Control					
		1 (high)	2	3	4	5	6 (low)
Age							
Less than 40	1055	40.2	23.9	12.1	22.0	1.0	0.8
40 to 59	1263	24.8	24.0	17.8	27.6	3.2	2.6
60+	711	19.6	24.8	23.5	26.2	3.7	2.4

Gamma = 0.21 p = 0.0000
Tau C = 0.16 p = 0.0000

and the public value index are not greatly affected by the age of the respondent.

Political Identification

The effect of political identification on the public value index for pollution control was also examined. It makes little difference with which of the major political parties the respondent identifies (Table 8). Independents are somewhat more likely to have a higher ranking on the public value index than either Republicans or Democrats. A better predictor of the public value index is how the respondent perceives himself on the conservatism-liberalism dimension of the political spectrum. Self-identification as a liberal or a radical is strongly associated with a higher public value for pollution control.

In summary, it was found that the allocation of more public resources for pollution control efforts is highly valued, ranking second only to crime prevention and control, among the 15 areas studied. The high value is uniformly held by persons living in areas of varying pollution levels. Although persons living in areas where pollution levels are thought to be higher are more concerned about air and water pollution in their local communities, this concern is not translated into a higher public value. But, for individuals, the higher their concern, the higher their public value tends to be. Finally, a person is more likely to hold a high public value for pollution control if he is better educated, highly skilled, more affluent, and considers himself a liberal or radical.

For those concerned with preventing further environmental degradation the findings may suggest both encouragement and despair. The findings that persons do not have to live in areas where pollution is great in order to hold a high value for pollution control

TABLE 8.　Relationship of Political Identification to Public Value Index for Pollution Control (Percentage)

Political Identification	N	Public Value Index for Pollution Control					
		1 (high)	2	3	4	5	6 (low)
Political Party[a]							
Republican	823	28.9	27.1	13.5	26.0	2.2	2.3
Democrat	1103	24.8	23.7	19.6	27.3	2.2	2.5
Independent	1001	34.2	21.5	17.1	23.5	2.7	1.1
Other	73	21.9	28.8	20.6	20.6	6.9	1.4

$$x^2 = 51.4^b \quad p = 0.0000$$
Contingency coefficient = 0.13

Political Orientation[c]							
Conservative	1066	25.0	27.9	13.7	28.1	2.8	2.6
Middle-of-the-road	1324	26.7	23.7	17.8	28.1	2.0	1.7
Liberal	509	42.4	18.9	20.2	15.1	2.0	1.4
Radical	46	45.7	17.4	23.9	8.7	4.4	0.0

Gamma = 0.13
Tau C　= 0.09　p = 0.0000

[a]These categories are the response alternatives provided for the following question: "Which do you consider yourself to be?"
[b]The chi-square statistic is substituted because of the inappropriateness of the gamma and Tau C statistics for categories which cannot be ordered. It is a test for differences. The contingency coefficient is an index of association based upon the chi-square.
[c]These categories are the response alternatives provided for the following question: "Which of these best describes your usual stand on political issues?"

suggests that the development of a favorable social climate for bringing about pollution control may occur without more geographic areas being subjected to the ill effects of pollution. In fact, the social climate appears quite favorable at the present time. It appears that citizens are becoming convinced that pollution is a threat to them even though it is not seen as a local community problem. Encouragement may also come from the finding that those best equipped to provide articulate leadership and resources to action efforts (the younger, better educated, and more affluent) hold the highest public value for pollution control.

Despair may come from the finding that although concern about pollution as a community problem is higher where pollution levels are higher, concern in these areas does not result in a higher overall public value. This could mean that as pollution levels increase, accommodation rather than a change in values takes place. For this reason, increases in pollution levels may not necessarily lead to a more favorable social climate for action efforts.

Past research on the public's sentiment toward pollution control has tended to focus much more on *concern* with pollution as a community problem rather than the *value* held for control efforts. Present findings suggest that if one of these were to be used as a basis to predict readiness to accept control measures, different conclusions would be forthcoming, depending on which was used. This suggests the need to consider both in future research and their relationships to actual behavior.

Future research would also profit from the development of more refined measures of actual pollution level and an exploration of the effects of other variables: for example the mass media, local community identification, and membership in voluntary associations on the development of the public value for pollution control.

REFERENCES

Blalock, Hubert M.
   1960 Social Statistics. New York: McGraw-Hill.
Breslow, Lester
   1956 California Health Survey. Sacramento: California Department of Health, Bureau of Chronic Diseases.
Catton, William R.
   1966 From Animistic to Naturalistic Sociology. New York: McGraw-Hill.
Crowe, Jay M.
   1968 "Toward a 'definitional model' of public perceptions of air pollution." Journal of the Air pollution Control Association 18:154-157.
de Groot, Ida
   1967 "Trends in public attitudes toward air pollution." Journal of the Air Pollution Control Association 17:679-681.
Harris, Louis, and Associates, Inc.
   1970 "The public's view on environmental problems in the state of Washington." Prepared for Pacific Northwest Bell Telephone Company.
Hays, William L.
   1963 Statistics for Psychologists. New York: Holt, Rinehart & Winston.
Kluckhohn, Clyde
   1951 "Value and value-orientations in the theory of action: An exploration in definition and classification," in T. Parsons and E. Shils (eds.), Toward a General Theory of Action. Cambridge: Harvard University Press.
Medalia, N. Z., and A. L. Finker
   1965 "Community perception of air quality: an opinion survey in Clarkston, Washington." Environmental Health Service, Public Health Service Publication No. 999-Ap-10.
Morris, Charles W.
   1964 Signification and Significance: A Study of the Relations of Signs and Values. Cambridge: M.I.T. Press.
Mueller, Eva
   1963 "Public attitudes toward fiscal programs." Quarterly Journal of Economics 77:210-235.
Mueller, J., K. Schuessler, and H. Costner
   1970 Statistical Reasoning in Sociology. New York: Houghton Mifflin.

National Wildlife Federation
  1970 "More for natural resources . . . less for space, defense, and foreign aid." National Wildlife 18:18-20.

Nye, F. Ivan
  1967 "Values, family, and a changing society." Journal of Marriage and the Family 27:241-248.

Rankin, Robert E.
  1969 "Air pollution control and public apathy." Journal of the Air Pollution Control Association, 19:565-569.

Rokeach, Milton
  1968 "The role of values in public opinion research." Public Opinion Quarterly 32:547-559.

Schmid, Calvin F., and Stanton E. Schmid
  1969 "Growth of cities and towns: state of Washington." Washington State Planning and Community Affairs Agency.

Schusky, J.
  1966 "Public awareness and concern with air pollution in the St. Lewis metropolitan area." Washington D.C.: Dept. of Health, Education and Welfare, Public Health Service.

Smith, W. S., J. J. Schueneman, and L. D. Zeidberg
  1964 "Public reaction to air pollution in Nashville, Tennessee." Journal of the Air Pollution Control Association. 14:418-423.

Washington State Office of Program Planning
and Fiscal Management, Information Systems Division
  n.d. Projected Census Statistics for the State of Washington: 1968. Olympia, Washington.

Wilson, William J., and F. Ivan Nye
  1966 Some Methodological Problems in the Empirical Study of Values. Washington Agricultural Experiment Station Bulletin 672, Pullman: Washington State University.

SECTION V
Authority Systems and Decisions About Nature

An understanding of man's approach to the nonhuman environment requires us to consider one of his ubiquitous social tools—human social organization. Man has developed the capacity to extract from his small, naturally occurring social groupings those elements which enable the coordination of behavior among substantial numbers of persons. The mobilization of such numbers on a sustained basis for particular purposes is without parallel among other species, even the extraordinarily effective social insects.

Interestingly, men create social organizations to routinize social decisions, yet often this very routinization becomes maladaptive for dealing with unanticipated problems or changes in beliefs and attitudes. When this occurs, more amorphous, looser associations of people begin to form around a common base of ideas or leaders, or sets of felt needs, in order to challenge prevailing organizational forms. However, to ultimately effect their goal, members of a social movement more and more must shape their desires into the organizational mold that they are attempting to overcome.

Morrison, Hornback, and Warner provide a theoretical analysis of the nature of such processes. They illustrate that environmental issues, as other social problems, are imbedded in the tissue of social decision making and are likely to follow certain regularized patterns observed in other issues. The authors trace how, in the development of a social movement, various pressures combine to alter the nature of strategies, to tighten organizational structure, and, to an increasing extent, to shape the movement into the form of its "enemies."

257

The eventual settling into traditional organizational patterns may be partly accounted for by the conditional constraints which cultural continuity imposes and by the social strata which furnish the largest proportion of participants. Of interest is the authors' suggestion that very often those strata least affected by a particular social problem are those most active in supporting the social movement. (The McEvoy and the Dillman and Christenson studies in Section IV provide further data on this matter.)

Gale's study indicates that there are certain parallels between earlier social movements and the environmental movement. However, he provides an important caution: just as all individuals of a species share certain similarities, they also express certain unique character- istics, and so do social movements. As studies earlier in this volume illustrate, culture is not static but ever changing. This, as the variation introduced by the nature of the issue and the participants in the movement, can provide distinctive patterns. Gale indicates some of the ways in which the environmental movement may be distinctive.

Miller's study of priorities held by members in the hierarchy of established organizational patterns may indicate some of the reasons why the environmental movement may need to be distinctive. The necessarily closed nature of human social organizations is seen in his study. As previously noted, while a culture may be more or less open-ended, the substitution of new meanings within an existing moral order is a complex and long process. However, the same degree of openness to permeability does not exist in human social organizations. A change in the moral order of an organization has direct consequences for the allocations of power, status, and responsibilities among participants. Thus, the organization is always slow to adjust to the process of cultural change through adjustments in the social order. It is not a matter of cultural lag, but a matter of simple power distribution in a society. The same phenomenon occurs in the community when new meanings are granted ready acceptance, only when existing social arrangements are not likely to be drastically altered. It is not the intransigence of the organizational format which delays an accommodation to the emergence of new meanings. It is in the fundamentally different natures of culture, society, and man. Evolution is a time-consuming process, measured in eons, as far as we can presently discern, with reference to biological variations in particular species. So, too, is evolution a time-consuming process with reference to cultural variation. In the world view of ecoactivists, such a time frame for change may no longer seem permissible.

PAPER 13

The Environmental Movement: Some Preliminary Observations and Predictions

DENTON E. MORRISON
KENNETH E. HORNBACK
W. KEITH WARNER

In the last few years there has been a great mobilization of rhetoric, activity, and organization around environmental problems in the United States. Hundreds of new, independent, voluntary citizens' groups have sprung up at local, state, and national levels. Many new efforts have been instituted as parts of universities and of governmental agencies at all levels. Older, established environmental-oriented citizens' groups have recruited large numbers of new members and have developed new programs. Business and industry have shown new interest in these problems, and have incorporated into their advertising an awareness of the sensitivity regarding this subject among the general population. Communications media have given extensive attention to environmental problems.

This greatly increased level of general, societal concern with _Definition_ problems in the realtionship of man and his environment is what is meant by the "environmental movement." It is most visibly manifest in the activities of those persons who mobilize and organize to bring about changes presumed to solve the problems. That is, the movement is most clearly and easily seen in the beliefs and actions of the "environmentalists" and their organizations.

The general focus of this analysis is on the environmental movement: we will describe some of its current characteristics, and

We are indebted to David Chaplin, Riley Dunlap, Richard Gale, Thomas Herberlein and Edward Silva for helpful comments on an earlier draft. We also wish to acknowledge Ariel Maas for newspaper clipping. Our research is supported by the Michigan and Wisconsin Agricultural Experiment Stations; the paper (Michigan Agricultural Experiment Station Journal Article No. 5472) was written while the senior author was in residence in, and supported by, the Wisconsin Station, January–June 1971.

attempt to anticipate some of its developments over the next few years. In doing so, we will give special attention to the environmentalists and their organizations, including the nature of their concerns, the changes they seek, their strategies and modes of organization, and their demographic and attitudinal characteristics.

Most of our notions come from rather general kinds of information available on these groups—for instance, from the public statements of their leaders, from reports in the mass media of their activities, and from literature emanating from the groups themselves. In addition, the two senior authors have been involved in collecting and processing data from a national survey of the mailing list generated by the organization that coordinated Earth Day, 1970. In part our observations come from some general and qualitative impressions gained from these as yet incompletely analyzed data (Environmental Resources, 1971). We have also tried to use some of the accumulated ideas about other social movements to understand this one. Consequently, our ideas are quite preliminary and tentative. We spell out some expectations about the development of the movement over the near future in enough detail, however, that time should soon tell something about their general accuracy.

THE CONCERNS OF THE
MOVEMENT AND THE CHANGES SOUGHT
Historical Context

Concern with man in relationship to his environment is not new in this country or elsewhere. The conservation movement that blossomed vigorously here around the turn of the century has, despite some loss of visibility in the interim, maintained vitality to the present. It has also provided some important organizational and ideological undergirdings for the present environmental movement. In fact, most of the concerns of the present movement can be found among the writings of the earlier conservation leaders, including the diversity of viewpoints on ends and means that characterizes the present movement.

Basically, the concerns that developed as central in the conservation movement were more narrowly circumscribed than are those in the present movement, and the earlier concerns are somewhat more easily characterized. Generally, these concerns can be termed "preservationist" and "utilitarian." Since the beginning of the conservation movement, these two orientations have been at odds with each other, and both have been, in different degrees, at odds with the commercial and other interests that were defined as favoring a laissez faire approach to the natural environment.[1]

The preservationist's concern was to keep unique features of the natural environment from alteration and from use except for man's aesthetic and controlled recreational enjoyment. Preservationist interests were (and are) represented in groups such as the Sierra Club, the National Audubon Society, and the Wilderness Society. The utilitarians, on the other hand, took the view that the features of the natural environment that the preservationists wanted to protect generally should be considered candidates for economic use, but that these natural features must be used wisely, governed carefully, and renewed properly.

The utilitarian position, then, stood between the poles of conflicting interests represented by the preservationists and the "commercialists." Utilitarianism became organizationally manifest in various governmental agencies such as the National Park Service, the Forest Service, and the Soil Conservation Service. Such agencies compromised and mediated—and came into conflict with—the preservationists on one side, and the commercialist interests on the other.

The Current Environmental Movement Concerns

The current environmental movement incorporates many of the traditional conservationist concerns. But it also goes beyond them in at least four important ways.

First, the environmental movement involves a much broader conception of the features of the *environment* that are of concern. The earlier movement was primarily concerned with a rather limited segment of unique, nonrenewable, or only slowly renewable, natural resources—particularly forests, lakes and streams, wilderness and scenic areas, and their natural inhabitants, and, later, at least for the utilitarians, soil and water generally. The environmental movement involves concern with literally all aspects of the natural environment: land in general, all natural bodies and courses of water, minerals, all living organisms and life processes, the atmosphere and beyond, terrestrial and extraterrestrial space, the sun, climate, the polar icecaps, natural silence and natural sounds, and so on. The present

[1]These distinctions are implicit in much of the writing on the history of the conservation movement, particularly in McConnell (1954). See also Nash (1968), Jarrett (1958), and Burton and Kates (1965) for conservation history and analysis.

movement also involves concern with the man-made environment at both macro (urban) and micro (personal space, housing) levels as well as concern with the relationship of man-made and natural environments.

Second, the present movement takes a broader view of *man*. In addition to the earlier, more or less straightforward concern with the problem of the *supply* of natural resources (with *demand* or at least the increasing rate of demand more or less assumed to be constant), there is now great concern with the nature, sources, and amount of man's demand for resources. More specifically, there is concern with how values, institutions, technology, social organization, and, in particular, population, influence the long- and short-term quality and quantity of all resources available. Demand for resources is now considered an important potential variable rather than a constant.

Beyond the broader conceptions of man and of his environment, the current movement also involves a scientifically much more sophisticated notion of the *relationship* of man and his environment than was generally the case in the conservation movement. In the environmental movement this relationship has increasingly come to be understood in ecological terms: the belief that all living organisms, including man, are in complex and delicately balanced systems of interrelationship with each other and with their environments. And, much more than in the earlier movement, environmentalists are concerned that man is upsetting this balance through uncontrolled population growth, resource consumption, and technological development. Whereas the conservation movement was concerned with safeguarding certain natural resources against use and overuse on the general grounds of prudence or an esthetics, the environmental movement includes this but goes beyond it to be concerned with a much broader range of environmental phenomena on the grounds that the violation of ecological imperatives has reached the point where, at best, the quality of life is threatened and, at worst, the long-run survival of man is called into question.

Thus, the fourth point of comparison is that the note of general *crisis* in man's relationship with his environment is greater in degree, broader in kind, and wider in scope in the environmental movement than it was in the earlier conservation movement. Neither the crisis nor the movement is any longer the quiet one Udall (1963) described.

The foregoing is a constructed composite of the general ideology underlying a very broad and heterogeneous movement. One of the central themes running through this ideology is the notion of "ecological balance." However, the rhetoric of the movement provides no firm guidance as to what ecological balance is, or should be, in a highly complex, densely populated, urban-industrial society, nor does the ideology specify the kinds and rates of change necessary to achieve ecological balance. Consequently, the movement organizations vary across a wide spectrum of goals, and the means for achieving these goals are equally diverse.

The proposed solutions to the environmental crisis generally do not involve elaborate, systematic programs for broad societal restructuring around fundamental value, institutional, and technological changes. (A retreatist, rather than a fundamental reformist or revolutionary, variation of such a solution is, however, seen in some rural communes and back-to-the-land efforts by small groups that have organized around an ideology of fundamental social restructuring to achieve ecological balance.) Rather, the focus in the movement thus far has been mainly on increasing environmental awareness and understanding in order to solve more or less specific current and anticipated environmental *problems.* Mostly, the action programs and proposals of both older and newer voluntary movement organizations seek changes to restore and preserve air, water, and land quality, and to lessen demand on resources through population control.

ENVIRONMENTAL COSTS AND CONFLICTS: EMERGING ORGANIZATIONAL STRATEGIES, FORMS, INTERRELATIONS

Although the changes proposed by the environmentalists vary greatly in their specifics, we think the most important common denominator of many of the changes proposed, at least for the short-term course of the movement, is the fact that these reforms will involve substantial economic costs. Such costs include direct expenses of environmental clean-up, higher-priced consumer goods and services, expenses of developing alternative technologies with improved environmental impacts, foregone opportunities that can be translated directly into economic terms, and other costs in convenience, effort, planning, and research.

The environmentalists argue that these costs are justified on the grounds that they are mainly short-term costs, and that the costs of *not* immediately engaging in environmental reform will eventually be much greater than the present costs of such reform. They also argue that many of the costs of environmental degradation are social and psychological in nature, and cannot be interpreted or defended on economic grounds alone. Examples would include consumer frustration and wasted effort involved in product obsolescence, the social costs of the disorganization, mental problems and alienation involved in crowding, and costs to personal development involved in a lack of contact with nature.

The notion of the costs to economic development involved in environmental protection has always been and continues to be apparent in more or less traditional conservation concerns, as, for instance, in the preservation of the forest or the prevention of a wild river from being dammed to provide hydroelectric facilities. But general public realization of the cost implications of the newer, broader environmental concerns, for instance in halting or reducing air and water pollution, is only beginning.

From Participation to Power Orientation[2]

It is also being realized by the environmentalists that individuals, families, firms, and communities will, in general, tend to resist engaging in environmental reforms and bearing these costs voluntarily. In addition to the magnitude of the costs is the fact that the benefits from the changes being proposed are often not immediately or clearly visible, particularly when participation in the changes is not universal. The lack of universality in participation is related to the fact that many of the proposed changes are interpreted simply as matters of value preference rather than as ecological imperatives for survival. Although most people favor clean air and water in the abstract, many people are not convinced that the benefits of environmental reform are worth substantial concrete costs to them, or at least are unwilling voluntarily to undertake the costs to receive such benefits.

Thus, the environmentalists are increasingly turning to *power* strategies (attempting to achieve sufficient group influence to coerce changes) and away from *participation* strategies (educating and urging people voluntarily to make changes).[3] Power strategies played a major role in the conservation movement, but the early phases of the environmental movement have seen a strong—though by no means exclusive—emphasis on participation strategies. Some examples are the many efforts of environmental groups to get people to stop littering, use returnable bottles, use pollution-free detergents, buy nonleaded gasoline, reduce water and pesticide use, tune up their autos, and so on.

These participation strategies are aimed mainly at the level of individual and family consumption decisions. Developing power

---

[2]A theoretical explanation for the changes described in this section is described by Olson (1965).

[3]The power-participation distinction in social movements is theoretically developed in Killian (1964).

strategies involves efforts to coerce change at higher public and private decision-making levels that affect the production and distribution of goods and environmental management. Some examples include: attempts to prevent land developers from desecrating wildlife refuges by litigation proceedings, restraining orders and sit-ins; letter writing, boycott, and law enforcement campaigns to force local industries to reduce polluting effluents; lobbying and other pressures on state and local governments to outlaw the sale of nonreturnable bottles, polluting detergents, certain pesticides; and so on.

It is likely that, as a power-oriented movement, efforts will increasingly aim at the political and legal spheres, in terms of both new laws and stronger enforcement of existing ones, and that such changes will increasingly be national in scope rather than state or local. Since environmental reform will call for greater production costs in many instances, firms in competition will not be willing or able to make the changes individually. Therefore, considerable emphasis will be given to attempting to make it illegal for all firms to pollute so that all producers and consumers will participate in the greater costs. Similarly, it will be more fully recognized that it is insufficient to pressure only one community that is polluting a stream to purify its effluent, and efforts will be made to take a more comprehensive approach toward regulating all communities that pollute a given body of water.

Participation orientation will, of course, continue to exist in the environmental movement, but it seems likely that, in addition to declining in relation to power orientation, participation strategies will take the direction of providing auxiliary support to power strategies by attempting to influence people to change their *values and attitudes* (rather than changing their environmentally relevant individual *behavior*) about the necessity for the public policy and legal changes that are promoted in the power strategies. Indeed, a necessary part of power strategy will be to "bring the people along." In addition, participation strategies will be encouraged by actual and potential private targets as well as public targets of the movement in order to avoid and delay more threatening changes through power tactics—for example, the recycling efforts of bottling companies and the attempts to promote sales of nonleaded fuel.

From Consensus to Conflict

Thus far the environmental movement has been largely a consensus movement, with broad, general support from the population at large. But because conflict will be a concomitant of power usage, we expect it rapidly to become a movement of conflict between the environmentalists and those who stand to suffer economically by the costs of environmental reform.

More specifically, we think those who are the most directly, immediately, and drastically threatened by the costs of environmental reform will be those who will first and most strongly resist the reforms. Such conflicts will first involve the environmentalists with firms that are directly threatened by the increased costs of pollution-free technology or, simply, the technological inability to conform to new environmental quality standards and social norms.

Already we see the beginnings of these conflicts in various places, for example, a headline expressing the view of one threatened employee of the pulp mill considering closure in the face of inability to operate profitably under the costs required to clean up its discharges: "To Hell With Environment" (Madison, Wisconsin *State Journal*, 1971). On a national scale, another example is seen in the reverberations from the congressional defeat of the SST Program in early 1971.

The effects of such economic threats from pressures of the environmental movement might be particularly severe for relatively small, localized firms and for communities that are economically dependent on single firms that are threatened. Nevertheless, the economic threat and reactions will not be, or remain, only localized. Within these contexts the conflicts will occur in political, judicial, and mass media arenas.

To some extent, of course, increased costs can and will be passed on to consumers, particularly over a period of time. However, this doubtless will be a less attractive first strategy than efforts by firms to resist incurring the costs. The limits and risks of consumer price increases are difficult to assess, there are often numerous possibilities for product substitution, and there are problems of differentially enforced local and state environmental quality standards. This resistance will involve battles with, and negative polarization of, attitudes toward environmentalists both prior to, and after, the affected firms engage in curtailed operations, shutdowns, and location shifts.

In addition to price increases on certain products, large blocks of consumers will feel the costs of environmental reform in other ways, probably most immediately in higher utility prices and higher property taxes as communities and firms are required to make technological changes to conform with higher standards for waste, heat, and smoke disposal. Environmental reform might, in fact, have two general costs simultaneously: higher costs for goods and services, and higher unemployment rates.

Most of the economic cost claims of the environmentalists (that short-term costs will bring long-term benefits, and that failure to undertake these costs will result in greater long-term costs) are unassessable on the basis of evidence currently available. The same is true of the noneconomic claims. Many of the latter and some of the former probably are ultimately questions of values and preference—for instance, whether people prefer wild rivers or hydroelectric facilities to run urban air conditioners. As a consequence, many of the conflicts will center around claims and counterclaims regarding the short- versus long-term costs and benefits (economic and otherwise) of environmental reform, as well as around rates at which specific reforms should take place.

Voluntary and Institutional Movement Organizations

A common traditional view of social movements has implied that individuals pursue their movement activities "outside" the context of central institutional structure. Similarly, that view implies that the concerns regarding problems and programs for change lie in voluntary associations rather than in central institutional agencies. This is not an adequate picture of the situation in the present moment. It draws a false dichotomy between voluntary associations and institutional agencies reagrding their involvement in the environmental movement.

Regardless of where the first or major impetus for many of the changes originates, many of the organizations that are concerned about environmental problems and that are working toward changes that will help solve these problems are institutional agencies of various kinds. These include special governmental districts, municipal units of various kinds, local, state and federal agencies of a wide variety, educational institutions, some commercial groups, and so on. Thus we recognize that at least two broad categories of organizations are involved in the environmental movement: (1) voluntary movement organizations and (2) institutional movement organizations. Both types are intimately involved, but play quite different roles in the environmental movement.[4]

One of the reasons that governments have been so quickly and extensively involved in the movement is that many governmental

[4]The distinction we draw is not necessarily intended to imply that some important common processes of growth, decay, change, and influence do not operate in both types of movement organizations, but only to point out that any important differences in these processes are usually missed because most analyses of social movements implicitly dwell only on voluntary organizations (see Zald and Ash, 1966; Devall, 1970b).

agencies already existed for environmental protection, research, control, and development. Thus, governmental agencies in particular are increasingly called upon to provide the substantial research necessary for assessing environmental claims and counterclaims, and for otherwise establishing a basis of information and evidence on which to build legislation, regulations, policies, organizational machinery, and other requirements of dealing with the costs and benefits of environmental management. It is too early to tell how adequately such research will be encouraged, supported, and used.

Governmental movement organizations can thus be expected to increase in the number and scope of their programs, and in power. It is important to note, however, that these agencies will occupy a *range* of points on the continuum between the poles of the more radical varieties of voluntary movement organizations and the commercial and other interests favoring a laissez faire approach to the environment. Also, government agencies *other* than movement organizations are involved in programs closely aligned with commercialist interests. Thus, we may expect that institutional movement organizations will become involved in (1) conflicts with commercialist interests as well as with other govenmental agencies and lower levels of government organization, and (2) coalitions with certain voluntary movement organizations in order to gain the power needed to engage successfully in these conflicts. It is likely, however, that, because of the range of positions occupied by the governmental environmental agencies, they will also become involved in periodic conflicts with some voluntary movement organizations.

Organizational Cooperation and Conflict

The environmental movement is likely to undergo changes in its mode and scale of organization to achieve the power necessary to bring about environmental reform by the strategies outlined above. We expect an increase of relationships and interactions among the voluntary movement organizations. This will take *both* a cooperative form, in which the organizations will form temporary coalitions around particular issues or cooperate toward common objectives in other ways, *and* a conflict form in which ideological and power rhetoric and activities will be turned against each other.

The increase of power orientation will require increased organizational resources, which can be obtained, in part, by cooperation with other environmental organizations. There are issues on which some of the organizations, at least, have common views and objectives, and this makes cooperation possible. The wide range of diversity and the complexity of environmental problems, the extremely complex and fragmented public and private institutional-organization structure that deals with such problems, and the diversity and intensity of individual and group interests at stake, all make cooperation among environmental organizations necessary—if they are to have long-term visible successes. The traditional, powerful conservation groups such as the Sierra Club are taking a leading role in coalescing the potential power of the newer environmental groups.

Environmental issues are not, however, defined similarly by all persons who identify with the environmental movement, and they are not issues around which there will be complete unity or consensus. Some persons who think of themselves as "environmentalists" would not be regarded as such by others with a similar self-identification. The same is true of organizations. Further, there are within the environmental movement great differences of viewpoint over the appropriate methods for problem solving (as, for instance, between participation and power strategies). Therefore, the more the environmental issues move from abstract rhetoric to operational delineation of problems and solutions, the more will agreement subside and conflict emerge within the movement.

Additionally, if economic conditions remain austere, as in 1971, environmental organizations will come into conflict with groups focused on other "causes" in society, such as those associated with poverty, and various minority group problems. The environmental "cause" already is in competition with those salient concerns and the movements that represent them. Adverse economic conditions will likely catalyze and sharpen this competition into conflict.

Organizational Change

The more successful environmental organizations will in time become more "conservative" in significant ways. Two consequences of this will be that such organizations will become targets of criticism by those persons and groups representing a more radical approach to problems, and new "splinter groups" will be formed by persons dissatisfied with these "established" environmental organizations (Warner, 1971).

The general process of the institutionalization of new groups, and the increasing conservatism of successful and enduring groups, is not simply a linear one, however. One of the important consequences of a social movement is to provoke a more "liberal" response from established organizations. Therefore, the outcome of movement organization efforts is not visible simply in their own accomplishments, but also in the responses they bring about from other organizations. The greater emphasis on power strategies by movement organizations should intensify this process of evoking reactive change on the part of established organizations. Consequently, we expect that, at least in the near term, established organizations and agencies concerned with the environment will formulate and pursue more active and liberal policies and programs than they have undertaken in the past. In fact, because established public and private organizations will in general have more resources as well as greater organizational and political power, we may expect the major changes affected by the movement to take place through their auspices. The lengths to which these processes will go will, in the short run, be constrained by economic conditions in the country and by the outcome of organizational competition in representing environmental issues among other issues in the context of national priorities

In the next section of the paper we shall offer some observations that will sharpen and supplement some of the above analysis by examining the causes and composition of support for the environmental movement.

CHARACTERISTICS OF THE PARTICIPANTS
AND CONDITIONS FOR THEIR MOBILIZATION

Who are the environmentalists? What are their characteristics? Who espouses the ideology and claims that the costs of environmental reform should be paid, that the problems require solution now? What are the conditions that tend to mobilize potential participants to awareness and action?

The Participation Paradox and Relative Deprivation

One of the paradoxes of social behavior is the fact that those persons who are objectively most deprived of the goals that social movements seek are not, in general, those who initiate and provide the early support for the movements. Social movements tend to emerge among and receive their early support from those who have come to expect a substantial measure of the movement's goal, but who also have come rather suddenly and unexpectedly to perceive substantial blockage in the existing, conventional routes to reaching or maintaining that goal. These are the persons who develop the special degree and kind of discontent that predisposes them to join with others in the urgent attempts to bring about the changes that are the generic characteristic of all social movements.

Expectations for a given goal (in contrast with simply "desire" for that goal) generally do not develop—first, at least—in those contexts where some persons have not experienced some genuine gains with respect to the goal in question. That is, expectations do not develop in contexts where desires are more or less continuously blocked. Thus, blockage brings the degree and kind of discontent involved in social movement participation only when it is sudden and unexpected. If the blockage were continuously present, an abstract desire would not turn into a concrete and reinforced expectation.

This, in brief, is the essence of the social psychological theory of "relative deprivation" that has been advanced, and in general supported, to account for the participation paradox mentioned above (see Morrison, 1971).

The paradox also operates in the environmental movement, and the theory of relative deprivation would appear relevant for explaining it. For instance, although the United States is a prime locus of the environmental crisis and the environmental movement, it is extremely doubtful that the average citizen in this country (or the average environmentalist!) could be persuaded to trade environments with the average citizen in one of the underdeveloped countries where the inhabitants apparently perceive little or no crisis in the environment. Moreover, many of the policies aimed at "developing" these countries seem likely to produce environmental problems similar to those here.

The above is not stretching the meaning of "environment" but only recognizing that a generic interpretation of the term and of the movement must include *all* aspects of the situation in which we exist, and especially that the causes of the environmental crisis we perceive are at the same time the causes of many environmental features that are generally valued highly. This, in fact, is the essence of the social dilemma and of the social conflicts inherent in environmental reform.

In absolute terms, then, and on balance, most people in this country, environmentalists included, would rate their environment vastly superior to those of persons in underdeveloped countries. The environmental crisis in this country is defined relative to our generally high expectations for our environment and, particularly, relative to the quite sudden and unexpected perception that we have acquired of severe threats to (blockage of) those expectations.

What has brought people to perceive threat or blockage of their expectations? Some of the factors are illustrated by the following. The last decade has witnessed a great outpouring of documentation, warning, and doomsaying on environmental problems from scientists, scientific popularizers, political figures, and others, especially in the writings and pronouncements of Rachel Carson, Stewart Udall, Barry Commoner, and Paul Erlich. Along with this, generally visible environmental deterioration in the form of polluted rivers and lakes and air has taken place in recent years. Further, certain dramatic events such as the Santa Barbara oil spill have received heavy mass media coverage, serving to stimulate general public awareness of environmental problems. Indeed, the mass media capabilities and appetite of this country, and the taste for crises that the mass media nourishes, together with general public and media weariness with campus, war, and racial crises, probably go far toward explaining why the environment has so rapidly become a crucial issue here.

The Paradox, Relative Deprivation, and Social Class

The paradox of the environmental movement having its locus mainly in the country whose environment many other countries would like to emulate is paralleled by the fact that within this country the main participants in the environmental movement are those persons who presently or potentially live in or have access to the better rather than the poorer environments. The movement received its initial impetus from persons of relatively high actual or potential educational status: scientists, teachers, government officials, professionals, and students.[5] The bulk of the movement's base of support remains considerably above the median educational level. Again, it would be hard to persuade these environmentalists, who also generally enjoy relatively high socioeconomic status, to trade their work or leisure time environments with those of the working class, or the ghetto, or the rural poor.

The crisis perceived by the environmentalists is relative to their higher expectations for their environment as compared with the expectations of those of lower socioeconomic status, and it is especially relative to the perceptions of rapid environmental deterioration they have acquired by virtue of their more sophisticated environmental education (formal and otherwise) as well as their broader and more salient exposure to and appreciation of a variety of environmental phenomena. To the extent that people are poor, they can be expected to have only limited concern with such problems as oil on the beaches, the destruction of the wilderness, or the long-term problems of survival threats due to environmental pollution. Most of those with average or less affluence will not have many opportunities to enjoy the beaches or the wilderness, and their concerns must necessarily focus on the day-to-day problems of survival and comfort in, as well as escape from, environments that directly threaten their health, welfare, and security.

Thus, the environmentalists have largely solved certain basic economic problems and have both the leisure and the conceptual

[5]Some quantitative evidence that supports this claim is provided by Harry et al. (1969) and Devall 1970a).

tools (through their formal education and their extent and kind of media exposure) to take a broader, longer-range view of the environment to gain the perceptions of crisis that such a view implies. In addition to perceiving and accepting the necessity of some general loss of societal affluence to bring about environmental improvement, they are personally better prepared both economically and mentally to accept the costs of environmental reforms than those of lower socioeconomic status. The latter group increasingly has high expectations for their environment, but their expectations are probably not as high as the environmentalists, and, moreover, they define an improved environment in exactly the terms the environmentalists are increasingly questioning: higher levels of consumption and material convenience. The less affluent segments of the population also perceive blockage in their attempts to reach their expectations, but such blockages are not defined in broad ecosystem and environmental protection terms as much as in terms of features of social arrangements that keep them from getting a larger share of the pie. Indeed, we expect that certain less affluent segments of the population will come in time to view the costly efforts at environmental reform as a primary source of blockage for their economic expectations.

Threat from Environmental Reform

The conflicts in the environmental movement cannot be expected, in general, however, to take simple, clear, or extreme class lines. In particular, the poorest segment of the population lacks organizational and thus the political power to resist environmental reforms that threaten them economically. Thus it seems likely that high economic threat from environmental reform will bring a coalition of medium- and higher-level socioeconomic groups whose economic fate is largely tied together and who have the organizational ability to wield political power and other forms of power to resist environmental reforms—specifically, organized labor, management, and ownership of threatened industries. In terms of Table 1 this will mean a coalition of those in cells G and H and a conflict of these with those in cells B and D. The latter cells, because of the general correlation of economic and educational status, and because high education is the hallmark of the environmentalists and their supporters, will be the ones from which the environmentalists will be mainly recruited. To some extent environmental issues and the environmental movement will provide professionals and others in biological, health, and resource-related fields of government, schools and colleges, and certain industries with vehicles for upward

TABLE 1. Relationship Between Threat from Environmental Reform, Organizational Ability, and Socioeconomic Status

Threat from Environmental Reform	Organizational Ability (or, Power)	Medium	High
		Socioeconomic Status	
Low	Low	A	B
	High	C	D
		Conflict	
High	Low	E	F
	High	G Coalition	H

individual and group power mobility, that is, ability to move from cell B to cell D.

Some industries, of course, will be in a position to profit by research, development, manufacturing, construction, and servicing related to demands for new environmental technology. Hence our notion of "threat" is necessarily somewhat vague at this point and must undergo considerable operational specification. Nevertheless, it is apparent that certain major industry groups such as automotives, steel, aircraft, lumbering and paper, mining, chemicals, heavy manufacturing, and agriculture are increasingly feeling specific threats of the kind we indicate.

Youth and the Environmental Movement

Thus far little mention has been made of the age characteristics of the environmentalists. Yet it is clear that the movement is heavily supported by the young, particularly students of both college and lower levels. (However, the proportion of youth support in the environmental movement may not be any greater than for other movements such as the civil rights movement or antiwar movement, given the fact that the traditional conservation groups and their supporters have effectively blended into the environmental movement.)

Students, by virtue of the fact that their education is generally aimed at preparing them for middle class and higher status, have high expectations for their environment. They also have acquired a keen sense, through the knowledge they have gained by their direct and indirect contacts with the academic and scientific leaders of the movement, that these expectations are presently or potentially blocked. Their sense of blockage is probably made even more keen by the fact that many aspects of the environmental crisis are protracted for the future—the time period which they, more than their elders, have a direct stake in protecting.

But student participation in the environmental movement also fits in with and reflects student activism generally, particularly its counterculture theme of questioning material acquisition values and technology, as well as reflecting some specific antiwar themes connected with defoliation, environmental desecration, and general national priorities. In addition, white students who have been politically active in other movements have found roles in the environmental movement particularly attractive since their displacement from the civil rights movement (this movement has been taken over by blacks) and the partial decline of the disillusionment with war issues. And, because until recently the environmental movement has been more consenual and less threatening to the American power structure than other student issues, there has been considerable encouragement and facilitation of youth participation in voluntary movement organizations by teachers, administrators, and the older generation generally.

Equally and perhaps more important is the extent to which environmental education has been formally instituted in courses and curricula in schools and colleges. This, in fact, probably represents one of the most profound long-term impacts of the movement. It is doubtful that the high state of youth activism and mobilization around environmental issues that has characterized the last two years (1969-1971) can be maintained for long. However, the fact that students are receiving and will continue to receive a substantial amount of environmental education will provide—as the current 12-22-year-age cohort obtains economic and political influence over time—the condition of "structural conduciveness" (Smelser, 1963) for programmatic, continuing environmental reforms in the future. This group will also provide the basis for rapid revitalization of the movement for more dramatic reforms if and when dramatic environmental crises occur. In many ways, the recent emphasis on environmental education is structurally similar to the shift to heavy emphasis on mathematics, physics, electronics, chemistry, and engineering that followed Sputnik in 1956. Environmental education also emphasizes science, but now the focus is on the biological and life sciences, and is heavily flavored with analysis of the moral and social implications of "ecological imperatives" (see, for instance, Potter, 1971).

Because students have and will continue to have a great awareness of environmental reform, we expect that, as the movement changes from consensus to conflict, students will play active roles in this conflict. It seems likely to us that, in comparison with older persons, youth will press for quicker and broader reforms and by more militant tactics. Thus, youth participation in the movement will be an added source of the general polarization and conflict of the generations, both within the movement and between the movement and those who stand outside as targets. Just as youth will make radical environmental reform demands on society at large, their influence within the movement—both in voluntary movement organizations and in institutional organizations in which they will seek careers will be a radical one. There is, however, some evidence that youth (and, by inference, others) of the far Left have not generally become involved in the environmental movement (Dunlap and Gale, 1971). Indeed, many followers of the far Left, including the young, have viewed the environmental movement as an attempt by the "establishment" to co-opt young people and channel their activism away from campus, war, poverty, and racial reform issues, as well as from "revolution" generally.

For some youth the state of the environment will be just another factor in their general alienation from the larger society. To some extent, then, we may expect this alienation to result in retreat and isolation from the larger society in subcultural developments, probably most notably in communes that will be built around an ideology stressing ecological balance. These efforts, on any scale, can be expected to generate as much antagonistic response in the larger society (especially in the communities where communes are located) as does youth involvement in radical attempts by the environmental movement to bring about social change—particularly since such communes are likely to incorporate youthful attitudes toward sex, the family, drugs, authority, and so on.

Institutional Involvement of Participants

Finally, it is important to recognize that the participants in the environmental movement are not all people "outside of" the institutional agencies whose activities consist solely of campaigns against what those agencies are doing. As indicated earlier, some views of social movements convey the notion that the movement participants are indeed somehow outside of the central institutional structures of society. One traditional view is that they are people without much power or organizational status who must mobilize and organize into voluntary associations in order to bring about some change in the institutional structures or programs (Hoffer, 1951). But whatever may be the case regarding other movements, this is not an adequate picture of the current "environmentalists."

Many of the persons who can properly be regarded as participants in the current environmental movement are employees and officials in a wide variety of governmental agencies, educational institutions, and other societal institutional agencies, as well as members and leaders of various voluntary associations concerned with the environment. Many of them are concerned with environmental problems as a part of their job in these agencies, as well as through their concerns as private citizens and by means of their membership in private associations. This fact, of course, helps to account for the heterogeneity of the participants' characteristics and ideologies. It also means, in turn, that the environmental movement cannot be characterized by only the ideologies and actions of the voluntary associations that have some special identification with the environment, or the speeches and writings of a few individuals.

CONCLUSIONS

What happens to the environment is not simply a consequence of the workings of ecological, technological, or economic forces. The environmental movement is, itself, a significant force in affecting the way environmental problems are defined and addressed.

Our observations are tentative because the movement is very broad and diverse; also, developments in the movement are rapid and far flung. Indeed, the rapid growth of the movement is one of its singular characteristics; another is the rapid extent to which the environmental movement has, in comparison with other social movements such as the labor and the civil rights movements, been influential in effecting changes. The environmentalists have quickly become a powerful force for change in our society.

The general level and scope of mobilization, rhetoric, and activity managed by the environmental organizations will decline from the 1970 level, we think, and will tend to sharpen and focus. Mobilization will periodically rise and fall in response to scattered environmental issues and crises, but in the long run we expect to see the influence and power of these organizations increase.

We regard it as both scientifically and practically important to make observations of the movement even though our data, analysis, and thinking are, to a great degree, incomplete, and thus our statements are in risk of being greatly in error. Sociologists and other social scientists need to be encouraged to research this movement, to use it for developing general knowledge about movements and to use general knowledge about movements to understand it, and we hope our notions will be heuristic in this regard.

We do *not* take the view that movements are mainly, or even substantially, irrational or emotional phenomena, but it would be naive to think that there is not some noteworthy measure of excessive claims in the rhetoric and ideology of every movement. As necessary as such excesses may be to bring about needed changes, they also create excessive reactions to the movement. Polarization occurs as issues, persons, and groups become defined in black-and-white terms, and conflicts ensue as much over pseudoproblems as over real ones. Thus, policy makers inside and outside the movement, public and private, as well as the citizens who must pay for and live with policy decisions, need the views and interpretations of those who are relatively (and we realize *only* relatively) objective and analytic if the problems a movement addresses are to be approached in a way that minimizes the undesirable secondary effects of a new set of problems generated by the excesses of the movement and its targets.[6]

REFERENCES

Burton, Ian, and Robert W. Kates (eds.)
    1965 Readings in Resource Management and Conservation. Chicago: University of Chicago Press.
Devall, William B.
    1970a "Conservation: An upper-middle class social movement: A replication." Journal of Leisure Research 2(Spring):123-126.
    1970b "The organization and integration of the social movement." Paper read at the Annual Meeting of the Rural Sociological Society.
Dunlap, Riley, and Richard P. Gale
    1971 "Politics and ecology: A political profile of student eco-activists." Paper read at the Annual Meeting of the Pacific Sociological Society.
Environmental Resources
    1971 National Directory of Environmental Organizations. Washington, D.C.: Environmental Resources.
Harry, Joseph, Richard P. Gale, and John Hendee
    1969 "Conservation: An upper-middle class social movement." Journal of Leisure Research 1(Summer):246-254.
Hoffer, Eric
    1951 The True Believer. New York: Harper & Row.

[6]We would take as evidence for the truth of our claim that every movement involves excessive claims the fact that some environmentalists who read this will doubtless label us as "against" the environmental movement, or at least as having an antimovement bias. We categorically deny this, of course, and recognize that this denial is also evidence for our notion!

Jarrett, Henry (ed.)
  1958 Perspectives on Conservation. Baltimore: Johns Hopkins University Press for Resources for the Future.
Killian, Lewis
  1964 "Social movements." Pp. 426-455 in R. E. L. Faris (ed.), Handbook of Modern Sociology. Chicago: Rand-McNally.
McConnell, Grant
  1954 "The conservation movement—past and present." Western Political Quarterly 7:463-478.
Madison, Wisconsin State Journal
  1971 "Mill town scared for jobs: 'To hell with environment'" (January 10):1-2.
Morrison, Denton E.
  1971 "Some notes toward theory on relative deprivation, social movements and social change." American Behavioral Scientist (May/June).
Nash, Roderick (ed.)
  1968 The American Environment: Readings in the History of Conservation. Reading, Mass.: Addison-Wesley.
Olson, Jr., Mancur
  1965 The Logic of Collective Action: Public Goods and a Theory of Groups. Cambridge: Harvard University Press.
Potter, Van Rensselaer
  1971 Bioethics: Bridge to the Future. Englewood Cliffs, N.J.: Prentice-Hall.
Smelser, Neil
  1963 Theory of Collective Behavior. New York: Free Press.
Udall, Stewart
  1963 The Quiet Crisis. New York: Holt, Rinehart & Winston.
Warner, W. Keith
  1971 "Structural matrix of development." Pp. 94-115 in George M. Beal, Ronald C. Powers, and E. Walter Coward (eds.), Sociological Perspective of Domestic Development. Ames: Iowa State University Press.
Zald, Mayer N., and Roberta Ash
  1966 "Social movement organizations: Growth, decay and change." Social Forces 44(March):327-341.

PAPER 14

From Sit-In to Hike-In: A Comparison of the Civil Rights and Environmental Movements

RICHARD P. GALE

Will Green Panthers replace Black Panthers? Will "environment" become the major social movement of the seventies, overshadowing the civil rights movement of the sixties? There are several possible ways of assessing the evolution of the environmental movement and predicting its future development. One is to examine it in light of the various classificatory schemes developed for the study of social movements. This task, however, would be both premature, given the relatively early stage of development of the movement, and somewhat difficult, given the lack of systematic data on it. A second approach is to compare the environmental movement with another, more mature, movement. This paper will use such an approach, comparing the environmental movement to the civil rights movement. It will focus on several key elements of the two movements: their early development, the major actors and publics involved, and the evolution of tactics. The purpose of this paper is not to present a detailed description of either movement. Rather, the intent is to look at critical features of both movements with the hope of contributing to a comparative analysis of social movements, and to develop a basis for predicting the future of the environmental movement.

EARLY DEVELOPMENT

In sketching the early development of both the civil rights and the environmental movements, we will look at the nature and scope of the goals sought, the organization base of the movements, and the degree to which each movement attempted to mobilize large numbers of people in support of its goals.

I am grateful to Riley E. Dunlap for his helpful comments on an earlier version of this manuscript. I am also indebted to the Center for Urban Ecology at the University of Oregon for research and secretarial assistance.

Early Development of the Civil Rights Movement

Born in the stirrings which led to the Civil War, the civil rights movement passed through a relatively quiet adolescence during the last quarter of the nineteenth and the first half of the twentieth century, and emerged as a major social movement in the fifties.[1] The 1954 Supreme Court desegregation order and the Montgomery bus boycott in 1955 marked the beginning of the contemporary thrust. There were three notable features of the movement during the early fifties. First, though implicity linked to the larger goal of racial equality, specific "status goals," such as voting rights and public accommodations, were pursued and efforts concentrated on certain localities or regions. Only later did the movement turn to a national campaign focusing on the achievement of "welfare goals," such as employment and housing. The goals of the early movement were well defined, limited, and, some would argue, primarily symbolic.[2] Attainment of the rights to vote and to use public facilities did not represent a significant challenge of the power structure. Further, pursuit of these early goals did not emphasize the similar structural position of other "Third World Peoples" in the United States.

Secondly, when civil rights emerged as a major social movement in the mid fifties, much of the activity was channeled through established organizations, such as the National Association for the Advancement of Colored People. These organizations were influential

---

[1] For historical analyses of the civil rights movement, see Muse (1968). In addition, the volume edited by Franklin and Starr (1967) is useful because it contains many of the documents, speeches, and other materials which have been important in the development of the civil rights movement since the beginning of the twentieth century.

[2] Some maintain that the civil rights movement limited its ability to recruit a mass following by focusing on status goals—public accommodations and voting—rather than on welfare goals, employment, and housing. Others argue that this interpretation is incorrect, and that an early focus on welfare goals would have made it difficult to produce the mass mobilization which was needed later in the movement. "By stressing welfare goals, the civil rights movement would have directed itself to a population which is very difficult to recruit, while failing at the same time to attract middle-class elements, thus missing both the moderately and the severely deprived. Furthermore, because welfare goals are harder to obtain—whites resist more in this area and the locus of power is more diffuse—the efforts of the movement would probably have resulted in failure, creating an image of weakness and thus further inhibiting recruitment. The concentration on status goals may thus have been tactically sound. It permitted the movement to give an image of strength necessary for long-run recruitment" (Pinard et al., 1969). On the other hand, some believe that the civil rights movement "was a dismal failure for the masses of black people," and that, nearly a decade after the Supreme Court desegregation order, the movement "had done little or nothing in the crucial areas of jobs, housing, and education" (Frazier and Roberts, 1969:53).

long before their intensified action brought them to the forefront of an expanded movement. The NAACP dates from 1910, the Congress of Racial Equality from 1942.[3] Some of the organizations which are usually associated with the more activist phase of the movement were not even formed until well after the 1954 Supreme Court decision. The Student Nonviolent Coordinating Committee, for example, was started in 1960, but did not emerge as a viable organization prior to 1964.

Third, achievement of early civil rights victories did not require mass mobilization. In fact, significant victories were attained through the involvement of a relatively few middle-class black professionals who were experienced in the operations of nonviolent voluntary associations. Prior to the Montgomery boycott, and even on that issue, the courts were more important than the street corner.[4]

In summary, the civil rights movement did not begin as a radical, militant movement striving for broadly defined social and economic rights. It was neither led by nor dependent upon disenfranchised and deprived blacks. Although the formal statements of purpose of organizations such as the NAACP and CORE included wide-ranging goals, effort was directed to specific issues, and the tactics used to pursue them were relatively conservative. But with the sit-ins and mass demonstrations of the sixties, directed protest became a central element; new militant organizations began to guide the movement, and poor blacks and white college students became active participants in a national effort to pursue the welfare goals of education, employment, and housing.[5]

[3]For capsule histories of the major civil rights organizations, see the special issue of the Annals of the American Academy of Political and Social Science on "Negro Protest" (1965).

[4]Later conflict over the use of sit-ins to desegregate lunch counters led to the emergence of new leadership. According to Lomax (1962:126), "The sit-ins were a major and decisive victory; they were a rousing triumph over segregation and a clear-cut vindication for the proponents of direct and mass action. And for these very reasons, the sit-ins marked the end of the great era of the traditional Negro leadership class, a half-century of fiercely guarded glory." (Quoted in Frazier and Roberts (1969).

[5]College-student involvement during the early sixties was heralded as a new stage in the movement. "For the first time in our history a major social movement, shaking the nation to its bones, is being led by youngsters. [The Negro revolt] a long-time marching out of the American past, its way suddenly lit up by the Supreme Court decision, and beginning to rumble in earnest when thousands of people took to the streets of Montgomery in the bus boycott, first flared into a national excitement with the sit-ins by college students that started the decade of the 1960s" (Zinn, 1964:1).

Early Development of the Environmental Movement

Two themes in American culture—resource conservation and outdoor recreation—were important in the formation of the contemporary environmental movement. Some of the earliest expressions of concern about resource conservation came from Teddy Roosevelt and Gifford Pinchot around the turn of the century. Alarmed at the wanton destruction of forest, game, and soil, Roosevelt pushed for strong governmental support of a "conservation-wise use" policy which emphasized "rational planning to promote efficient development and use of all natural resources" (Hays, 1959:2). And, in the 1890s, a number of private citizens became alarmed at the despoiling of unique features of the natural environment and at the commercial exploitation of wildlife. In the west, a variety of threats to the new Yosemite National Park prompted several University of California faculty members to join other San Francisco area professionals in forming the Sierra Club in 1892 (Jones, 1965; Nash, 1967). On the east coast, persons objecting to the use of bird feathers and animal pelts in the manufacture of clothing founded the first state Audubon Society in 1895. This "conservation-preservation" emphasis was frequently at odds with the "conservation-wise use" philosophy so often expressed by government resource management agencies. Though advocates of both perspectives considered themselves "conservationists," the preservation and protectionist orientation sharply contrasts with the management and development orientation of the "wise use" conservationists. Arnold Green (1964:16) summarizes the preservation conservationists' philosophy in this way:

> *What may be called the idealistic conservationists reject the recreational-consumption values shared by most of their fellow citizens, and they denounce or deplore the technical and economic requirements of the builders and producers. They implore that what remains of the natural setting be preserved intact, and that as much as is feasible of the already upset ecological balance be restored.*

Outdoor recreation as an important leisure activity was a second major factor in the development of the environmental movement. Especially in those regions which offered high-quality outdoor recreation, persons joined together to enjoy outdoor sports in a group setting and to train others in outdoor skills. On occasion, these groups actively defended a favorite recreational area or other natural resource which was crucial to the continued enjoyment of the recreational activity. Some of the organizations were national—like the Izaak Walton League and Ducks Unlimited—which others were regional or local—like the Seattle Mountaineers, Appalachian Mountain Club, or Association of Northwest Steelheaders. On the west coast, a number of these organizations, some of them almost as old as the Sierra Club, formed the Federation of Western Outdoor Clubs in 1932. Though at times it appears that the more consumptive varieties of outdoor recreation merely accelerate environmental degradation, the contribution of outdoor recreation to the environmental movement is significant in three ways: (1) strong personal attachment to an outdoor-recreation activity can lead to an equally strong commitment to protect those features of the environment which contribute directly to enjoyment of the activity; (2) the emphasis on getting out into nature has made it easier to expose large numbers of individuals to disputed areas through well organized field trips; and (3) since many outdoor-recreation organizations are organized on the community level, environmentally aware members may have some linkage with the local power structure, as well as an intimate knowledge of the threatened resource.

In terms of its maturity as a social movement, the environmental movement is still quite young. The older preservation movement reached a point of major political influence in the "Conservation Congress" of 1968 which created the North Cascades and Redwoods National Parks, halted plans to dam the Grand Canyon, and established a Wild and Scenic Rivers System and a National Trails System (McCloskey, 1968). Though there had been some prior interest in environmental issues which were outside the traditional preservationist concerns (for example, the Sierra Club became concerned with "urban amenities" and thermal pollution in the late sixties), the environmental movement was launched in the fall of 1969 with the nationwide coordination of activities culminating in the first Earth Day on April 22, 1970. If one considers the period 1966-1970 to be embryonic, the movement does bear some similarity to the formative period of the civil rights movement prior to 1955. We will look at the environmental movement in terms of the three factors which were previously used to describe the civil rights movement: the goals it pursued, the extent of its reliance on established organizations at the point of emergence as a major social movement, and the nature of its leadership and degree of mass support.

When early environmentalists did become politically active, they tended to confine their interest to classic preservationist issues, such as preserving a back-country area or blocking a dam, or to equally specific but more urban environmental issues, such as cleaning up rivers and lakes or pressuring industries to install adequate pollution abatement equipment. Organizations like the Sierra Club were primarily concerned with back-country recreation and wilderness preservation, and only occasionally participated in campaigns dealing with air or water pollution, or population.

In a sense, effort was directed toward the achievement of the environmental counterparts of "status" goals rather than "welfare" goals by focusing on the preservation of remote areas and the promotion of a type of recreation enjoyed by a relatively small segment of the population. Such specific goals were of great importance to those intimately acquainted with an area, but did not have the universal appeal of environmental "welfare" goals, such as clean air and water, easy-access outdoor recreation, and readily available birth control information. Many organizations limited their involvement to environmental issues which had a direct impact on the outdoor recreation activities enjoyed by their members. Others were primarily concerned with regional problems, such as the North Cascades Conservation Council, or were issue-specific ("Save the . . .") groups formed to deal with a particular environmental problem.

Although a large number of national, regional, and local environmental organizations have recently been formed, the older, established organizations at all levels played key roles in the early stages of the environmental movement. It is significant that six of the nine national environmental organizations listed in the first annual report of the Council of Environmental Quality were formed prior to 1937.[6] These organizations provide continuity between the older preservationist interests and the emergent environmental movement. Organizations such as the Sierra Club and the Audubon Society thus resemble older civil rights organizations like the NAACP in that they were important contributors to the expansion of the movement. One important difference, however, is that the older environmental organizations have not yet been challenged by more militant groups, in the manner in which the traditional Negro "leadership class" was challenged in the Montgomery bus boycott of 1955 (Lomax, 1962:126).[7] The Sierra Club did experience a potentially disruptive

[6]The nine national environmental organizations mentioned in the annual report are as follows with founding dates given in parentheses: National Wildlife Federation (1936), National Audubon Society (1905), Izaak Walton League of America (1922), National Recreation and Parks Association (1966), Wilderness Society (1936), National Parks Association (1919), Sierra Club (1892), Friends of the Earth (1970), and Zero Population Growth (1969) (Council on Environmental Quality, 1970:215-216).

[7]There have, of course, been a number of criticisms of the environmental movement by the Left. In May 1970, Ramparts magazine published a special issue on ecology. Also of interest are articles by Weisberg (1970) and Fuchs (1970).

jolt in the club's hotly contested election of 1969 (Devall, 1970a). Some believed that without the aggressive leadership of the club's Executive Director, David Brower, the club would decrease its involvement in environmental issues and would return to a society of "companions on the trail." And when Brower resigned as Executive Director and formed a new environmental organization, Friends of the Earth (FOE), some predicted that it would soon outdistance the Sierra Club in membership and aggressive action on environmental issues. At least as of early 1971, there had been little, if any, decline in the influence of the Sierra Club, and relations between the two organizations were complementary, rather than competitive.

The conservation-preservation movement was the epitome of an upper middle class movement, which neither attempted to define goals in a way to make them palatable to a wider, more heterogeneous public, nor made efforts to mobilize mass support for their achievement. Given the relatively high class position of outdoor recreationists who participate in the types of outdoor recreation most closely linked to preservationist concerns (for example, mountain climbing and back packing), and taking into account the fact that voluntary association membership and participation has repeatedly been shown to be related to social class, it is not surprising that members of preservationist organizations were disproportionately drawn from the well educated and professionally employed (Harry et al., 1969; Devall, 1970b). Though at times forging alliances with fishing, hunting, or other mass recreation organizations, the early environmentalists were perhaps even more removed from "the masses" than were those early civil rights leaders who fought for the right to use hotels and restaurants.

The older, established organizations which played an important role in the development of the environmental movement thus resemble many of the older civil rights groups. Few engaged in militant action, and many retained a relatively narrow focus. Few began by pursuing the types of goals which were later to attract mass support, and the leadership reflected a somewhat elitist bias.

THE SOCIAL MOVEMENT ACTORS

All social movements focus on some feature of the existing order as their primary target. Some movements try to block continued evolution or change or attempt to alter the existing order by returning it to some previous state. Most social movements, of course, seek to alter the existing order to achieve some desired future state. Regardless of whether the goal of the movement is "progressive" or "regressive," three groups of actors are involved. One group, obviously, is composed of the most active participants in the movement—those who form a part of ". . . a collectivity acting with some continuity to promote or resist a change in the society or group of which it is a part" (Turner and Killian, 1957:308). Their goal is to alter some feature of the existing order. The second group is made up of those who oppose the efforts of the first group. This group could include members of other, competing groups who also wish to promote change, but it is more often composed of the dominant group within society and simply supports the continuation of the status quo. Because the dominant group opposing change usually appoints a third party to deal with those seeking some alteration of the existing order, these two groups—those who wish to alter the system and those who do not—typically interact with each other via intermediaries or mediators. These mediators or intermediaries constitute the third group of actors, although their autonomy may be limited by the fact that they are acting as agents of a larger, more diffuse, body of individuals who oppose the goals of the movement. We turn now to a discussion of the membership within, and interaction between, these three groups in the civil rights and environmental movements.

The Actors in the Civil Rights Movement

Although at no time in its history did the civil rights movement include all black Americans, it was black America which sought a basic transformation of the existing order. Being the targets of discrimination and prejudice, black Americans were, in simple terms, the racially "oppressed" and "subjugated." The second major group of actors—those who tended to oppose the goals of the civil rights movement—was white America, the numerically and ideologically dominant segment of society. Initially, only some segments of white America were seen as directly perpetuating segregation and discrimination. The majority simply accepted passively the values and practices which contributed to racial divisiveness in the United States. The notion of "white racism," however, enlarged the group which could be defined as "oppressors" and "subjugators" of black America.[8] The third group of actors—the numerous government

---

[8]Until recently, the specific targets of civil rights action have included only a small sector of white America. The primary "oppressors" were judges, businessmen, school superintendents, and hotel and restaurant operators. Such targets were relatively vulnerable and public, and the rest of white America could assure themselves that they were not directly responsible. The accusation of widespread institutionalized "white racism" was thus particularly disturbing, since a much larger segment of white America was thereby held responsible for

agencies and voluntary associations that attempted to play a mediating role—both helped and hindered relations between the two major racial blocks.[9] Police departments, election boards, personnel offices, state and federal employment agencies, and even the Armed Forces of the United States insulated black from white. The balance of power was such that even mediating agencies tended to act on behalf of whites, and to reflect the generalized prejudice against black America. It is, of course, many of these same mediating organizations which have been more recently entrusted with integrating black and white.

In an insightful and provocative essay, Ralph Turner (1969) observes that social movements rapidly gain stature when they are able to define a specific problem or misfortune as indicative of a more generalized "sense of injustice." Black America, together with some prominent whites, has been able to define the denial of social, political, and economic equality as a grave injustice, inflicted by a white America which often used government agencies and voluntary associations to perpetuate racial inequality. In nearly all instances, the injustices were felt by individuals and resulted in a deprived or degraded *human condition*.

The Actors in the Environmental Movement

Three groups of actors are also involved in the environmental movement, although the structure of interaction between them varies from that in the civil rights movement. Participants in the environmental movement constitute the first group of actors. In their desire to transform the existing order, they are similar to black

---

(Footnote 8 *continued*)
discrimination. Many more whites thus became potential targets, being defined as "oppressors." One notes a similar trend in the environmental movement. Government agencies, corporations, and individuals were initially singled out as the major causes of environmental degradation, and action focused on certain companies and agencies. But to be told that "pollution is everybody's problem" directs attention away from specific targets. Such an emphasis diffuses the influence of environmental organizations in that "the public" is a far more elusive target than a pulp mill or the Atomic Energy Commission. Interestingly, some of the major proponents of the "everybody contributes to pollution" idea are industries.

[9]Except for organizations with some history of civil rights activism, few existing voluntary organizations in the black community were in a position to exert much influence. One study found that most associations in the black community were linked to the church and dominated by women (Seals and Kolaja, 1968). In contrast, many existing voluntary organizations have become involved in environmental issues. Many go beyond the mere endorsement of a position or the formation of a "study group," as was the case when white community organizations became "involved" in civil rights.

America. But in terms of a felt "sense of injustice," it might be argued that they have little in common with black America, in that the inconveniences which result from polluted air or loss of a recreation area are hardly of the same magnitude as being unable to obtain adequate housing or maintain a sufficient diet. A different view, however, is that human beings, along with plants, animals, and other features of the natural environment are in fact "environmentally oppressed." Grave injustices have been thrust upon animals, lakes and rivers, and plots of land. Further, the attachment to, or dependence upon, an animal, river, or plot of land is often such that injustices inflicted on these nonhuman targets are interpreted as harmful to their human protectors. This man-resource linkage is reflected in the names of some environmental groups, such as the Defenders of Wildlife, Friends of the Three Sisters (in the Oregon Cascades), and Friends of the Earth. Moreover, it is increasingly apparent that humans are likewise victims of environmental degradation, as in the case of air pollution, and DDT and mercury contamination. Yet, as with the civil rights movement, only a small segment of the "oppressed," or their representatives, become directly involved.

The second group of actors in the environmental movement is "utilizationist" America, whose pursuit of development, growth, laissez faire industrialization, and the conquest of nature have often led to a deprived or degraded *environmental condition*. In terms of the structure of the environmental movement, the role played by the "utilizationist" majority of our society parallels that of white America relative to the civil rights movement. Of course, it is far easier to distinguish black from white, than environmentalist from utilizationist. Even environmentalists may adhere to, and materially benefit from, much of the utilizationist philosophy. Although one may point to polluting industries, manufacturers of environmentally damaging products, and those dedicated to the short-term exploitation of natural resources as specific perpetuators of environmental injustices, relatively few individuals, or organizations, can clearly be considered as always belonging to the "oppressors," or the "oppressed." A foul-smelling pulp mill does, after all, consume wood chips which would otherwise be disposed of in polluting burners.

Between environmentalists and utilizationists stands a multitude of government agencies, ranging from local park and planning commissions to the U.S. Forest Service and Bureau of Land Management. This third group of actors has a more active role in the environmental movement than did their counterparts in civil rights. This is due, in part, to the fact that resource management agencies, such as the Forest Service and National Park Service, were defined as the stewards of public resources. No agency ever assumed a stewardship role regarding black Americans, though some have accused the Bureau of Indian Affairs of exercising a near-stewardship of American Indians. Paralleling the agencies charged with the protection of minority rights, government agencies which are theoretically "keepers of the environment"—claiming to give primacy to the protection of the environment—may actually operate on behalf of those exploiting the environment, as some civil rights agencies became vehicles for the continuation of discriminatory practices. Further, those who are targets of agency decisions, or others who may wish to argue that a specific agency decision is environmentally damaging, may find it difficult to challenge the autonomy and decision-making processes of the agency.

In both movements, the interaction between the three groups of actors (oppressed, oppressors, and mediators) is a function of many variables. Two obvious ones are the relative degree of challenge to the status quo implicit in the goals of the movement—whether activitists are pursuing "evolution" or "revolution"—and the actual posture of the "mediating" agencies—whether they merely reflect the perspective of those in power or, at the other extreme, advocate the views of the oppressed. A third variable is the amount of support given to activists in the movement, either through increased involvement by unorganized segments of the oppressed, or by the occasional defection of a sometime oppressor to the side of the oppressed. Influencing each of these variables is the relative balance of power among the three groups. And one of the best indices of the state of this balance is the form of tactics used in the movement.

EVOLUTION OF TACTICS

The dominant strategies or tactics of a social movement have often been viewed as indicators of its maturity. Laue (1965), for example, refers to legalistic, educational, and activist strategies in describing the civil rights movement. In a general discussion of social movements, Cameron (1966:121) refers to nonviolent, quasi-violent, and violent methods of social action. Analyses of changing tactics usually attempt to assess the extent to which a movement has become violent in its tactics and revolutionary in its aims. More specifically, analysts of changing social movements are interested in answers to two questions. First, how does a movement utilize, and respond to, those types of strategies considered legitimate for proponents of evolutionary social change? Second, at what point does a movement utilize protest, either violent or nonviolent, as a dominant strategy? The first question taps the degree of commitment to legitimate and institutionalized channels for action, and the second relates to the transformation of the movement "from politics to protest."

Tactics in the Civil Rights Movement

The transformation of the civil rights movement is clearly reflected in progressive changes in its dominant strategy. The legalistic emphasis in the early stages of the movement was part of what Bailey (1968:28) has termed a "middle class politics" strategy. Litigation, lobbying, and seeking change through elected officials were major activities for the NAACP and the Urban League (American Academy of Political and Social Science, 1965). Though the use of these tactics reflected some naive assumptions about uniform enforcement of laws, the responsibility of elected officials, and the power of the ballot box, such "establishment" or "within the system" activities did facilitate the development of white support outside the South, and made it difficult for opponents to discredit civil rights action by labeling it violent or illegal. Moreover, utilization of tactics long accepted by much of the white majority made it easier for whites to directly participate in the civil rights movement, although some argue that such participation may have contributed to cooptation of black leaders and organizations by white activitists.

What Wilkinson (1970:17) calls "activism," in contrast to the previous legalistic strategy, characterizes the second major stage of the civil rights movement. During the first part of this stage, sit-ins were used by *CORE* and the *SCLC* to force negotiation on a number of very tangible demands. In the latter part of this stage, 1961-1963, nonviolent methods expanded to economic boycotts, freedom rides, and mass demonstrations (Frazier and Roberts, 1969). It was in the third stage, beginning with the Birmingham riots of late 1964, that violence became an increasingly common component of civil rights action, although it was often provoked by the reaction of police and others entrusted with preventing violence.[10]

The contemporary civil rights movement retains some commitment to "middle class politics," though increased militancy characterizes other segments of the movement. In addition, there is little agreement on whether the civil rights movement has made any substantial gains (for example, welfare) for the majority of black Americans. Jackson (1960), for example, documents the impact of the civil rights movement on social change which was beneficial to black Amer-

[10]For a discussion of the evolution of black militancy see the chapter on this subject in Skolnick (1969:125-176).

icans in all major social institutions. Frazier and Roberts (1969), on the other hand, maintain that "the civil rights movement was a dismal failure for the masses of black people . . . in part because it looked upon the problems of black people as being solvable merely by acquiring civil rights."

Tactics in the Environmental Movement

Tactically, or strategically, the environmental movement in 1971 resembles most closely the civil rights movement in 1954. That is, most past environmental action has been well within the confines of middle class politics. Although there are some radical ecology groups, such as Berkeley's Ecology Action, and occasional militant acts such as those of the University of Texas students who were arrested for their attempt to save several trees from the bulldozer's blade, litigation, lobbying, and electioneering continue to be the dominant forms of environmental action. However, the environmental movement does differ from the older conservation-preservation movement in terms of its more generalized concern, its overall intensity, and its increased emphasis on specific varieties of middle-class politics, such as legal action. Yet, the use of middle class politics by environmentalists differs in significant ways from their use in the civil rights movement of the fifties.

First, the legal framework governing most environmental and resource management agencies provides for the management and protection of resources in a manner which is, theoretically, responsive to the public interest and supportive of resource conservation. Inspection of the bureaucratic vocabulary of many agencies would lead one to this conclusion. The Multiple Use Act directed the Forest Service to administer lands to provide "the greatest good of the greatest number in the long run" (for a critique, see Behan, 1967). The "primary project purpose" of specific projects undertaken by the Corps of Engineers was not designed to exclude other benefits. Further, review and appeal procedures are well defined, and, in addition, many agencies look to citizen advisory boards as possible linkages to a vaguely defined "public." Because of the existing administrative framework, and because the stewardship of such a large portion of the total physical environment rests with government agencies, environmentalists are far more likely to focus on the behavior of government agencies than were civil rights activists.

Further, the existing legal framework for the protection of the environment is considerably more comprehensive than that which dealt with civil rights in 1955. The Wilderness Act, federal air and water pollution statutes, and the National Environmental Policy Act are all on the books, and, while pressure to pass new laws and strengthen existing statutes continues, much more energy is directed to the adequate enforcement of existing laws. Civil rights activists, in contrast, could rely in the early days on a minimally tested section of the U.S. Constitution and assorted state and local statutes, many of which did little to protect minority rights. The task for civil rights activists was thus to press for additional legislation, and to direct attention to private bodies which violated existing statutes. For environmentalists, although legislative change is important, monitoring and challenging the administrative decisions of public agencies is perhaps a more critical task, since, within general policy guidelines, there may be dramatic variations in implementation, particularly in the extent to which agencies themselves directly monitor private exploitation and development of public resources. The existing framework of environmental law also has implications for the use of legal action by citizens and citizen groups. In the civil rights movement, government agencies brought suit against individuals and other government agencies, and individuals took other individuals to court for the violation of specific statutes. Use of the courts in civil rights matters was hampered by an "individual case emphasis," the frequent inability of the courts to issue an injunction, and excessive delays in bringing cases to trial (Lockard, 1968). In the environmental movement, on the other hand, in addition to suits brought by government agencies, individuals and organizations have brought action against government agencies for alleged violations of both environmental law and administrative procedure. Frequently, environmentalists are able to obtain injunctions which halt the environmentally damaging practice while the issue is being adjudicated. And, as a further extension of legal power, several states now permit individuals and groups who do not have a direct economic interest to bring suit against any other "legal entity" which fails to provide for the "protection of the air, water and other natural resources and the public trust therein from pollution, impairment or destruction" (statement from Michigan Environmental Protection Act, quoted in Pearce, 1970:123). The total impact of existing environmental legislation is that, at the present time, it is more effective to go into court than into the streets.

A second major difference in the use of middle class politics is in the relative importance of national, state, and local legislation. Legislation dealing with both civil rights and environment exists on all three levels of government. But in the case of civil rights, although states and communities adopted a number of antidiscrimination laws dealing with employment, housing, and public accommodations, it was usually the federal statutes which set the tone for change, and often superceded more restrictive, and at times unconstitutional, state and local laws. The situation for environmental legislation differs in several ways. First, although some state and local laws do apply to features of the environment which are under federal jurisdiction, the division of labor is somewhat clearer than for civil rights legislation. The U.S. Forest Service has no control over forests owned by the individual states, although states may apply their own water quality standards to bodies of water which pass through federal lands. Second, where state and local laws do conflict with federal environmental statutes, as in the case of radiation standards, it is usually the state or local laws which are more favorable to the environment. Environmentalists may thus have far better success with state and local legislation than did civil rights activists. Where the trend is to delegate more and more environmental control to states and localities, environmentalists may find that middle class politics go a long way in obtaining desired legislation.

A third major difference in the use of middle class politics by the two movements is that blocking or delaying a proposed alteration of some aspect of the natural environment is frequently hailed as a victory by environmentalists, whereas the delay or postponement of an action was seldom similarly defined by civil rights activists. On many environmental issues, to delay, or to preserve the status quo, may yield precisely that: the preservation of a remote area or flowing river. Although delay is not always a victory for environmentalists—as in the case of pollution legislation—it is much more difficult to point to issues for which delay would have been defined as a victory by civil rights activists. Not implementing school desegregation plans, preventing the adoption of employment quotas, or blocking the use of federal funds for urban core projects are not positive achievements, except when the proposed action has the potential for reversing prior achievements (see Geschwender, 1968b:134). Convincing legislators that an environmentally unsound bill should be killed, or that an agency should "go slow" on a planned development, is far more susceptible to the varieties of middle class politics than trying to obtain passage of a fair-housing ordinance or a minority program.

The differential consequences of delay or opposition as a primary tactic in the two movements may be indicative of other, more fundamental differences. Two frequent observations about environmentalists are relevant. First, the environmental movement has, to a considerable extent, continued to maintain the nonpartisan posture of the preservation movement. It was almost impossible to determine if preservationist campaigns were Democratic or Republican, and it was equally difficult to place them on any sort of liberal(now radical)-conservative political continuum. Except in the South, it was the Democratic party, particularly its liberal wing, which was far more likely to endorse civil rights goals. A second observation might suggest that environmentalists are nearer the conservative pole. An antidevelopment, preservationist philosophy implies a more conservative perspective. Though certainly some environmentalists advocate rapid and dramatic social change, it is often environmental activists who accuse society of going too fast, while in the civil rights movement it was more often society which argued that civil rights activists were moving with excessive haste.

These fundamental differences between the two movements in both orientation toward change and linkage with the political system may be related to the social conditions which gave rise to the two movements. In a systematic review of five major hypotheses about the rise of social movements, Geschwender (1968b) maintains the Davies' "rise and drop" theory and the "rising expectations" theory are particularly helpful in understanding why blacks became involved in the civil rights movement. He goes on to point out that these two perspectives, along with the "relative deprivation" hypothesis, all deal with dissatisfaction resulting from a comparison of actual conditions with anticipated conditions. Movements which result from such pressures are typically oriented toward the future, and tend to be "progressive" or leftist. Not all movements, of course, result from this type of pressure. The "downward mobility" hypothesis, for example, suggests that action is triggered by a decline in an individual's objective material position. While this hypothesis may add little to our understanding of the civil rights movement, it does, however, explain why wealthy Saskatchewan wheat farmers acted as agitators in stimulating unrest and protest activities among other farmers (Geschwender, 1968b:130). The "downward mobility" perspective describes dissatisfaction which results from comparing present conditions with a better situation in the past, and is thus more likely to be associated with "regressive" or rightist protest movements (Geschwender, 1968b:134).

It might be argued that the conservation-preservation movement resulted from a perceived decline in an objective environmental condition. Campaigns to preserve areas stress the need to allow individuals to experience nature "as it was," before widespread settlement and development. There is an emphasis on "returning to nature" and "restoring" the natural qualities of an area. Even efforts to protect birds and animals aim at the replenishment of "endangered species." Thus, in the portion of the environmental movement which represents an extension of the older conservation-preservation movement, a more conservative perspective may prevail, and blocking or delay may be a successful tactic. However, in that portion of the movement which aims at new environmental policies, such as industrial siting and the use of comprehensive land-use planning, one would expect to find a future orientation, somewhat greater in similarity to the civil rights movement in terms of the political orientation of activists, and a willingness to seek innovative solutions to pressing environmental problems.

In terms of the evolution of tactics, then, the civil rights movement can be characterized as having employed a number of different tactics throughout its recent history. Civil rights moved from politics and litigation to protest in the late fifties and early sixties. Some sociologists (Rustin, 1965) maintain that in the late sixties the movement went from protest to politics, although others would cite the emergence of the Black Panthers, black separatism, and a linkage of black activists with the New Left, as evidence of a further move from politics to protest. One cannot yet point to a similar evolution in the environmental movement. There has been no "protest era" in the environmental movement. Speculation regarding the future of the environmental movement constitutes the next section.

THE FUTURE OF THE ENVIRONMENTAL MOVEMENT

Green Panthers, "eco-tactics," hike-ins, and a growing radical ecology are, together with an occasional advocacy of violence, indications of disillusionment with the older middle class politics. Citizens who are compelled to take political action because of an environmental crisis, as occurred in Santa Barbara during the oil spill in 1969, may find that traditional tactics accomplish little. Harvey Molotch (1970:141) quotes one irate citizen, the president of an international research and development firm with headquarters in Santa Barbara:

> "We are so God-damned frustrated. The whole democratic process seems to be falling apart. Nobody responds to us, and we end up doing things progressively less reasonable. This town is going to blow up if there isn't some reasonable attitude expressed by the Federal Government—nothing seems to happen except that we lose."

Yet, in spite of similar feelings of frustration on the part of many environmentalists, no environmental equivalents of Stokely Carmichel or Martin Luther King have stepped forward, no militant environmental organization has successfully challenged the leading role played by established organizations such as the Sierra Club and the Wilderness Society, and no environmental campaign has brought about a nationwide mass mobilization. Further, the environmental movement has remained nonviolent, using public pressure as a means of forcing negotiation on specific environmental issues.

It would be naive and simplistic to merely predict that the environmental movement will follow much the same evolutionary path as the civil rights movement. Furthermore, there are some general trends in the level and type of political involvement in the United States which suggest that the future tactics and strategies of environmentalists may develop in a somewhat different direction. One of the most important is what James Laue (1970) calls "the Movement." The Movement refers to the variety of separate "causes," such as civil rights, peace, Red Power, and Student Power, that have evolved into a generalized challenge of economic and political control in the United States. Two features of the Movement are directly relevant to an understanding of the future of the environmental movement: the proliferation of new voluntary organizations, often formed for a single purpose by individuals with little experience in such organizations, and the emergence of protest as a legitimate political tactic.

Escalation of the environmental movement has meant a rapid growth of both issue-specific and generalized ecology action organizations. Though some of the organizers and activists in these new groups are veterans of either preservationist organizations or other voluntary organizations, with only indirect contact with environmental concerns, many are political novices. The instrumental, political goals of the group may be lost in "technical" questions (for example, the color of a bumper sticker), and goals may become redefined so that the major task of the group is to raise funds for some ill-defined campaign. Organizers may lack experience in dealing with environmental agencies, the press, and industrial interests. And, infiltration and cooptation by industry and government agencies are typical of many recently formed environmental organizations.

Yet, one positive consequence of this growth in the number of different organizations is the involvement of new participants and the emergence of new constituencies. In the older conservation-preservation movement, most interorganizational linkages were limited to preservationist organizations which shared an interest in a remote area or animal species. Preservationist campaigns could count on few additional allies; for example, mass recreation organizations objected to the exclusionist philosophy implied in proposals which would "lock up" vast areas. Industrial and professional organizations typically did not define the issue as relevant to their interests, or opposed the "antidevelopment" emphasis of the preservationists. But the extension of the movement to the urban environment, and the use of increasingly elaborate political and legal tactics, has produced alliances between quite diverse organizations on specific issues. Organizations which had little interest in preservationist campaigns now become actively involved. Farmers may join environmentalists to fight a nuclear power plant which would turn agricultural lands into cooling ponds, though these same farmers may oppose environmentalist efforts to restrict the open burning of grain stubble. Industries which are the target of local restrictions may lobby with environmentalists to make sure that restrictive legislation is at least statewide.

A strategy which stresses operating through voluntary organizations, and which seeks political power through organizational alliances, can have quite diverse effects on the movement and on the individual participants. On the organizational level, environmental organizations may be unwilling to pay the price of a series of temporary alliances with nonenvironmental organizations. One such price would be entering subsequent campaigns with a greater willingness to compromise. Further, continually forming new organizations requires the commitment of scarce resources to essentially internal matters. To the extent that the environmental movement relies on publicity and operates essentially in a public arena, the continual formation of such organizations may assist specific environmental campaigns. But where action involves negotiation with government agencies or fighting environmental battles in the courts, merely adding the name of one new organization to a list of supporters may accomplish little. Though each new organization does attract new participants, much of the organizational effort may be carried on by persons active in a number of other environmental organizations, and by those who are actively involved in nonenvironmental groups. The impact of these "multiple memberships" will depend on the range of the total constellation of memberships for the individual. Compounding memberships in like-minded environmental organizations could further reinforce one's commitment to the goals of the movement. On the other hand, if an individual's memberships included organizations with a minimal interest in the environment or with a philosophy which was sometimes in disagreement with that of most environmental organizations, the effect of these "cross-cutting" memberships could be to restrain the individual's involvement in the environmental movement.

As the civil rights movement expanded, several voluntary organizations such as White Citizens' Councils, were formed specifically to oppose the goals of the movement. Given the widespread acceptance of many of the goals of the environmental movement, few organizations have been formed to contest specific goals, although many existing organizations have directly challenged environmental organizations. Industry associations, professional groups, such as the Society of American Foresters, and local and regional economic development groups have been especially active. Anti-civil rights organizations often matched the tactics of the organizations they were opposing. "Nonviolence [in the civil rights movement] brought forth the same retaliatory modes of action with only slight modifications observed in the emergence of organizational structures such as White Citizens Councils" (Wilkinson, 1970:18). When antienvironmental organizations appear, they sometimes take the form of "pseudo" citizens groups which try to appear as representatives of the general public (Krizek, 1970). The timber industry and representatives of the Forest Service joined together to form the now defunct "Public Resources Council of Oregon." The campaign of the Citizens for the Orderly Development of Electricity *(CODE)* which unsuccessfully supported a proposed nuclear power plant in Oregon included the publication of a list of some fifty "subcommittees," such as "Engineers for Nuclear Power" and "Physicians for Nuclear Power." While these organizations may confuse the public and some public officials, they do not pose a major threat to the environmental movement. They find it difficult to endure as a "pseudo" citizen's group, particularly since their leadership is often more skilled in operating industrial or trade associations than in guiding a grass roots, voluntary citizens organization. Along with the proliferation of voluntary associations, environmentalists will continue efforts to increase the accountability of government agencies and public officials. Since accountability and vulnerability to "public" influence typically go together, environmentalists often see themselves as representing a vaguely defined "public" or constituency of an agency or elected official. Demanding the establishment of citizens advisory boards and overseeing the operation of such boards, "show-me" visits to existing and planned projects, and the systematic "watchdogging" of legislators, legislative committees, and government agencies are a few of the tactics which are increasingly employed.[11] Such tactics, however, remain those of an "outsider"; the basic power relationship between environmental organizations, keepers of the environment, and economic interests often remains unchanged. In the civil rights movement,

> ... *the early legal victories of the NAACP, the successful feats of non-violent resistance, and the violent confrontations have had the combined effect of altering many of the structural relations between blacks and whites and of increasing the vulnerability of the whites and of increasing the vulnerability of the white power structure and various "gatekeepers" of discrimination to certain kinds of pressure tactics (Wilson, 1970:43).*

Though federal agencies are increasingly vulnerable to environmentalist pressure, more general structural relationships which typically operate against the environmentalist remain unchanged. Increasingly militant environmental action has the potential for altering the relationship, and thus increasing vulnerability and accountability. It could also produce a "utilizationist backlash."

It is most difficult to predict the extent to which the environmental movement will become more militant. At best, one can only suggest some of the factors which would increase the probability of it adopting less legitimate, more violent tactics, and to also indicate some reasons why the environmental movement might not evolve in this direction. Most supportive of a trend toward the use of violent tactics would be a spillover from tactics used in other "causes." To the extent that "the environment" becomes linked with other basic social problems, and where this linkage is reinforced through the participation of more radical groups, such tactics could become part of the environment movement as well. Thus far, however, the radical wing of the environmental movement has remained relatively undeveloped. A second factor is the simple increasing legitimacy of protest as a means of political action. The scenario for protest is becoming well defined, and groups can

---

[11]To effectively challenge the policy or decision of an agency usually requires one to move beyond a general critique. Doing so often requires expertise, and such expertise is often available only to the agency or to economic interests. Few nuclear engineers do not have some type of linkage with the Atomic Energy Commission. In the environmental movement, most experts are either employed by, or in other ways linked to, agencies and industries. Such was not the case with civil rights. Most experts in the field of race relations were academics, and thus the needed expertise was somewhat more accessible.

effectively predict the type and scope of response to the protest. Where an environmental issue is of a nature to demand maximum public awareness, use of protest might be the effective channel. A third factor is the increasing frustration which results from the use of traditional means of political action: what appear to be environmental "victories" later turn out to be little more than government agency propoganda, while a simple victory in the legislative realm turns into a defeat due to lack of funding or to administrative action. The best example of this was the blocking of the Timber Supply Act in Congress, and the later administrative order to dramatically increase the cutting of soft wood on government lands.

Several other factors suggest that the environmental movement will not become violent. A primary reason is the social and educational background of the contemporary participants in the movement. Upper middle-class professionals are unlikely to resort to violent tactics on behalf of the environment. Should the major participants in the movement dramatically change, however, and should the movement be guided instead by those less integrated into the existing social order, the environmental movement could quickly move beyond the limits of traditional political action. In the past, the relative homogeneity of the leadership in the environmental movement was due, in part, to the close linkage between active participation in certain types of outdoor recreation and an intense interest in the environment. Formerly, mountain climbing, back packing, and excursions into remote areas appealed primarily to well-educated professionals. As different segments of the society come to participate in these forms of outdoor recreation, we might expect a greater heterogeneity among those participants in the environmental movement who are attracted to the movement by a love of the outdoors.

A second factor which would tend to limit the potential for violence in the environmental movement is that violent political action may be uniquely inappropriate to many of the causes espoused by environmentalists. That most civil rights issues are political is readily apparent, and, once politicized, civil rights activists may find themselves endorsing, or using, ever more violent tactics. It is much less apparent that saving forested valleys, protecting animals, and cleaning up rivers are also basically political problems. Environmental activists may resist "making it all political," and may fail to understand the political interests involved in attempts to preserve a remote area. Given some reluctance to become overtly politicized, environmentalists may be expected to further resist the use of more dramatic political tactics.

Third, the likely targets of environmental action are such that societal reaction to violence could be far more harsh than was the case for those instances in which violent action was utilized by civil rights and peace activists. Though there would be little difference in a riot over a racial incident and an environmental rally which became a riot, the targets of directed violence would be quite different. In the civil rights movement, frequent targets were police stations, government offices, and allegedly exploitive small businesses, usually located in the ghetto. Military installations on college campuses, and selective service offices, were prime targets for antiwar protesters. Should the environmental movement engage in directed violence, two categories of targets are likely. Just as blacks became unhappy with the performance of such mediators as police departments, environmentalists could conceivably become as discontent with the environmental counterparts of the police: the keepers of the environment. In this case, air and water pollution authorities, agencies charged with administering federal lands, and even local zoning or planning commissions could be defined as viable targets. Public reaction to an explosion in a local forest service office, for example, would be somewhat more pronounced than a similar action directed against a police department. A high level of risk is expected of police, but not of forest rangers.

When civil rights activists went straight to the oppressors, they rarely went beyond the confines of the ghetto. It was difficult to point to specific *producers* of discrimination, although some did look to some large corporations for their failure to hire blacks. Specific producers of pollution are far more identifiable. In many communities, several large corporate polluters are responsible for much of the pollution, other than that attributable to vehicle exhaust. Pulp mills, chemical and petroleum-processing plants, saw mills, metal refineries, and even large subdivision developers could become targets of directed violence. Such action would probably be defined as tantamount to industrial sabotage, and the negative reaction would be dramatic and intense. It is for this reason that it is doubtful that many environmentalists would endorse this type of action, either against the keepers of the environment, or against those more directly responsible for environmental degradation.

Finally, environmentalists may look at the accomplishments of the civil rights movement, and wonder if the use of violence played an important role in those accomplishments. They might also speculate as to whether the accomplishments would have been greater with even more, or substantially less, violent action. If experienced environmentalists are moved to consider the use of violence, it will no doubt be at a point of tremendous frustration and fatigue. At that point, withdrawal may be as appealing a response as further escalation of tactics. Less experienced environmentalists may bring a quite different perspective. If they come to the environmental movement with experience in what they define as the successful use of more dramatic tactics in other movements, or the Movement, they may more readily endorse the application of these techniques to environmental campaigns.

This paper has explored only a few of the many possible points of comparison between the civil rights and environmental movements. Many questions about the environmental movement await the collection of systematic data. And, while the environmental movement is much in the limelight, one must not forget that the civil rights movement continues to fight on behalf of an ever-widening segment of our society, which now includes American Indians, Mexican Americans, students, and welfare recipients.

The most critical question about any social movement is whether it will endure long enough to have a significant impact on society, defined as an alteration of the balance of power in the society. Cooptation, fatigue, and deliberate attempts to turn activists away from dealing with potential structural change were common problems in the civil rights movement, and may be expected to provide similar challenges for environmentalists. As the environmental movement matures, its successes will be measured, in part, by the extent to which it can remain in that middle ground between the despair which usually leads to inaction and withdrawal, and the frustration which would suggest that Green Panthers offer the only viable alternative for action.

REFERENCES

American Academy of Political and Social Science
    1965 "Negro protest." Annals 357(January).
Bailey, Harry A., Jr.
    1968 "Negro interest group strategies." Urban Affairs Quarterly 4(September):26-38.
Behan, R. W.
    1967 "The succotash syndrome or multiple use: A heartfelt approach to forest land management." Natural Resources Journal 7(October):473-484.
Burton, Ian, and Robert W. Kates (eds.)
    1965 Readings in Resource Management and Conservation. Chicago: University of Chicago Press.
Cameron, William Bruce
    1966 Modern Social Movements: A Sociological Outline. New York: Random House.

Council on Environmental Quality
  1970 Environmental Quality: The First Annual Report of the Council
      on Environmental Quality. Washington, D.C.: Government Printing
      Office.

Devall, William B.
  1970a The Governing of a Voluntary Association: Oligarchy and
      Democracy in the Sierra Club (unpublished Ph.D. dissertation).
      Eugene: University of Oregon.
  1970b "Conservation: An upper-middle class social movement: A
      replication." Journal of Leisure Research 1(Summer):246-254.

Eynon, Thomas G.
  1970 "Black equality: revolution from the movement." Sociological
      Focus 3(Spring):23-32.

Franklin, John Hope, and Isadore Starr (eds.)
  1967 The Negro in Twentieth Century America. New York: Random
      House.

Frazier, Arthur, and Virgil Brothers
  1969 "A discourse on black nationalism." American Behavioral Scientist
      (March-April):47-49.

Fuchs, Sanford
  1970 "Ecology movement exposed." Progressive Labor 7(Sep-
      tember):50-63.

Geschwender, James A.
  1968a "Civil rights protest and riots: A disappearing distinction." Social
      Science Quarterly 49(December):474-484.
  1968b "Explorations in the theory of social movements and revolutions."
      Social Forces 47(December):127-135.

Green, Arnold W.
  1964 Recreation, Leisure, and Politics. New York: McGraw-Hill.

Harry, Joseph, Richard P. Gale, and John C. Hendee
  1969 "Conservation: An upper-middle class social movement." Journal
      of Leisure Research 1(Summer):246-254.

Hays, Samuel P.
  1959 Conservation and the Gospel of Efficiency. Cambridge: Harvard
      University Press.

Jackson, Maurice
  1969 "Civil rights movement and social change." American Behavioral
      Scientist 12(March-April):8-17.

Jones, Holway
  1965 John Muir and the Sierra Club: The Battle for Yosemite. San
      Francisco: The Sierra Club.

Krizek, John
  1970 "How to build a pyramid: A kit of PR tools helps win San
      Francisco's approval for a new high-rise office building." Public
      Relations Journal 26(December)17-21.

Laue, James H.
  1965 "The changing character of Negro protest." Annals of the
      American Academy of Political and Social Science 357(Janu-
      ary):119-126.
  1970 "The movement: Discovering where it's at and how to get it."
      Urban and Social Change Review 3(Spring):6-11.

Lockard, Duane
  1968 Toward Equal Opportunity: A Study of State and Local
      Antidiscrimination Laws. New York: Macmillan.

Lomax, Louis
  1962 The Negro Revolt. New York: Harper & Row.

McCloskey, Michael
  1968 "Four major new conservation laws: A review and a preview."
      Sierra Club Bulletin 53(November):4-10.

Molotch, Harvey
 1970 "Oil in Santa Barbara and power in America." Sociological Inquiry 40(Winter):131-144.
Muse, Benjamin
 1968 The American Negro Revolution: From Nonviolence to Black Power, 1963-1967. Bloomington: Indiana University Press.
Nash, Roderick W.
 1967 Wilderness and the American Mind. New Haven: Yale University Press.
Pearce, Susan
 1970 "Michigan environmental protection act of 1970." Journal of Law Reform 4(Fall):121-134.
Pinard, Maurice, Jerome Kirk, and Donald Van Eschen
 1969 "Processes of recruitment in the sit-in movement." Public Opinion Quarterly 33(Fall):355-369.
Rogin, Gilbert
 1969 "All he wants is to save the world." Sports Illustrated (February)24-29.
Rustin, Bayard
 1965 "From protest to politics: the future of the civil rights movement." Commentary 39(February):25-31.
Sax, Joseph L.
 1970 "Legal redress of environmental disruption." Architectural Forum 132(May):50-51.
Seals, Alvin M., and Jiri Kolaja
 1968 "A study of Negro voluntary associations in Lexington, Kentucky." Phylon 25(Spring):27-32.
Skolnick, Jerome H.
 1969 The Politics of Protest. New York: Simon and Schuster.
Turner, Ralph H.
 1969 "The theme of contemporary social movements." British Journal of Sociology 20(December):390-405.
Turner, R. H., and L. M. Killian
 1957 Collective Behavior. Englewood Cliffs, N.J.: Prentice-Hall.
Weisberg, Barry
 1970 "April 22: A one day teach-in is like an all day sucker." Liberation 15(April):38-41.
Wilkinson, Doris Yvonne
 1970 "Tactics of protest as media: The case of the black revolution." Sociological Focus 3(Spring):13-22.
Wilson, James Q.
 1961 "The strategy of protest: Problems of Negro civic action." Journal of Conflict Resolution 5(September):291-303.
Wilson, William J.
 1970 "Revolutionary nationalism 'versus' cultural nationalism: dimensions of the black power movement." Sociological Focus 3(Spring):43-52.
Zinn, Howard
 1964 SNCC: The New Abolitionists. Boston: Beacon Press.

PAPER 15
The Allocation of Priorities to Urban and Environmental Problems by Powerful Leaders and Organizations

DELBERT C. MILLER

THE PROBLEM OF PRIORITIES

In industrialized society, urban problems rush upon us in great number and in great intensity. The awareness of our plight can induce melancholy or pessimism in those easily defeated, and anger or violence in the frustrated who seek quick action. Sober counsels pledged to a peaceful pattern urge a drastic change in national priorities. As defense expenditures eat away the national substance, these counsels point to the urgent problems of race relations, unemployment and poverty, education, housing, urban renewal, public education, crime, transportation and parking, planning and zoning, roads and streets, drug abuse, family planning, child welfare, health problems, civil rights, police-community relations, tax revision, restructuring of government, status of women, prison reform, buttressing of private education, labor relations, judicial reform, student protests, and university reform. This long list is not exhaustive. Note that environmental problems were omitted. A supplementary list could include noise abatement, sign control, air pollution, water pollution, depletion of natural resources, waste disposal and litter, illuminary and olefactory pollution, protection of open land, conservation of beaches and wilderness areas, protection of birds and wild animals, beautification of city and countryside, provision for parks and playgrounds, new cities, amenities for pedestrians and bicyclists, and so on.

John W. Gardner has written: "There is so much that needs to be done. There are so few who are properly organized to do it. We must end the war. We must bring about a drastic change in national priorities. We must renew our attack on poverty and discrimination. And we must keep at it until we build a new America."[1]

The focal points for urban action are usually identified as government (federal, state, and local), private organizations, and urban leaders. Each is asked to intensify their activity in ameliorating, remedying, or solving urban problems. Each response awakens the need for greater resources and effort. Any new allocation among the competing priorities arouses new contests. Both organizations and leaders are caught in the whipsaw of competing demands.

THE OBJECTIVES OF PRIORITIES RESEARCH

This research report is directed at some crucial questions which explore the nature of competing problems and the responses to them by government, private organizations, and urban leaders in Megalopolis. In 1968 research was begun in the northeastern seaboard of the United States, embracing the five principal metropolitan areas of Boston, New York, Philadelphia, Baltimore, and Washington, D.C. The aim was to examine power and decision making affecting urban and environmental problems. Resources for the Future, Inc., supported the research. The supporter wanted to know how decisions were made relative to environmental problems and whether a regional attack on these problems was commensurate with political and social inclinations of leaders in Megalopolis. The research required answers to questions such as: Who are the business, labor, political, religious, and civic leaders of this region? What are the urban problem interests and activities of these leaders? What priority do they give to environmental problems? Are leaders working together on urban problems, from Boston to New York to Philadelphia to Baltimore to Washington, D.C.? A similar set of questions was developed for private and governmental organizations. What organizations in Megalopolis which deal with urban and environmental problems are most powerful? What are their urban problem interests and activities? What priority do they give to environmental problems? Are organizations working together on urban problems in megalopolis? These research questions have been carefully studied and reports made (Miller, 1970).

In this paper special attention is paid to new research findings. The first survey of 400 powerful leaders in Megalopolis was made in May 1969. A resurvey of the same 400 was made in July 1970. The

---

[1]From a nationally circulated letter urging the formation of a new, independent, nonpartisan organization to be known as *Common Cause* (1970). The organization reported approximately 200,000 members on its rolls in 1971.

object of the resurvey was to find out if the increased public attention to environmental problems had brought about changes in the urban problem interests and activities of leaders. An accompanying objective was to explain any changes that might have occurred. In the discussion that follows, these interests and activities of leaders are described. A parallel analysis of organizations is made to examine organizational priorities. We shall begin with an analysis of the powerful leaders because it is widely believed that leaders are the major agents for change. Organizations, both private and public, regard themselves as instruments of collective interest groups and wait for leaders to legitimate action and provide initiative and support for organizational policy. This assumption heightens a need to identify the powerful leaders. This is not a simple task and research must begin here.

THE IDENTIFICATION OF POWERFUL URBAN LEADERS

An initial decision was made to select leaders from five occuptional groups—business, labor, government, religion, civic, and civil rights. These are the same five groups used by the National Urban Coalition. It is assumed that these groups of leaders are important in building a consensus of public opinion.

The identification of leaders began with a documentary search followed by interviews of selected judges in each of the five principal cities—Boston, New York, Philadelphia, Baltimore, and Washington, D.C.[2] The number of leaders sought was based on the size of the cities and the size of the occupational groups. Once the five leadership groupings of the five major metropolitan areas were established, a matrix of 25 cells was constructed. The matrix is shown as Table 1. It designates the number of leaders chosen to

[2]The documentary search included a review and evaluation of Easterners who were nominated as top national policy-making leaders as shown in Floyd Hunter's study, *Top Leadership, U.S.A.,* University of North Carolina Press, 1959, pp. 196-198: policy board members of the Business Council, National Industrial Conference Board, Committee for Economic Development, National Urban Coalition, Urban America, National Alliance of Businessmen; Eastern leaders on U.S. government commissions concerned with such matters as urban problems, civil rights, civil disorders, sources of violence, equal opportunity, and intergovernmental relations; Wealthiest Easterners, heads of 25 top corporations, national political contributors, Eastern trustees of the major foundations, national labor leaders active in urban problems, the most influential Eastern educators as listed by Theodore White in *Halls of Power* and Daniel S. Greenberg in *The Politics of Pure Science,* influential civil rights leaders in social welfare, 11 mayors and governors in the major cities and states of Megalopolis.

TABLE 1. Urban Influential Leader Matrix

Metropolitan Areas	Business	Labor	Political- Governmental	Clergy	Civic Civil Rights	TOTAL
New York	20	10	10	10	20	70
Philadelphia	10	5	5	5	10	35
Boston	5	5	5	5	10	30
Baltimore	5	5	5	5	10	30
Washington	5	10	5	5	10	35
NUMBER	45	35	30	30	60	200

occupy each cell.[3] Two hundred leader spaces were allocated. The plan was now to locate those urban-oriented leaders in Megalopolis who should be able (1) to work with other business, labor, religious, and civic leaders; (2) to commit themselves to the work required; and (3) to be able and willing to influence others. A brief description of this search for leaders will be made after a final design decision is reported.

The cost and effort to provide a replication population of leaders appeared relatively small. In the search for the most influential leaders it was obvious that many leaders would be named and those who received a lower number of nominations could easily be included in the research inquiries of the study. The plan was to fill the influential leader matrix with the 200 individuals receiving the greatest number of votes. These leaders would in all probability be of great influence because they would be drawn from large reservoirs of leadership. In order to maintain a proper perspective on the leader populations, the first group winning the greater consensus was called key leaders; the second group, top leaders. Altogether, 400 leaders were sought and similar research inquiries were planned.

Interviews were held with judges in the five urban areas. The senior investigator lived successively in Washington, D.C. (three months), New York (three months), Philadelphia (two months), Boston (one month). Only Baltimore was omitted as a place of residence. It was reached from Washington, D.C.

[3]Size was considered as an important variable, so the New York area was given a maximum representation. Philadelphia was given just one-half as many leader spaces as New York. Boston, Baltimore, and Washington were given further reductions in leader spaces because of their smaller sizes. The largest total representation of leaders in any grouping was given to civic and civil rights leaders because their grouping is very broad, encompassing educators, civil rights leaders, association and foundation leaders, and social welfare leaders.

Final Evaluation of Leaders by Selected Judges

Judges were selected on the basis of their knowledgeability and their range of contact. An ideal judge was one who knew all the persons he was asked to judge and could add names of influential leaders not yet on the list. Judges were drawn from the following sources: national and local Urban Coalition officers; association and foundation officers in labor, civil rights, education, business, government, and religion; company public relations and urban affairs officials; and retired influentials. In each city a panel of five to ten judges were selected and asked to evaluate various groups of leaders. The 200 leaders winning highest consensus were selected as key leaders; the 200 of slightly lesser consensus were retained as top leaders [4]

SURVEYS OF URBAN-PROBLEM INTERESTS AND ACTIVITIES, (1969, 1970)

In May 1969 a 10-page questionnaire was sent to all 400 leaders. From all leaders the final return after two follow-up requests was 178 or 45 percent (key leaders, 50 percent; top leaders, 39 percent). Each wave of these returns was carefully examined for any evidence of bias. No significant deviations were detected. In July 1970 a resurvey of the same leaders was initiated to examine the interests and activities in urban problems with the same format as that of the first survey. After one follow-up, final results showed that 167 responded or 42 percent (key leaders, 40 percent; top leaders, 44 percent). Of the initial respondents in May 1969, 114 or 75 percent responded again in July 1970. The responses of the repeaters were carefully checked against the total sample and no significant deviations found. The representativeness of the two samples are accepted as true patterns of the larger populations.

A copy of the questionnaire as set in July 1970 appears on p. 311. It is identical to one part of the 10-page questionnaire sent in May 1969 except for the questions added on changes of interest and activity.

Survey Findings

The profile of urban-problem interests for key and top leaders is shown as Figure 1. The profile reveals the interests of 178 key and

[4]Senators, congressmen and U.S. cabinet officers were not included (as is the practice of the Urban Coalition) because these leaders are seen as those who must be pressed to move toward new priorities. Governors, mayors, and local political leaders were included as persons capable of exerting pressure on federal decision makers.

EASTERN LEADERSHIP AND ENVIRONMENTAL QUALITY STUDY

DEPARTMENT OF SOCIOLOGY — INDIANA UNIVERSITY

BLOOMINGTON. INDIANA 47401

Sponsored by:
RESOURCES FOR THE FUTURE
1755 Massachusetts Avenue, N. W.
Washington, D. C. 20036

URBAN PROBLEM INTEREST AND ACTIVITY PATTERN OF CIVIC LEADERS IN THE BOSTON TO
WASHINGTON URBAN REGION

(1) Check problems in which you have the highest personal interest.
(2) Mark the <u>one</u> problem on which you are currently working most intensively.

(Note: The researcher is seeking to estimate the degree of interest and current
activity pattern of civic leaders engaged in urban problems. All information is
confidential and each person will be recorded by code number.)

I have Most Interest In	I Am Currently Working Hardest On	URBAN PROBLEMS
		1. AIR POLLUTION
		2. CONTROL OF LAWLESSNESS AND CRIME
		3. IMPROVEMENT OF PUBLIC EDUCATION
		4. WATER POLLUTION
		5. IMPROVEMENT OF TRANSPORT, TRAFFIC MOVEMENT, AND PARKING
		6. WASTE (GARBAGE, LITTER, AND DUMPS)
		7. IMPROVEMENT OR ELIMINATION OF POOR HOUSING: RE-BUILDING OF CITIES
		8. IMPROVEMENT AND MAINTENANCE OF ROADS AND STREETS
		9. PLANNING AND ZONING OF LAND; PRESERVATION (OR IMPROVEMENT) OF PARK AND OTHER NATURAL AREAS; BEAUTIFICATION
		10. UNEMPLOYMENT AND POVERTY
		11. RACE RELATIONS
		12. OTHER (PLEASE SPECIFY)

Have you changed your interests and activity in urban problems during
the past year? [ ] yes   [ ] no

If yes, what interests and activity have changed?

INTEREST CHANGES   ACTIVITY CHANGES
(Indicate by number of problem
as shown above.)

_____   _____

_____   _____

How would you account for these changes?

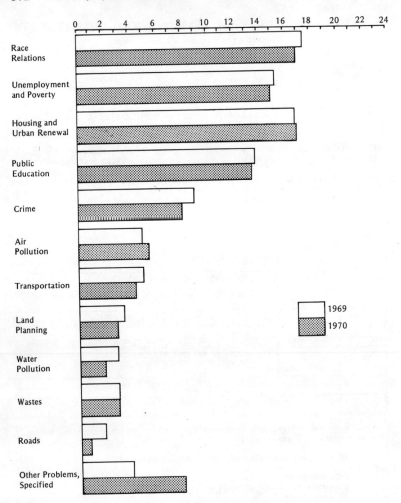

FIGURE 1. Urban Problem Interest Profile of Key and Top Leaders (N = 178) of Megalopolis in May 1969, Compared with the Resurvey of Key and Top Leaders (M = 167) in July 1970 (Scale in Percentage[a])

[a]Each percentage is based on the number of interests marked for each problem over the total number of interests marked for all problems (in 1969, f = 561; in 1970, f = 505).

top leaders of Megalopolis in May 1969 and compares a similar profile based on the resurvey of these leaders in July 1970. Note that major attention in both 1969 and 1970 was concentrated on race relations, housing, unemployment and poverty, public education, and crime. Air pollution, water pollution, and waste ranked in sixth, ninth, and tenth position among the eleven problems. We may conclude that *no significant change in interest patterns occurred in the 14-month interval.* The increase in a variety of other interests develops some significance as the survey of activities subsequently reveals. Figure 2 is based on the answers to the instruction: "Mark the *one* problem on which you are currently working hardest." In answering, some did not restrict their activity to one problem and named more than one in some cases. The resulting pattern of activity shows the true focus of effort. The results again indicate that *there is a high similarity of activity in the 14-month period.* The big five remain: race relations, unemployment and poverty, housing, public education, and crime. However, there is slippage in race relations and unemployment and poverty, while activity in housing increases. Activity in environmental problems is low, with water pollution, air pollution, and waste in eighth, ninth, and tenth rank. Notice a large rise in *Other problems* and that the list given below the figure is a long one. When asked if they had changed their interests and activities during the past year, 17 percent said yes and 83 percent said no. This was followed by the questions: "What interests and activities have changed? Why?" Some conclusions can be drawn about the changes.

1. The intrusion of additional problems weakens activity in the older problem areas.
2. Activity in race relations and unemployment and poverty has been weakened.
3. Activity in housing and crime problems has increased.
4. Activity in environmental problems has certainly not been heightened by all the public attention centered on them.

Reasons for Changes in Interest and Activity

Those relatively few leaders who did say that their interests and activity had changed during the past year were asked to account for these changes. Their answers reveal six different reasons.

1. Appointment to positions which arouse and focus new interest and activity.
2. Search for a different, more comprehensive approach rather than specific concentration on a given "project."
3. Disenchantment, frustration, blockage.

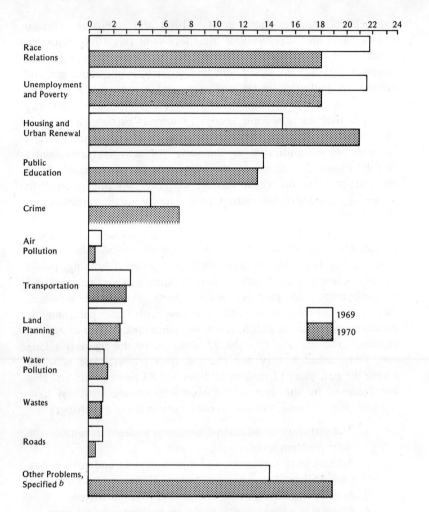

FIGURE 2. Urban Problem Activity Profile of Key and Top Leaders (N = 178) of Megalopolis, May 1969, Compared with Resurvey Responses of Key and Top Leaders (N = 167) in July 1970 (Scale in Percentage^a)

^{a}Each percentage is based on the number of activity checks (the problem a respondent is currently working hardest on) over the total number of activities marked for all problems (in 1969, f = 277; in 1970, f = 239).

^{b}Other Problems, Specified: Reduction of drug abuse; family planning; economic development of ghetto; private university education; child welfare; creation of new value system; developing new cities; black participation in decision making; educating black youth; peace; consumer education; guaranteed work and income; alienation of youth; revision of New York State social service law; police brutality; preparation of cities for absentee ownership; black

4. Awareness of new problems and a shift of interests to them.
5. Increase of intensity in the listed problems which arouses new interest but not necessarily activity.
6. New activity aroused in the listed problems due to change of public attitudes and support.

Examples and discussions of each of these reasons for change will be set forth. They are important, for if changes in environmental priorities are to occur, then these reasons for change provide an understanding of how priority shifts come about.

Appointment to Positions

This reason seems to dominate all others. A growing number of professional full-time and lay voluntary positions now draw more persons directly into contact with responsibilities for urban problems. A professional who takes a full-time position of responsibility cannot duck his new responsibility. Nor can lay persons do so even though they work only part time. The following illustrations all show that involvement arouses new interests and commitments.

> *"My interest and activity changed with my appointment to the Justice Coordinating Board last year. That has focused my efforts on control of lawlessness and crime."*

A respondent who has shifted from activity on urban health problems to civic legal assistance for indigents says,

> *"[I] left law practice where I was chairman of the board of Municipal Hospital to become Dean of University Law School."*

A respondent describes his addition of housing and crime to his activity in race relations.

> *"I received an opportunity to participate in a specific housing project in my immediate area. This has motivated my addition of housing. And, awareness of local crime has added control of lawlessness and crime."*

(Footnote *b continued*)
liberation by any means necessary; structure of social services; improvement of education for government services; improving urban government; improvement of Philadelphia and Pennsylvania political climate; establishing a reading center for a public elementary school; health problems; recreation research, planning, and programming; civil legal assistance to indigents; status of women; student activism and judicial process in the university; legalization of abortion; civil liberties; court administration and judicial practices; vocational rehabilitation; police-community relations; training for prison inmates; private elementary and secondary education; labor relations; regional organization for air, water, and mass transit; and so on.

Another respondent reports that he changed his interests to water pollution and race relations.

> *"I became interested in water pollution because it is business-related. I became involved as a speaker bringing about government changes. My work in race relations began when I accepted a regional chairmanship for the National Alliance of Businessmen. The immediate demand is to find a meaningful program and result."*

And still other respondents—

> *"My interest and activity was changed to court administration and judicial practices when I became professionally employed to study the criminal courts. My interest had been previously aroused by newspaper investigations of poor and illegal judicial procedures."*

> *"As I learn more through my activity as chairman of the League of Women Voters in my city, I have become more interested in transportation. Transportation is the main two-year program item of the League, continuing now into its second year."*

Search for a Different, More Comprehensive Approach

A number of leaders report changes or shifts in emphasis due to a desire for more effective answers to urban problems. Many report their discoveries of overlap and interrelatedness of problems and want to find more effective ways to get to basic or root causes. The illustrations express this common yearning and searching.

A respondent who has shifted to economic development of low-income areas says,

> *"I have been searching for a more comprehensive and effective solution to economic problems. I am working more intensively now and seeking wider understanding and acceptance of this approach."*

A religious leader writes that he has shifted his interest on the housing problem from being most active in discrimination in housing to working for an increased housing supply. He says,

> *"As a white activist, I feel that nondiscrimination in housing and race relations will proceed on its own, if minorities take a more militant role and improve their income earning and if housing supply increases for low-income groups and for the elderly. The indifference of the white middle class to damage*

and dangers of excessive suffering and hardship requires inten-
sive united action for planning and massive federal and state
investment in housing as a public utility."

Another respondent reports that he is working hardest on the structure of regional government.

"I feel that one of the greatest needs in this region is the
establishment of area-wide governments, and an objective
analysis of entities, the taxes imposed, and, based on this
analysis, an approach to an improved system of government
operation, services, and taxes. If environmental problems are
to be licked, we better know what level of government would
be responsible for 'what' and the funds needed to support
them."

"I believe there has been some change in the quality of my
interests—but no shift in checking the listed categories. I am
more interested now in the interrelationship of problems and
how citizens can grasp and express the wider implications of
the immediate concrete issue presented. My growing interest
in environmental quality turns not to listed items, but to how
we can clarify and simplify our values so that we use less of the
valuable, natural resources and thus have less to clean up."

"I have changed from working directly on urban problems to
political activity as the way to bring about social reform."

A religious leader writes,

"My interests have not changed substantially; however,
a greater interest is now being shown by us in dealing with
problems of our own people in urban areas (that is, control
of lawlessness and crime) and, as well, a new interest in the
white ethnic American working class. In essence, there is less
focus on black problems specifically, and greater focus on a
broader range of problems and for other minority groups as
well."

Disenchantment, Frustration, and Blockage

The three psychological causes are well depicted one by one in the three following excerpts.

"My faith in the system responding to the needs of black
people is drastically changing. I have real fears regarding police
repression and genocide of black people."

This respondent is working hardest on unemployment and poverty, race relations, and public education but reports most interest in police-community relations.

A respondent reports that he has shifted from a direct agency attack on housing through the Model Cities program to a college position developing new nonprofit, modular housing and delivery systems and is assisting in changing the "exploitative housing market."

> *"I left the Model Cities program. I found the city political system impossibly rigged by putrid, political interests."*

Another respondent switched to work on race relations.

> *"I am less active in the problems of unemployment and poverty because of restrictions inherent in the recession."*

Awareness of New Problems

The rise of new problems (or old problems with new public awareness) has been cited as one of the compelling drains of time and energy from the so-called list of major problems. A few illustrations indicate how shifts to these new problems produce new concentrations of interest.

> *"My interest has shifted from crime and race relations to drug abuse. I believe that the drug situation, which has moved from the ghetto to the colleges and now to the secondary schools, is the most serious threat to the country."*

A respondent writes,

> *"Abortion has become a 'hot' issue in D.C. and I am involved in it actively."*

Intensification of Listed Problems

A few leaders express new interests in many of the listed problems but do not indicate activity. Environmental problems tend to fall in this category. New interest is reported most commonly in air pollution, water pollution, and waste—in that order. But activity does not follow.

> *"I have increased interest in air pollution."* But respondent reports: *"I am currently retiring early from present job to work full time on housing."*

Another respondent, who is working hardest on improvement of public education, says he has added control of lawlessness and crime to his list of interests—other interests are unemployment and poverty, and race relations.

> *"I have added control of crime because of the increase in lawlessness and crime."*

A respondent who is working hardest on unemployment and poverty says that he has a new interest in air and water pollution. When asked to account for these changes, he writes,

> *"Improving knowledge about pollution."*

New Activity in Listed Problems

It would be hoped that broad public encouragement would increase awareness and support. Only one leader mentions this as a cause for his change. Perhaps others are influenced more than they have realized by this factor.

A leader writes that he has shifted his interests from purely local issues to problems of overall environment. When asked how he accounts for this change, he writes,

> *"Greater public support of environmental problems."*

Summary of Reasons for Change

These six reasons for change suggest that personal interest and activity is aroused in many different ways. Some hypotheses may be proposed to account for changes.

1. Interest arousal must precede activity investments.
2. Position responsibilities at the professional or lay level greatly increase activity on urban problems.
3. The psychological states of disenchantment, frustration, and blockage induce shifts of interest.
4. Shifts from concentrated attention on "projects" to a search for a broader, more comprehensive approach will accompany individual efforts to solve urban problems as time elapses and his efforts are applied.
5. New problems as they intensify will drain efforts away from the formerly high priority problems even though these problems are not solved or remedied.

A final question must be asked. Why do patterns of interests and activity remain relatively stable? This is an important question because it applies to the overwhelming majority of leaders. Unfortunately, the leaders were not asked that question. However, a few did volunteer information. Their answers included these reasons:

1. Position requires attention to all urban problems or
stabilizes attention upon those they have responsibilities for.
2. Interests are stabilized on national priorities which are
perceived as relatively stable.

Perhaps they would have added (if asked) that they have made
commitments and do not see any reason to change them. Some of their
responses follow.

A business leader writes of concern with all urban problems,
saying,

*"As a large corporation, we are working with local, state,
and federal governments in all phases of urban problems."*

A labor leader who has been working hardest on unemployment
and poverty says he has put greater emphasis on housing needs and
solutions, but he writes,

*"As a labor union official my major activity in poverty and
unemployment is most time consuming and my time does not
allow for major activity in other areas."*

Another respondent says,

*"Running a Chamber of Commerce, as I do, all of these
urban problems have been major interests for several years.
They don't change—they intensify."*

A labor leader writes that his interests have been stabilized on
public education, housing, and jobs because

*"National priorities should be education, housing, and jobs.
I see no reason to change."*

IDENTIFYING POWERFUL
URBAN-ORIENTED ORGANIZATIONS

The most powerful urban-oriented associations were identified
by methods similar to those used in the identification of leaders. A
list of more than 70 private and public organizations was assembled
by documentary and panel techniques. Thirty-seven government
organizations and private associations won the highest ranking from a
panel of five knowledgeable judges thoroughly familiar with these
organizations. The list of these organizations was prepared for a
rating by organizational officials. Twenty-five well-qualified raters
were asked: *Regardless of the positions they take or how you feel
about them, which of these organizations would you rate as the most
powerful in initiating, supporting, or vetoing activities affecting urban
programs and policies in the Boston to Washington area or the nation
generally.*[5] Table 2 shows the 20 most powerful organizations.

TABLE 2. The Top Twenty Most Powerful Urban-oriented Organizations

Rank	Type of Organization[a]	Organization
1	G	U.S. Department of Housing and Urban Development
2	V	U.S. Conference of Mayors
3	G	U.S. Office of Economic Opportunity
4	V	National Urban League
5	G	U.S. Department of Health, Education, and Welfare
6	V	AFL-CIO
7	V	Ford Foundation
8	G	U.S. Department of Labor
9	V	National Association for Advancement of Colored People
10	V	National Urban Coalition
11	V	National Alliance for Businessmen
12	V	National League of Cities
13	V	U.S. Chamber of Commerce
14	V	International City Manager's Association
15	V	National Association of Manufacturers
16	V	National Association of Counties
17	V	League of Women Voters
18	V	Congress of Racial Equality
19	V	Urban America
20	V	Council of State Governments

[a]G = Government; V = Private association.

[5]The raters who were interviewed include: (1) Legislative Director, Council of State Governments; (2) Legislative Director, National League of Cities; (3) Director of Community Relations Service, U.S. Conference of Mayors; (4) Division Director, Office of Economic Opportunity; (5) Assistant Director of National Relations, National Urban Coalition; (6) Urban Affairs Director, U.S. Chamber of Commerce; (7) Assistant Urban Affairs Director, U.S. Chamber of Commerce; (8) Director of Urban Affairs, League of Women Voters; (9) Director of Public Affairs, Urban America; (10) Assistant Director of Urban Affairs, National AFL-CIO; (11) Program Director, W. E. Upjohn Institute for Employment Research; (12) Staff Research Associate, Potomac Institute; (13) Vice President, Director of Industrial Environment, National Association of Manufacturers; (14) Director of Public Relations, National Urban League; (16) Assistant Executive Director, NAACP; (17) Manager, Civic and Governmental Affairs, National Industrial Conference Board.

The following raters responded by mailing the interview schedule: (18) Executive Director, National Association of Counties; (19) Executive Secretary, National Association of Broadcasters; (20) Executive Director, American Institute of Planners; (21) Executive Secretary, Business Council; (22) Director of Task Force on Urban Education, National Educational Association; (23) Executive Director, National Federation of Business and Professional Women's Association; (24) Executive Director, International Association of City Managers; (25) Executive Secretary, Washington office, American Bankers Association.

URBAN PROBLEMS CHECKLIST

Please (1) indicate the order of importance or ugency that *your organization* assigns to the following eleven urban problems which prevail in Megalopolis (the Boston-New York-Philadelphia-Baltimore-Washington urban complex); (2) check problems in which your organization has the highest personal interest; (3) mark those on which your organization is currently working.

	Urgency Ranking	Interested In	Currently Working Hardest On
Urban Problems			
1. Air pollution			
? Control of lawlessness and crime			
3. Improvement of public education			
4. Water pollution			
5. Improvement of transport, traffic movement and parking			
6. Waste (garbage, litter, and dumps)			
7. Improvement or elimination of poor housing; rebuilding of cities			
8. Improvement and maintenance of roads and streets			
9. Planning and zoning of land, preservation (or improvement) of parks and other natural areas			
10. Unemployment and poverty			
11. Race relations			

Organizational problem priorities,
interests, and current work activities

The 25 organizational raters were provided with an urban problem checklist and asked to rank the problems in three ways. (The checklist and ranking instructions are reproduced on p. 322.)

The data on such a measure are difficult to collate because the respondents exhibit many different patterns. An official of the National Alliance of Businessmen may check "Unemployment and poverty" in all three columns: Number 1 in "Urgency," "Most interested in," and "Currently working on," and decline to check any others as outside the scope of his association. On the other hand, the official at the National League of Cities or at the League of Women Voters may insist that they put a high priority on almost all the problems and that in the organization comprehensive efforts are being made by interested and responsible staff members. Between these two extremes are those who do rank all problems from 1 to 11 in priority and specify interest and working activities of the organization. An examination of all data indicate that the 11 problems fall into six distinct priority levels or categories.

Level 1: Unemployment and poverty

Level 2: Public education; Housing and urban renewal; Race relations

Level 3: Crime

Level 4: Land planning and preservation; Transport, traffic and parking

Level 5: Roads and streets; Air pollution; Water pollution

Level 6: Solid wastes or refuse

Table 3 shows the frequencies for "Most interested in" and "Currently working on" as the 25 organizational raters reported for their urban-oriented organizations.

The table shows how interest and work patterns relate to the designated priority levels. Especially important to the environmental concerns of the study is the ranking of air pollution, water pollution, and solid wastes. These problems are at the bottom (Levels 5 and 6) in priority. They do not fare as badly in interest and working activity. Here, they show an equivalence to Level 4.

TABLE 3. Priority Levels Assigned by Twenty-five Organizational Raters and the Frequencies for Interest and Working Activities

		Frequency for Most Interested in (N = 25)		Frequencies for Currently Working Hardest On (N = 25)	
	Priority Levels	Frequency	Percentage	Frequency	Percentage
Level 1:	Unemployment and poverty	17	68	14	56
Level 2:	Public education	13	52	11	44
	Housing and urban renewal	15	60	13	52
	Race relations	10	40	11	44
Level 3:	Crime	9	36	10	40
Level 4:	Land planning and preservation	6	24	8	32
	Transport, traffic, and parking	8	32	9	36
Level 5:	Roads and streets	4	16	3	10
	Air pollution	8	32	9	36
	Water pollution	8	32	10	40
Level 6:	Solid wastes or refuse	6	24	8	32

It can be seen that the priorities established by powerful urban organizations correspond closely to the same activity rankings of powerful leaders.

IDENTIFYING POWERFUL ENVIRONMENTAL-QUALITY ORGANIZATIONS

A list of some 200 organizations concerned with the quality of the environment was assembled and rated by qualified raters. Raters were organizational directors and officers of 130 such organizations. Table 4 shows the top 33 organizations reputed to be most powerful. They are rated according to influence scores as raters ranked each organization as very powerful (1), powerful (2), not so powerful (3), and don't know (0). The highest rating is indicated by the lowest score. A score of 1 means that particular organization rated it as being "very influential." The lowest rating included in this top group is 1.9.

Note that Table 4 is divided into two sections, containing 8 and 25 organizations, respectively. While all these organizations should be viewed as having a reputation for being "very influential," there is a cutting point separating the two groups which will be referred to as Group A and Group B.

Observe that all 33 organizations listed in Table 4 represent either segments of the legislative and executive branches of the federal government or national voluntary associations. In Group A, the highest rated organizations, the dominant organizations, are in the government.

But powerful urban-oriented organizations can be identified in the list. It may be noted that the overlap of the urban-oriented and environmental-quality organizations includes such urban-oriented associations as the U.S. Chamber of Commerce, the National Association of Manufacturers, the League of Women Voters, the National League of Cities, Council of State Governments, National Association of Counties, and the U.S. Conference of Mayors.

The following question was asked of all the powerful environmental organizations: *Does your organization have a unified program which combines problems of air pollution, water pollution, solid wastes and/or others?* Of 26 reporting, five said that they were working on environmental quality problems (air pollution, water pollution, and solid wastes) only, 3 said they combined work on environmental quality problems with planning and zoning, and 18 reported environmental quality programs combined with activity on other urban problems.

TABLE 4.   Reputed Top Thirty-six Most Powerful Environmental Quality
Organizations (1968)

Power Score	Organization
	GROUP A
1.0	Federal Water Pollution Control Administration (now designated as Federal Water Quality Administration)
1.0	U.S. Senate Committee on Public Works
1.0	U.S. Senate Committee on Interior and Insular Affairs
1.0	U.S. House of Representatives Committee on Public Works
1.0	U.S. House of Representatives Committee on Science and Astronautics
1.1	U.S. Army Corps of Engineers
1.2	Bureau of the Budget, Natural Resources Division
1.3	U.S. Chamber of Commerce
	GROUP B
1.5	Citizens Committee on Natural Resources
1.5	The Conservation Foundation
1.5	Federal Power Commission
1.5	National Association of Manufacturers
1.6	Izaak Walton League
1.6	League of Women Voters
1.6	National Rivers and Harbors Congress
1.6	U.S. Forest Service
1.6	Fish and Wildlife Service
1.7	Water Resources Council
1.7	National Air Pollution Control Administration
1.7	National League of Cities
1.7	American Iron and Steel Institute
1.8	Manufacturing Chemists' Association
1.8	Bureau of Mines
1.8	Wildlife Management Institute
1.8	Council of State Governments
1.8	National Audubon Society
1.8	Sport Fishing Institute
1.8	National Association of Counties
1.9	Water Pollution Control Federation
1.9	Sierra Club
1.9	Bureau of Outdoor Recreation
1.9	U.S. Conference of Mayors
1.9	National Coal Association
—[a]	National Parks Association

[a]The National Parks Association received a rating of 1.0, but it was based on so few ratings that the score was not considered representative enough to justify its inclusion in Group A. It is an organization that has wielded strong veto power and cannot be ignored. It is tentatively placed in Group B.

Figure 3 presents the working relationships between the seven urban-oriented organizations which are among the top environmental quality-residuals organizations and 19 other top-reputed environmental quality organizations. In the center of the figure are the seven urban-oriented organizations: League of Woman Voters, U.S. Chamber of Commerce, National Association of Manufacturers, National League of Cities, National Association of Counties, Council of State Governments, and the U.S. Conference of Mayors. The lines connecting the organizations represent working relationships as reported by the seven urban-oriented organizations only. Reciprocal choices are not included. Solid lines represent supportive contacts and dotted lines represent informative contacts. The organizations at the top of the figure represent private organizations and those at the bottom represent executive and legislative committees and agencies within the federal government. This pattern represents the report of an official representing each of the seven urban-oriented organizations. It must be regarded as an illustrative rather than a definitive statement. Note that *supportive* means that the rater indicated that the supporting organization works with or supports his organizations on issues of environmental quality; *informative* means that there is a contact or exchange of ideas about environmental quality with the informing organization.

Table 5 presents the working relations between the urban-oriented and the government and private organizations presented in Figure 3. The working relationships are described in terms of coefficients of interaction, and they are divided into informative, supportive, and total categories. The coefficient of interaction is the actual number of contacts between the classes of organizations divided by the total number of possible contacts between two classes of organizations.

The interaction coefficients reveal that the urban-oriented organizations tend to have a wider range of total contacts with the

TABLE 5. *Interaction Coefficients Between Seven Urban-oriented Organizations and Other Organizations with Environmental Quality Programs, as Reported by the Urban-oriented Organizations*

	Contacts with Seven Urban-oriented Organizations		
	Informative	Supportive	TOTAL
Governmental (N = 11)	0.26	0.27	0.53
Private (N = 8)	0.13	0.23	0.36

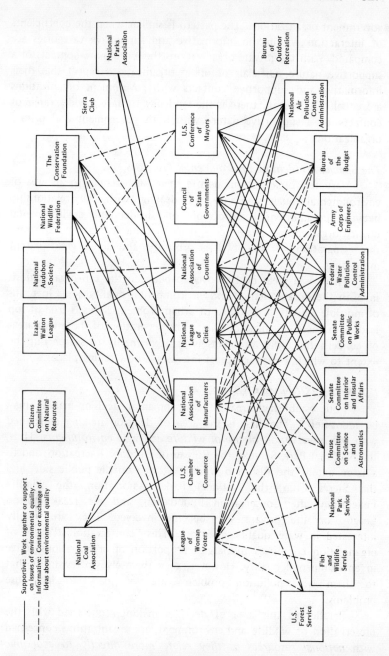

FIGURE 3. Working Relationships Between Urban-Oriented Organizations and Other Environmental Quality Organizations as Indicated by Urban-Oriented Organizations Only.

government organizations. The pattern is similar when the coefficients of interaction within the informative and supportive categories are compared. With the private organizations there are more contacts of a supportive nature. Officials of urban organizations report that their informative and supportive contacts with government organizations are equal. Yet overall, there is the tendency to have a wider range of contacts of a supportive nature with both government and private organizations.

The Special Problem of Environmental Priorities
      Very few organizations devote their full energies to an area of environmental quality. Hence, in dealing with the relationship between urban-oriented associations and leaders and environmental quality organizations and leaders, it has become increasingly apparent that separation of the two is arbitrary and to a great extent misleading.

There is a great deal of overlap between the top organizations in both the urban-oriented and environmental quality areas in terms of multiple activity in the field of urban problems. This is true of top leaders in these organizations also. The separation of these two areas of concern for urban problems is made primarily to search out the extent to which a coalescence of interests is now taking place.

FOUR DECISION-MAKING AREAS
      Four established areas of environmental decision-making may be identified.[6] The first is the area of decision making concerned with *the preservation or use of wildlife and wild environments.* Thus, the National Park Service, the Bureau of Outdoor Recreation, and to a large extent the Fish and Wildlife Service on the public side, and the Sierra Club, the National Parks Association, the Wildlife Federation, the Conservation Foundation, and the Izaak Walton League on the private side become involved. They are usually interested in water quality questions. This "conservationist" type of organization comprises the largest proportion of organizations active in environmental quality. However, they themselves often insist that to them water pollution problems are secondary to land use problems.

Parallel to this area of decision making, concerned with the preservation of wildlife and environment, are organizations concerned with *national resources as they relate more directly to economic*

[6] I am indebted to my research associates, James L. Barfoot, Jr., and Paul D. Planchon for many of these ideas and for research on the environmental organizations.

exploitation. This draws into the field such organizations as the Bureau of the Mines, the Army Corps of Engineers, the Congressional Committees on Public Works, the National Rivers and Harbors Congress, the National Coal Association, and the American Petroleum Institute. It is important to point out, however, that, for all of these, environmental quality is very much a secondary concern.

These two areas of decision making intersect with those concerned in a third area—*environmental quality as it is identified within the general setting of urban problems.* Thus, organizations whose primary interests are in urban problems (or civic interest in general) are drawn into the field of environmental participants. Examples are the organizations of state and local governments—the National League of Cities, the Council of State Governments, the National Association of Counties, and the U.S. Conference of Mayors. Other examples would include the League of Women Voters.

The fourth area of decision making which intersects with that of environmental quality comes from *business and industry.* Because the assimilative capacity of the environment is a resource to industry, and therefore a concern of business, they are drawn into the field if for no other reason than that pollution abatement is likely to become another cost of doing business. Business and industry appear anxious that equitable and economically sound decisions are made about environmental quality. At least, they are concerned that decisions are not made which place an intolerable burden upon them. Thus, the Chamber of Commerce becomes involved, as does the National Association of Manufacturers, the Manufacturing Chemists Association, and many individual firms. Industry, as well as business indirectly, finds itself in the structural position of having to respond to the environmental quality challenge as the demand for it increases. Organizations, including firms or individuals in business and industry, may take a defensive position designed to avoid the costs of pollution abatement as long as possible, or they may take varying degrees of positive action. Action, however, tends to be directly toward the problems specific to the concerns of the industry or firm. The findings show that industry seldom directs its attention to public policy decisions, and when it does its desired outcomes are often distinctly different from those of others taking part in the decisions.

The findings indicate that the significant characteristic distinguishing urban and environmental areas of organizational and leadership structure is simply the lower priority which environmental quality is receiving in the total context of urban problems and the demands for effort and funds. This brings different levels of leaders to the fore with top ranking, urban-oriented leaders gravitating to problems of race, unemployment, housing, education, and crime, and leaving environmental quality to lower ranking and generally less powerful leaders. Fortunately, powerful governmental leaders have emerged to buttress support for environmental quality. Governmental leaders in a democracy, no matter how powerful, need wide popular backing. This is especially true if upward shifting of priority for environmental quality means less resources for urban problems that are regarded as more critical.

THE COALESCENCE OF URBAN
AND ENVIRONMENTAL LEADERS

As environmental quality reaches to higher priority, it is expected that the distinction between urban oriented and environmental quality leaders will become less meaningful. At this time, the extent of their mutual involvement is a significant indicator of the commitments made to the importance of environmental quality. In January 1970 the President created a new Council of Environmental Quality of three men headed by Russell Train, then Assistant Secretary of Interior. Robert Cahn of the Christian Science Monitor and of Boston is a second member from the Megalopolis appointed to the new council. The other member is Dr. Gordon J. F. McDonald of California. The President said that this council would report to him directly. It is to advise him and to serve with respect to environmental quality as the Council of Economic Advisors serves in economic matters affecting the nation.

Other contact points of importance are those around the Federal Water Resources Council and the Federal Air Pollution Control Council. Common lobbying activities of urban-oriented and environmental quality leaders are another important sector of contact. The new Environmental Protection Agency should play an increasing role as a center of activity.

A systematic analysis of committee work on environmental problems in trade and voluntary organizations, on government boards, commissions, and councils would reveal urban-oriented leaders who are growing in experience. Studies of interest and motivation of such leaders would provide the knowledge necessary for development of new leaders. It is probably safe to say that nobody knows today how leaders develop their commitment to environmental quality problems—especially those influentials who are badgered by competing demands for their services.

REFERENCES

Miller, Delbert C.
> Top Leadership and Organizational Power in Megaloplis. Forthcoming.

Miller, Delbert C., James L. Barfoot, Jr., and Paul B. Planchon
> 1970 Decision Making in Megalopolis with Special Reference to Environmental Quality Problems. Resources for the Future, Inc., Washington, D.C. (Copies available upon request.)

SECTION VI
Overview

Though man's invention of organized, verifiable, cumulative knowledge—his science—can extend his ability to manipulate his habitat, it can also serve as a trained incapacity. Klausner indicates that quite different problems emerge when natural systems are more extensive than social systems, rather than when the social system is more extensive than the natural system. But in both cases our theories are unable to provide appropriate answers. If we attempt to reduce social issues to biological measures, our answers will be no less accurate than if we attempt to account for biological issues on the basis of animistic conceptions.

Klausner's analysis of recent works dealing with environmental problems illustrates how, when we deal in terms of systems, we are always confronted with boundary problems even though our very interest is to transcend such problems. His study is a strong reminder that disciplines of knowledge, like other subcultures, have adaptive strengths and weaknesses. He suggests some useful research directions which may help us to minimize such weaknesses.

PAPER 16

Some Problems in the Logic of Current Man-Environment Studies

SAMUEL Z. KLAUSNER

NEEDED: A SOCIAL-SCIENTIFIC LANGUAGE FOR ENVIRONMENTAL STUDIES

An industrial city enclosed in a chamber with only the air above it would stifle itself with waste and asphyxiate itself. This ominous thought introduces Howard T. Odum's (1971) book on nature and man. Indeed, if industrial societies are so environmentally gluttonous, we ignore the warning at our peril. Ascertaining the validity of Odum's warning must assume high priority. Though oxygen and waste are elements of the physical environment, the validity of the warning cannot be assessed through inspection of biophysical processes alone. An industrial city is an organization of human activities around machines, materials, and land. The environmental problem is set at the boundary of human action and its physical environment, a point at which physical processes mesh with processes of human action.

An examination of the biological organism's need for oxygen and of industry as a complex of material-transforming machines provides but a part of the information needed to assess the issue. The behavior of industrial workers, the knowledge which guides their work, the marketing of their products, and their commitment to their families are as much aspects of the industrial system as are machines, oxygen, and waste. To assess the threat identified by Odum, we must understand the mutual articulation (or disarticulation) of biological, physical, and social processes in an industrial setting.

This is a publication of the research program on Society and Its Physical Environment of the Center for Research on the Acts of Man, Philadelphia, Pennsylvania. Randall Kritkausky's perceptive reading of an earlier draft of this paper preserved it from even more errors than it presently contains.

Today, environmental problems tend to be pinpointed in terms of the temperature and oxygen content of a lake, or the decibel level of a sound. Yet, the depletion of a lake's oxygen or the production of noise is but a link in a chain of events—some of which are social. Environmental amenities tend to be described in terms of forest and seacoast settings rather than in terms of the human activity which takes place in those settings. It is a complex of social events which defines a forest as a vacation setting. Some current ecological writings of engineers and biologists (for example, Commoner, 1970) analyze the physical aspects of environmental problems and conclude with the piety that social action holds the key to their solution. This salient perception precipitates a call for consideration of the "total" environment: physical, biological, and social. Now, no one can study the total environment. Further, it is not obvious how one would link the physical, biological, and social aspects of even a fragment of society with its physical environment.

Not unusually, the plea for a total study of the total environment functions as ideological rhetoric. Generally, the engineer's definition of the problem in terms of particulates in the air, or micro organisms in a stream, are the dominant conceptions. Social scientists who attempt to work directly with such physically defined environmental variables soon become mired in low-level abstraction and offer studies of low generalization. Effective environmental research requires the ability to link propositions stated in the language of the natural sciences to propositions stated in the language of the social sciences. However, physical science concepts such as eutrophication and density of SO_2 make strange intellectual partners for such traditional social science concepts as role or motive. What is the nature of the conceptual incompatibility and what may be done about it?

This paper will attempt to specify the nature of the dilemma of man-environment research and suggest a temporarily viable way of skirting the dilemma—though not of resolving it. The second section will argue the incommensurability of current social and natural scientific languages. It will follow that social action and natural processes cannot be thought of as constituting a single socioenvironmental system. An illustration will be presented in the third section showing the problems which arise from a disjunction between the use of space in a palpable physical system and the orientation to space of a palpable social system. Some adjustments by the social system to stem environmental deterioration will be introduced. The fourth part of the paper reviews two ways in which researchers have attempted to develop a more general understanding of social and physical adjustments without stumbling on the problem of incommensurability. One approach is to deny the need for two theoretical languages by reducing both social and natural events to a single natural science language. A second approach is to set aside the requirement for a theoretical language and develop models describing the behavior of manifest social and natural events, perhaps creating an environmental monitoring system as is common among operations researchers. The final major section proposes that we cope with the theoretical problem by dealing with either social or natural variables alone while treating the processes in the other system as constant conditions. This allows for the development of a theory of social action oriented to the physical environment. The patterning of social events with respect to the physical environment differs from their patterning in more traditional sociological work. An exploration of some of these differences leads into a discussion of analyses which focus on orientations to physical objects as opposed to those focusing on an analysis of roles which emerge in virtue of the orientation to physical objects. The last pages review three social science concepts that have been useful in describing social behavior at its environmental boundary. These are the concepts of selective perception, externalities, and interest groups. Almost all of the material presented in this paper to illustrate its arguments is gleaned from books and articles on society and the physical environment published during 1970. The works were not selected as a representative sample, but simply as a source of examples from writings current at the time of the publication of this book.

THE INCOMMENSURABILITY OF SOCIAL
AND PHYSICAL SCIENCE LANGUAGES

When volcanoes throw ash into the atmosphere or seacoasts rise and ebb with tidal or geologic motion, men may shift their dwellings or build protective walls. The events are a spontaneous activity of nature, but the response of men rests on their understanding of the laws describing these natural events. The natural sciences, physics, chemistry, and biology, codify these laws. Problems of air and water quality or problems of the allocation of natural resources are more likely to be caused by human intervention in nature than to result from the spontaneous activity of nature. Environmental remedies involve additional intentional intervention. On the one hand, the environmental consequences of human intervention ramify according to the laws of natural science. On the other hand, the intervention itself is affected by the exigencies controlling human behavior. Social science may clarify why a man drops a ball from a tower, but the description of its fall is given in terms of the laws of gravity. To understand the occasion for the intervention, or why a particular form of intervention was selected, we appeal to principles of motivation, to laws about social organization, and to rules by which knowledge and other cultural directives inform action. The social sciences, sociology, psychology, economics, anthropology, and political science codify these laws and apply them to the understanding of recreational behavior, resource managerial organizations, and the emergence of environmental law.

Current theories explaining the behavior of physical and social systems are constructed within disparate frames of reference and, as a result, their elements are incommensurable. They are analogous to propositions relating, say, apples and oranges.[1] Physical and social theories differ in their definitions of units and sometimes in the types of relations which their laws express among these units.[2] The units of a physical or biological system are conceptualized in a space-time frame of reference. Each unit is an object located in space and described in terms of objective attributes such as mass, length, temperature, and elasticity or in terms of its potential for entering into a bond with another unit. Fundamentally, these objects interact through exchanges of material or energy. The preferred type of law expressing a change in the relations among these objects is a deterministic rule which may be formulated algebraically or in terms of the differential calculus.

Models of human action are constructed around an actor dealing in meanings. These meanings define acts and purposes. The direction of behavior is influenced by personal and culturally proffered choices. An actor is assumed able to take into account the purposes and choices of others and to modify his own on the basis of experience. Symbols expressing goals and rules of behavior are internalized in individual personalities and institutionalized in collectivities. The laws expressing relations among these units may be deterministic or probabilistic. Generally, the deterministic form is

---

[1]Odum (1971) sidesteps the problem of incommensurability by expressing both social and natural events in a common biophysical language. Human societies may be considered as equivalents of physical nature because, as Odum says, human intitutions have a calories-per-day value. The question of reductionism will be taken up later in this section.

[2]The logical structure of social science and natural science theories have much in common. Both state relations among variables in if-then propositions. Both proceed inductively in the "context of justification." They differ in the character of nonlogical elements, or substantive categories. The use of symbolism as a substantive referential form and as a form of relating units in a proposition in the social sciences distinguishes them in logical structure from the natural sciences. More will be said about this below.

considered a heuristic of the theoretical language rather than an attribute of relations among real social factors. Elements both in the theory and in real action may be related to principles of symbolic reference. The latter laws are complexes of meanings rather than dynamic models of events.

Natural and social systems are not easily grasped within a single supertheory—the appeal of ecological totalists notwithstanding.[3] Some so-called unified theorists of ecosystems treat physical elements which happen to have been produced in connection with some human activity as if they were social variables. The analyst measures gaseous effluents from automobiles as a function of the number of drivers, or the amount of phosphates dumped in a stream as a function of housewives' use of laundry detergent. This is a physical analysis. The human origin of the physical quantities does not turn it into an analysis of human behavior. No reference is made to concepts of role, motive, norm, reference group, or style of life as would be the case were social action the referent. Such societal concepts cannot be variables in a physical analysis. The characteristics of the human system from which the gases or the phosphates come do not affect the mechanisms by which they are processed in the physical system. The human environment of a physical system affects the physical parameters, the quantities of material being processed.

In analyzing human behavior, the constraints imposed by the physical system become relevant in terms of orientations, attitudes, cultural values, or norms. The physical elements themselves do not become variables in the social science equation. The variables are the rules affecting human behavior with respect to those elements.

Man-environment studies explore points of tangency between the natural and the social orders, and it should follow that this tangency be definable in the theoretical systems developed to model each order. However, unlike the mathematical notion of a point of tangency as a shared point, this tangency does not imply incorporation within the same system. The theoretical language used to study the physical component of the man-environment event is incommensurable with the language for describing the social component. This may be illustrated by examining the point of tangency in the light of what we mean by a system. In a single

[3]Two principal attempts at developing unified theory spanning the special sciences have been the semiotics of Charles Morris and general systems theory, including cybernetics, as described by Anatol Rapaport and Norbert Weiner. Both of these approaches are significant contributions to scientific methodology because they identify the common logical structures of the specialized sciences. They are less helpful when the problem is to state substantive relationships—to describe concrete events.

system elements are, in principle, mutually related. If variable A influences variable B which, in turn, influences variable C, then we would expect A to influence C. In other words, in a chain of propositions, the final terms should not be unrelated to the initial term.

Suppose a relationship is established between climatic temperature, a physical measure, and intensity of social interaction, a social measure. The relation between the physical and social variables is the point of tangency between the systems. As the weather grows warmer, people more often venture out of their homes to associate with their friends. The temperature does not cause the increased interaction. Rather, people contemplate the climatic change and decide to behave in a certain way in relation to it.

We may follow a hypothetical chain of social-scientific statements beginning with the social variable "intensity of social interaction." Increasing intensity of social interaction may, for one thing, lead to an increase in the suicide rate. The increase in the suicide rate may, in turn, affect conceptions of social order and the willingness of people to institute measures of social control. The intensity of social interaction, the initial variable, and attitudes toward social control, the terminal variable, are related. This relation may be statistically weak but should, in principle, exist. Suicide rate mediates the relation. A system, by definition, is constituted by such closed linkages.

Similarly, a chain of propositions may be developed from the concept of temperature in a physical frame of reference. Seasonal change in temperature is related to the angle of the sun's rays or, in other words, to the tilt of the earth's axis with respect to its plane of revolution about the sun. This angle is, in turn, related to the pattern of masses and distances of bodies in the solar system. Here, too, is a closed system of propositions. Temperature changes, the initial variable, and the pattern of masses and distances in the solar system, the terminal variable, are asociated. (In causal terms, the direction of association is reversed.) However, while the social and physical initial terms, temperature and intensity of social interaction, are spoken of as related to one another, no relationship exists between the termini of the propositions in the two systems. The distribution of sun and planets has no relation to attitudes toward social control. It is not that the correlation is low, as it might be between termini of two chains in the same system, but that it makes no sense to speak of the relation.[4]

---

[4]The incommensurability of terms in the social and physical frames of reference becomes apparent when the propositions are looked at deductively. If

It also makes no sense to speak of the initial relation between temperature and social interaction unless a transformation term is inserted between them. No causal nexus exists between temperature and social interaction. For the social analysis, the former is related to the latter as an object of orientation. The relation is symbolic.[5]

Hoary theories of the relations of climate to personality and to society are in disrepute, and appropriately so.[6] Perhaps some scholars are seduced into these theories by observing, for instance, that some measures of a physical event vary in some lawful way with measures of some human event—at least in some limited sample of observations. The distinction must be made between the referents of the theoretical concepts which are held to be related and a relation observed between some selected indicators or measures of the concepts. Any two observable phenomena undergoing secular change in the same time period, say the price of bread in New York and the oxygen content of Lake Baikal between 1960 and 1969, would produce a correlation coefficient, in this case a negative one. Joint occurrence is insufficient for verification of causality without specification of some understandable mechanism connecting the two phenomena. The scientist is not concerned with the specific price-oxygen relation. He might be concerned with a relation between economic processes and eutrophication for which the specific observations are proxy measures.

(Footnote 4 *continued*)
the termini are taken as the major premises, one can deduce the initial condition in the same frame of reference. If one posits a rule about the masses and the distances between them in the solar system, then one can deduce, by passing through the other terms, the element of temperature. Temperature itself is not included in the major premise, but it is a relational outcome of a given juxtaposition between the sun and the earth, among other conditions. None of the social referents is derivable deductively from the major premise or any of the minor premises in the chain of reasoning from the physical variables.

[5]A temperature extreme could, of course, affect the physiological organism and thus its competence to act.

[6]Modern aspirants to global ecological theories encompassing a "total," "sociobiological," or "sociophysical" environment are not the original perpetrators of the sin of correlating the noncorrelatable. Part of the classic tradition in man-environment studies blithely states propositions joining a physical to a social variable. Examples of such theories from St. Thomas Aquinas and Ibn Khaldun to the present day are cited in my *On Man in his Environment: Social-Scientific Foundations for Research and Policy* (Klausner, 1971) as "theories that failed." In recent times these include Albert Leffingwell's (1892) correlation of seasonal variation in solar light and heat with the incidence of passionate behavior. Henry L. Moore (1923) related economic and rainfall cycles against the backdrop of the eight-year cycle of interpositions of Venus between the sun and the earth. The critique of these physical-social correlations is also not original with the present author. Durkheim's chapter on "Suicide and Cosmic Factors" in his *Suicide* is a model for the argument here advanced.

Even in the absence of a specifiable mechanism, the analyst could gain some assurance that the relation was not spurious by testing it under a series of control conditions. Also, he would want to know whether the relation would be found repeatedly in a wide sample of 10-year periods—between 1900-1909, 1910-1919, and so on, before concluding that the correlation coefficient attests to the discovery of a new general proposition.

In the process of meeting these conditions, one is dealing with the problem of incommensurability. Principally, the specification of the mechanism mediating between the social and physical facts involves the identification of a transformation term. A discussion of such transformation terms would take us too far afield. As a rule of thumb, the analyst of socioenvironmental relations should be most wary of propositions relating a social and a physical term.

THE SOCIAL ORIENTATION TO SPACE AND ITS PHYSICAL COGNATE: AN ILLUSTRATIVE PROBLEM

The incommensurability of the theoretical terms used to describe the natural and social orders poses a problem for the development of abstract socioenvironmental generalization. Theories are designed to explain observed, palpable events by generalizing about processes which account for the observations. Abstract concepts and the analytic propositions formed of them transcend any particular place or time. The intensity of illumination of an object is inversely related to the square of the distance between the object and the light source, whether they are found in New York or Hong Kong. A particular physical event, however, takes place in a particular locale. Such an observable event is not raw sensory input but also conceptualized. It is conceptualized according to "common sense" rather than abstracted in terms of a scientific frame of reference. Such palpable, observable events may also be studied as organized systems. A theoretical system may be given coherence definitionally. That a set of palpable events hangs together as a system is a matter to be demonstrated empirically.

The observable things which people do in particular places are the events reported by history and by newspapers as constituting everyday life. The boundaries of palpable natural systems are, in part, set in terms of the reach and intensity of physical, chemical, or biological effects. The boundaries of social systems are established on the basis of social definitions of inclusion and exclusion. Under the artificial conditions of a space capsule, the boundaries of the natural and social system are coterminous.

Odum, in the image with which the paper opened, is concerned with a disjunction between an industrial system, considered biophysically, and a natural ecosystem, imagined to be in a closed capsule. Imbalances are due to the relative rates of various processes within the boundary. Similarly, Commoner (1970) is concerned with a major incompatibility between our system of productivity and our environmental system. The disjunction between the boundaries of the industry's physical processes and the implicated social system of the same industry is a frequent source of environmental problems. Factory fumes affect communities beyond that of the industrial workers. In the spreading of these fumes, a physical process, working according to its laws, cuts across the boundaries of several social systems, organized according to their rules. In this section, we explore some problems which arise when there is a disjunction between the scope of some natural ecosystem and the boundaries to which the social systems related to it are oriented. We will note some of the planned and unplanned adjustments of palpable social systems to such problems.

The size of a natural system may vary greatly. The damp underface of a rock may be a natural ecosystem as may the biota of an isolated island. At the other extreme, the astonishing distances covered by herring or salmon between spawning and dying illustrate the great reach of ecosystems. Whatever the size of a biophysical system, its boundaries are defined by physical and biological processes. Social systems are socially bounded and extend from two-person dyads to vast empires.[7] Explicit orientation to a spatial boundary is not always a significant factor in defining group membership; a small group in a storefront church defines its members in terms of orientation to a religious system. There may be secondary, implicit, spatial criteria for inclusion and exclusion. Geographic proximity is a flexibly interpreted constraint.[8] It is

[7]The artificial boundary exerted by the hull of a submarine is atypical in that it exerts an absolute constraint on the maximum scope of interaction. Actually, the crew of a submarine may subdivide into groups oriented to a spatial boundary more restricted than that defined with respect to the hull. At the same time, members of several subgroups may be interlaced being oriented to the same spatial boundary.

[8]Young and Larson (1970) sought to discover the sociospatial boundaries of a neighborhood. They began by defining the legal limits of its school district. They then asked residents to cite the locality to which they look for schooling, trade, and work and found that residential location is the strongest determinant of perception of the community boundary. Residence is, in turn, related to occupation, which, in its turn, influences participation in formal organizations. These, in turn, affect one's attitude toward informal social life which, in its turn, again affects residential location. Neighborhood boundaries need not coincide with legal boundaries.

important to remember that the concept of spatial boundaries of a social system is an elliptical expression referring to the behavioral rules governing action with reference to physical space.

The problem of balancing the relation of natural and social systems is complicated when there is a boundary disjunction. The nature of the complication and its possible remedies differs according to whether the spatial boundaries of the natural system are more or less extensive than those to which the relevant social system is oriented.

For instance, the boundary of noise, a natural event, extends beyond that of its associated social event. Here the natural system is more extensive than the social system. Noise need not be especially oppressive to members of the social system generating it. Revelers would feel uncomfortable were drinks served amid funeral-parlor quiet. A pilot is comforted by his engine's roar and the weekend gardener using a power mower may feel thrilled by the sound. Occupants of a neighboring apartment, residents in the vicinity of the airport, or nongardening neighbors are more likely to be annoyed. In each case, the noise makers and unwilling noise receivers are participating in different action systems. Sound stretches from one to another, breaking across social boundaries. A parallel example involving water pollution is that of an upstream community using a river as a receptacle for its sewage while a downstream community treats the river water for drinking. The natural system, consisting of water, organic materials, organisms, oxidizing processes, is quite oblivious to the economic and political fences established by the human communities.

The same social system that originates a destructive natural process may be the one to suffer the damage, as in the Odum image, while, at the same time, its products befoul another social system. Cattle put to pasture scatter their wastes over a considerable area. These wastes, through the nitrogen cycle, are converted to humus. The constraints of competition and the norm of rational efficiency may lead to assembling the cattle in feedlots. The wastes pile up and produce ammonia and nitrate which may seep into water supplies. The cattle managers, as well as some innocent community sharing the same underground water, may be affected. Another instance in which the initiating social system as well as others suffer arises in the disposal of nonbiodegradable detergents. Particular households or factories release them into the river system. The oxygen cycle which ordinarily cleanses the water fails, and organic debris accumulates in the water denying it to others—perhaps to the very same individuals who dumped the original detergent into the waterways.

The examples of noise, cow dung in feedlots, and the release of nonbiodegradable detergents illustrate a case in which natural systems are more extensive than social. The natural processes traverse the boundaries of several social groups. The adjustment tends to be made by the social system. The social system may, through some change in rules, extend itself to encompass the natural system. What the economist calls internalizing the externalities illustrates this adjustment. The definition of the market is extended so as to include both the noise maker and the noise receiver. The former may pay the latter for the disbenefit imposed by the noise. Or an overarching regulatory system may be developed controlling the spillage of detergents. The factory spilling the detergent and the community affected are socially joined by the ordinances concerning waste disposal. In this sense, the boundaries of the social system or some aspect of it are extended to enclose those of the natural system. The entire natural event then takes place within a single social framework and so may be managed within it.

Another case is that in which the social system is more extensive than the physical or biological system. Parrack (1969) traces food-energy relations among various biota and living creatures in an area of rural West Bengal. From the physical point of view, sunlight is the main input to the ecosystem, while heat, migrating animals, cow dung, cremation of corpses, and wood fuel are the outputs. The sale elsewhere of jute fibers, rice, vegetables, and livestock are additional outputs particularly dependent on human intervention. Because the market is more extensive than the bioecological community, trade with other areas produces a net loss to the biotic community. Reserves of soil, for instance, are being used faster than they are replenished. Typically, soil depletion is compensated by allowing the land to lie fallow and replenish itself, by rotating crops which make differential demands on the soil or by use of artificial fertilizer. The decisions to apply these procedures are social acts which intervene in the natural system.

An agricultural economy, a social system, may be spread over a wide area. For reasons of efficiency and economies of scale, as well as for reasons of soil and climate, specific tracts may be planted in single crops. The dedication of extensive tracts to a single crop is called monoculture. Within each tract, an ecological imbalance may develop. Monoculture is a response to functional requirements of a social system. Mumford's (1970) argument that a monoculture is not only deleterious bioecologically, if no compensating step is taken, but is also socioculturally disfunctional, fails to appreciate this point.[9] Monoculture may be economically rational for a social system by improving its position in the trade market. However, to enjoy such an advantage without suffering a bioecological deterioration requires a social adjustment.

Social action may adjust the natural system to the social in response to problems arising when the social system is more extensive than the natural one. Fertilizer may be brought from one part of the social system to another. Natural products are introduced into the deprived ecosystem on the basis of social decisions. Ultimately, therefore, as in the previous case, an adjustment in the social system is strategic. In this case, the adjustment is internal to the affected social system. In the previous case, with the social system smaller than the natural, relationships must be established externally with other social systems to solve the problem.

REDUCTIONISM AND OPERATIONS RESEARCH: SOLUTIONS WITHOUT SOCIAL SCIENCE

We have found that the call for a study of the total socioenvironment is utopian—if not unnecessary. The incommensurability of the languages currently in use for thinking about society and about the natural environment is a stumbling block to integrated theory. Our illustrations of disjunctions between palpable natural and social systems with respect to spatiality have revealed certain concrete, though ad hoc, social responses.

If we are not to be bound solely to ad hoc adjustments, we need some more general way of thinking about socioenvironmental

[9]Mumford (1970) observes that our technology, emphasizing power, standardization, and mass production, tends to decrease variety in favor of quantity. A variety of habitats—primeval, communal, domesticated, and urban—are necessary not only for the ecological system and for an ecological balance, but also for the development of man. Presumably, each habitat provides its specific stimulation, which enlarges the quality of life. The Mumford analysis tends to be reductionist. Were variety of habitat a cause of intellectual growth, nomads would be brighter than either valley or mountain dwellers. Human learning takes place through symbolic interactions in the context of social institutions. Potentials for living are abilities to symbolize rather than evironmentally induced adaptations. Modern man has an aptitude for encapsulating himself in a standard environment almost regardless of the natural environment in which he finds himself. A variety of habitats may challenge man to develop more variegated cultural solutions. The ingenuity required to deal with various environments may have some developmental impact on culture. Whether variety contributes to cultural growth depends upon an already existent cultural ingenuity.

relations. If we cannot combine terms from the two orders, what can we do? Three approaches have been used. One approach has been to claim that both man and environment may be examined with the same conceptual tools. This is the reductionist approach. Second, some scholars choose to ignore the problems of theory and deal only with associations among manifest events. This is the approach of practical modeling, especially as found in operations research. Finally, students of man-environment relations may accept the need for an integrative theory but refuse to abandon the traditional concepts of physical and social science prior to such a formidable theoretical breakthrough. Their solution is to study one system at a time while holding the other constant as a "condition."

In analyzing social interaction with respect to the physical environment, physical environmental factors may, as it were, be held constant. In analyzing changes in the natural environment, consequent upon receipt of materials from the social system, the social factors related to the production of those materials may be held constant.

Reductionist approaches attempt to dissolve the problems by denying that disparate theoretical languages are needed for the natural and social orders. A single *overarching* socioenvironmental theory is not reductionist. The reductionist claims either that the natural science framework is appropriate for social analysis or vice versa. No serious postmedieval scholar has extended the animistic conceptions of social science to the natural world. It is not unusual, however, to find contemporary scholars using the physical science frame of reference for sociology. Up to a point, there are advantages. Demography develops population models using the physical science frame of reference. Individuals are enumerated as if they were objects located in space. These objects may have attributes of sex or age and may be aggregated into a whole equal to the sum of its parts. The problem arises when an attempt is made to account for behavior of the individuals. This requires the introduction of terms such as motives, norms, or values. These resist a spatial frame of reference. This may be called perspectival reductionism.

The most serious flaw in reductionism is not in its misapplication of a frame of reference. The confusion of physical and social content is more serious. The content reductionist will hold that the substantive categories used to describe the physical world are adequate for describing and explaining human behavior. Bioecologists are sometimes drawn into this type of reductionism in their efforts to extend their analysis to encompass the human component. Odum (1971), mentioned earlier, measures the effect of social factors in bioecological energy terms and so is reductionist in this sense. He conceives of nature as consisting of animals, plants, microorganisms, and human society, all joined by chemical materials that cycle round and round as potential energies flow over all of them. Information exchange, through human language, and economic exchange are measured in terms of material equivalents expressed in quanta of physical energy. Man and machine both become part of a system engaged in controlling or processing energy. Insofar as this approach represents society in terms of energy, it is reductionist. Insofar as it is dealing only with energy spin-offs from social activity, there is no analysis of society itself, and no pretense of social analysis is permissible. In either case, despite the use of the term *human society*, the biophysical system alone is subject to analysis. This may be called reductionism by translation.

The metaphor of the spaceship earth leads implicitly to reduction of the social to the biological. A spaceship is a self-contained system having an adequate source of energy, an adequate food supply, pure air and water, systems for reprocessing wastes, and a crew who observe the rule that it must not increase and must remain unified (Caldwell, 1970). All but the last concept suggest a bounded biological system. Members of the crew participate in this system as processors of biological material, not as social actors. Their role in the ecology of the spaceship complements that of the machines which reverse or recycle the material processed by them. The requirement that they remain unified is a social element which may affect the conduct of their mission, but remains as a dangling unanalyzed term in this complex. Whether crew members love or fight, the energy and material balances remain about the same. This may be termed reductionism by elimination. Social variables tend not to be considered.

The spaceship analogy is helpful for a bioecological analysis as such. Nothing inherent in the model prevents a sociological analysis. This is suggested by the fact that the context in which the metaphor was introduced by Kenneth Boulding and Barbara Ward was that of a social-scientific discussion.[10] Were it to be extended to sociological analysis, it would be limited to the study of small groups. The exclusion of institutional complexities which arise in larger groups limits the generalizability of a sociological analysis based on it. The

[10]Adlai Stevenson popularized the analogy. As with so many ideas developed in the political arena, its thrust is more ideological than scientific. It urges environmental action on the basis of an image of the interdependence of organisms and of the immediacy of the threat of exhaustion of our life-support system.

spaceship analogy, as an artificially closed biological system, is a good heuristic of situations without externalities, that is, impacts on systems external to the one under consideration.[11]

In the above examples, social facts were reduced to biological and physical facts. Reduction may be in the reverse direction. The analyst may seem to be dealing with the natural world when, in reality, his statements contain only social terms. Economists sometimes speak in this way and are usually aware of the ellipsis. Gudrey and Stoevener (1970) develop a demand model to assess benefits accruing from use of a resource for outdoor recreation. Measures of demand include recreation or visitor days. The socioeconomic characteristics of the user population enter as a control variable. The language of the presentation suggests that the physical characteristics of the facilities are the factors influencing demand. Relevant characteristics of recreational facilities include remoteness, level of site development, and opportunities for fishing. The measures of these characteristics may actually be the number of structures on a plot, the availability of toilets, or the number of fish caught. The economist seems to be focusing on physical facilities. These items, however, are but proxies for economic variables. The economic variables (demand for a good or utility of a service) are functions of the roles these elements play in a social system. These reflect the desire of the individual to obtain rights (a social variable) in the resources. Physical facilities are transformed in terms of their relevance to a social system before they are associated with the concept of demand. Remoteness is not an attribute to the facility but an expression of life style, of the character of human activity around a site. Similarly, it is not site development and fish which enter the equation, but the implications of site development and fish for the

[11]The reduction of social to biological categories is sometimes justified on the ground that man is but a more complex animal. Work in biological ecology tends to limit itself to those characteristics which man shares with animals. Paul Shephard, in a selection from his work on the subversive science (1970), says we should look at the world as a part of our body. Referring to overwhelming evidence of the likeness of men and animals, he says that affirmation of its own organic essence would be the ultimate test of the human mind. Shephard faults the conception of human uniqueness for a great mass of pseudodistinctions such as language, tradition, culture, love, consciousness, history, and the awe of the supernatural. Most sociologists would hold that the study of man requires concepts referring to symbolic behavior, an acceptance of human uniqueness. The popular mind relates the debate on human uniqueness to an ideological statement about the moral responsibility of man for nature. Scientific statements are factual, whether they refer to natural or to social systems. Scientifically speaking, neither the claim of human uniqueness nor the claim that man is but a complex animal implies an assertion about morality.

personal and social drama the individual would play out in that setting.

Allowing physical terms to enter economic discourse as a *façon de parler* has, undoubtedly, eased the dialogue between economists and resource managers. At the same time, it has, as Gudrey and Stoevener point out (1970), led some economists to mistake a physical object for a single good when, in reality, the demand may attach to a package of attributes or to several attributes each of which may be differentially in demand.

Reductionism, while denying the need for two theoretical languages, asserts the need for one, unless the reduction is to the palpable rather than to a theoretical level. Discussion about man-environment relationships may and does proceed without benefit of theory—at least, without self-conscious, systematic scientific theory. This differs from reductionism to a palpable level because no claim is made for underlying explanation. A theoretical statement rests upon observables which are treated as indicators of more general, nonobservable concepts. The observed events may, however, be taken for what they are, that is, as "common sense" conceptualizes them. For instance, a study of junked autos (Barnes, 1970) observes the process from automobiles to junk to scrap iron. A theoretical analysis attempting to generalize about this process in order, perhaps, to anticipate its future, might introduce social concepts about attitudes toward driving old cars, social purposes for which cars are used, including the economic implications of such use, and physical concepts about strength of materials and rates of oxidation. One may, on the other hand, describe the process and predict, with tolerable accuracy, the amounts of material arriving at each stage. Knowing the number of automobiles sold and the rates at which they are discarded provides a mortality estimate. Application of the mortality rate to any subsequent sales figure would predict the number flowing into the junk pile in successive years. These extrapolations from past to future approximate theory when repeated regularities are discovered. These regularities may be expressed as empirical generalizations either in verbal form or in the form of mathematical models. Using these mathematical models as a base line, a monitoring system may be developed. Succeeding observations may be used to detect a deviation from the now established regularity. A monitoring system signals changes in the process permitting appropriate adjustive action. The principle is like that of the governor on a steam engine. The monitoring system does not depend on an understanding of the underlying process. A basic social change affecting the process would require revision of the monitoring models. Some forms of operations research follow such a modeling and monitoring procedure.[12]

This method, though, permits a description of an ongoing process and the implementation of procedures to deal with that process without awaiting more fundamental understanding. Slobodkin (1970) notes that the use of a monitoring system to assess environmental quality deterioration is at a disadvantage because it would react to but might not anticipate a change in the significance of its variables, and because variables not significant at first glance may be overwhelming empirical significance under certain circumstances. Assessing the changing significance of variables requires additional general theory. Procedures to correct the monitored process must grow out of some theory about how the process works. Proceeding without systematic theory may offer temporary relief, improve the efficiency of systems in use, and provide a way of dealing with everyday management problems. There is no assurance, however, that the monitoring model is the optimal one.

TOWARD A SOCIAL-SCIENTIFIC LANGUAGE FOR ENVIRONMENTAL STUDIES

At best, reductionism provides an illusion of a sociophysical system while the research is, in fact, working on either social or physical variables. At worst, it may produce meaningless results by imposing an inappropriate frame of reference. The atheoretical models of operations research offer immediate managerial practicality, but do not offer the kind of understanding of underlying social and physical mechanisms needed to develop a long-range program and to anticipate contingencies not manifest in a current model. The development of an overarching theory in which both man and environment may be treated seems to be utopian at this point.[13] A

---

[12]The contention that operations research models are atheoretical rests upon a special definition of theory which excludes the statement of an empirical regularity, even when in mathematical form. Theoretical statements have a higher level of generality than the protocol statements they explain.

[13]The work in psychophysics of S. S. Stevens offers transformation equations between physical and psychological events that have some important, though limited, application to the solution of the problem of bridging concepts in the two systems. Stevens has established a relationship between the intensity of physical phenomena and the intensity with which those phenomena are experienced. An objective measure of sound level in decibels has a known relation to experienced loudness. For sound, the expression is $\Psi = K^{0.6}$ where Ψ is the psychological and ϕ the physical magnitude. Experienced loudness increases at a somewhat slower rate than increase in the decibel level. The decibel measure is based on sound pressure. A given sound level implies a given pressure on the eardrum and the nerve follicles. The exponential function states

third approach to man-environment research which manipulates the variables of one system at a time while looking to the other for parametric inputs or as an object of orientation, as the case may be, seems the most promising. We may study natural systems in the light of human intervention. We may study social systems in the light of physical and biological constraints and the personal and social orientations toward those constraints.

Physical Parameters and Social Variables and Vice Versa

Examples of physical system analysis occur in the literature in which social events are treated as parameters rather than variables. More precisely, a social proxy is offered for some quality of physical input to a physical system. Coale (1970) discussed air and water pollution against a background of economic activity, technological practices, and population size. The amount of physical materials produced by participants in the social system under these various social conditions is explored. The size of the population is relevant to the amount of pollutants—the accumulation of trash deposited in the environment. As a result, the question of population control, a social problem, is examined in the light of its impact on the physical environment.

As another example, Barry Commoner (1970) discusses the circularity of ecosystems within a bioecological frame of reference. Individuals in the social system become relevant to the analysis insofar as their aggregate affects the biological environment of other species. These are, of course, hidden social forces. The amount of trash deposited by a human population and the biological pressure it exerts on other species are not simple functions of number and some standard consumption levels, but are a function of its culture and the way its members are organized. Cultural and social organization, however, do not appear as variables in the analyses of Coale or of Commoner.

(Footnote 13 *continued*)
the relationship between the amount of physical stimulation and the psychological apprehension of the physiological response to this stimulation.

Other meanings which affect the psychological judgment of loudness are excluded from the equation. An item in the everyday environment has little chance of appearing as a discrete stimulus, such as a pure tone or nonsense syllable. The stimulus is encapsulated in culturally given meanings, the event interpreted. Psychophysical relations offer a baseline for evaluating psychological and social responses. Stevens' exponential functions give the mathematical transformation needed to enter a physical event as a parameter in a social or a psychological analysis.

Examples are also available of physical events treated as objects of orientation in a social analysis. Technology is knowledge about the behavior of natural systems. It is an aspect of culture and depends, in part, on other cultural elements and upon the exigencies of social interaction. Moncrief (1970), pursuing a cultural analysis, relates physical quantities of waste to population and production, technology, and urban concentration. His analysis begins with cultural values or styles of life. From these, he draws implications for the output of physical material. The democratic ideals of the French revolution produced a redistribution of the means of production and a reallocation of natural and human resources. A larger proportion of the population became involved in the production process. The technological revolution amplified the productive capacity of each worker several times. The integration of democratic and technological ideals led to more equitable distribution of this increased wealth. Consumption rises with income. Waste, in turn, increases with level of consumption. This particular analysis says nothing about the physical production processes. This is a social system analysis. Its variables are political change, economic ideology, and styles of life. Together, they produce a physical environmental impact. The physical material is an output of the social activity. It could be treated as an input quality for the physical system.

How to Pattern Physically Oriented Social Acts

How would an analysis of a social system oriented to the physical environment differ from an analysis of any other social system? One important difference is in the solution to the problem of relevance. Any social observation takes in a wide variety of acts. The problem is how to form them into some meaningful pattern either by organizing contemporaneous acts into a structure or by specifying a meaningful filiation of sequential acts.

Acts may be patterned around an object of orientation which may be an idea, a group goal, a norm, or a physical entity. They may also be patterned around a relationship, around a role. The important thing is that the pattern of acts along with their object, or acts along with their focal role, constitute a meaningful system of action. Social action with respect to the physical environment is distinguished by special objects of orientation, a physical element, and organization around a special set of relationships. These relationships may have emerged in virtue of the object orientation.

Physical objects of orientation lead to different types of social structures than do social or cultural objects. Aside from many commonalities, organizations differ according to the type of goal they pursue or object around which they are oriented. Industrial organizations oriented to natural resources differ from religious organizations oriented to cultural objects such as a doctrine, and both differ from a political organization oriented to power in social relations. The social organization of a factory is responsive to the technology it is applying, which, in turn, is devised with reference to the characteristics of the material being processed and the nature of the product envisioned.

Not only is organizational structure responsive to objects of orientation, but the history of a group as perceived by its members is influenced by the object of orientation. A group centered around a cultural commitment such as, say, Christianity, has a different history from that of a group centered around a territory. The Church of Antioch and the Council of Trent are events in the history of Christianity. The Church of Antioch and the Islamization of Seljuk Turks are events in the history of Anatolia.

Alternatively, the social life or interactional patterns of the group itself may be the focus. For instance, by applying the principles of institutional evolution, the sociologist traces the history of the family from its extended to its nuclear form. Certain continuities in role definitions and social functions define the descent of the nuclear from the extended family. The change in a religious movement from a sect with charismatic leadership to a formal church organization is explained in terms of internal organizational exigencies. A palpable church is considered the successor or descendant of a palpable sect because of its members' consciousness of historical continuity. Continuity is related to a development of the network of roles or relations rather than to the persistence of an object of orientation.

As another illustration, the developmental psychologist picks a single individual and links the events in which that person is involved. He follows the child through family, school, peer group, the successive institutions oriented to his development. History centered on an object rather than on roles is less than modal in sociology, in general, but is more common in tracing social groups with respect to the physical environment. Policy discussions about the environment almost always center on the material object and run through the social acts or groups patterned around it.

Barnes (1970), for instance, details the successive social actors oriented to junked autos and their sequelae. In 1966, when some 30 million junked auto bodies had accumulated, Senator Douglas of Illinois proposed the Junked Auto Disposal Act which would subsidize processors of the junk. The scrap iron industry testified against using public funds to subsidize the processors. Rather, they suggested that Congress address itself to the bottleneck at the consumption end of the scrap cycle where processed scrap is converted into raw steel. They also suggested removing the road blocks to the collecting and transporting of car hulks to the processor. Then, the scrap industry, the vendor—and the steel industry, the customer—could achieve equilibrium. Thus, focusing on a bit of the material environment, in this case the auto, social groups successively oriented to it are linked filiatively. One might begin with the material at the mine tracing it through the metal-manufacturing process, into auto production, driver use, junking, reprocessing, and back to auto production, where it is again targeted for the scrap market.

A pattern of social relations is contextual at each stage. The collector of car hulks may, on one side, deal directly with the last driver or some proxy appointed for disposal of the car. On the other side, the collector of hulks may deal with the processor who receives car hulks from him. Here the junkyard, the community of drivers, and the processors constitute one complex of relations focused around the automobile. At the next stage, the processor deals with his suppliers, the earlier collectors of the hulks, and then deals with the steel industry to which he sells the crushed materials for conversion into reclaimed steel. The second complex of relationships consists of supplier, processor, and steel industry. The steel industry works on the metal in the light of its relationship to the processor, to the purchaser of ingots, to stockholders, and so on.

Two factors distinguish between the filiative pattern around a physical object and a history of internal institutional development, as that from sect to church. First, the series of social groups around the processing of junk consists of almost discrete, socially discontinuous collectives. The successive clusters of groups are linked to their predecessors in virtue of a common concern with the commodity being processed. The social cluster supplier-processor-steel industry is not an organic development of the prior cluster junkyard-drivers-processors. The market relationship between the driver who disposes of his automobile and the steel mill that produces ingots is indirect and not immediately apparent from the individual transactions.

Second, in a traditional, social organization analysis, successive incumbents of a given set of institutional roles are linked. All the incumbents are interested in realizing a persistent goal. In following metal from scrap to steel, one encounters a series of discrete organizations, each with its own goals. The course of the metal, it is important to note, is not that of the natural system. We are not following iron to ferrous oxide. It is physical material carried through some social system in a culturally specified direction. The channel becomes possible because of some coordination among the groups along the route. The existence of this coordination implies the existence of an overarching social system. This system revolves around the economics of metallic resources and the technology for processing them.

Linking social events around a physical series, while unusual as a social science model, is comparable to the food chain model of biological ecology. The path of DDT may be traced from slight concentrations in a river bed to slightly greater concentrations in small organisms feeding there, then on to somewhat greater concentrations in fish that ingest small organisms, and lastly to markedly greater concentrations in birds that eat the fish. The organisms, the fish, and the birds are not a single developing organism—as is the sect becoming a church. These discrete biological systems are related through consumption of their predecessors.[14]

The focuses on objects of orientation or on role relationships in linking events sequentially are not mutually exclusive. Action with respect to an object of orientation implies certain social positions which are created in virtue of the relations to that object. A persistent object of orientation implies a persistence of roles. This may be illustrated with respect to the division of labor. The sociologist is accustomed to tracing complementary relations between functionally differentiated roles—mother and father, worker and supervisor. This is the social division of labor with roles differentiated with respect to social functions—aspects of social institutions. One role may evolve specializing in instrumental functions and its complement specializing in expressive functions. The development of specialties in a manufacturing process, such as that between an iron smelter and the fabricator who draws the metal into iron beams, reflects a technical division of labor. Specialties emerge around orientations—here technologically shaped orientations—to a physical item. Those divided by the social division of labor are related by interactive cooperation—the connection between them is intrinsic. With the technical division of labor, the specialists are related sequentially in dependence on the technological process. They need

[14]Territorial history follows this model of filiation on the basis of common orientation to a land. The history of Palestine connects its successive conquerors—Canaanites, Phoenicians, Philistines and other Semites, and then Egyptians, Babylonians, Greeks, Romans, Crusaders, Arabs, and Jews. The developmental history of any one of these peoples would follow social currents cutting across many locations.

not even know one another. The social positions, or roles, created by orientation to the technical process lead to their own principle of filiation—a history of crafts or the professions.

Any palpable social action must be understood in the light both of patterns of relations and of objects of orientation. However, one is sometimes more determining than the other. The following section discusses the case in which outside, nonevironmentally determined relations are crucial and some implications for environmental policy.

When Relations Are More Important than Orientations

In most of the examples presented above, the physical and social events were conceived as standing face to face, to occur at some point of tangency of physical and social systems. Under all circumstances, the character of social action with respect to the physical environment is affected by constraints imposed by the physical elements as well as culturally influenced orientations to those constraints. This relation to nature itself generates social relations such as those of the technical division of labor. A social system oriented to nature is, at the same time, subject to the personal, social, and cultural exigencies affecting all social action. It is, after all, a group in a wider world of groups.

Where the social actors are directly involved with a natural element, the set of factors specifically related to the man-nature relation (for example, constraints of the physical elements, orientation to those constraints, and roles generated in virtue of the relation to nature) will be relatively more important determinants of social action than will the general relational factors affecting all action. For instance, the structure of roles will be relatively more responsive to the technical than to the social division of labor than would be the case for a group not directly involved with nature.

Social organizations established to formulate environmental policy are generally not oriented to the environment directly but to other social organizations which, in turn, may be directly implicated in the environment. Market mechanisms and the organizations controlling them may be thought of as at a second remove from the actual productive and consumptive organizations. The brokerage firm handling stock of a mining corporation is less influenced by the characteristics of the work in the mine than are the operators at the mine head. As a consequence, policies established by the brokerage firm will be less responsive to physical system processes than will the policies of the mine operators. It does not follow that more bioecologically advantageous decisions are made at a mine head than in a New York office. On the contrary, the latter may take a longer range and less geographically specific view.

Gilpin (1970) shows how the impact of technological change, advances in air and sea transportation, improvements in radio, telephone, and television communication may facilitate the emergence of a global market. Pressure may be exerted upon the natural system as new products are introduced and transported throughout that market. Gilpin is concerned with adjusting the theory of international trade so that it can deal with market structures more independent of local resource conditions.

Here the social system is more extensive than the natural system of reference. The principal distinction, however, is not that the international market is oriented to a series of local resources but that it is oriented to a series of markets of lesser scope which, in turn, are oriented to resources. Social action in this system, as in those directly facing the resources, is a joint function of the constraints of the physical world and the exigencies arising at the social organizational level. At this socially coordinating level, general market considerations and the social factors determining them enter the resource policy decision.

Environmental policy organizations also do not generally respond directly to environmental constraint, but to symbols about the environment. These may be generated, in part, by organizations more directly related to the environment. These latter transmit selected information about the physical environment. Policy groups will, therefore, be more responsive to social system exigencies arising from the complex of social organization relations than to constraints of some specific physical system.

Government-established formal organizations for the management of specific aspects of the environment tend to be designed to fulfill social tasks set by broad sociopolitical rather than by literal environmental requirements. Although the distance afforded by this arrangement may, in effect, increase the overall efficiency and equity of environmental decisions, because a wider range of factors may be considered and decisions reached free of the specific press of one of them, this advantage is not necessarily realized. Caldwell (1970) describes a situation in which public responsibility for the environment is divided among congressional committees and executive agencies in a way inconsistent with the organization of bioecological processes in the natural environment. The decision about whether to allocate a forest area for recreation or for harvesting of commercial timber may involve the Bureau of Land Management, National Park

Service, Fish and Wildlife Service, Bureau of Outdoor Recreation, Forest Service, and the Corps of Engineers. Wandesford-Smith and Cooley (1970) point out that no congressional committee or executive department has responsibility broad enough to encompass proposals as diverse as the protection of endangered species and the elimination of automobile junkyards.

Influences on resource decisions not directly resource related are manifold. Different locales and different levels of government may press for divergent policies respecting the same resource. McConnell (1970) argues, for instance, that the citizens of Arizona might benefit from electrical power generated by harnessing water in the Grand Canyon. The interest of the larger society in its recreational value overrides the needs as perceived locally. Wandesford-Smith (1970) traces the effect on environmental policy of industry, conservation groups, and representatives of local interests, their effectiveness in manipulating policy depending upon their access to those who establish policy.

Government agencies themselves may have a vested interest in maintaining the independence of their particular environmental responsibility. The Corps of Engineers, for example, has opposed the reorganization of the Department of the Interior as the Department of Natural Resources. A bill introduced into the 90th Congress by Senator Nelson to create a Council on Environmental Quality in the Executive Office of the President proved to be a threat to the Office of Science and Technology within the circle of Presidential advisors. Thus, even if various pressure groups form on the basis of a direct orientation to the environment, the forces which control them may be relatively independent of direct environmental constraints. As Wandesford-Smith and Cooley (1970) say in their concluding essay, Congress is prone to choose environmental issues according to its own internally defined values rather than relative to values appropriate to the issues. Here the amount of slippage between natural and social systems can be stultifying.

When Marx analyzed the relation of workers to the means of production, he was concerned with the impact of their direct involvement in the productive process on their socioeconomic and cultural lives. The direct involvement is expressed in social rights of ownership in the resource as well as through social relations which the worker acquires in virtue of his relation to production. Marx ascribed deleterious social consequences to estranging the worker from the tools of production. The present discussion reverses the vision. Looking at the disjunction between society and its environment, this estrangement, by influencing the character of human intervention, also influences the environment. Doubtless this influence is also often deleterious, but it need not be.

Three Current Social-Scientific Terms

One advantage in analyzing one system at a time is that it allows the analyst to draw upon his disciplinary heritage for tried and tested conceptual tools. Three concepts in current use will illustrate the utility of such tools in describing social and psychological adjustments to environmental press. These are the concepts of selective perception from psychology, externalities from economics, and interest group from political science. The concepts refer to mechanisms of adjustive, tension-reductive, social, or personality change. As formal models, they may also be used to describe change which is not tension reductive.

The concept of selective perception was evolved in the context of equilibrium theory to account for the maintenance of a steady state. The tropistic behavior of the moth around the flame, which has profuse human analogies, illustrates the point that perception may select out suicidal opportunities as well as defensive opportunities. The concept of growth involves selective perceptual processes which increase environmental impact and, in consequence, the tension level. Selective perceptions or avoidance of certain contacts are among those social filtering mechanisms which an organism or society may employ to regulate the number of intensity of its relationships with the environment. Selective perception is part of the natural armory of defense which springs into action even without conscious planning. The model is one of adjustment through monitoring the boundary by gatekeeping.

Milgram (1970) analyzes the role of selective perception in managing psychological and social system overload. The term overload, though reflecting environmental input, and despite its physical metaphor, is an attribute of the social or personality systems rather than of the physical system. Thus, the physical input, environmental press, is treated parametrically while the social and psychological processes are analyzed. Milgram uses the concept of overload to describe how people in cities redraw the boundaries of their social transactions so as to reduce stress. Overload does not refer to the boundary-adjusting mechanisms themselves, but rather to the occasion or signal for pressing adjustive mechanisms into service.

The concept of externalities describes a mechanism by which one socioeconomic system relates to others when they participate in a more extensive natural system. The economist uses the concept to show this linkage—usually operating negatively for one of the systems. He abstracts the costs imposed by one social system on another and then shows that the difficulty may be alleviated by allocating the cost between them, that is, by changing the market boundary. This adjustive mechanism, called internalizing the externalities, is generally presented normatively as a recommended, planned move. Natural market mechanisms do not, by themselves, resolve externalities.

The model is one of adjustment by reallocating elements among systems. It may be used to analyze situations in which costs are not equitably balanced. For instance, in a parasitic relation, one system increases its externalities at the expense of another. Internalization of the externality involves a bioecological system broader in scope than the relation of parasite and host. The concept of externalities suggests the exploitation of one system by another as in the case of an industry dumping waste in water for which it does not pay and thereby imposing the cost on someone else. This is implicit in the analogy of parasite and host. However, the notion of exploitation is not necessarily implied by the model. For example, urban congestion and environmental pollution both involve externalities. In neither case is there intermediation of a market to enable affected parties to confront their tormentors (Rothenberg, 1970). In all forms of congestion, more than one agent is attempting to share a type of service not furnished in a separable unit earmarked for each user. That service is a form of "public good."[15] For instance, traffic becomes congested when the medium is used by all in much the same way. Abusers are indistinguishable from victims. The essence of pollution is that some users (polluters) abuse the medium, while others (the public) are relatively passive victims of such abuse. Congestion does not involve exploitation but pollution may.

A political move may be required to adjust the economic market so as to internalize the externalities. A downstream community might attack the upstream community by political means, forcing them to adjust market boundaries. The upstream community might pay a fee to cover the downstream community's cost of a water purification system, or absorb the cost of an alternate waste disposal system for the upstream community. The political boundaries are not redefined, but political action may be involved in readjusting market boundaries.

[15]Economists call a public good that part of a natural system, for instance, air or a river, which is not subject to exclusive rights of some specific individual or group. The concept of public good does not refer to an attribute of the physical system but to the social rules which govern the behavior of people with respect to the good. It defines an attribute of social relations and enters as a variable in propositions about social relations.

Political unification may not, by itself, guarantee an adjustment of the market. A superordinate polity or economy may help but is not sufficient for articulating natural and social systems. A difference in subsystem goals may be enough to maintain a disjunction. Goldman (1970) illustrates this in the case of the Soviet Union. It has been assumed, he says, that if all factories in a society were state owned, the state would insure protection of the interests of the general public. But the Russians too have been unable to adjust their accounting systems so that each enterprise pays not only its own direct costs of production for labor, raw materials, and equipment, but also its social costs of production arising from such by-products as dirty air and water. State officials are judged almost entirely by how much they increase their region's economic growth. A number of pulp mills, constructed on the shores of Lake Baikal, discharge effluents into the lake and so, implicitly, treat it as a free or undervalued good.

The political science concept of interest group explains both a disjunction between social and natural systems and a mechanism for adjusting them to each other. Except for specifically environmentally oriented interest groups, the scope of interest of these groups is not homologous with a natural environment system. The concept of interest group reflects the notion of flexibility in the distribution of power and the notion of temporary crystallization of concern. By and large, the concept has been used in the environmental field by political scientists to account for obstructive behavior in the adjustment of groups. An industrial interest group may block plans for air pollution abatement. There then emerge pro-abatement citizen interest groups in opposition. An interest group forms around an "issue," a problem as publically perceived.[16] The concept refers to a political mechanism which redraws the boundaries of power cutting across natural groups such as the family and relatively stable artificial groups such as church and party. The concept calls attention to an ephemeral consensus around a problem as perceived through the prism of social relations.

The concept of selective perception is constructed on a gatekeeping or boundary model, that of externalities on a model of the allocation of elements among systems. The interest group model

[16]Issue is a concept in current use among policy-oriented political scientists. It refers to some social consensus around a consciously perceived problem. An issue will emerge where there is an experience of tension. However, the issue need not present a clear or objective diagnosis. It is an interpretation of the situation influenced by the culture and social position of the individuals expressing it. As an object of orientation for political action, it is a focus around which an interest group may develop.

reflects group formation around an integrative focus. Concepts useful for dealing with boundary, allocation, and integrative problems take us a long way toward the development of theories of social and individual behavior with respect to the physical environment.

REFERENCES

Barnes, Robert J.
1970 "Junked autos: Embodiment of the litter philosophy." In Richard A. Cooley and Jeffrey Wandesford-Smith (eds.), Congress and the Environment. Seattle: University of Washington Press.

Caldwell, Lynton Keith
1970 Environment: A challenge for modern society. Garden City, N.Y.: Natural History Press.

Coale, Ansley J.
1970 "Man and his environment." Science 170(October 9, 1970): 132-136.

Commoner, Barry
1970 "To survive on the earth." In Robert Disch (ed.), Ecological Conscience: Values for Survival. Englewood Cliffs, N.J.: Prentice-Hall.

Gilpin, Robert
1970 "Technological strategies and national purpose." Science 169(July 31, 1970):441-448.

Glacken, Clarence J.
1970 "Man's place in nature in recent Western thought." In Michael Hamilton (ed.), This Little Planet. New York: Scribner.

Goldman, Marshall I.
1970 "The convergence of environmental disruption." Science 170(October 2, 1970):37-42.

Gudrey, L. J., and H. H. Stoevener
1970 "The role of selected population and site characteristics in the demand for forest recreation." Report No. 2 of the Cooperative Regional Research Technical Committee, An Economic Study of the Demand for Outdoor Recreation, Reno, Nev. (June 1970).

Klausner, Samuel Z.
1970 Society and its physical environment. Annals of the American Academy of Political and Social Science 389(May 1970).
1971 On Man in His Environment: Social-Scientific Foundations for Research and Policy. San Francisco: Jossey-Bass.

Leffingwell, Albert
1892 Illegitimacy and the influence of seasons upon conduct. London: Swan Sonnenschein.

McConnell, Grant
1970 "Prologue: Environment and the quality of political life." In Richard A. Cooley and Jeffrey Wandesford-Smith (eds.), Congress and the Environment. Seattle: University of Washington Press.

Milgram, Stanley
1970 "The experience of living in cities." Science 167(March 13, 1970):1461-1468.

Moncrief, Lewis W.
1970 "The cultural basis for our environmental crisis." Science 170(October 30, 1970):508-512.

Moore, Henry L.
1923 Generating Economic Cycles. New York: Macmillan.

Mumford, Lewis
    1970 "Closing statement." In Robert Dishch (ed.), Ecological Con-
        science: Values for Survival. Englewood, Cliffs, N.J.: Prentice-Hall.
Odum, Howard T.
    1971 Environment, Power and Society. New York: Wiley-Interscience.
Parrack, Dwain W.
    1969 "An approach to the bioenergetics of rural West Bengal." In
        Andrew P. Vadya (ed.), Environment and Cultural Behavior:
        Ecological Studies in Cultural Anthropology. Garden City, N.Y.:
        Natural History Press.
Rothenberg, Jerome
    1970 "The economics of congestion and pollution: An integrated view."
        American Economic Review (Papers and Proceedings of the 82nd
        Annual Meeting of the American Economic Association) (May
        1970):114-121.
Shephard, Paul
    1970 "Ecology and man—A viewpoint." In Robert Disch (ed.), Eco-
        logical Conscience: Values for Survival. Englewood Cliffs, N.J.:
        Prentice-Hall.
Slobodkin, Lawrence B.
    1970 "Aspects of the future of ecology." In Robert Disch (ed.),
        Ecological Conscience: Values for Survival. Englewood Cliffs, N.J.:
        Prentice-Hall.
Wandesford-Smith, Jeffrey
    1970 "National policy for the environment: Politics and the concept of
        stewardship." In Richard A. Cooley and Jeffrey Wandesford-Smith
        (eds.), Congress and the Environment. Seattle: University of
        Washington Press.
Wandesford-Smith, Jeffrey, and Richard A. Cooley
    1970 "Conclusions: Congress and the environment of the future." In
        Richard A. Cooley and Jeffrey Wandesford-Smith (eds.), Congress
        and the Environment. Seattle: University of Washington Press.
Young, Ruth C., and Olaf F. Larson
    1970 "The social ecology of a rural community." Rural Sociology
        35(September 1970): 337-353.

INDEX